Teaching Strategies That Create Assessment-Literate Learners

Teaching Strategies That Create Assessment-Literate Learners

Anita Stewart McCafferty | Jeffrey S. Beaudry

Foreword by Rick Stiggins

FOR INFORMATION:

Corwin
A SAGE Company
2455 Teller Road
Thousand Oaks, California 91320
(800) 233-9936
www.corwin.com

SAGE Publications Ltd.
1 Oliver's Yard
55 City Road
London EC1Y 1SP
United Kingdom

SAGE Publications India Pvt. Ltd.
B 1/I 1 Mohan Cooperative Industrial Area
Mathura Road, New Delhi 110 044
India

SAGE Publications Asia-Pacific Pte. Ltd.
3 Church Street
#10-04 Samsung Hub
Singapore 049483

Program Director: Jessica Allan
Associate Editor: Lucas Schleicher
Editorial Assistant: Mia Rodriguez
Production Editor: Amy Schroller
Copy Editor: Megan Markanich
Typesetter: C&M Digitals (P) Ltd.
Proofreader: Dennis W. Webb
Indexer: Sheila Bodell
Cover Designer: Anupama Krishnan
Marketing Manager: Nicole Franks

Printed in the United States of America

ISBN 978-1-5063-8209-8

This book is printed on acid-free paper.

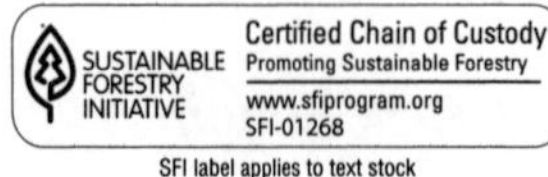

SFI label applies to text stock

18 19 20 21 22 10 9 8 7 6 5 4 3 2 1

• Contents •

• Foreword •

To introduce Anita and Jeff's book, let me share a brief history of the evolution of my thinking about the role of assessment in American education. This retelling leads directly to *Teaching Strategies That Create Assessment-Literate Learners.*

When I entered the profession in the 1970s, the dominant vision of excellence in assessment held it to be the process of gathering evidence of student achievement in a dispassionate scientific manner. This was to be a precise act as free of bias and other sources of measurement error as possible. Previous decades had spawned a rigorous set of quality control standards intended to sharpen the focus and consistency of measures. These standards were developed for universal application in the rapidly emerging domain of large-scale standardized testing. They were codified in conceptual and mathematical models intended to bring the field of educational measurement to the same levels of scientific rigor and respect attained by other recognized sciences.

Upon graduating from the doctoral program at Michigan State, I embraced these tenets of modern and classical test theory and practice, building my early career around teaching and applying these accepted principles of psychometrics in the standardized testing domain. I was intent on the mission of contributing to the advancement of the accepted vision of excellence in assessment.

But then something startling—indeed, career changing—happened. This personal event caused me to realize that my professional training, thinking, and work was being carried out in a stratosphere located miles above, and completely out of touch with, the teaching and learning processes of America's classrooms and schools. What happened was that I became a dad.

As our child proceeded through the elementary grades, we had a front-row seat from which to view and understand how the real, continuous classroom assessment process impacted the learning life and academic self-concept of our growing child. The vision of assessment unfolding before us was not a pretty one. Not only were the assessment quality control standards I had learned about at Michigan State not being applied but our local teachers had never heard of them. And more importantly, the emotional dynamics of the assessment experience—based in large part on intimidation and the perpetuation of anxiety—were doing as much harm to student learning success as good!

So I left the world of large-scale standardized assessment behind forevermore with the mission of translating complex technical standards of good practice into commonsense ideas that any teacher could learn to apply as a matter of routine in her or his classroom assessment processes. In addition, part two of this new mission was to understand the emotional dynamics of assessment from the student's point of view with sufficient depth to see how to shape the classroom assessment experience in ways that would promote confidence and a sense of academic well-being for *all* students, thus opening the door to the promise of universal academic success.

As it turned out, others across the country and, indeed, around the world also were striving to link the classroom assessment process to more productive teaching and learning. Among the early joiners of the crusade were Jeff and Anita. They began their work by internalizing a practical view of excellence in assessment used *for* learning that they have shared with teachers and school leaders. Their practical vision of quality assessment used to support and certify learning is spelled out in this book.

But they didn't stop there. They continued to develop, collect, and expand upon concrete strategies that teachers can use to *cause*—not merely measure—student learning. This book represents an up-to-date status report to teachers, school leaders, and the measurement community about the state of the art in using classroom assessment as a teaching and learning tool. And my sense is that their collection of strategies will continue to grow.

Two important and interrelated features of their presentation are worthy of mention here at the outset. One is their success in taking assessment for learning strategies into specific subject matter contexts with clear and relevant examples. This brings the reader to a focus on applications that truly are ready for prime time. The second key feature is the mode of teaching they have adopted. The depth and clarity of their applications and illustrative graphics, again, make their strategies come alive for the reader. In a very real sense, they model for the readers the very teaching and learning process those readers can apply in their classrooms.

Above all, this is a book for teachers, revealing through sound pedagogy ways to bring the learner into the assessment process as full partners in ways that help them learn to manage their own learning. If we don't define the foundations of "lifelong learner" in those terms, I don't know how we define it. But it is also a book for school leaders who seek to balance the long-standing assessment for accountability movement with the classroom level of assessment for learning.

—Rick Stiggins
Portland, Oregon

• Acknowledgments •

We would like to acknowledge our spouses, family, colleagues, and friends for their support and patience during the writing of this book.

We are indebted to the following colleagues for their editing and revision support: Hal Earle, Andrea Jarvis, Joanna Martel, Erica Mazzeo, Anthony Luke Stewart II, and our Corwin team.

We have been privileged to be surrounded with an amazing cast of educators with whom we have been able to learn and grow. These dedicated educators have allowed us to teach, learn, and experiment with ideas, strategies, and tools. They have taken concepts and applied them to their own classrooms, schools, districts, and organizations in unique ways; they have adapted the principles to fit the learning needs of those they teach. We are grateful for the continued support of the following organizations who opened their doors time and time again to engage their educators with our work around Assessment for Learning (A4L): Maine Arts Leadership Initiative (MALI), Maine Center for Research in STEM Education (RiSE Center), Midcoast Superintendents' Association, MSAD 6, North Woods Partnership, Penobscot River Education Partnership (PREP), RSU 67, Southern Maine Partnership (SMP), and Washington County Consortium. We have been privileged to work with dozens of other districts and schools on this project and are grateful for the unique learning opportunity each one provided.

Additionally, we have a host of individual educators who have contributed their work to this book through Practitioner Spotlights and specific classroom examples. The inclusion of their work is our way of paying homage to the larger pool of talented, innovative educators with whom we have been privileged to work and learn. Please see the complete list of all contributors, following the publisher's acknowledgements.

We would also like to thank our incredible Educational Leadership and Professional Educator graduate students at the University of Southern Maine for their contributions in applying ideas, grappling with assessment for learning concepts in varying contexts, and expanding our thinking through their insight and questions.

We would also like to thank Jan Chappuis and Rick Stiggins for sharing with us their wisdom, books, presentations, support, and friendship. Your work is an inspiration to us!

Publisher's Acknowledgments

Corwin gratefully acknowledges the contributions of the following reviewer:

Susan D'Angelo
K–5 Math Program Specialist
Sarasota County School District
Sarasota, FL

• List of Contributors •

Erika Allison, former project director, Maine Center for Research in STEM Education (RiSE Center)

Zach Arnold, high school science teacher, Orono High School

Ashland Middle School sixth-grade English language arts team, Principal Steve Retzlaff, and Assistant Principal Katherine Holden, Ashland, Oregon, Ashland School District

Anita Bernhardt, director of curriculum, instruction, and assessment, York School Department

Betty Bickford, fifth-grade teacher, Mattanawcook Junior High School, RSU 67

Rachel Bourgeois, elementary teacher, Teague Park Elementary School, RSU 39

Beth ByersSmall, NSF teaching fellowship program coordinator, RiSE Center

Wendy Cole, middle school math teacher, Mattanawcook Junior High School, RSU 67

Tracy Cowan, high school English teacher, Mattanawcook Academy, RSU 67

Ryan Crane, assistant principal, Mattanawcook Academy, RSU 67

Sharon Crockett, kindergarten teacher, Ella P. Burr School, RSU 67

Scott Davis, high school social studies teacher, Mattanawcook Academy, RSU 67

Rebekah Drysdale, special education director, MSAD 52

Wendy Dunbar, middle school teacher, Mt. Jefferson Junior High School, MSAD 30

Tammi Edwards, kindergarten teacher, Ella P. Burr School, RSU 67

Jim Fratini, middle school science teacher, Hermon Middle School, Hermon Schools

John Goater, high school English teacher, Mattanawcook Academy, RSU 67

Gus Goodwin, middle school teacher, King Middle School, Portland Public Schools

Jim Gorman, high school physics teacher, Northbridge High School, Northbridge School District

Kirsten Gould, first-grade teacher, Buxton Elementary School, MSAD 6

Sarah Holmes, doctoral student, University of Southern Maine

Chris Hughes, assistant principal, South Portland High School, South Portland School District

Lisa Ingraham, elementary arts teacher, Madison Elementary School, MSAD 59

Emma Jarvis, middle school student, Mattanawcook Junior High School, RSU 67

Jessica Johnson, high school English teacher, Mattanawcook Academy, RSU 67

Nancy Kinkade, music teacher, RSU 67

Cathlyn Langston, first-grade teacher, Falmouth Elementary School, Falmouth Public Schools

Sonya Laramee, first-grade teacher, Chelsea Elementary School, RSU 12

Holly Leighton, high school art teacher, Mattanawcook Academy, RSU 67

Dean Libbey, high school mathematics teacher, Mattanawcook Academy, RSU 67

Lincolnville Central School K–2 team, Five Town School District, Union 69

Joanna Martel, graduate assistant, University of Southern Maine

Laura Matthews, middle school teacher, Reeds Brook Middle School

Molly Mingione, kindergarten teacher, Steep Falls Elementary School, MSAD 6

Argy Nestor, director of arts education, Maine Arts Commission (MAC)

Heather Oakes, fifth-grade teacher, Granite Street School, Millinocket School Department

Jamie Peters, kindergarten teacher, Ella P. Burr School, RSU 67

Lindsay Pinchbeck, founder and director, Sweet Tree Arts/Sweetland School, and Maine Arts Leadership Initiative (MALI) design team member

Kristi Raymond, middle school STEM teacher, Mahoney Middle School, South Portland School District

Melissa Roberts, professional learning and data/assessment coordinator, RSU 57

Heather Rockwell, director of curriculum, RSU 67

Sarah Ritz-Swain, curriculum coordinator, Connecticut

Mick Roy, assistant superintendent, MSAD 6

Stephanie Shocki, elementary teacher, Camden-Rockport Elementary School, Five Town School District, MSAD 28

Patricia Simon, kindergarten teacher, Steep Falls Elementary School, MSAD 6

Jake Sturtevant, music educator, Falmouth High School, and MALI design team member

Deb Taylor, director of curriculum and technology, RSU 12

Nathan Theriault, high school social studies teacher, Edward Little High School, Auburn School District

Raymond Tilton, high school English teacher, Mattanawcook Academy, RSU 67

Aaron Ward, high school social studies teacher, Mattanawcook Academy, RSU 67

Mary Wellehan, middle school studio arts teacher, King Middle School, Portland Public Schools

Polly Wilson, eighth-grade science teacher, King Middle School, Portland Public Schools

Carla Wright, high school teacher, Mattanawcook Academy, RSU 67

Katie Wright, high school science teacher, Houlton Middle/High School, RSU 29

• About the Authors •

Anita Stewart McCafferty is Assistant Professor of Educational Leadership at the University of Southern Maine and serves as Department Chair. She also serves as Co-Director of Southern Maine Partnership, a university-preK–12 consortium of more than 30 districts and the USM Educational Leadership Department. Dr. Stewart McCafferty is passionate about professional learning done well. Her research interests include assessment literacy; the impacts of technology and social media on the work-life balance of principals; teacher and principal feedback and evaluation processes and results; middle level education; and experiential learning/service learning. Prior to joining USM, Anita served as a middle school principal, assistant principal, professional development provider, and classroom teacher. She can be reached at anita.stewart@maine.edu or by Twitter @AnitaStewartMcC

Jeffrey S. Beaudry is Professor of Educational Leadership at University of Southern Maine. Dr. Beaudry spends his time focusing on high-impact classroom assessment and leadership strategies. He is passionate about the use of visual thinking and assessment for learning. Since 2009 he has co-authored numerous publications, books, and articles about critical thinking, visual representations, and concept mapping. As an instructional designer, he enjoys going deeper into assessment for learning (formative assessment). He is most proud of his time as co-director of the Southern Maine Partnership, a regional collaboration of schools and the University of Southern Maine, and the collaboration with other regional partners in Maine (Penobscot River Educational Association, and the Northwoods Partnership).

Anita dedicates this book to her dad, the late Dr. Rev. Jack Stewart, the most impactful teacher and leader she has been privileged to know.

Jeff dedicates this book to his wife, Judy, who supports his scholarly spirit, and to his mother, Jeanne, his visual mentor, and his father, Steve, and his gentle guiding force.

Introduction to #assessmentliteracy

Key Takeaways

Assessment literacy is not an initiative. It's a foundational essential competency for all teachers, school leaders, and students.

Learning and teaching are the context for effective understanding of assessment for learning.

Curriculum and leadership are the sources for big picture and effective change in creating assessment-literate educators and learners.

As assessment-literate educators, we must understand the use and abuse of formative assessment, especially concerns about commercialization of formative assessment products.

Assessment for learning focuses on the key roles of the teachers and students.

Assessment Literacy

Assessment literacy is not an initiative, not just another fad or bandwagon to jump on or off. It's a foundational and essential competency for all school leaders, teachers, and students. For us, assessment literacy is foremost about learning and secondarily about teaching. As assessment-literate educators, we are able to make instructional decisions about the strategies, tools, techniques, and resources we use to improve the learning for *all*. Assessment-literate learners, which includes educators, know (1) where they are headed, (2) where they are now, and (3) what their next steps are in order to help them achieve their learning goals (Chappuis, 2012). In their progress toward these goals, educators can help students become self-regulated lifelong learners by empowering them to develop assessment literacy for themselves. Hattie (2012) referred to this idea as assessment-capable learners. Educators need to see assessment as feedback of their teaching (and leading) and use this evidence to create and modify learning environments that positively influences achievement and growth (Hattie, 2012).

In our work in classroom assessment, we begin with these essential questions as points of reference to both differentiate and sustain our discussions:

- What is good learning?
- What is good teaching?
- What is good assessment?

PAUSE AND REFLECT

- Take a few moments to reflect on and respond to each of these questions that were just given.

Share your answers with a colleague, create a visual representation, or go to our forum #assessmentliteracy on Twitter to post comments and questions.

The exclusive focus on assessment has the potential consequence of isolating this powerful concept from teaching and learning. The tight connection to teaching and learning is best kept at the center of all discussions about assessment in order to keep teachers and students as the key partners in the assessment process (Stiggins, 1994).

At the risk of overcomplicating the discussion, we have added two more essential questions to get a bigger picture of the context of assessment.

- What is good curriculum?
- What is good leadership?

We will discuss the essential connections with curriculum and leadership throughout the book, but curriculum is a theme in Chapters 2 and 4. Professional learning and instructional leadership, including that of teachers, building leaders, and district level positions, is the focus of Chapters 10 through 12. By incorporating these latter two essential questions, teachers and leaders greater understand the value of their professional expertise and can see the connections of learning and teaching with curriculum, leadership, and assessment. We see teachers as the leverage point if professional learning is to have an impact on learning in our classrooms and schools. We provide numerous examples of teacher-led professional learning in Chapters 10 and 11.

We will use the term *assessment for learning* to mean the following:

> A set of high-impact strategies that collect evidence to show learners where they are, where they are going, and what's the next step. These strategies focus on moving the learner forward *during* the learning process instead of the summative postlearning grading process.

Classroom teachers have a remarkable understanding of instruction and develop wisdom of practice throughout the tenure of their careers. We acknowledge and applaud the passion, skills, and commitment of the great teachers with which we know and work. While our profession has come a long way in its development, when it comes to assessment literacy, we still have a way's to go on the journey.

Classroom Assessment: A Brief History of the Impact of the Field

In the relatively brief history of classroom assessment, Bloom's mastery learning model put assessment in understandable terms and provided us with the notion of immediate feedback to improve performance. The term *classroom evaluation* (Crooks, 1988) was replaced by *classroom assessment* in the 1990s. This underscored the shift to the balance between classroom strategies *for* learning and grading. In 1992, Stiggins and Conklin completed a study of the amount of time teachers spent on classroom assessment tasks, demands and functions, and teacher preparation for these competencies. They found that teacher preparation programs summarily lacked sufficient courses to produce assessment-literate teachers. Stiggins (1994) followed

FIGURE 1.1 ● The Classroom Assessment Tree

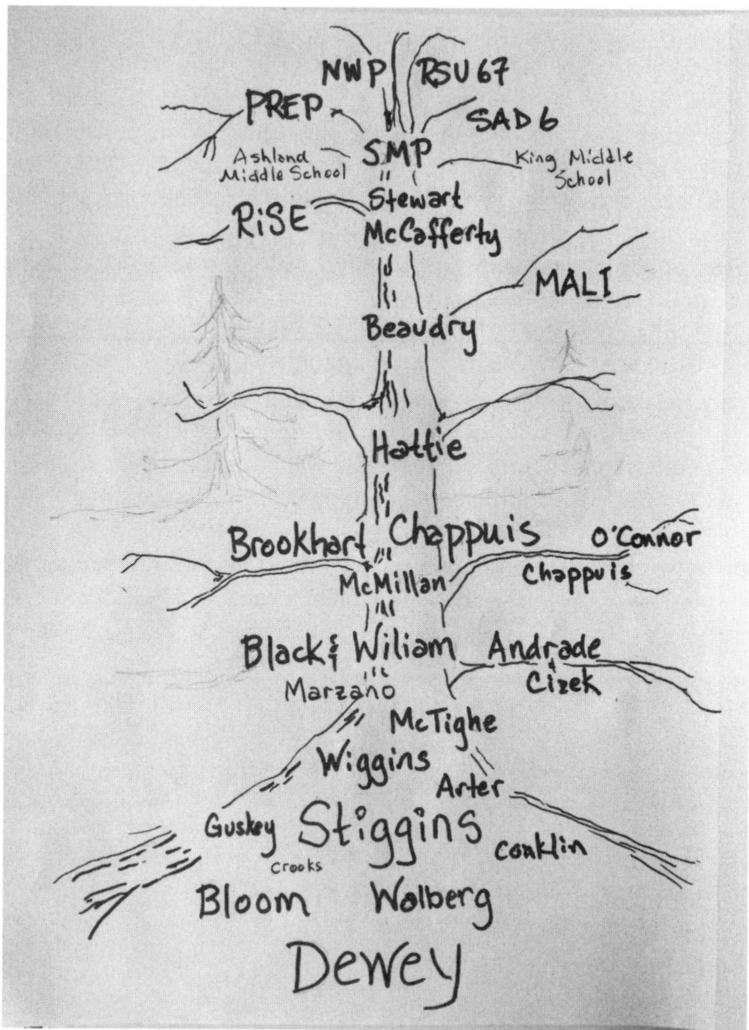

up with a notion that radically departed from teacher-centered strategies by articulating direct student involvement as one of five standards of quality for classroom assessment. His book helped establish the need for more attention on clear purposes and focused on the potential connection of assessment and learning by (1) intentionally bringing students inside the assessment process, (2) requiring students be able to self-assess and communicate their learning to a variety of audiences, and (3) the need to counteract the dominance of high-stakes testing by balanced use of teachers' classroom assessment practices. In rapid succession, textbooks on classroom assessment by McMillan (2004), Oosterhof (1999), and many others appeared. Teacher and leader preparation programs have benefited from these resources and have, in turn, created areas of excellence within the field of classroom assessment that have benefited the profession as a whole. Yet, there are far too many teachers and leaders who graduate from our colleges and universities without foundational competencies in assessment literacy demanded by today's classrooms, schools, and districts. There are far too many students who leave our schools believing that assessment simply means grading and therefore miss the powerful connections to her or his own learning and growth.

Scriven's term *formative assessment*, which focuses on process and improvement, helped to set it apart from summative assessment, which primarily focused on evaluative judgment, scores, and grades. One of the issues we often encounter is that the term *formative assessment* is often seen as a product, like a common assessment or something a teacher gives as practice for the summative assessment. As a product, formative assessments often get a grade or score and therefore masquerade as a way to use a score to focus feedback. In doing so, the attempt is made to demonstrate the principle that timely, focused feedback has an impact on learning. As a practice, it is understandable to convey the message to students that "everything counts." However, there are limitations in the rigor of what can be measured, and there are often unintended consequences for learners and parents who only equate learning with a score. The study by Butler (1988) is a prime example of feedback; it compares the impact of comments, grades plus comments, or comments only. Chapter 6 examines effective feedback strategies that move beyond the use of points, grades, or scores.

The careful use of empirical evidence from research marked the next phase in classroom assessment: the shift to the impact of classroom assessment practices. Black and Wiliam (1998) used research evidence from meta-analysis to support their argument that feedback and quality questioning, if done well, could have a high impact on student achievement. Brookhart (2008) continued to clarify the connection between instruction and assessment, and Cizek and Andrade (2010) provided more discussion in the *Handbook of Research on Formative Assessment*. The presence of research signified that classroom assessment was becoming a field of study, drawing the attention of practitioners who want to see improvements in their classrooms that promote and deepen learning.

Books, articles, tweets, and blogs now are helping to shift the focus to learning and assessment and fill in new portions of the landscape of accountability and data literacy.

PAUSE AND REFLECT

- Why are you interested in classroom assessment?
- Upon what aspects of your practice as a teacher and a leader do you hope to improve?

Share your answers with a colleague, create a visual representation, or go to our forum #assessmentliteracy on Twitter to post comments and questions.

Classroom Assessment: Today's Dialogue About High-Impact Practices and Strategies

For us, the recognition of an empirical research base for high-impact strategies is exciting, because it builds a bridge between theory and practice and shows us what is possible for learners and learning. At the policy level, assessment-literate teachers and leaders are vital to navigate and build our education systems and shape educational policy. Practitioners understand that at the heart of classroom assessment are concerns about student engagement, feedback, collection of appropriate evidence of student learning, and appropriate communication about students' proficiency with standards. In Chapter 2, the role of assessment-literate leaders is discussed and carried through the book as a theme.

The Era of Rapid Response: Our Concerns About the Commercialization of Formative Assessment

Our goal is to inform and empower educators to deepen their classroom assessment practices, to become designers of high-quality assessment for learning, and to be very critical consumers of commercial products that may contain the term *formative assessment*. Empowering educators to be their own best resources is a tremendous challenge that requires an investment of time and human resources in building assessment literacy competency of all educators.

PAUSE AND REFLECT

- What is your definition of *assessment for learning*? What is your definition of *formative assessment*?
- Think about this statement: Formative assessment is not the same as assessing formatively.

Share your answers with a colleague, create a visual representation, or go to our forum #assessmentliteracy on Twitter to post comments and questions.

The rapid commercialization of formative assessment and the rebranding of standardized tests as formative assessment tools should set off alarms in your head! The corporate wolf is already inside the classroom door. One of our biggest concerns is that commercial vendors and testing companies, with the power of technology and the new opportunity to produce rapid response data systems, are now investing millions and millions of dollars to capture the formative assessment market. These commercial formative assessment systems are being purchased by leaders and teachers in state and local school systems before teachers and leaders have really become assessment literate (see Chapter 2 for a discussion of the importance of knowing WHY we assess before we decide on HOW or WHAT).

> In fact, classroom assessments, including formative and other kinds that are not state-mandated, represent nearly a $1.6 billion market this year, compared with the almost $1.3 billion that will be spent for state-mandated tests. Expected to grow by 30 percent through 2020, the classroom-based sector is the fastest-growing of the two. (Molnar, 2017)

PAUSE AND REFLECT

- How should we balance teachers' classroom assessments with standardized assessments?
- Think about this prompt: Testing companies have finally got it right. They need to go where the impact really is, formative assessment.
- What are the benefits and drawbacks of commercial standardized formative assessments?

Share your answers with a colleague, create a visual representation, or go to our forum #assessmentliteracy on Twitter to post comments and questions.

On the one hand, you might think, "Well... finally these testing companies have got it right." Are these testing companies now building the perfect assessment system? We fear that *assessment for learning* is being co-opted and sold as another software tracking and reporting system in the hands of commercial data collection providers. In order to maximize the benefits of new systems, assessment-literate teachers and leaders should have a thorough understanding of assessment *for* and *of* learning in order to think critically about investing precious resources. We cannot simply purchase the answer or buy our way into high-impact on student learning.

Assessment Literacy: It's About the Teachers and Their Leaders

The message we want to convey is that the first investment needs to be in teachers and school leaders and in helping them become more assessment literate. Judging from our ongoing discussions and observations of teachers and school leaders, this first step is far from complete. Assessment-literate educators can help create balanced assessment systems (Chappuis, Commodore, & Stiggins, 2016; Stiggins, 2017) that have appropriate foci on assessment *for* learning, interim benchmark assessments, and state-mandated tests or other large-scale standardized tests. When our assessment systems are in balance, our learners win. With the proper emphasis on learning and how best to support their progress, learners win.

Educators must stay ahead of the testing and publishing companies that are filled with computer-based tracking programs and solutions. We want to capitalize on the realization that there is still so much for teachers to learn and do with students in the area of formative assessment. We propose that teachers and students are the key users, and as such, they are the ones who need to have the greatest and most consistent involvement in developing, designing, and differentiating high-impact strategies for teaching, learning, and assessment.

The thirteen chapters about creating assessment-literate learners are organized by these questions and topics:

Chapter 1: Introduction to #assessmentliteracy—Why is assessment literacy the essential link between learning and teaching?

Chapter 2: Contextualizing Assessment Within Curricula and Instruction—What does it mean to be an assessment-literate learner and leader? How do we design curriculum, instruction, and assessment to help our learners succeed in and beyond our school walls?

Chapters 3–9: What are the high-impact strategies of assessment for learning? How do teachers and learners work with assessment for learning strategies?

- **Chapter 3: The Convergence of Research and Practice: Seven Strategies of Assessment for Learning Meets High-Impact Strategies**—What is the research base for high-impact strategies? What are the connections between research evidence and assessment for learning strategies?
- **Chapter 4: Clear Learning Targets: Clarity Is the Goal**—What is meant by clear learning targets and teacher clarity, and why are these strategies important?
- **Chapter 5: Mapping, Visual Literacy, and Assessment for Learning**—What is the role of visual learning in critical and creative thinking, and how does visual literacy support clear learning targets and other high-impact strategies?
- **Chapter 6: Putting Feedback Into Action**—What is descriptive feedback, and how does it work in the classroom?
- **Chapter 7: Metacognition, Self-Assessment, Goal Setting, and Reflection: GPA Matters! (Goals, Plans, and Actions, That Is!)** — How do we get the most out of the learner-centered strategies, self- assessment, goal setting, and reflection?
- **Chapter 8: Diagnosing Student Learning Needs During the Learning Process**—Why do teachers need to understand and be able to use diagnostic assessment for all learners? What is the role of familiar strategies like classroom discussion and questioning techniques in the assessment for learning model?
- **Chapter 9: The Whole Learner and Nothing But the Learner**—What are the connections between learners' attributes and high-impact strategies that help to develop assessment-literate learners?

Chapters 10–13: How do we develop assessment-literate learners and leaders?

- **Chapter 10: High-Impact Professional Learning Principles and Communities of Practice: Let's Get It Right!**—What does high-quality professional learning look like?

FIGURE 1.2 ● Thirteen Chapters of Teaching Strategies That Create Assessment-Literate Learners

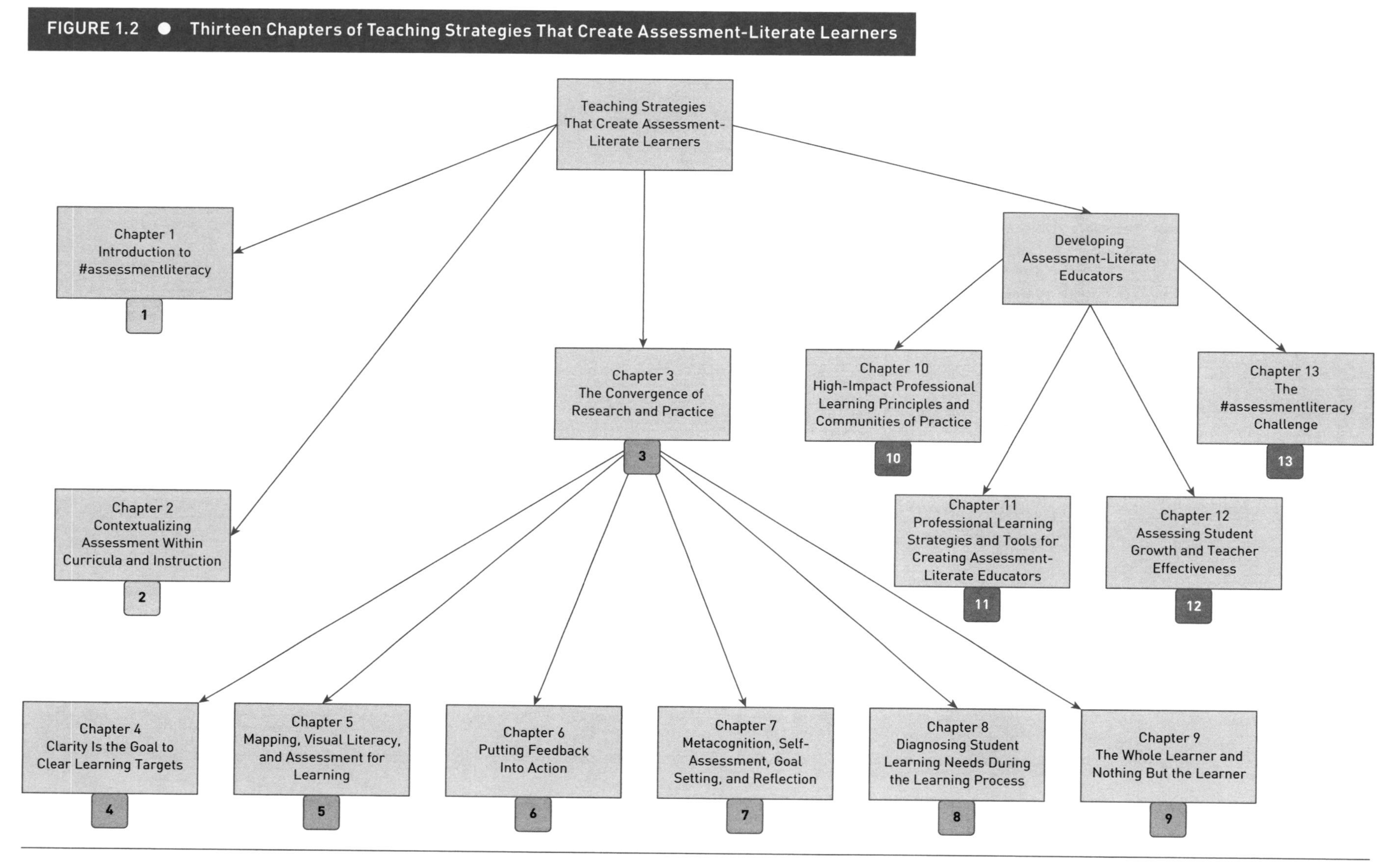

- **Chapter 11: Professional Learning Strategies and Tools for Creating Assessment-Literate Educators**—What examples do we have of high-quality professional learning strategies, tools, and resources?
- **Chapter 12: Assessing Student Growth and Teacher Effectiveness**—Why is assessment literacy essential to create and maintain effective teachers and leaders? How do we assure that educators and their systems incorporate evidence-based practices into their procedures and protocols for teacher evaluation, including assessing student growth?
- **Chapter 13: The #assessmentliteracy Challenge**—What are our next steps?

Take a Deep Dive to Further Your Understanding

The media landscape for assessment literacy is vibrant and interactive with social media tools like blogs, Twitter, and massive online courses. What do these new powerful influences have to offer us when it comes to assessment for learning? For example, *Twitter* offers "microbloggers" 280 characters, and it works by following people who post their ideas and share resources (the fun way to grow networks), like @AnitaStewartMcC or @BeaudryJeff or by going straight to a specific topic or hashtag by searching for #assessmentliteracy. Either way, there is a learning community already interacting. You can ask questions, debate solutions, share and re-share resources, and highlight information. Information sharing is now instantaneous through web-based tools, which has made media like CD-ROMs a relic of the past. We will come back to the social media landscape in the concluding chapter. For now, we invite you to make comments on Twitter as you read and use the material in these chapters. See you at @AnitaStewartMcC or @BeaudryJeff or leave a message with #assessmentliteracy.

Contextualizing Assessment Within Curricula and Instruction

Key Takeaways

We can assess anything; make sure students are learning worthy content. Before focusing on classroom assessment practices, first consider the answer to this question: What is essential for our students to know, be able to do, understand, appreciate, and be like in order to be successful in life beyond our classroom walls—in the workplace, in higher education, in relationships, and in their community lives?

Planning with the end in mind is necessary in a proficiency or standards-based context. What understandings, skills, and dispositions (e.g., standards, learning outcomes, transferable goals) will students be learning? What does it look like to do those things in a proficient manner? With the answer to those questions, teachers can turn their focus to designing for learning, not just designing the summative or culminating assessment.

Assessment is much more than a product, outcome, or thing; it is a collection of strategies and processes that help learners become better learners and educators become better educators.

Assessment literacy is a fundamental competency for all educators. Teachers need assessment-literate school leaders who can guide and support their development and who understand deeply the complex acts of teaching and learning.

WHY, WHAT, and HOW

While we will spend most of this book sharing high-impact strategies, tools, and recommendations for how to engage learners (whether they be professional educators or students) in ongoing assessment for learning that yields improvement in achievement and increased learner involvement and ownership, we will first turn our attention to WHY we focus on WHAT we teach, and HOW we teach the WHAT to our learners.

We are confident that we can assist educators and students in accurately assessing their progress toward learning and becoming proficient of any WHAT; however, assessing irrelevant and less than rigorous curricula seems to be a worthless endeavor for all involved. Because we are convinced that learning worthy content, skills, and dispositions is crucial to the learning equation, we do not want to gloss over the importance of establishing shared purpose, powerful curricula, and sound instructional approaches before or simultaneous to turning one's attention to using sound assessment strategies and keys to quality.

Why We Focus on What We Teach

> "When will we ever have to know this?"
>
> "What's the point of learning this?"
>
> "Why do I need to know this anyhow?"
>
> "When will I ever use this in the real world?"

If these questions do not sound familiar to you, you are a rare breed of enviable teacher! For most of us, we dare speculate, these questions have been uttered by numerous students and perhaps even by ourselves at times.

Simon Sinek (2009), in his best-selling book *Start With Why: How Great Leaders Inspire Everyone to Take Action* and riveting TED Talk, reminded us of the power of beginning with the WHY and communicating that to others before launching into the WHAT or HOW. Although Sinek writes and speaks about successful marketing of companies and organizations, he also speaks about the successful distribution of ideas. In summation, his "golden egg" notion suggests that one needs to communicate first the organization's compelling purpose and beliefs, then move on to communication of HOW the organization will accomplish the WHY, and finally describe WHAT the organization makes or sells. To align this thinking with learning organizations, we find it pertinent to first consider our shared purposes (i.e., the WHY we exist as schools or districts, our shared beliefs as educators), the strategies we will use to engage our learners and help fulfill our shared purposes (the HOW), and finally outline the important learning outcomes needed for our students' future success (the WHAT).

For instance, if our WHY revolves around an intense belief in preparing *all* learners, including disenfranchised students, to participate fully in our democracy by making contributions to their communities, engaging in the civic and political aspects of society, and making informed decisions about the world in which they live, we will carefully consider our pedagogy (the HOW) so that it is congruent with our WHY. As we consider WHAT we teach, we will ensure that we include critical thinking skills, media literacy, opportunities to engage in solving problems in our communities (e.g., service learning opportunities), perspective consciousness skills, etc., in addition to the content or factual examples we teach. We will create ample opportunities for our students to practice their civic engagement skills instead of leaving it to those who self-select to volunteer or participate in community service projects. Our WHY will drive our HOW and our perspectives on the WHAT. See Figure 2.1.

Establishing the WHAT

WHAT is most valuable for students to learn? Why do we believe it to be most essential? Says who? For what purpose is it being learned? Are we helping to create college, career, and civic readiness in our students? Is the WHAT essential beyond what is needed simply for the next grade level, to do well on the mandated testing, and beyond how the school or district will be held accountable on the state grading or rating of schools or districts? These questions and a host of others need to be well debated and clearly established before we proceed to assessment strategies. After all, we can teach folks to assess and report out on *anything*. Why not make sure the WHAT helps serve our larger WHY!

FIGURE 2.1 ● Start With Why Express-a-Book Sketch

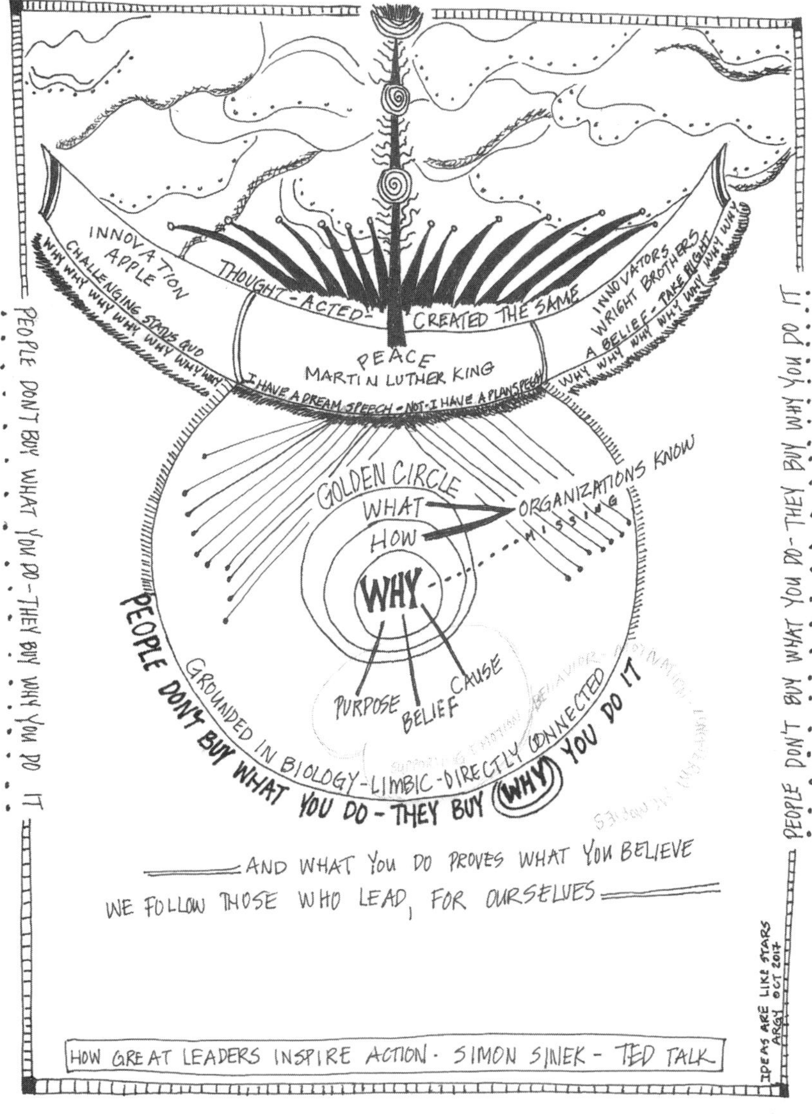

Source: Argy Nestor, director of Arts Education, Maine Arts Commission (MAC).

PAUSE AND REFLECT

While considering WHAT we should assist our students in learning, consider the following questions:

- What is essential for our students to know, be able to do, understand, appreciate, and be like in order to be successful in life beyond our classroom walls—in the workplace, in higher education, in relationships, and in their community lives?
- How do we explicitly teach reasoning skills, habits of work and learning (HOWLs), and metacognitive skills?
- How do we use rigorous and relevant content or factual examples to build a conceptual understanding of crucial crosscutting concepts and big ideas?
- How do we make sure that content becomes the vehicle for learning and that we provide feedback

(Continued)

(Continued)

about essential thinking skills, reasoning skills, and HOWLs in addition to the acquisition of knowledge?

- What are the graduation standards? What do we hope our students will become by the time they graduate? What are the incremental steps along the way to help achieve these outcomes? Do businesses and higher education recommend the graduation standards we have established? Do our graduation outcomes represent the understandings, skills, and dispositions required for success beyond our school walls?

Consider these recommendations when determining your WHAT:

- Ensure that WHAT we value as most essential is WHAT we teach, assess, and report. Avoid the pitfall of focusing on content or factual knowledge because it is what seems easiest to assess or what has been traditionally assessed, scored, and reported out to external stakeholders.
- If you believe critical thinking is most essential, unpack the skill, allow students ample opportunities to practice the skill using a variety of content, provide descriptive feedback during the learning, engage students in self-assessing and goal setting for next steps, assess the skill using agreed upon success criteria and articulated levels of performance, have learners collect evidence of their progress, and report progress with regard to the acquisition and proficiency of the skill. The same holds true for perseverance to produce quality work, or communicate effectively, or the ability to work productively with others. All of which, by the way, are identified by businesses as skills needed for success in the workplace.
- Focus on teaching students strategies *for* learning. The old Chinese proverb of the importance of teaching people to fish for themselves holds true with learning; when we teach students metacognitive skills and how to learn for themselves, we have changed their lives forever, truly helping them become self-directed lifelong learners. When students know how to learn for themselves and when clarity is achieved, we dramatically cut down on the long lines at our desks with students asking, "Is this what you are looking for? Is this what you want?"
- Consult your standards documents as part of determining WHAT is taught, but be sure to also focus on industry or workforce development standards as well. Engage community, business, and higher education members on each curriculum team. Seek their input, expertise, and resources.
- Organize curriculum into units of study that are relevant to learners and life in the future (not just relevant within the walls of school). We encourage schools and districts to eliminate, when at all possible, artificial content containers (e.g., math, English, social studies, science, art, career education, physical education, music, world language) and instead to organize curriculum around authentic problems, tasks, guiding questions, or outcomes. Model collaboration and effective communication by working with other educators with different content knowledge or skill sets around meaningful curriculum. Better yet, invite community, business, and higher education partners to engage with you and your students.
- Ensure that students are not simply learning discrete parts or facts but have deepened their understanding of and skill sets with big ideas, enduring understandings or transformational goals, crosscutting concepts, complex thinking and reasoning skills, and dispositions or habits of work and learning (HOWLs) that guide all of their learning units and standards.

HOW do we teach and learn WHAT we believe to be essential and enduring?

- The strategies and approaches you invest in using and learning more about through high-quality professional learning opportunities need to be those best suited for accomplishing the WHY (purpose) and the WHAT for your particular demographic.

- How you organize the learning progression or units of study around worthy questions can help facilitate the HOW you help students best learn.
- Will you invest in project-based learning, expeditions, service learning, or outdoor education as instructional strategies or approaches for accomplishing more than content alone? For instance, if we believe that collaborating with others with diverse opinions is an important ending outcome, then we will carefully organize the HOW in ways that help teach and assess those skills, rather than only through teacher-directed lectures or demonstrations.

PRACTITIONER SPOTLIGHT 2.1

CREATING MEANINGFUL CROSS-CURRICULAR UNITS OF STUDY USING ENGAGING PEDAGOGY AND SOUND ASSESSMENT FOR LEARNING STRATEGIES

What?

Our district has invested several years in clearly articulating our curriculum standards and summative scoring guides. In addition, we have been involved in a multiyear professional learning experience around assessment literacy. With the work behind us of identifying standards for reporting, we have invested our intellectual energy into examining and implementing project-based learning experiences for our high school juniors. We created a collaborative project-based learning unit of study for our learners around the critically essential skills of media literacy, engaged citizenship in a democracy, and effective communication by

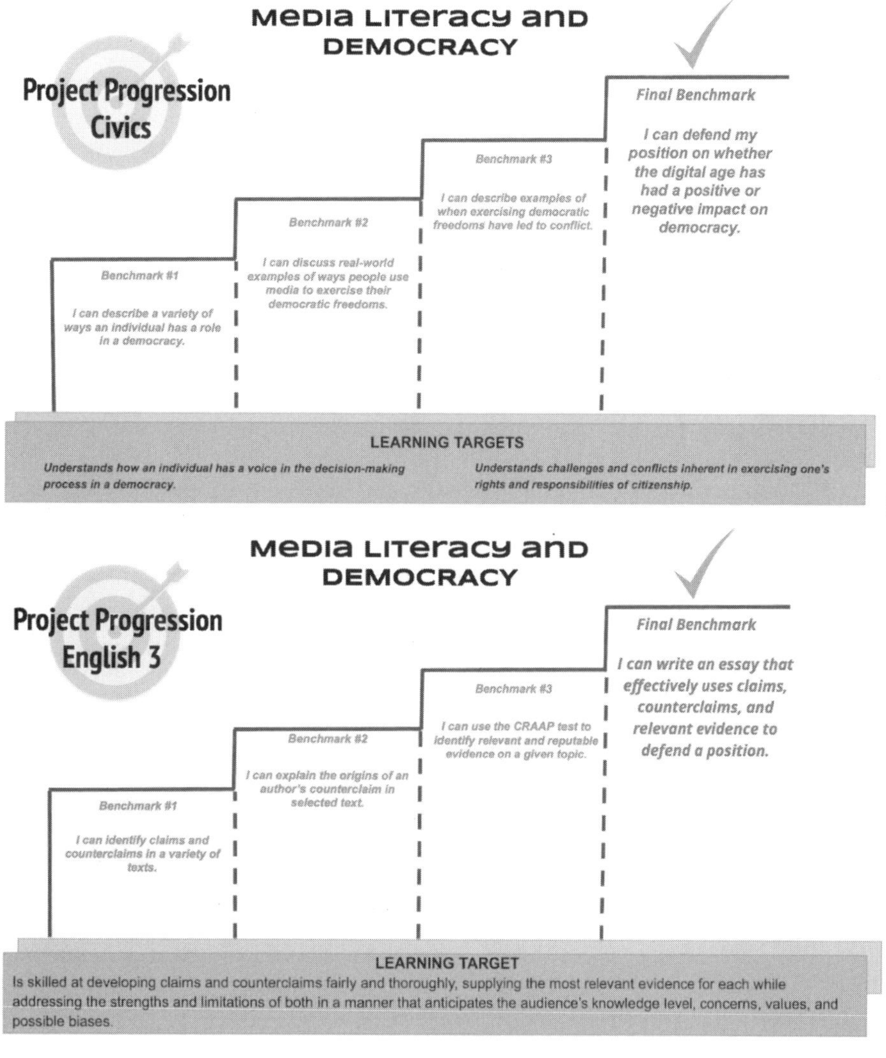

(Continued)

(Continued)

combining civics and English 3 standards and proficiency expectations. By doing so, we took what could be discrete learning targets or standards and combined them in meaningful and relevant ways. Another of our goals is to clearly articulate the learning targets for and with our learners and give them tools and strategies for self-assessment and tracking their progress. (See Chapter 4 for a more detailed examination of Stars and Stairs and other graphic organizers for articulating learning targets.)

We have been working with the Stars and Stairs rubric in our project-based civics class but calling it a "target progression." We have also been reading about evidence-based assessment. Our approach has been to break the associated targets down into learning objectives ("I can . . ." statements) and have students collect evidence in a folder throughout the project to demonstrate what they have learned and what it is they need to learn. We are also encouraging students to bring in artifacts they come across outside of class to put in their folders to use as evidence. At the end of the project, we are having students use their collections of evidence to reflect on their learning and self-assess.

Learners are working in groups of five to create a learning experience and an original informative video for a specific target audience (elementary, middle school, high school, or adult). The groups are learning from experts about iMovie from NESCOM and about lesson design from our curriculum coordinator. Each group will be teaching a lesson on digital media literacy at the end of the project.

So What?

As a result of our collaborative project-based learning unit and clear target progressions for learners, we are noticing that learners are more engaged and are exhibiting increased depth in their abilities to analyze and develop claims and counterclaims with evidence. By examining varied real-world examples of the way citizens use media to exercise their democratic freedoms, we have removed the questions about relevancy of the standards. We have also made a concerted effort not to score every assignment our learners submit; instead, we focus on providing effective feedback and continuously ask the question, "How is this work evidence of your understanding of the learning goal/target?" We strongly feel our decision to substitute feedback for scoring has allowed our learners to focus more of their energy on the learning rather than accumulating and maintaining points. Learners are clear from the get-go about what types of evidence they need to provide to demonstrate proficiency on the identified graduation standards.

Now What?

We are excited to continue learning more about project-based learning and about how to help our learners effectively "own their learning" as they collect and examine evidence of their proficiency of meaningful learning targets. We are leading a professional learning team around project-based learning and are looking forward to more of our colleagues within our high school and across our district joining us. An additional next step for us is to share our target progressions and students' evidence folders with our colleagues and encourage them to use or adapt the tools for use in their classrooms.

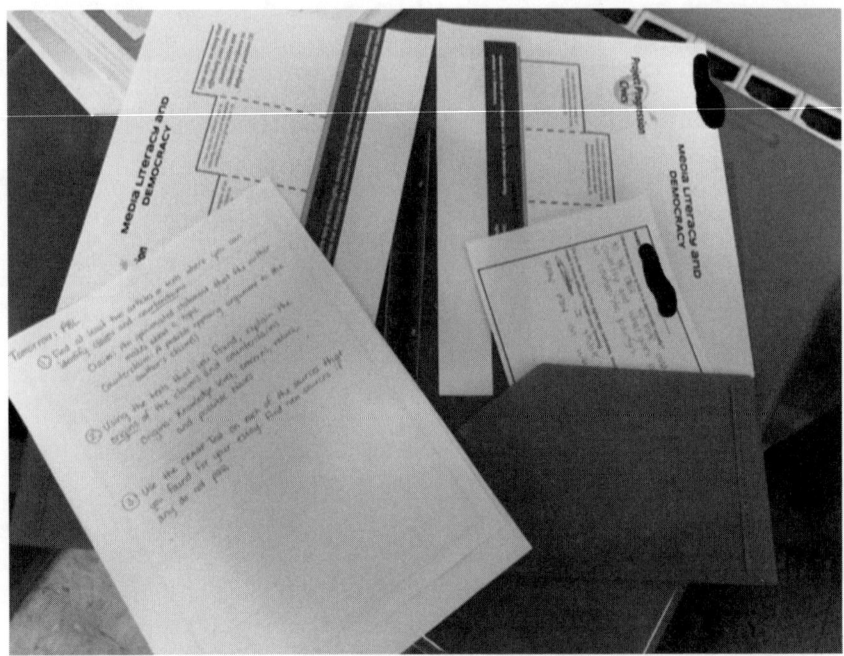

Source: Contributed by Ryan Crane, assistant principal and civics teacher, and Tracy Cowan, English teacher, Mattanawcook Academy, RSU 67.

Backward Planning in a Proficiency-Based or Standards-Based Context

In our home state, we have encountered many misconceptions about how to best assess in a standards-based or learner-centered system. From working with others across the United States and beyond, we know that these misconceptions are not particular to Maine. For instance, we have encountered many well-meaning educators and systems that fail to (a) differentiate between unpacking curriculum and (b) determine what needs to be assessed, scored, and reported on summatively. These two tasks (i.e., unpacking curriculum and assessing summatively) for many have become one and the same. This has led many educators to believe that every discrete knowledge segment and microskill needs to be formally assessed and reported upon in order to ensure that students do not have any gaps in their learning. In fact, some curriculum documents are really only summative assessment plans. These districts have taken the idea of "viable curriculum" to the extreme. In doing so, the curriculum is then left to either individual teachers or teams, or the purchased programs become the de facto curriculum. Sometimes it seems to educators that there are multiple competing curriculum—the program plus the district assessment or reporting plan—referred to by leadership as the curriculum.

Districts and learning organizations have spent years of professional learning time deconstructing Common Core State Standards, Next Generation Science Standards (NGSS), and other state and national standards in ways that parcel out all the pieces involved in learning the complex standard(s). Attention was then turned to designing scoring guides that hold students to learning "foundational skills" before "leveling up" to the standard. Others have created complex reporting systems where students are responsible for demonstrating hundreds of discrete learning targets multiple times in the name of triangulation or trend scoring or power law. Many of these systems fail to have students put all the pieces and parts together to demonstrate proficiency of the original rich, complex standard. They have mistaken a sum of the parts for the whole.

Wiggins and McTighe (1998) helped us think about backward planning in their seminal work, *Understanding by Design*. As part of that original design, we learned to create culminating tasks and rubrics for those engaging tasks tied to identified standards before planning individual lesson plans. We are grateful for this work and its evolution over the past several decades (Wiggins & McTighe, 2005, 2011). Surprisingly, we still find many educators and systems that either do not engage in backward planning, or if they do, they are stuck in 1998 in their thinking on the topic. We are grateful for the evolution of our understanding of backward planning to include the three-stage process advocated by Wiggins and McTighe (2011): Stage 1: Desired Results, Stage 2: Evidence, and Stage 3: Learning Plan. Assessment evidence should be aligned to and stem from clarity around the desired results, and as Wiggins and McTighe have reminded us, understanding is demonstrated when learners make meaning and transfer their learning through authentic performances.

In a standards-based or proficiency-based landscape, once we have identified the worthy outcomes and standards we are helping our students learn and have determined what it means to be proficient with regard to the standard(s), we are well on our way to planning with the end in mind. The evolution that has taken place with backward planning over the past twenty years, as we see it, is an opening up of multiple ways that students can learn and demonstrate their learning. This is opposed to all students engaging in the same culminating task or common summative assessment or the same series of teacher-directed lessons. Backward planning to us means educators agree collaboratively with others in their disciplines, teams, schools, states, and professional organizations about what it means to be proficient with worthy standards. They then distinguish between the varying levels of performance. Educators consider what kinds of evidence will demonstrate students' proficiency of the standards. Then, the real work begins. Instead of spending all professional learning time debating the semantics of the rubric or creating the perfect common summative assessment, educators turn their attention to planning HOW they will help learners engage in meaningful ways with the standards and HOW they will teach them strategies for learning. These educators know that they need to spend more time designing learning opportunities and feedback loops around clear targets and success criteria. In this way, backward planning includes both backward design and what we have come to call forward design.

When we plan with the end in mind, we become very clear about what outcomes we seek and what standards are to be learned and assessed, what the varied levels of performance look like, and how the learning will be transferred or applied. Any standard, skill, disposition, appreciation, or understanding worth acquiring is complex and multifaceted. While we deconstruct standards into chunks to ensure that we help students gain the specific knowledge, understanding, and skills needed to become more proficient, we cannot lose sight of the forest for the trees. We cannot forget our WHY and how the WHAT fits into it. We cannot forget that we need learners to not only be able to complete the parts satisfactorily but, most importantly, want them to show their growing proficiency with standards in authentic, meaningful, and rigorous ways.

PRACTITIONER SPOTLIGHT 2.2

LEARNING TRACKER: FROM PARTS TO WHOLE

What?

After reading *Seven Strategies of Assessment for Learning* by Chappuis (2015) and attending the Assessment for Learning Conferences at the University of Southern Maine, I set about to incorporate the research of Chappuis into my high school social studies classroom. As I reflected on my practice, I realized that in service of proficiency-based education, I had placed far too much emphasis on summative assessment. As I adapted my assessment practices in service of proficiency-based education, I began assessing my students multiple times so that I could evaluate a student's body of evidence to determine if he or she demonstrated mastery with respect to a certain thinking skill.

Reading Chappuis helped me to notice that while my approach was an improvement over traditional practice, it prioritized summative performance, which flew in the face of assessment research. The challenge, then, was to modify my teaching and assessment practices to emphasize formative assessment. I started first with a U.S. History course.

The process is best illustrated with a concrete example. I began by looking at my course outcomes, one of which calls for students to be able to analyze reasons the United States has entered into a conflict or war. To make this more concrete, I decided that I wanted students to analyze perspectives for why the United States went to war with Spain in 1898. To go beyond the standard, I wanted students to demonstrate deeper thinking rather than analyzing multiple perspectives: In this case, I expected them to demonstrate decision-making capacity with respect to the situation at hand. Next, I conceived of my performance task, minding the need for the task to incorporate both types of thinking. I settled on a briefing memo, a document solicited frequently by presidents to gather context regarding particular issues and used to inform their decision-making.

From there, I started to build a rubric. My goal was a rubric that would break each layer—the content, the two thinking skills (analyzing perspectives and decision-making), and the product format—into teachable parts. It is worth noting here that rubric writing and unit planning became inseparable. See the Chapter 2 appendix for the complete task and rubric.

So What?

This primary advantage of this approach is that it simulates real-world learning processes. I've long heard that teachers should adopt the methods of coaches, but I've never found a means to successfully adapt that analogy to a classroom. Now, in creating

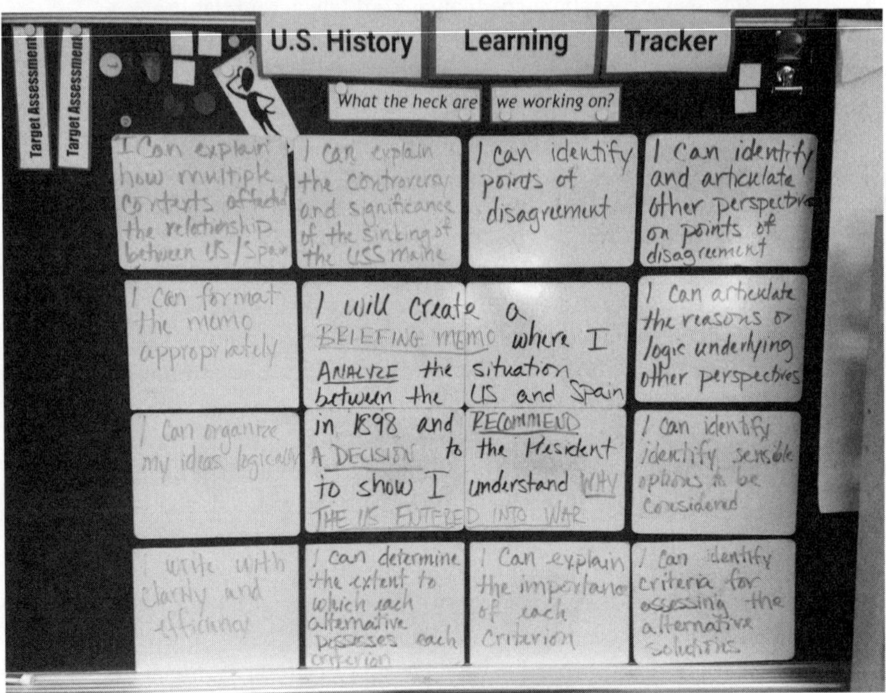

the performance task and using it as an anchor for my daily instruction, I feel myself acting like a coach, breaking down a whole skill, action, or movement into constituent parts so that students can learn the proper "mechanics." This is similar to how baseball coaches teach hitting, how track coaches teach running form, and how football coaches teach various techniques.

Secondly, this approach insists that I create risk-free learning opportunities that invite formative feedback. What is more, I can share this responsibility with students since the daily learning is so focused. Since students come to understand the performance task as "game day," they are more willing to make and fix mistakes in our daily learning.

Now What?

There are still several things I need to refine in my adoption of this approach. To create a loop between our daily learning and our final task, I created a learning tracker, which I use to introduce each rubric skill. I also use it as a review tool so that students see connections across their daily learning. Still, once I distribute the rubric, I find myself referencing the learning tracker and regularly directing students' attention to the most important parts to keep them focused on what matters. To me, this means that the rollout and or format of the rubric needs refinement. It also means that more needs to be done to create a shared understanding between teacher and student of how the parts relate to the whole and a clearer sense of what mastery looks like.

Moving forward, I also need to develop more tasks for my classroom practice, which I expect to get easier with each application.

Source: Contributed by Nathan Theriault, high school social studies teacher, Edward Little High School, Aurburn School District.

Designing Forward and Backward

Based on the work of Chappuis, Stiggins, Chappuis, and Arter (2012), there are five keys to high-quality classroom assessment that have guided our work and helped us deepen our assessment understanding. These keys to quality assessments include clear purpose, clear targets, sound design, effective communication, and student involvement. The keys to quality have assisted us in our understanding of how to create classroom assessment experiences that yield accurate information and evidence of learning while informing instructional decisions and learners' next steps. Over the past decade, we have come to see these keys to quality morph and our foci change as our experiences and explorations have led us down paths of discovery about the complex acts of teaching, learning, and leading.

We view these keys to quality as depicted in Figure 2.2. You will note that we see clear learning targets as a necessary focus for gathering evidence of learning. We have renamed student involvement as "assessment-literate learner" to convey our idea that the goal of the learning and assessment process is to help develop and create learners who truly own their learning. Hattie refers to this concept as "assessment-capable" learners, as do Moss and Brookhart (2012). For us, assessment-literate learners are as follows:

- Learners who know how to collect and use assessment evidence about their learning to help guide their next steps
- Learners who have strong metacognitive skills and can accurately appraise their learning based on success criteria
- Learners who possess clarity about the learning targets and what proficiency looks like
- Learners who exhibit growth mindsets around seeking and implementing feedback
- Learners who regularly reflect on their learning and advocate for their learning needs
- Learners who see assessment evidence as an essential part of the learning process
- Learners who know that there is always a next step to take
- Learners who are not caught up in simply collecting points, grades, or scores or in completing tasks

We believe that backward planning couldn't be more true for today's proficiency-based or standards-based context. Whether intended or not, backward planning for many of us has commonly resulted in a fixation around creating an engaging culminating or common summative task and the corresponding rubrics or scoring guides.

FIGURE 2.2 ● Keys to High-Quality Classroom Assessment Concept Map

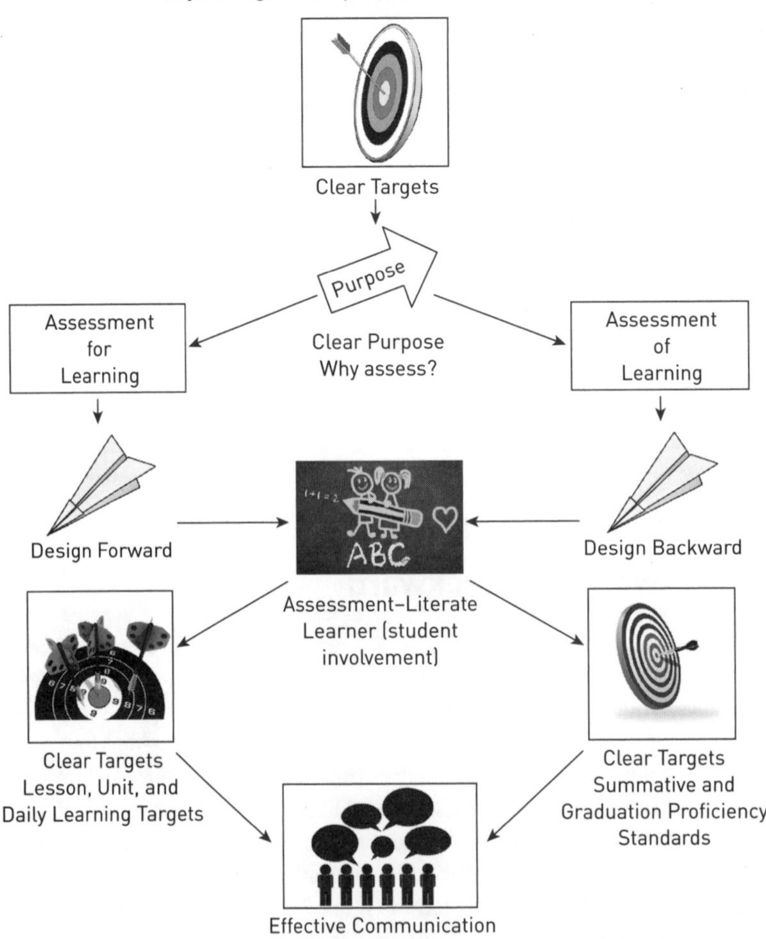

Source: Adapted from Chappuis et al. (2012).

From our personal experiences and those shared with us by many educators, we have noted a trend in backward planning that results in most of our professional planning time with colleagues being spent around the assessment *of* learning task, leaving little time for planning how to engage our learners in high-impact assessment *for* learning strategies. We have also noted that backward planning of culminating tasks has resulted oftentimes in providing only one way of demonstrating knowledge and skills of the particular standards being assessed. With more emphasis placed on encouraging different ways for students to demonstrate their proficiency around standards, we have noted a trend of creating several choices in culminating tasks. These added assessment options seemingly satisfy the call for more "voice and choice." While it does allow for deviation from one common summative assessment or culminating task, it still emphasizes the majority of planning time be spent around creating summative or culminating tasks (designing backward) instead of focusing on what happens during the learning, which is our understanding of the intent of Understanding by Design (UbD).

We believe that in a proficiency-based or standards-based education context, once you have established clear learning targets and outcomes and a common understanding of what it means to be proficient with standards, then you have engaged in backward design thinking. In other words, you have established what students will be expected to know, do, and/or become by the end of the unit of study—what it means to be proficient with the standards being assessed. Clear learning targets is an essential first step to sound design, regardless of whether you move to the assessment *for* learning or assessment *of* learning side of sound design first. We posit that in our current educational context, backward planning does not have to include the design of a culminating performance task or a common summative assessment as a first step. Instead, designing backward means that we must be very clear about the standards, outcomes, or targets we will be teaching and, most importantly, what students will be learning as well as what it means or looks like for students to become more proficient or to become masters of those learning outcomes. How and when our students show evidence of proficiency can be very different from one student to the next. We believe that multiple pathways to achieving worthy standards, differentiation, and the collection of multiple pieces of evidence is much more than allowing various products for the summative assessment (e.g., an essay, rap or song, poem, skit, multimedia production, oral presentation, demonstration, blog, meme, cartoon, diorama, selected response test, one-on-one interview).

Assessment Traps

There are many potential traps educators can fall into around classroom assessment. We feel passionate about waving the warning flag to help other educators avoid these pitfalls or at least to help them avoid staying ensnared for too long.

Trap 1: Viewing Assessment as a Product or Outcome

One trap is a product or outcome orientation kind of thinking regarding assessment. By this, we mean focusing on assessment as a product, a thing educators create or purchase, a thing learners produce or have done to them. When we fall into the product or outcome trap, we focus the vast majority of our assessment attention on creating a better assessment task, rubric, or scoring guide; we focus too much attention on the product students create to demonstrate their learning. Focusing instead on assessment for learning strategies help keep the learning (and therefore assessment) process healthy and productive. Formative assessment then becomes process-oriented and a way to learn, not simply an outcome or a product. Avoid the trap of viewing formative assessment as simply the practice for the summative (e.g., the homework or quiz before the test, the practice essay or oral presentation before the on-demand essay or presentation). When we view formative assessment as a thing (a noun), we miss much of its potential for positively impacting learning. Instead, we challenge educators to view assessing formatively as an action verb—an active learning process, a set of strategies, techniques, and tools to use to further learning.

Trap 2: Viewing Assessment for Learning as Another Initiative

Another trap is viewing assessment literacy or assessment for learning as an initiative or another thing on educators' proverbial plates. Initiatives come and go and are often associated with legislative mandates or new district or building leadership. Initiatives are usually top-down and are rolled out as a way to "fix" something educators are doing incorrectly. As a result, initiatives are often associated with a sense of instability and feelings of resistance or resentment on the part of educators who are already overwhelmed with the number of initiatives they are expected to implement. Educators experience initiative fatigue. If you have been in the profession for very long, you have seen initiatives come and go, and it is easy to develop a mindset of "this too shall pass." Assessment literacy is not an initiative, as we have stated, it's a fundamental competency for all educators and learners. Assessment literacy is foremost about the learning and how educators can create learning environments and conditions for learning by the strategies they choose that promote learning for all. Learning *is* our profession, and as such, assessment for learning is not another thing on an educator's plate; it is the plate. Assessment for learning is how we teach our students and professionals to learn for themselves. It is how we know where our learners are in the process, so we know what our next steps need to be.

Trap 3: Focusing to a Fault on the Reporting System

Be careful not to allow the tail to wag the dog when it comes to either purchasing or creating student data management systems for tracking and reporting student achievement of established standards. Student data management systems, often expensive, overbuilt, and time-intensive to maintain, can all but undo the best intentions of teacher and curriculum leaders. If the reporting system requires the summative evaluation of too many moving parts, standards, or discrete learning targets, then a district is almost guaranteed that classroom assessment and other instructional practices will suffer. The emphasis will be placed on collecting evidence of whatever needs to be reported out in a summative nature. If metacognition, reasoning skills, dispositions, and HOWLs are not formally reported out on, they will fall by the wayside in attempts to satisfy the demands of the data required by the reporting system. If the data management system requires summative scores or grades for each established learning target (not just essential or power standards), the sheer amount of summative evidence needed will skew classroom assessment practices. No matter how often teachers are told they need to focus on the learning and engage in formative assessment strategies, the requirements of the data management system (the tail if you will) will wag the dog and emphasis will be placed on assessment *of* learning not *for* learning.

If what a district or school says is their WHY (purpose) and what they believe about learning does not match the structures in place, the structures will always communicate the loudest. Communication experts tell us that only 7 percent of what we communicate is through what we say; the rest of what we communicate comes from our tone, paraverbals, nonverbals, and actions (Mehrabian, 1972). When our actions as educators and as educational systems do not match what we say we believe about learning and teaching, our actions will always speak louder than our words. Make sure that what your system reports out matches what you established as the worthy curriculum. Ensure that the sheer quantity of gatekeeping summative evaluations does not hinder HOW learning is approached in classrooms.

Trap 4: Focusing on Summative Assessment as the Means to Become a Standards-Based System

With the HOW in mind, we are reminded of another trap—that of becoming so focused on becoming a proficiency-based or standards-based system (where decisions are based on learners' proficiencies with established standards) that we shift most of our attention to the assessment of learning, or summative assessment. In such systems, the focus is on deconstructing the standards, creating learning progressions and scoring guides or rubrics, determining acceptable evidence, establishing levels of performance, teaching educators and families how to use the student data management system, building the diploma and transcript analysis, and so on, instead of upon creating learner-centered, innovative, inspiring learning environments that will engage our learners in authentic, meaningful, and rigorous experiences with the standards in which we wish them to be proficient. Sadly, we have seen teachers, schools, and entire districts turn from a focus on powerfully impactful approaches to learning, such as service learning, project-based learning, expeditionary learning, place-based learning, outdoor education, or reflective inquiry learning. Instead, they turn their attention and emphasis to building a proficiency-based system with a focus upon the assessment evidence and the reporting of the data instead of upon creating rich learning environments in which the standards are learned and applied in authentic and relevant ways.

Trap 5: Underutilizing High-Impact Instructional and Assessment Strategies

A fifth trap we often see ensnaring dedicated educators is related to the previous trap. Many dedicated educators, in an attempt to connect with the worthy idea of accommodating variety in student pacing, implement tools such as capacity matrices or organized packets (either digital or hard copy) that indicate the learning targets and tasks to be completed in order to obtain certain performance levels or to demonstrate proficiency with specific learning targets. The permeating learning assumption is "all students can learn just in different ways and at different rates." We could not agree more. Another learning assumption is that allowing students "voice and choice" will result in student ownership of their learning and create self-directed learners—an outcome we very much value. We are concerned however that the implementation strategies used are too often not high-impact strategies, as is often true in the organized "packets" we see students working on at their own seats.

In an attempt to differentiate and personalize learning for students, educators have created structures and systems in their classrooms and schools that allow students to learn at their own pace (or teacher pace if prodding or assistance is required). Often the implementation of this learning proposition results in students working independently on the tasks at the level they are on, perhaps while watching a video lesson, completing an online tutorial, reading a text, working at a learning station, monitoring their data, or working in small groups with an adult in a guided reading workshop or a mini lesson. While not the intent, teachers have often become managers of the assessment evidence, making sure that students who can race through the levels, targets, and activities have more to do to keep moving on to the next targets. What we and others have noted is that while students have shown the evidence of becoming proficient with the learning targets, they often do not possess a deep grasp of the concepts or skills. They have not fully developed collaboration and perspective consciousness, or they have missed many opportunities to learn with and from others. Teachers have often felt pressure to forfeit powerful learner-centered approaches, such as project-based learning, service learning, expeditionary learning, and so on, in lieu of a more individualized approach to collect learning target evidence. These concepts are not mutually exclusive. It is possible to have well-articulated, worthy standards and learning targets while still engaging students in the learning using high-impact strategies. One critical element is not to overbuild the reporting system.

Need for Assessment-Literate Leaders

> Just as leaders can have a positive impact on achievement, they also can have a marginal, or worse, a negative impact on achievement. When leaders concentrate on the wrong school and/or classroom practices or miscalculate the magnitude or "order" of the change they are attempting to implement, they can negatively impact student achievement. (Waters and Cameron, 2007)

In order to help teachers avoid classroom assessment traps and to become more assessment literate, there is a great need for assessment-literate leaders. Over the past few decades, school leaders have had many responsibilities added to their roles, including that of instructional leadership. School leaders feel the pressure of managing their schools and districts, meeting the demands of increasing mandates with decreasing budgets, as well as leading the learning of their staff and students in impactful ways. Turnover and burnout rates for school administrators, like teachers, are alarmingly high. The job of a school leader is enormous and often overwhelming. Their responsibilities are great, as are their potential for impact on their staffs, students, and communities. With the demands of the role, how does a school leader decide which strategies to use and how to prioritize time and resources effectively? We believe that investing in professional learning done well around high-impact teaching and learning strategies is part of the answer. We will talk more about effective professional learning in Chapters 10 and 11. In order to lead their organizations effectively, school leaders need to be champions of professional learning done well.

What Is Effective School Leadership?

PAUSE AND REFLECT

- In your experiences, what does it take for school leaders to be effective?
- Which leadership strategies are most impactful to student learning?

Let's take a look at some of what the literature and studies tell us about effective school leadership.

Types of School Leadership

There are many different ways to categorize school leadership, but two of the most common are instructional leadership and transformational leadership. Hattie (2012) described instructional leadership

FIGURE 2.3 ● High-Impact Instructional Leadership Strategies

High-Impact Instructional Leadership Strategies	
Effect Size	**Specific Strategy**
.91	Promoting and participating in teacher learning and development
.91	Evaluating one's impact as a leader and getting colleagues focused on evaluating their impacts
.84	Focusing on high-impact teaching and learning
.77	Being explicit with teachers and students about what success looks like
.74	Planning, coordinating, and evaluating teaching and the curriculum (e.g., direct involvement in the support and evaluation of teaching through regular classroom visits and ongoing formative feedback to teachers)
.60	Strategic resourcing
.57	Establishing challenging goals and high expectations for everyone (staff and students)
.49	Ensuring an orderly and supportive environment both inside and outside the classroom

Source: Adapted from Hattie (2015).

in the following way: "Principals are engaged in instructional leadership when they have their major focus on creating a learning climate free of disruption, a system of clear teaching objectives, and high expectations for teachers and students." He went on to describe transformational leadership "as an emphasis on inspiring teachers to new levels of energy, commitment, and moral purpose such that they work collaboratively to overcome challenges and reach ambitious goals" (Hattie, 2012). According to Robinson, Lloyd, and Rowe (2008), when considering the impact the type of school leadership has on student achievement, instructional leadership has an overall effect size (or ES) of 0.42, while transformational leadership has an overall effect size of 0.11. Please note that a comprehensive explanation of effect sizes can be found in Chapters 3 and 7.With the aforementioned research in mind, it is important that school leaders interested in influencing student outcomes employ instructional leadership strategies. See Figure 2.3 for specific high-impact instructional leadership strategies.

"The more leaders focus their influence, their learning, and their relationships with teachers on the core business of teaching and learning, the greater their likely influence on student outcomes" (Robinson et al., 2008).

In order for school leaders to greatly influence teacher practices that improve student learning, they must engage in the teaching and learning process, model impactful strategies, observe classrooms regularly, provide ongoing formative feedback, and set high expectations. They must understand the place of assessment for learning in student and professional learning and be sure that their feedback to staff adheres to principles of assessment literacy, evidence-based learning, and teaching strategies. In other words, they must be assessment literate.

> The high-impact leader creates a school climate in which everybody learns, learning is shared, and critique isn't just tolerated, but welcomed . . . There's mutual agreement that any interventions that don't achieve the intended impact will be changed or dropped. This means moving from anecdotes and war stories to solid evidence. (Hattie, 2015)

In a collaborative report *Leadership Matters: What the Research Says About the Importance of Principal Leadership*, the National Association for Secondary School Principals (NASSP) and the National Association for Elementary School Principals (NAESP; 2013) highlighted research completed by the Wallace Foundation (2011) about the key functions of effective school principals:

- Shaping a vision of academic success for all students, one based on high standards
- Creating a climate hospitable to education in order that safety, a cooperative spirit, and other foundations of fruitful interaction prevail

- Cultivating leadership in others so that teachers and other adults assume their part in realizing the school vision
- Improving instruction to enable teachers to teach at their best and students to learn at their utmost
- Managing people, data, and processes to foster school improvement. (NASSP & NAESP, 2013, pp. 3–4)

We have been fortunate in our assessment literacy work to encounter and benefit from several assessment-literate school and district leaders. As a result of their effective use of high-impact leadership strategies, they have been able to set their schools and districts on a pathway of instructional reform. These leaders understand that having individual assessment-literate teacher or school leaders is not nearly as impactful as focusing on the collective. As a result, they work simultaneously on improving the assessment literacy of all of their teachers, instructional coaches, and administrators through collaborative leadership approaches and high-quality professional learning opportunities for their educators. See Practitioner Spotlights 10.1 and 11.2.

Conclusion

We can assess anything; we need to make sure students are learning worthy content before we begin focusing on assessment. Before focusing on classroom assessment practices, first consider the answer to this question: What is essential for our students to know, be able to do, understand, appreciate, and be like in order to be successful in life beyond our classroom walls—in the workplace, in higher education, in relationships, and in their community lives? Planning with the end in mind is necessary in a proficiency or standards-based world. What understandings, skills, and dispositions (e.g., standards, learning outcomes, transferable goals) will students be learning? What does it look like to do those things in a proficient manner? With the answer to those questions, teachers can turn their focus to designing for learning, not just designing the summative or culminating assessment. Assessment is much more than a product, outcome, or thing; it is a collection of strategies and processes that help learners become better learners and educators become better educators. Assessment literacy is a fundamental competency for all educators. Teachers need assessment-literate school leaders who can guide and support their development and who understand deeply the complex acts of teaching and learning.

Take a Deep Dive to Further Your Understanding

- Explore the Partnership for 21st Century Learning website: www.p21.0rg.
- Read the *College, Career, and Civic Life (C3) Framework for Social Studies State Standards* from the National Council for the Social Studies: www.socialstudies.org/c3.
- Read and apply *Understanding by Design, Second Edition* by Grant Wiggins and Jay McTighe (2005), *The Understanding by Design Guide to Creating High-Quality Units* (Wiggins & McTighe, 2011), and/or the UbD Template 2.0.
- Read "John Hattie on Effective School Leadership": http://visiblelearningplus.com/news/john-hattie-effective-school-leadership.
- Read *Evaluating Instructional Leadership: Recognized Practices for Success* by Julie and Raymond Smith (2015).
- Read the report *Leadership Matters: What the Research Says About the Importance of Principal Leadership*, authored by the National Association of Secondary School Principals (NASSP) and the National Association of Elementary School Principals (NAESP; 2013): http://www.naesp.org/sites/default/files/LeadershipMatters.pdf.

Chapter 2 Appendix: U.S. History Assessment Task and Rubric (See Practitioner Spotlight 2.2 for more detail.)

U.S. History: Reasons the United States Went to War With Spain

Section 1: What Learning Will I Demonstrate?

To successfully complete this task, a student will demonstrate that he or she does the following:

- Understands the reasons the United States has or has not entered into a war or conflict
- Understands how to analyze perspectives
- Understands how to make a decision
- Understands how to write a briefing memo

Section 2: Task Description

It is March 25, 1898. For months, there has been growing tension between the United States and Spain, whose weakening empire ranges from Cuba to the Philippines. Things came to a head on February 15, 1898, when the *USS Maine*, an American battleship, exploded in Havana Harbor, Cuba. That unfortunate event has placed tremendous pressure on President William McKinley to make a decision about what to do regarding Spain.

Here is your task:

Role	You are Charles James, secretary of war for President William McKinley. You have served the president for two years—since his election in 1896—and have become a close adviser. Recently, tensions with Spain are on the rise. The president is seeking help from his advisers.
Audience	President McKinley
Format	The president has asked you to write a briefing memo.
Topic	1. What are the contexts of the time? How can each help the president understand the situation? 2. Based on the evidence at hand, what do you think happened to the *USS Maine*? 3. In light of the explosion of the *USS Maine*, what courses of action are available to the president with respect to Spain? What good and bad could potentially come from each course of action? 4. Which course of action do you ultimately recommend to the president? Given other options, why is that course of action the wisest one?

Section 3: Additional Background Info

Here are some resources you might use to *learn* as much as you possibly can about the Spanish American War. Remember, it's March 25, 1898. You CANNOT use anything that happened after that date in your report!

- "Spanish American War" at the Smithsonian National Museum of American History: http://s.si.edu/2hayUZt
- *Spanish American War* by 3 Minute History: https://youtu.be/SmamZOAAJ0M
- "The Spanish-American War" by Khan Academy: http://bit.ly/2y8LtHX

- "The United States Becomes a World Power" by Digital History: http://bit.ly/2jBHS2p
- "The Spanish American War" by Digital History: http://bit.ly/2wzKP4O

Section 4: Rubric

	SKILL	Beyond	Meeting	Partially Meeting	Not Meeting
			Content Criteria		
Standard #1: **Understands the reasons the United States did or did not enter into a war or conflict.**	**SKILL** I can explain how multiple contexts affected the U.S. relationship with Spain.	I can explain accurately and in great detail how the impact of global, regional, and national events affect the relationship between the United States and Spain.	I can explain accurately how the impact of global, regional, and national events affect the relationship between the United States and Spain.	I can explain accurately the impact of some contexts on the relationship between the United States and Spain.	I can explain in limited or inaccurate ways the impact of contexts on the relationship between the United States and Spain.
	SKILL I can explain the controversy and significance of the sinking of the *USS Maine*.	I can detail what happened before and after the sinking of the *USS Maine* with sources and explain in depth why it matters.	I can explain accurately the controversy over the sinking of the *USS Maine* and how it relates to various contexts.	I can explain the controversy surrounding the sinking of the *USS Maine* but only parts of the significance.	I cannot explain the controversy or significance of the event.
			Reasoning Criteria		
Complex Reasoning: Analyzing Perspectives **The student properly executes (at least) the 3.0 skill to MEET PROFICIENCY.**	**SKILL** I can identify points of disagreement.	I identify and explain multiple contexts related to situation. I add accurate details beyond what we discussed in class.	I identify and explain multiple contexts related to the start of the Spanish American War.	I identify some explicit points of disagreement, but I identify other elements or points of agreement that are not.	I identify elements of an issue as points of disagreement that are not.
	SKILL I can identify and articulate other perspectives on points of disagreement.	I describe deliberately and precisely how each context relates to the situation.	I describe with accuracy how each context relates to the president's decision on how to deal with Spain.	I identify and articulate one perspective with few details or in a way that demonstrates some confusion or limited understanding of that perspective.	I identify and articulate one perspective in a way that demonstrates significant confusion and/or a lack of understanding of that perspective.
	SKILL I can articulate the reasons or logic underlying other perspectives.	I explain which context matters the most and which matters the least, and I justify and defend my reasoning.	I explain which context matters the most in this situation.	I articulate only the most obvious reasons or logic underlying a perspective and/or demonstrate some confusion or misunderstanding about the reasons or logic.	I simply restate or paraphrase the perspective or articulate reasons or logic that demonstrate significant confusion.

(Continued)

(Continued)

	SKILL	Beyond	Meeting	Partially Meeting	Not Meeting
Complex Reasoning: Decision-Making **The student properly executes (at least) the 3.0 skill to EXCEED PROFICIENCY.**	**SKILL** I can identify sensible options solutions to be considered.	I identify options that are seemingly equal and reflect an in-depth understanding of the obvious, as well as the less obvious, alternatives relevant to the situation.	I identify multiple sensible options for the president that reflect a realistic understanding of the circumstances.	I identify perspectives that are not all seemingly equal or that reflect confusion or limited understanding of the situation.	I identify perspectives that are not equal or that reflect significant confusion or a lack of understanding of the situation.
	SKILL I can identify the criteria for assessing the alternative solutions.	I identify the important decision-making criteria that should be considered as well as criteria that are less obvious. These criteria reflect a thorough understanding of the situation.	I identify the important decision-making criteria that should be considered. These criteria reflect a basic understanding of the situation.	I identify only some important decision-making criteria and/or criteria that reflect some confusion or a limited understanding of the situation.	I identify decision-making criteria that reflect significant confusion or a lack of understanding of the situation.
	SKILL I can explain the importance of each criterion.	I explain these criteria in a way that reflects a careful consideration of the relevancy of the criterion.	I prioritize decision-making criteria in a way that reflects consideration of the relevancy of the criterion.	I prioritize criteria in a way that reflects consideration of the relevancy of some criteria but a lack of consideration of the relevancy of others.	I prioritize each criterion in a way that reflects a lack of consideration of the relevancy of the criterion.
	SKILL I can determine the extent to which each alternative possesses each criterion and justify it.	I determine the extent to which each alternative possesses each criterion and justify this with information or knowledge at an unusual level of depth.	I determine the extent to which each alternative possesses each criterion and justify this with appropriate information or knowledge.	I determine the extent to which some of the alternatives possess each criterion or the extent to which all of the alternatives possess some of the criteria.	I inaccurately determine the extent to which each alternative possesses each criterion.
Product					
Format	**SKILL** I can format the memo appropriately.	N/A	Formatting includes date and full names and titles of author and recipient. The subject line is specific and informative. Headings are bold and capitalized as well as identify the focus of each section.	Formatting is inconsistent with expectations.	Formatting was disregarded throughout.

	SKILL	Beyond	Meeting	Partially Meeting	Not Meeting
Organization	**SKILL** I can organize my ideas logically.	N/A	Each paragraph relates to the purpose of the heading and the memo. Information is sequenced in a way that makes sense (main points are clear). It contains visual cues (headings, bullets, etc.) and guides readers. The recommendation follows from the body of the memo.	There is a disconnect at times between a few paragraphs and headings. The sequencing of information is confusing at times. The recommendation is confusing.	There is no relationship between the headings and my paragraphs. My sequencing of ideas is confusing and cannot be followed. The recommendation isn't provided or is illogical.
Writing	**SKILL** I write with clarity and efficiency.	There are no unnecessary words or phrases. I avoid jargon and use simple words throughout. I use active voice. All my sentences have a clear subject and verb. My tone reflects that I embrace the character throughout.	There are few unnecessary words or phrases. It avoids jargon and complex words when simpler words are available. It uses active voice often. Sentences have clear subject-verb relationships. The tone is suited to the situation.	I use unnecessary words or phrases to get my point across. I misuse some words and interfere with the reader's understanding in some places. My tone is inconsistent for the situation.	I am excessively wordy to the point that it is a distraction to the reader throughout the memo. I misuse words and obscure my meaning in many places. My tone is mostly inappropriate.

Section 5: Product

CLASSIFIED

FOR INFORMATION

Issue

Directions: In this section, you should clearly explain the question or issue that requires the president's attention. Refer to Section 2 if you are unsure what the issue is. This section should be short and sweet: no more than three sentences.

Background

Directions: In the background section, you should do the following:

- Describe the context and background information needed to bring the president up to speed on the issue.
- Explain what recent event(s) have brought us to this point.

Options and Considerations

Directions: In the considerations section, you should identify and explain three options available to the president to deal with the issue.

You should also explain the pros and cons of each option. Which groups will benefit from each option? How and why will they benefit? Which groups will lose out from each option? How and why will they lose out? What risks come with each option?

Recommendation

Directions: In the recommendations section, you should make a clear recommendation to the president about which option is the best and why. To convince him, you will have to explain why he should look past the risks and cons you identified in the previous section.

Respectfully,
Charles James
(Real name here)

The Convergence of Research and Practice

Seven Strategies of Assessment for Learning Meets High-Impact Strategies

Key Takeaways

Empirical evidence supports the claim of high-impact teaching, learning, and assessment strategies.

Teachers and leaders need a good grasp of evidence-based practices and need to continue to hone their beliefs and practices based on empirical evidence and experience. What is the balance of reflecting on practice (what we do) and research (what we read and hear)?

There is a strong match between *Seven Strategies of Assessment for Learning* by Chappuis (2015) and the empirical evidence from *Visible Learning* by Hattie (2009, 2012).

In order for learners to experience high-impact strategies, teachers and leaders need to understand their depth and complexity. Deeper understanding of these strategies is promoted by using visual forms like learning progressions, concept maps, and lists to self-assess and set goals for professional development (PD).

What is the evidence from research that supports and propels teachers' practices and students' accomplishments? In this chapter, we look at the body of evidence we are calling high-impact strategies of assessment for learning—in particular, the synthesis of research in Hattie's (2009, 2012) *Visible Learning*. We are at a critical point in assessment literacy, a point at which we can talk about evidence-based practice. The empirical research is more than just a study here and a study there; it is the accumulation of thousands of studies in rigorous research reviews. We have noticed a surprising convergence and consistency in the research findings prompting deeper discussions about things like teacher clarity, feedback, goal setting, and self-regulated learning. This comes at a time when there is an expectation for teachers and leaders to have a good grasp of evidence-based practices. In this chapter, we keep the focus on practices that yield results. To be effective and to support growth and learning, we all must find the right balance of reflecting on practice (what we do) and research (what we read and hear).

As we began to collaborate on our journey in assessment literacy, we were very excited as we merged research literature, models of assessment for learning, and instructional practices. One of the most repeated phrases that begins and punctuates professional dialogue is "research says," and the strong connection of research results with teaching, learning, and assessment is what caught our attention (Beaudry & Miller, 2016). One of our big "aha moments" that led us to write this book was the convergence of (1) research literature from Hattie (2009, 2012), (2) models of assessment for learning from Chappuis (2012, 2015), and (3) instructional practice (Dean, Hubbell, Pitler, & Stone, 2012; Marzano, 2001). We were most encouraged by the alignment of the seven strategies of assessment for learning with the high-impact strategies. See Figure 3.1 for the concept map that overlays the seven strategies with Hattie's effect sizes. We will unpack this concept map and discuss each of the strategies and how it is represented as a high-impact strategy. To interpret high impact, we need to explain effect sizes and fit them to the seven strategies of assessment for learning model. We provide a deeper understanding of each strategy by using a learning progression to explain just how each strategy may be transferred into practice. This work builds on the seven strategies model to visualize the intersection of teaching, learning, and assessment (Chappuis, 2015). See Figure 3.1.

So, how did we get from the seven strategies model to the high-impact assessment for learning model, and why is this important? Our first step was to analyze and evaluate the professional research on teaching, learning, and assessment. The accumulation of evidence from quantitative research, experimental, nonexperimental, and correlational studies was astounding. According to Hattie's (2009, 2012) work in *Visible Learning*, there are hundreds of thousands of studies not only stored in digital databases but coded and sorted in summaries of meta-analyses.

The next wave of researchers to use meta-analysis to support instructional models and help us create a better understanding of formative assessment were folks like Black and Wiliam (1998) and Marzano (2001). The key insights from meta-analysis reviews are (1) we have quantitative

FIGURE 3.1 ● Seven Strategies of Assessment for Learning

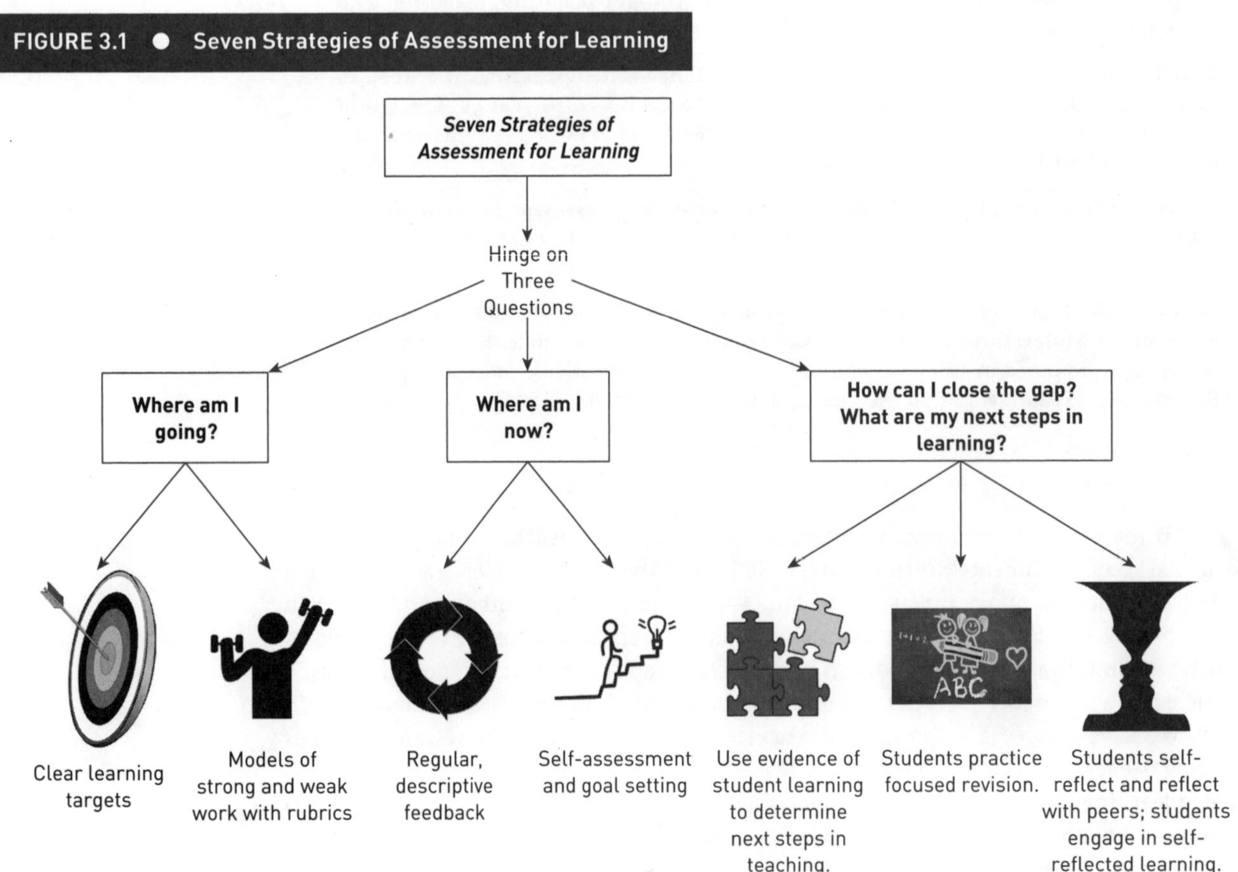

Source: Adapted from Chappuis (2015)

estimates of the impact of these practices from many studies that lead us to conclude that some strategies have greater value and (2) numerous examples of what the actual experimental studies and practices under study look like.

In 2009, Hattie and his research team released the first volume of *Visible Learning,* in which individual effect size estimates were calculated for over 130 different factors or influences related to teachers, teaching, students, schools, curriculum, and home. The total number and exact magnitude of the effect size estimates will be adjusted over time as new research becomes available and more studies are included, but they will remain good points of reference. As educators, we need to have a solid understanding of effect sizes, and be able to explain just what does the magnitude of an effect size really mean? There are no absolute standards to apply, and we urge you to be cautious when making inferences from individual quantitative studies and even from meta-analyses. Meta-analysis represents a preponderance of evidence—its validation of concepts with multiple studies, which is why the meta-analysis approach is so appealing to practitioners making decisions about taking action. The accumulation of evidence across numerous quantitative studies provides an overall estimate of the impact of a teaching strategy like effective feedback (effect size, or ES = 0.75) or a learning characteristic like persistence, concentration, and engagement (ES = 0.48). The effect size is a quantitative metric that estimates the overall impact of a treatment or factor in standard deviation units. Using Hattie's (2009) barometer of influence, effect sizes over 0.4 are in the "zone of desired effects" (see Figure 3.2). Effect sizes between 0.2 and 0.4 are about the range that can be expected in an average year of growth. An effect size that exceeds 0.4 is considered to be in the zone of desired effects, while effect sizes over 0.6 are considered to be large, which we label *high impact.*

An analogy we have found useful is to visualize three dump trucks. The smallest truck would be equivalent to a toy dump truck, medium would match a pickup truck, and large would be a full-size construction site dump truck. You can see that each one of them works, and each requires a set of skills. However, the truck with the greatest effect requires training and mastery of special skills. The work that can be done by a larger truck requires an investment in time, planning, and

PAUSE AND REFLECT

- What is an analogy for effect sizes that would help you understand and help you explain it to others?

FIGURE 3.2 ● Hattie's Barometer of Influences on Student Outcomes

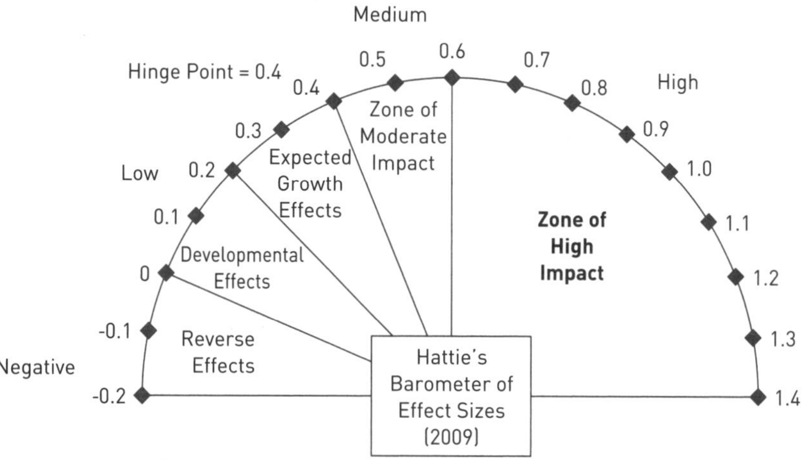

Source: Adapted from Hattie (2009).

infrastructure (big roads, loading docks, highly trained operators, and support) but has returns on the investment and may result in considerable time savings. What does a small effect size mean? It is arbitrary, but we could define 0.4 and below as small, from 0.4 up to 0.6 as medium, and 0.60 and above as large effects. For example, the effect size estimates for homework are ES = 0.29, whereas metacognitive strategies is ES = 0.69. This means that if you were to choose to spend the same amount of time on each, you would expect over double the impact on student learning. Or, said differently, you would expect to accomplish the same effects for effective feedback in half the time you would doing homework.

We suggest that a definition of a high-impact strategy is as follows:

- Specific action(s) or behavior(s) that can be used by teachers, learners, school leaders, or parents
- Summarized and reported in a formal meta-analysis with an effect size that is at least 0.40 or greater
- Recognized by teachers and leaders as something they can identify within their experiences and consider practical, useful, and feasible

The effect sizes offered a close alignment and validation with two of our essential questions: (1) What is good teaching? (2) What is good learning? Table 3.1 is a list in ranked order showing the teaching and learning strategies, and similarly, the factors that represent what is considered successful learning are in Table 3.2 (Hattie, 2009).

On the one hand, some of the strategies could be seen as a teaching strategy, like direct instruction. Strategies like classroom discussion, direct instruction, questioning, clear learning targets, and descriptive feedback are well known to most teachers. If not, it is an indicator of a goal you may want to set as part of your own learning as a professional. What we have found is that many teachers are familiar with instructional strategies but for whatever reason may not be keeping up with current practices enough to have mastery of them in their classrooms. For example, clear learning targets is a high-impact strategy with an effect size of 0.75, and teachers readily believe that clear learning targets means having the standard you are teaching

TABLE 3.1 ● What Is Good Teaching?

Effect Sizes	Teaching Strategies
0.90	Formative self-assessment (action research)
0.90	Teacher credibility
0.82	Classroom discussion
0.75	Teacher clarity/clear targets
0.75	Reciprocal teaching (peer teaching)
0.75	Descriptive feedback
0.72	Student-teacher relationships
0.71	Practice (spaced vs. massed practice)
0.64	Questioning
0.61	Problem-solving teaching
0.61	Not labeling students
0.60	Concept mapping
0.59	Direct instruction
0.58	Service learning
0.57	Worked examples
0.54	Peer tutoring (cooperative learning)
0.52	Interactive videos

TABLE 3.2 • What Is Good Learning?

Effect Sizes	Successful Learning Factors
1.33	Self-reported grades (learners' expectations)
0.65	Prior achievement (prior knowledge)
0.64	Self-questioning
0.56	Goal setting
0.53	Metacognitive strategie
0.48	Persistence
0.48	Self-motivation
0.47	Early intervention
0.45	Preschool
0.43	Self-concept
0.40	Reducing anxiety
0.36	Attitudes toward math and science
0.35	Creativity

displayed on a bulletin board, posted on a classroom website, or written on the assignment. What we know is that "clear targets on the wall are not targets in the head," a phrase we learned from Jan Chappuis at our Assessment for Learning and Leading conference in May 2017. Having students internalize clear learning targets is more complex than simply reading them in a task description or posting them on the whiteboard or on a classroom website. It consists of teachers' mastery and clarity, success criteria, and exemplars (Hattie, 2012). We will discuss some of the techniques for deeper student understanding of clear learning targets in Chapters 4 and 5.

Our next step in defining *assessment literacy* included aligning the research with the seven strategies of assessment for learning articulated by Chappuis, based on her interpretation of Sadler's notion of feedback and the "gap" to be addressed. We took each of the seven strategies and matched them with corresponding influences identified in Hattie's (2009, 2012) *Visible Learning* summaries. We saw a strong match with each of the strategies, indicating that there is empirical support for each of them and the potential for each to be a high-impact strategy. See Table 3.3 and Figure 3.3 for the concept map that overlays the seven strategies with Hattie's effect sizes. Each one of the strategies has an average effect size over 0.40, the point at which Hattie suggests the estimate goes from small to medium effects.

TABLE 3.3 • Combining High-Impact Strategies With the *Seven Strategies of Assessment for Learning*: The Outline

Where am I going?

1. Clear learning targets: teacher clarity (ES = 0.75)
2. Models of strong and weak work with rubrics (ES = 0.57)

Where am I now?

3. Timely, descriptive feedback that directly affects learning (ES = 0.75)
4. Student self-assessment and metacognitive strategies (ES = 0.69) and goal setting (ES = 0.50)

How do I close the gap? What are my strategies to get there?

5. Teachers use evidence of student learning to determine next steps (ES = 0.60)
6. Focused practice and revision (ES = 0.71)
7. Student self-reflection (ES = 0.62), tracking and sharing learning and progress with others (ES = 0.54; e.g., peers), learners' expectations (ES = 1.33)

Source: Chappuis (2015); Hattie (2012).

FIGURE 3.3 ● The Concept Map of the *Seven Strategies of Assessment for Learning* Plus Hattie's *Visible Learning* = High-Impact Assessment for Learning

Seven Strategies of Assessment for Learning

Hinge on Three Questions

Where am I going?		Where am I now?		How can I close the gap? What are my next steps in learning?		

Chappuis's Seven Strategies	Clear learning targets	Models of strong and weak work with rubrics	Regular, descriptive feedback	Self-assessment and goal setting	Use evidence of student learning to determine next steps in teaching.	Students practice focused revision.	Students self-reflect and reflect with peers; students engage in self-reflected learning.
Hattie's High-Impact Strategies	ES = 0.75 Teacher clarity Clear learning targets	ES = 0.75 Success criteria and examples	ES = 0.75 Descriptive feedback	ES = 0.40 Goal setting ES = 0.53 Metacognitive strategies	ES = 0.62 Teaching strategies ES = 0.68 Use of formative (diagnostic) assessment	ES = 0.71 Spaced versus mass practice	ES = 0.64 Self-questioning; ES = 1.33 Student expectations; ES = 0.55 Peer tutoring

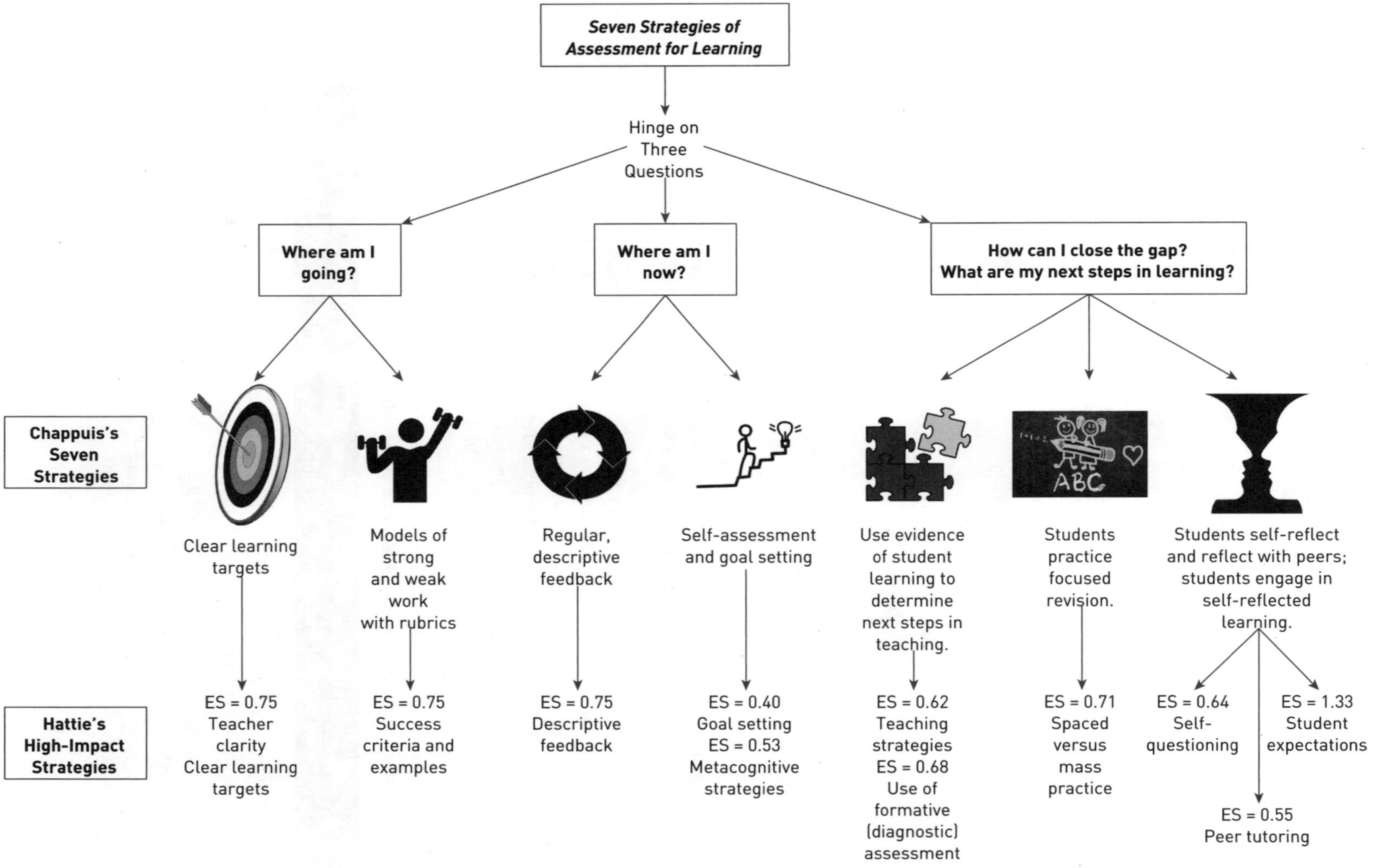

Source: Chappuis (2015); Hattie (2009, 2012).

As you can see, the seven strategies of assessment for learning are by and large in the high-impact zone! This kept us going and gave us validation that these strategies are likely to have an impact on learners and learning. Furthermore, the evidence of impact renewed our confidence that we were on the right track to improve teaching, learning, and assessing through the intentional, deliberate, persistent, and creative use of these strategies and associated tools.

By validating our essential questions—especially "What is good assessment?"—the literature is on our side and helps us to validate and map out a more complete model. While it is reassuring to have alignment with research, it is another thing to put it into practice, so it is our challenge to help learners get into the high-impact zone of influences. Our efforts blended with these studies of assessment for learning are continuously reflected on and filtered by our experiences as teachers, school leaders, and researchers. The ideas for the overlay of the effect sizes went through many iterations as a part of our learning and professional development (PD). For example, we displayed and modeled these ideas as poster gallery and digital slides as we endeavored to create concrete tools, techniques, and resources to help educators visualize the high-impact strategies in action in their classrooms. We tried out new ideas on assessment literacy means and continually asked teachers and school leaders to try the strategies and tools out in their classrooms to determine their impacts at the local level. The variety of PD processes and products, such as the visualizations in posters and the gallery walk, have been critically important to the development and refinement of learning modules, websites, and visual displays, as discussed in Chapters 10 and 11.

PAUSE AND REFLECT

Look at the effect sizes that are associated with these questions. What is good teaching, learning, and assessment? What do you see? How would you rate your mastery of the high-impact strategies? For the seven strategies of assessment for learning?

To talk more deeply about the list of the range of influences, try the Envelope Sorting Activity:

- Make a list of thirty to thirty-five influences using Tables 3.1 to 3.3, and add some of low- and medium-impact influences from Hattie's grand lists. Copy the list, and cut out each influence so it is on a separate slip of paper. Place all of the slips of paper (influences) in an envelope or a plastic sealable baggie.
- Ask participants to work in groups of no more than four. Disperse one envelope to each small group. Ask participants to sort the influences or strategies into low-, medium, and high-impact categories.
- The discussion that ensues is key. Reassure participants that it's okay if they are unsure about the specific meaning of a category (they can skip it and move on or make their most educated guess). Allow at least 10 minutes for the sorting.
- Debrief with the correct answers, remembering that effect sizes are estimates and derived from research with many individual studies combined to create an effect size.
    - Be prepared to provide definitions and details about the strategies, or make it a scavenger hunt and the learners go and find a definition and an example of an individual study.
    - Ask participants what two or three influences they really think they have mastered and what two or three influences they still do not understand or are not familiar with.

Another way to show the wide range of impact is to put the effect sizes on a horizontal scale, as shown in Figure 3.4. The range of effect sizes goes from low impact (homework, student retention, and integrated curricula programs) to medium impact (goal setting, classroom questioning, and peer tutoring) to high impact (teacher credibility, teacher clarity, and service learning). As you look through the lists of effect sizes for learning, teaching, and assessing, you may have some quick reactions—from "I already do this" to "Why is my favorite strategy rated so low?" The tables of effect sizes should be interpreted with care. And please remember that these effect sizes are estimates based from experimental research, not a certain statement on the actions of what they will do. We suggest further exploration and professional dialogue, so let's take a look at two examples: (1) homework and (2) integrated curricula.

FIGURE 3.4 ● Effect Size Estimates Placed on a Linear Scale

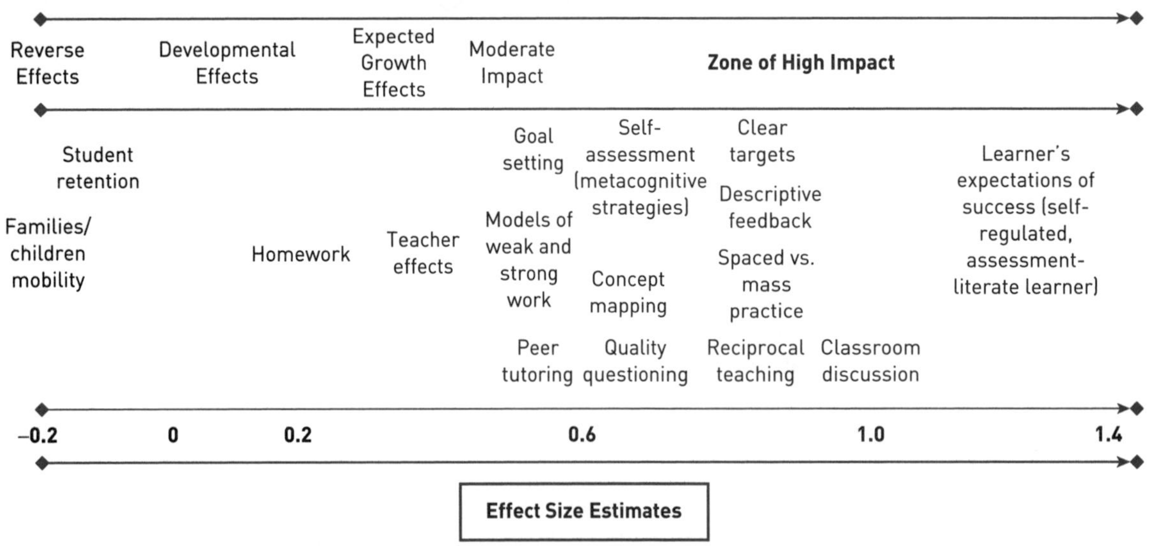

Homework practices are an entrenched practice but one that has been studied and analyzed thoroughly. Based on numerous studies and meta-analyses, there are differential effects of homework across grade levels, which makes the overall effect size of 0.29 somewhat misleading. The effects for elementary grades are much lower than for high school and postsecondary students. When homework is studied in conjunction with instructional strategies, the effects are greater when homework is linked with descriptive feedback, which we discuss in Chapter 6, and with the development of metacognitive strategies like self-assessment and goal setting, as we discuss in Chapters 7 and 9.

The overall effect size estimate for integrated curriculum programs is 0.40. Integrated curriculum is an area of intense interest currently, inviting a closer look. This effect size estimate comes from research in the 1980s and 1990s and looks at the combination of mathematics and science content. There are differential effects by subject, and integrated curriculum tended to be more "successful in elementary (0.56) and middle school (0.57) compared to high school (0.27)" (Hattie, 2009, p. 152). We believe that curriculum needs to be coupled with high-impact teaching, learning, and assessment as we discuss in Practitioner Spotlights from teachers involved in project-based, expeditionary learning programs in Chapters 4, 5, 6 and 9.

Learning Progressions for High-Impact Assessment for Learning Strategies: From Surface to Deep Practice

As we reflected on the high-impact strategies of assessment for learning, we were struck by how much time and work teachers must put into each one to realize the step up in outcomes with their students. As we sorted out the instructional strategies and techniques that go with each of the seven strategies, we made lists that were aligned with Chappuis's assessment for learning. As we deconstructed each strategy, we asked these questions: What are the actions that make these strategies work? What combination of actions and techniques deepen the learning? In the chapters about high-impact strategies (Chapters 4–8), each of the strategies is presented as a collection of more specific classroom strategies and techniques. Each strategy requires a focused, long-term commitment to master and to implement in PD over time, as discussed in Chapters 10, 11, and 12.

> The seven strategies are not a recipe to be followed step by step, although they do build on one another . . . The enabler strategies, especially Strategies 1 and 2, are generally

FIGURE 3.5 ● Learning Progression (Stairs and Stars) for Clear Learning Targets

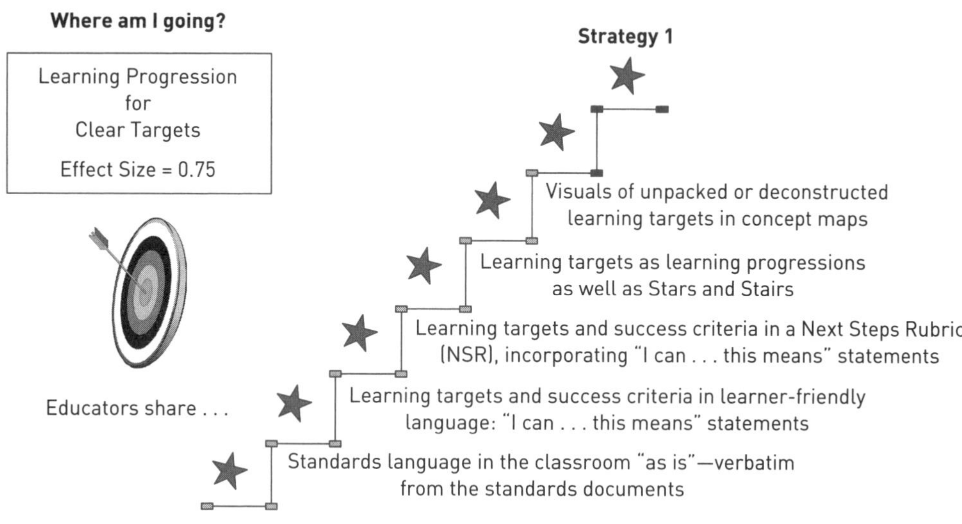

undervalued, and yet without them—without a clear picture of where we are going—it is hard to determine where we are now and even harder to identify actions to close the gap. (Chappuis, 2015, p. 10)

To visualize each of the seven strategies, we first tried to sort the steps in the list for clear learning targets into a sequence. With this focused list, we created a learning progression, a series of steps that it would likely take to get one to the high impact on learning outcomes. Our proposed learning progression for clear learning targets is Figure 3.5. The learning progression is based on Chappuis (2015) but goes further. The purpose of the learning progression is not to assert a predictable, sequential, step-by-step order but to represent the big picture and to provide a visual tool for self-assessment and goal setting. See Chapter 4 about clear learning targets and Chapter 7, which is about self-assessment, reflection, and goal setting for examples of other learning progressions. The learning progressions with their multiple steps suggest that classroom actions on the second, third, and fourth stairs are just as vital to get you and your learners to the highest impact possible.

Conclusion

The strategies and factors identified in meta-analyses may appear to be an oversimplification of the profession of teaching, or even misleading to some, especially because effect sizes cannot convey the qualitative complexities that we all know as our day-to-day classroom reality. We have found, however, that these strategies resonate deeply with teachers. Teachers often remark that they do some of the assessment for learning strategies already. They also say that they have not had the time to engage in the in-depth thinking and practice to really implement high-impact assessment for learning strategies. An active application of effect sizes is the use of a portable whiteboard. As we observed a strategy being used, we would write the effect size on a whiteboard and display it to the class or group. In this activity, we could demonstrate the relevance and prevalence of the strategies in everyday classrooms.

As we dive deeper into learning progressions for clear learning targets, descriptive feedback, and self-assessment and goal setting, we are reminded just how challenging teaching and learning truly are! These learning progressions helped us better understand what assessment literacy means, appreciate what it takes to attain as much impact as possible, and keep our focus on what is necessary for PD. In other words, the learning progression models helped us "chunk" the concept of clear learning targets into separate learning modules in order to build assessment literacy for and with teachers and leaders.

The synergy of the seven strategies model with the meta-analyses and effect sizes literature is very exciting because of the alignment and validation of practice and research. It continues to inspire us, helping us understand our next steps in the ongoing work to improve teaching, learning, and assessment for high impact as practitioners and researchers. We see them as fitting very well with standards of quality classroom assessment and will talk more about why they matter in following chapters.

Take a Deep Dive to Further Your Understanding

- In a book study, read *Seven Strategies of Assessment for Learning* by Jan Chappuis (2015).
- Take a look at the Visible Learning resources by reading John Hattie's (2009, 2012) *Visible Learning* in tandem with *Visible Learning for Teachers* and viewing the Visible Learning website (https://visible-learning.org) for more book choices.
- Dive into http://www.evidencebasedteaching.org.au.

Clear Learning Targets

Clarity Is the Goal!

Key Takeaways

Clear learning targets are foundational for both assessment *for* learning and assessment *of* learning. Clear learning targets provide the framework for all aspects of the learning, teaching, and assessment process.

Teachers need to know how to deconstruct standards in order to communicate learning intentions clearly to disparate student audiences. Standard documents are often not teacher-friendly, let alone student-friendly. As a result, teachers (preferably in teams) must take the time to carefully deconstruct the standards and transform them into learner-friendly language without losing the meaning of the original standard.

Teacher clarity, clear descriptions in learner-friendly language, success criteria, worked examples of strong and weak work, and clear communication in developmentally appropriate ways are crucial for helping learners achieve.

Learning targets need to be visualized for learners in a variety of ways, such as learning progressions, concept maps, graphic organizers like Next Steps Rubrics (NSRs), puzzle pieces, and other visual representations.

As you think about clear learning targets, imagine your students asking these essential assessment for learning questions: What am I doing? Why am I doing this? Where am I in my learning? How do I plan to get from where I am to the next step in my learning? To attain the most impact, students need to be able to answer these questions through self-assessment; with peers; and, of course, with you the teacher. The mantra for a successful classroom is this: it's all about clear learning targets.

PAUSE AND REFLECT

- How do you incorporate clear learning targets into your classroom?

Clear Learning Targets: The Progression of Strategies for High Impact

Clear learning targets consist of a collection of strategies that are the "what" of learning, especially in the classroom. We have come a long way from the sole reliance on experts in subject matter disciplines and textbooks to dictate required content knowledge, and we are more likely than ever before to be talking about standards, performance indicators, proficiency, skills, or guiding principles with our colleagues. Standards and clear targets are essential for (1) assessment *for* learning (formative), designing forward, and (2) assessment *of* learning (summative), designing backward (see Figure 4.1). Teachers help students move across the bridge between the big ideas and standards (derived from national goals, professional and discipline organizations, and state departments of education) and the learning targets for a successful classroom experience.

In our view of assessment for learning, clear targets or intentions are the day-to-day, minute-to-minute interactions of teachers and students about the "what" of learning.

Empirical evidence indicates that clear learning targets are a high-impact assessment for learning strategy with an estimated effect size (ES) of 0.75 (Hattie, 2009, 2012). Think about clear learning targets as an ongoing strategy, not just a display of the professionally written "as is" statements on the wall. One of the issues we see is teachers assuming that the clear learning targets work is done once they are written and posted. For school leaders doing observations, this may signify teachers' compliance with a school district policy to "show learning targets." Unfortunately, this practice alone is not likely to have a high-impact on the learning of all students and is reflected

FIGURE 4.1 ● The Role of Clear Targets in the Standards of Quality Assessment

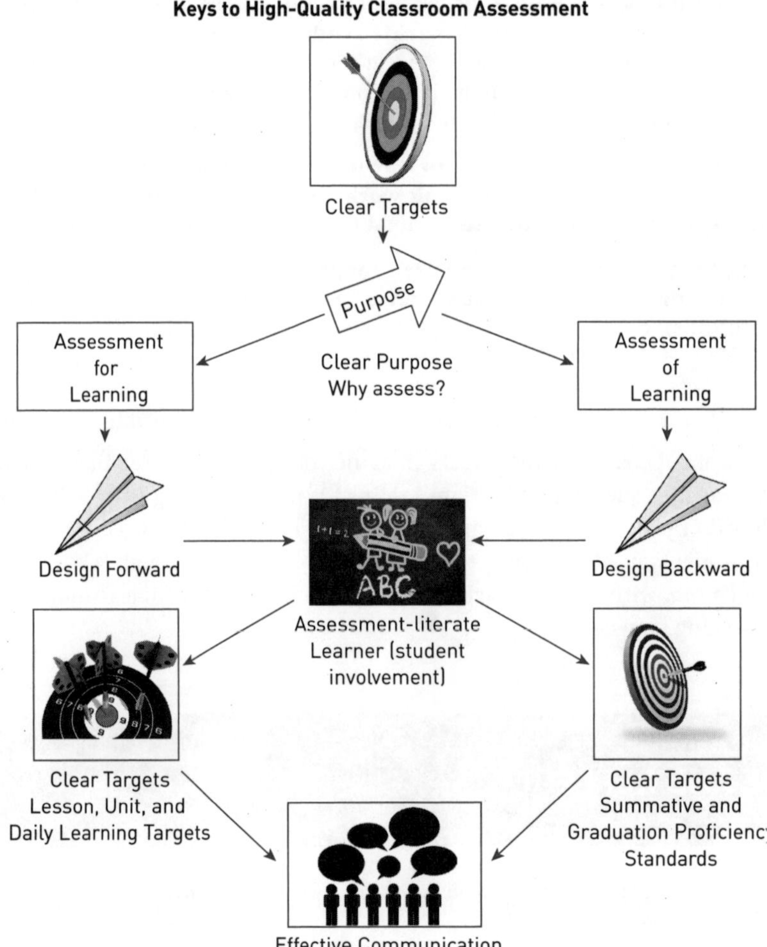

Source: Based on on Chappuis, Stiggins, Chappuis, and Arter (2015).

in one of Chappuis' most memorable phrases: "Clear targets on the wall are not necessarily clear targets in the minds of students."

These are four criteria that Hattie (2012) and Chappuis (2015) recommend:

1. Teacher clarity
2. Clear descriptions of learning outcomes or intentions
3. Clear success criteria
4. Worked examples of student work that model the learning progression from weak, developing to strong, proficient work

We will focus on teacher clarity, clear descriptions of learning outcomes, and clear criteria of success. We will use the terms *learning targets* and *learning intentions* to talk about the outcomes that classroom teachers build their teaching and collection of assessment evidence around and toward. Clear learning targets reflect worthy standards or proficiencies—those things we want students to understand in a deep manner and apply to authentic situations. Our examples of clear learning targets are what we want students to know and be able to do and what we want them to be able to self-assess and use to determine what their next steps in learning should be.

PAUSE AND REFLECT

- What terms do you use in your school district to get at the idea of clear learning targets or intentions?

Curriculum Context for Clear Learning Targets

Clear learning targets should emanate from good curriculum, not simply from a compilation of deconstructed standards and learning targets strung together in isolated, discrete activities that become assessments. Standards alone are the least common denominator of what good curriculum is. As discussed in Chapter 2, curriculum should help link together crucial skills, understandings, and habits in broader, more meaningful or transferable ways. Curriculum should purposefully help our students better understand the world in which they live and do so from a variety of perspectives. A well-designed curriculum should help learners master essential 21st century skills such as problem-solving and critical thinking skills, collaboration, effective communication skills, and processes for innovation and creativity. Such skills equip our learners for success in careers, college, communities, and healthful relationships. With a well-designed curriculum, students should be able to answer this broad question: Why am I learning this?

A Primer on Cognitive Models: Identifying, Organizing, and Communicating Clear Learning Targets From Standards Documents

We often think of standards as representing subject matter or being discipline specific, but it is essential to have a cognitive model to sort out the types of learning. Standards represent what we would like students to know, be able to do, and to become; therefore, they represent different levels of cognitive demands. Recent improvements were made to Bloom's taxonomy of cognitive demand (Anderson & Krathwohl, 2001). In this model and others, such as Webb's Depth of Knowledge, Marzano's taxonomy, and Stiggins's model of types of learning targets, cognitive demand is established as an essential ingredient in curriculum, assessment, and instructional design. Each of these models emphasizes the orderly classification of the ways we think, act, and create. Each classification is associated with strong verbs to represent the cognitive demands. There are many other versions of these cognitive models. We will use the label *clear learning targets* for our discussion because it is a flexible, learner-friendly term and is easily adapted to a variety of models.

Classroom Strategies to Influence Clear Learning Targets: From "As Is" Standards to "I Can . . . This Means" Statements

- Posting statements from standards on the wall or written on learning task templates AND
- Converting standards document language and format into learner-friendly forms by adding definitions, age-appropriate language, and student language, or a series of "I can" statements
- Converting standards document language and format into learner-friendly forms with success criteria by writing them in "I can...this means" statements
- Using concept maps to unpack and deconstruct standards incorporating nouns and objects as the nodes and strong verbs on the links or other visual metaphors
- Creating learning progressions by arranging the "I can . . . this means" statements in a graphic organizer or visual metaphor for students to see the continuum of learning or "what are my next steps?"—for example, Stars and Stairs, puzzle pieces, or pictures might be used
- Embedding examples of student work that display weak and strong work or "microprogressions" directly on learning progressions
- Directly connecting clear learning targets to feedback, self-assessment, and goal setting by adding space in the learning progressions or graphic organizers for students to check for understanding by self-assessment and goal setting

The classroom strategies are converted into a stairs learning progression in Figure 4.2. This is another way to show that the accomplishment of clear learning targets is a challenging, multifaceted endeavor, consisting of the first five steps we envision. This learning progression is shown as a stairs graphic. To make this graphic more active, you could put stars on each step and a line for the date completed, and it becomes a way to track progress (see Figure 4.3). While the steps in the progression appear to be linear, the steps can be taken in a variety of sequences and accomplish the goal of impact as long as the student works her or his way to the top of the stairs and masters the knowledge and skills.

FIGURE 4.2 ● Learning Progression for Clear Learning Targets

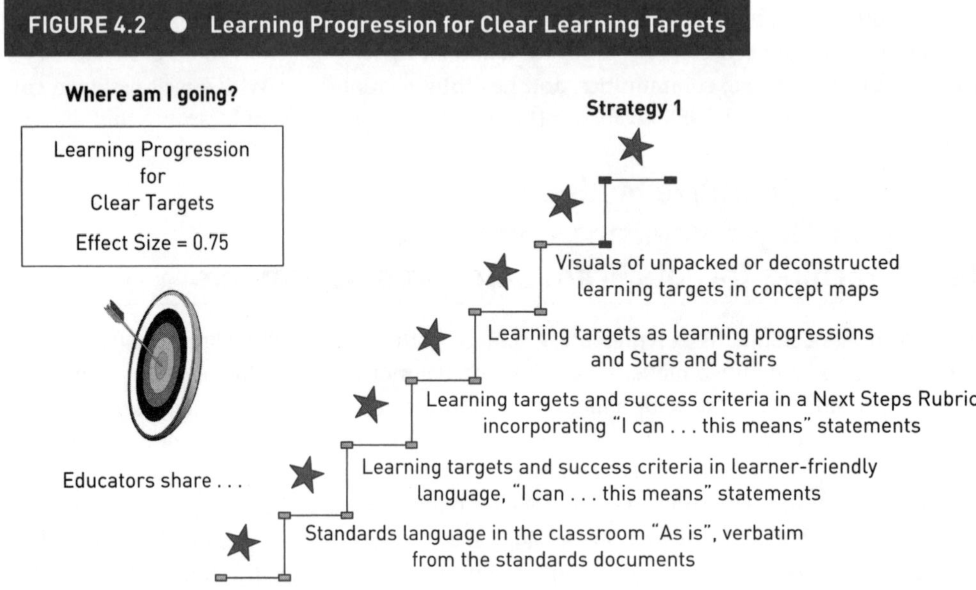

FIGURE 4.3 ● Tracking Evidence With Stars and Stairs Learning Progression for Clear Learning Targets

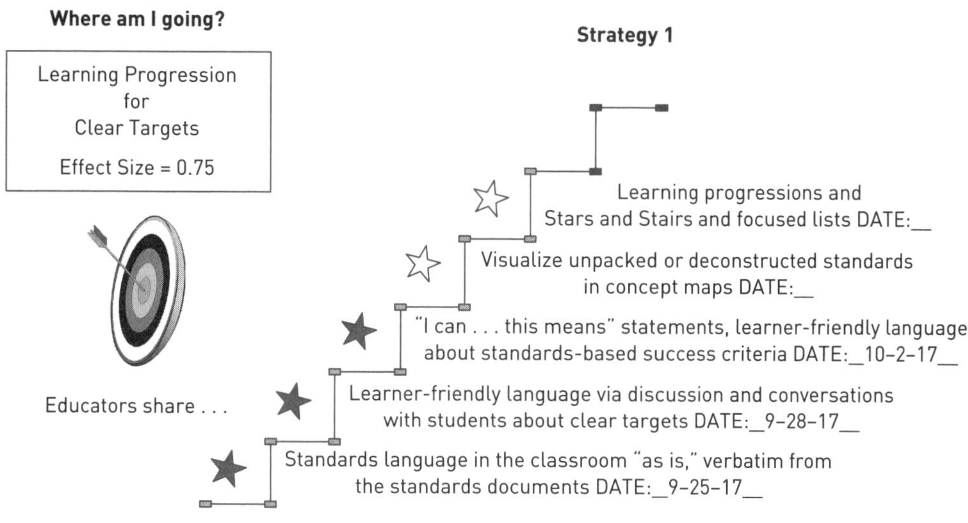

Learning Progressions

Learning progressions represent an effort to clarify content and performance standards or learning targets. For curriculum experts, learning progressions are usually a block of text and concepts arranged in a logical, time-bound sequence. The major advantage offered is a curriculum perspective that standards progress across grade levels (Heritage, 2012). To engage students in assessment for learning, these progressions can be visually displayed as Stars and Stairs, which show a sequential set of steps, and provide learners with a symbolic representation for accomplishing the learning target with a star. See Figures 4.4 through 4.7 for examples of Stars and Stairs for different content areas and grade-level standards.

FIGURE 4.4 ● Learning Progression for Solving Linear Equations

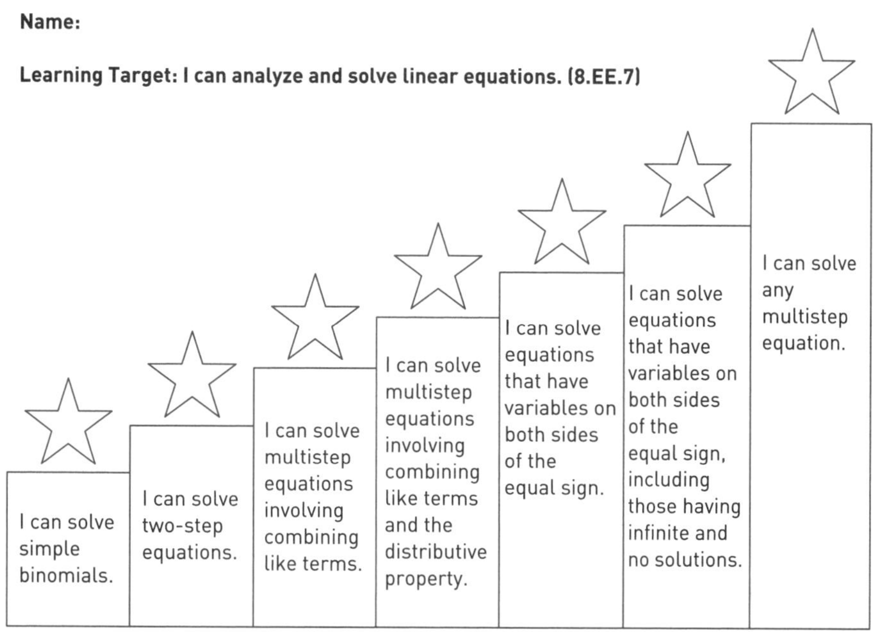

Tracking Progress by Learning Targets
Name:
Learning Target: I can analyze and solve linear equations. (8.EE.7)
I can solve simple binomials.
I can solve two-step equations.
I can solve multistep equations involving combining like terms.
I can solve multistep equations involving combining like terms and the distributive property.
I can solve equations that have variables on both sides of the equal sign.
I can solve equations that have variables on both sides of the equal sign, including those having infinite and no solutions.
I can solve any multistep equation.

Source: Contributed by Wendy Cole, middle school teacher, Mattanawcook Junior High School, RSU 67.

FIGURE 4.5 ● Learning Progression for Two-Dimensional and Three-Dimensional Drawing (Visual Arts Standard)

KINDERGARTEN
Art Targets
Stars and Stairs

Step 1	Step 2	Step 3	Step 4	Step 5	Step 6	Step 7
I can identify different kinds of lines in the world around me.	I can create different kinds of lines.	I can use a variety of 2-D media to draw or paint different kinds of lines.	I can use lines to make 2-D shapes.	I can use lines to make 3-D shapes.	I can use lines to make patterns.	I can use lines to make a drawing or composition that expresses meaning.
Date:	Date:	Date:	Date:	Date:	Date:	Date:

Source: Contributed by Lisa Ingraham, art teacher, Madison Elementary School, MSAD 59.

FIGURE 4.6 ● High School Weathering, Erosion, and Deposition Stars and Stairs

Standard ESS2-2: Use evidence to explain how natural processes have changed Earth's surface at varying time and sized scale.

I can explain how Earth's surface has changed over time, both fast and slow *and* large and small changes.

Name:

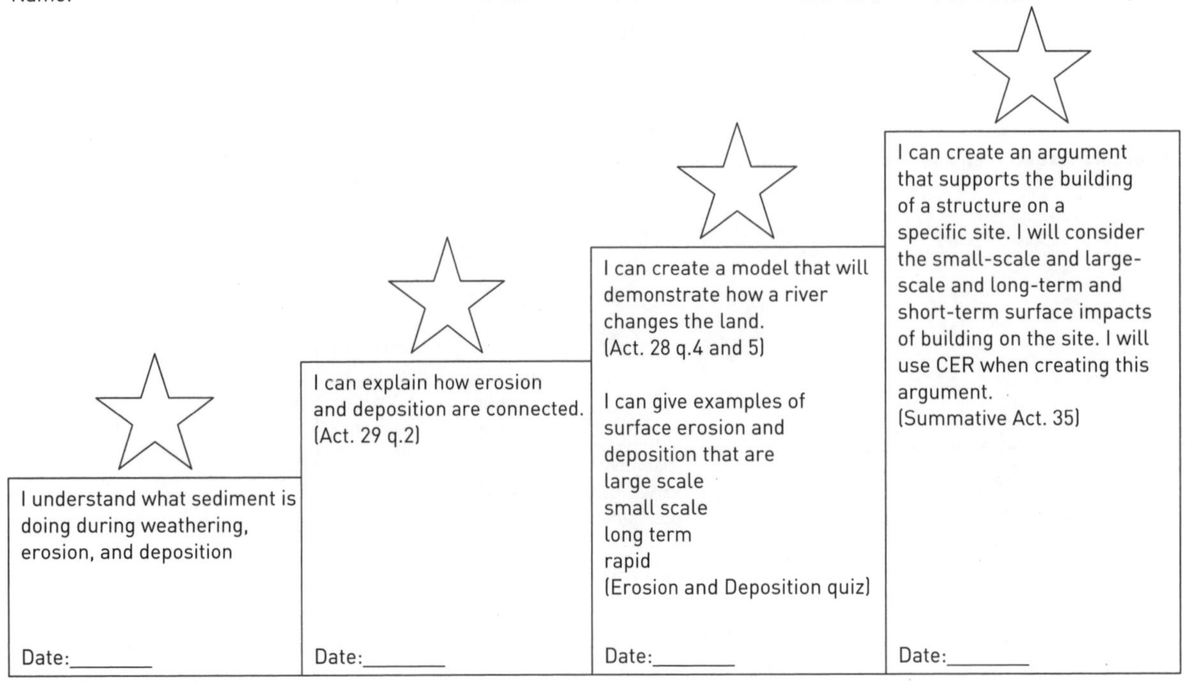

I understand what sediment is doing during weathering, erosion, and deposition
Date:________
I can explain how erosion and deposition are connected. (Act. 29 q.2)
Date:________
I can create a model that will demonstrate how a river changes the land. (Act. 28 q.4 and 5)
I can give examples of surface erosion and deposition that are
large scale
small scale
long term
rapid
(Erosion and Deposition quiz)
Date:________
I can create an argument that supports the building of a structure on a specific site. I will consider the small-scale and large-scale and long-term and short-term surface impacts of building on the site. I will use CER when creating this argument.
(Summative Act. 35)
Date:________

Note: CER = claim, evidence, reasoning.

Source: Contributed by Katie Wright, science teacher, Houlton Middle/High School, RSU 29.

FIGURE 4.7 • Speaking and Listening English Language Arts Stars and Stairs

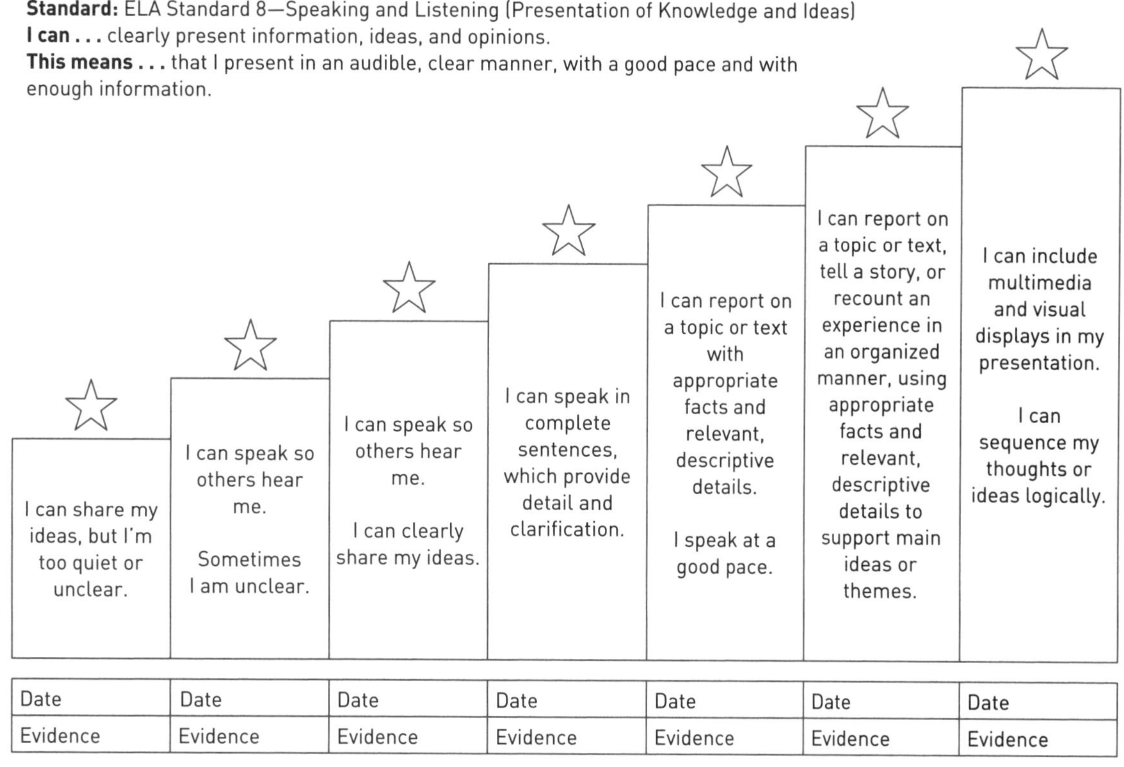

Stars and Steps
Standard: ELA Standard 8—Speaking and Listening (Presentation of Knowledge and Ideas)
I can . . . clearly present information, ideas, and opinions.
This means . . . that I present in an audible, clear manner, with a good pace and with enough information.
I can share my ideas, but I'm too quiet or unclear.
I can speak so others hear me. Sometimes I am unclear.
I can speak so others hear me. I can clearly share my ideas.
I can speak in complete sentences, which provide detail and clarification.
I can report on a topic or text with appropriate facts and relevant, descriptive details. I speak at a good pace.
I can report on a topic or text, tell a story, or recount an experience in an organized manner, using appropriate facts and relevant, descriptive details to support main ideas or themes.
I can include multimedia and visual displays in my presentation. I can sequence my thoughts or ideas logically.
Date
Evidence

Source: Contributed by Stephanie Shocki, elementary teacher, Camden-Rockport Elementary School, Five Town School District, MSAD 28.

Creativity in building graphics is motivating and fun. We have seen Stars and Stairs learning progressions with the images being replaced with rocket ships, hot air balloons, and roller coasters. In Figure 4.8, this veteran math teacher has called the graphic the "wealth of understanding" and has replaced the stars with denominations of money.

PAUSE AND REFLECT

- Take a close look at the graphic forms of the learning progression for clear learning targets; think about the standards you teach.
- What kinds of conversation could students have with peers, parents, or a classroom visitor to show her or his progress in terms of clear learning targets using these graphic depictions of the standards?

The Stars and Stairs visual representation may fit some learning targets, as a sequence of learning steps, while other learning intentions could employ a different graphic organizer, like an assembled puzzle or other visual metaphors. See Figures 4.9 through 4.16 for examples of puzzle piece visual representations of standards or learning intentions.

FIGURE 4.8 ● A Wealth of Understanding

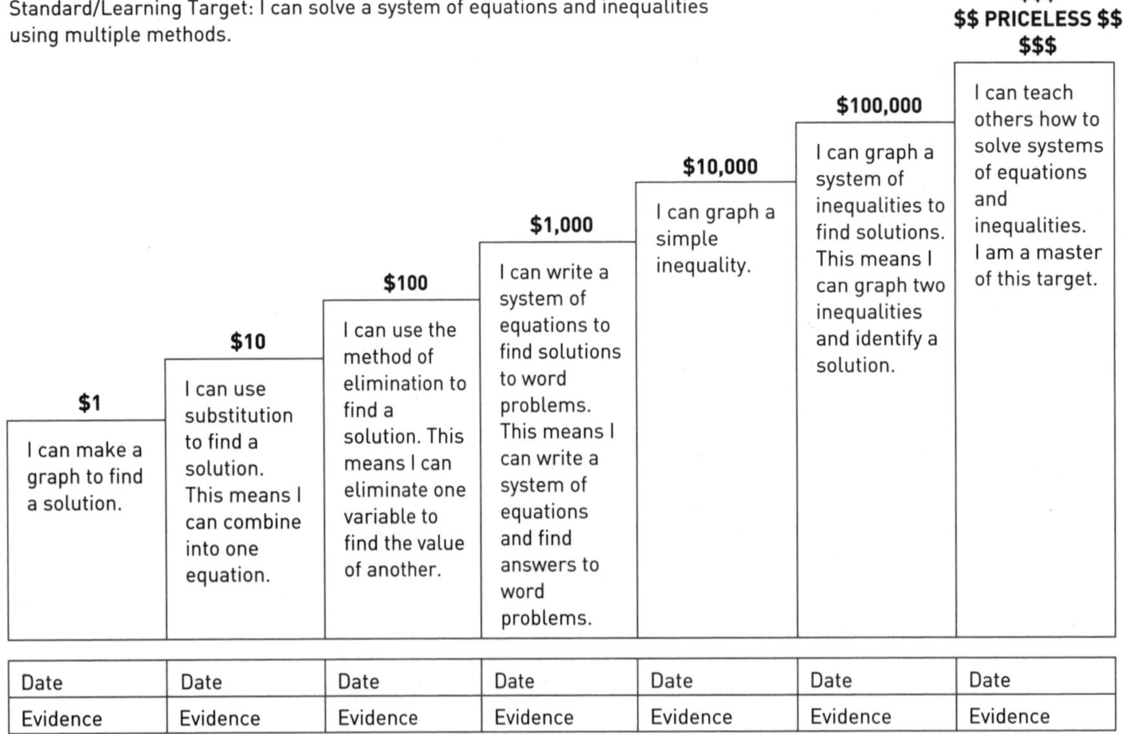

Standard/Learning Target: I can solve a system of equations and inequalities using multiple methods.
$1
I can make a graph to find a solution.
$10
I can use substitution to find a solution. This means I can combine into one equation.
$100
I can use the method of elimination to find a solution. This means I can eliminate one variable to find the value of another.
$1,000
I can write a system of equations to find solutions to word problems. This means I can write a system of equations and find answers to word problems.
$10,000
I can graph a simple inequality.
$100,000
I can graph a system of inequalities to find solutions. This means I can graph two inequalities and identify a solution.
$$$
$$ PRICELESS $$
$$$
I can teach others how to solve systems of equations and inequalities. I am a master of this target.
Date
Evidence

Source: Contributed by Dean Libbey, high school mathematics teacher, Mattanawcook Academy, RSU 67.

FIGURE 4.9 ● Learning Goal as a Puzzle Visual

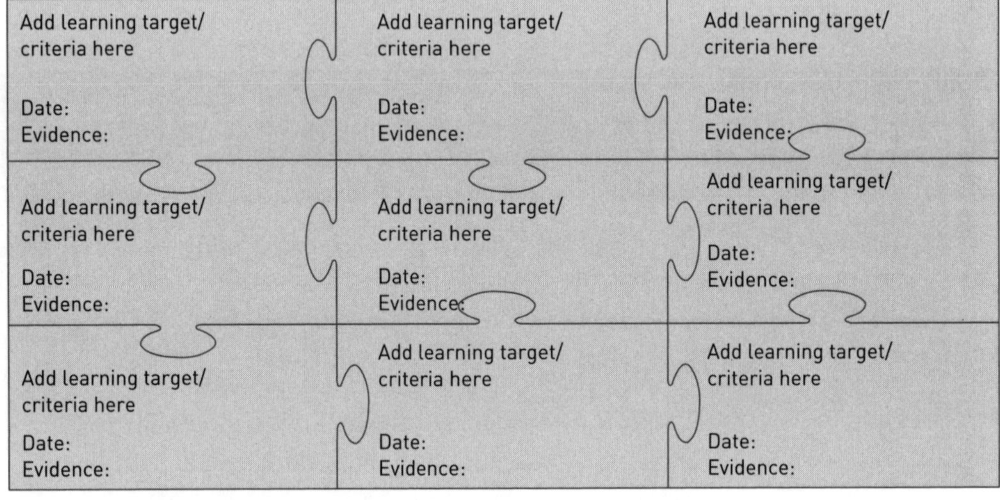

Overarching Learning Goal/Standard
Add learning target/ criteria here
Date:
Evidence:

Source: Contributed by Deb Taylor, director of curriculum and technology, RSU 12.

FIGURE 4.10 ● Grammar and the Writing Process Learning Targets in a Puzzle

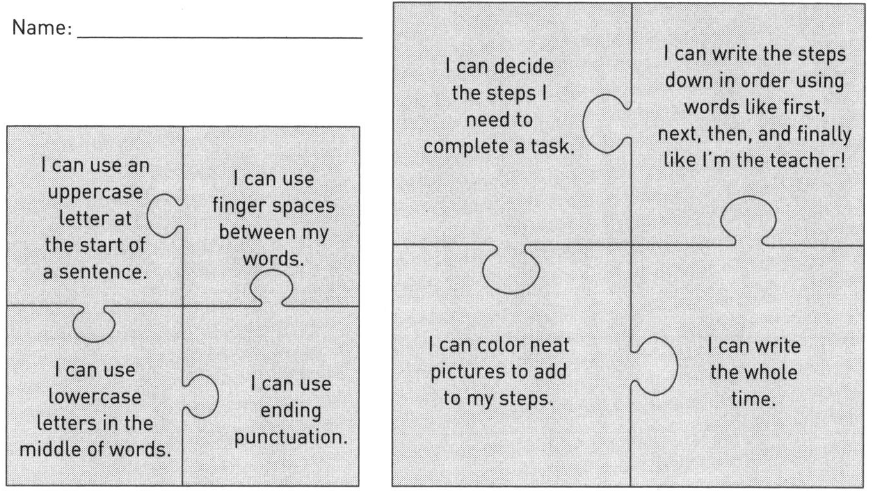

Source: Contributed by Kirsten Gould, first-grade teacher, Buxton Center Elementary School, MSAD 6.

FIGURE 4.11 ● Retell a Story Visual Representation

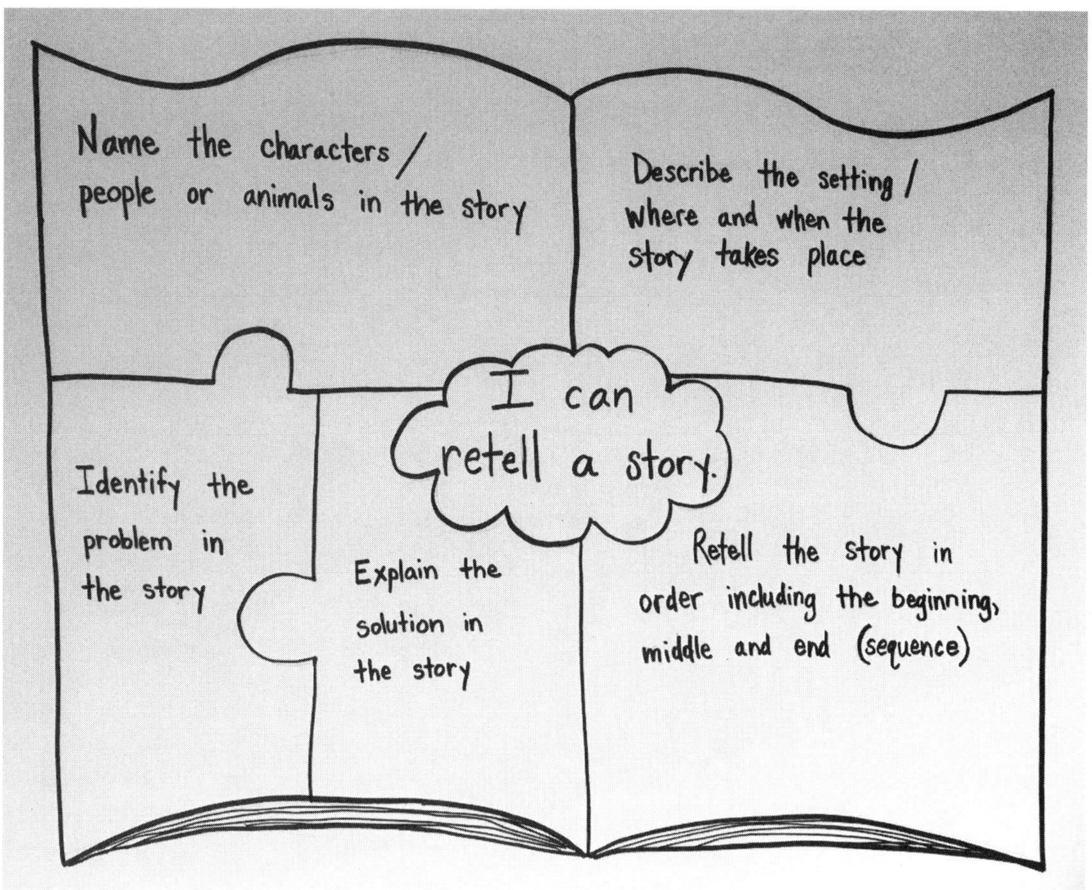

Source: Contributed by the Lincolnville Central School K–2 Team, Five Town School District, Union 69.

FIGURE 4.12 ● Learning Goals Circle Puzzle Piece

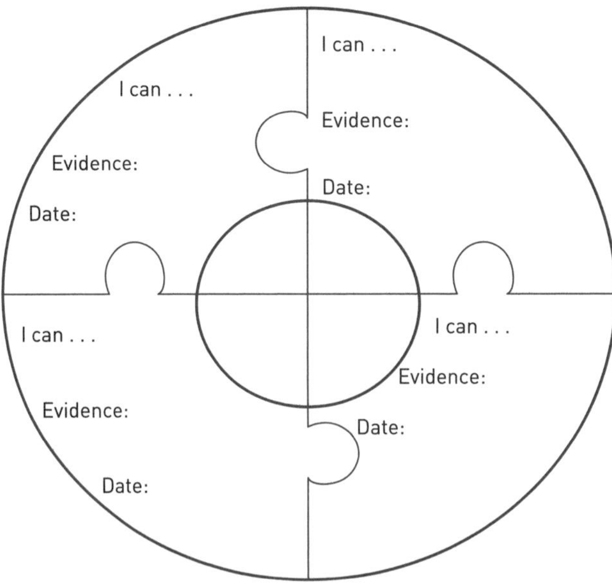

Source: Contributed by Sonya Laramee, first-grade teacher, Chelsea Elementary School, RSU 12.

FIGURE 4.13 ● Maine Geography Puzzle

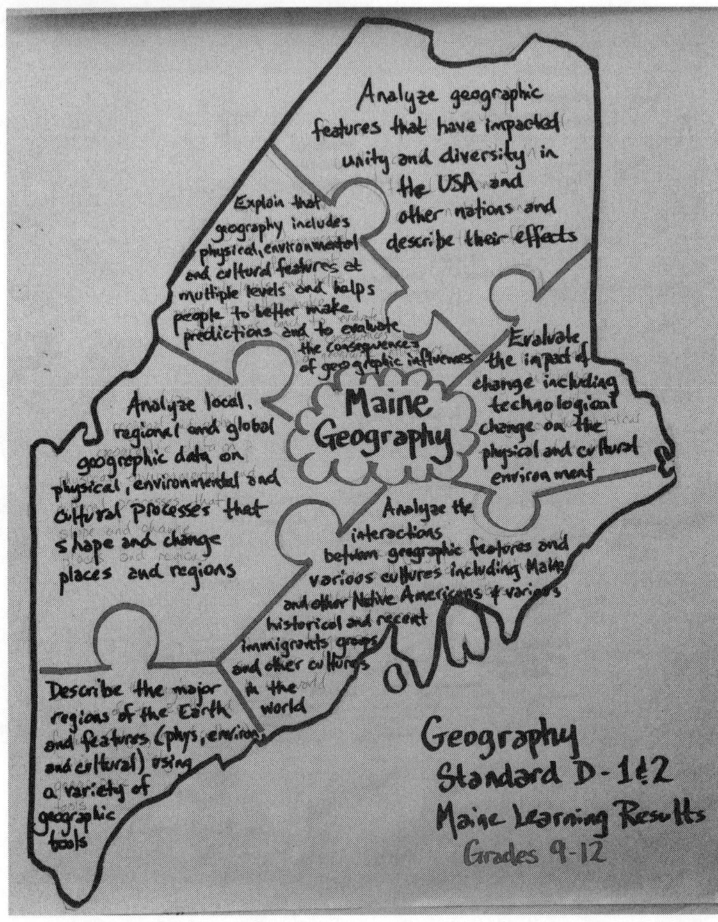

Source: Contributed by Jeffrey S. Beaudry and Anita Stewart McCafferty, authors

FIGURE 4.14 ● Identifying Uppercase and Lowercase Letters: Visual Representation

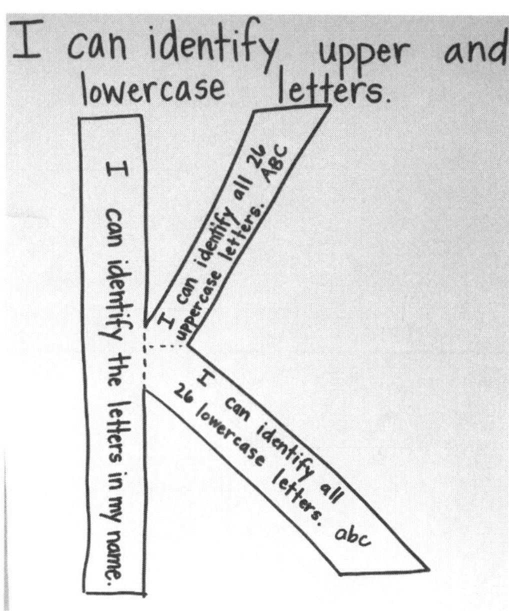

Source: Contributed by the Lincolnville Central School K–2 Team, Five Town School District, Union 69.

FIGURE 4.15 ● Chicka Chicka ABC Tree

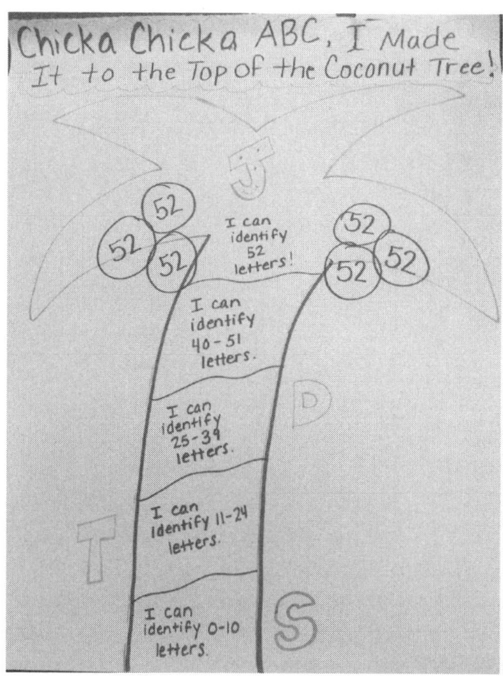

Source: Contributed by Sharon Crockett, Tammi Edwards, and Jamie Peters, kindergarten teachers, Ella P. Burr School, RSU 67.

Figures 4.14 through 4.16 are visual representations by three different kindergarten teams displaying the foundational concept of early childhood literacy: letter recognition. All of them focus on this learning target; however, the kindergarten teachers who designed "Oh! The Places We Will Go!" bulletin board, display three learning targets: (1) letter recognition, (2) letter sound recognition, and (3) high-frequency words. The bulletin board in Figure 4.16 shows the metaphor of learners hiking up three mountains, each one of them attached to an "I can . . . this means" statement and a learning progression.

FIGURE 4.16 ● Oh! The Places We Will Go!

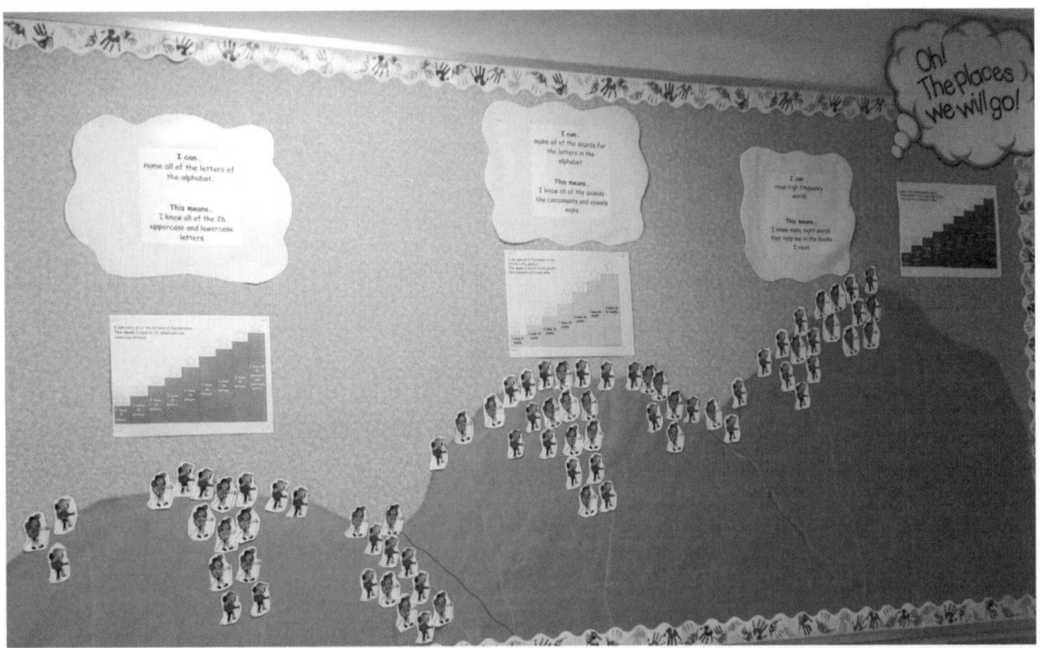

Source: Contributed by Patty Simon and Molly Mingione, kindergarten teachers, Steep Falls Elementary School, MSAD 6.

FIGURE 4.17 ● Effective Communication Guiding Principle

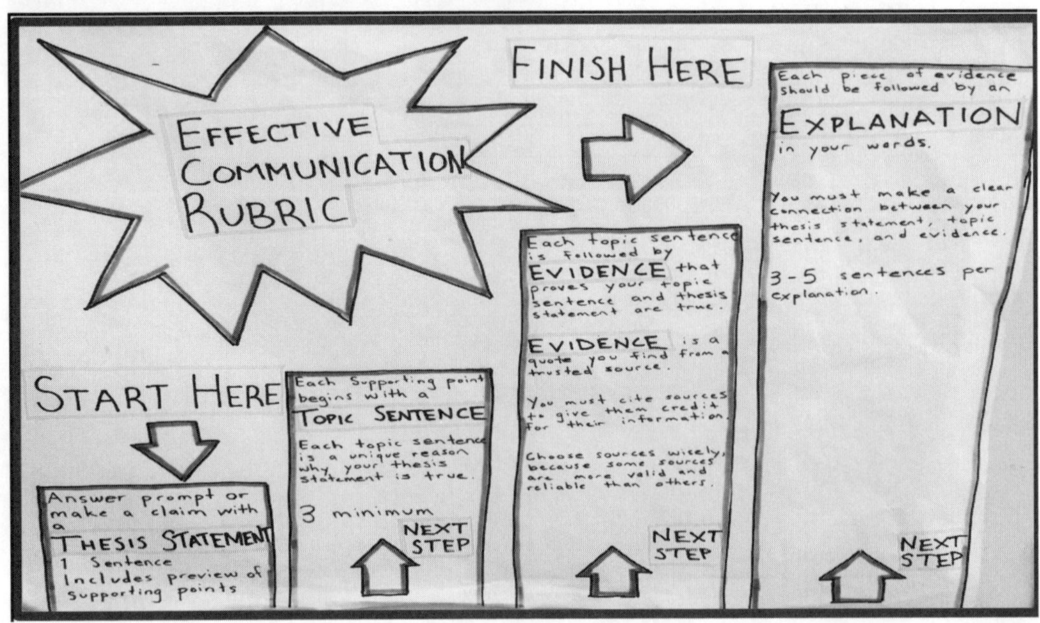

Source: Contributed by Scott Davis, high school social studies teacher, Mattanawcook Academy, RSU 67.

One of the high school teachers with which we have been privileged to work developed a graphic organizer to help his students visualize the steps they needed to take as they worked on becoming effective written communicators. While not a learning progression, it was an attempt to show the process in a visual way, illustrating the idea of taking one step at a time to complete a task and effectively communicate to others. The effective communication "rubric" in Figure 4.17 works to make clear the learning target to students.

PAUSE AND REFLECT

- As you look at the stairs and the puzzle visual representations, what do you see as relevant and useful for your classroom teaching?
- Are graphic organizers and visual representations developmentally appropriate for your classroom?
- Are visual representations an area of strength of yours? Or is it an area of needed development?

In our experience as learners and teachers, at times it has been easy to dismiss graphic representations like the stairs or the puzzles as too simplistic and juvenile. We have had our share of fixed mindset reactions to this and to other strategies that may seem to irritate and run counter to our sense of what learning is. When one feels that strong response (cognitive dissonance), that is a sign to "stop, drop, and reflect" on what this means for one's learners. The Universal Design for Learning (UDL) model suggests that educators are more likely to engage more learners if both the list (text only) and a visual representation in a graphic organizer are used and learners are allowed to use what works for them. With those tools in students' hands, there is a greater likelihood they will be used to communicate about learning targets.

A More In-Depth Look at Clear Learning Targets Using Next Generation Science Standards as an Example

We know that the "as is" standards language in documents are often the beginning of our deliberation. We know that teachers spend a great deal of professional-development time unpacking standards. Once you are in the stage of unpacked standards, you have entered the zone of learner-friendly targets. The goal of teaching and learning is for all students in your classroom to understand what clear learning targets are so that everyone can move quickly past the "why am I learning this?" and "what am I supposed to be learning?" and get to the challenging work of "what are my next steps in learning?"

The first example is taken from the middle school standards. Standards documents for the Next Generation Science Standards (NGSS) are written as frameworks and guidelines to organize complex and, in some cases, new bodies of knowledge. The purpose of standards is to organize curriculum, guide teaching, and help specify targets for assessment. NGSS uses a three-dimensional structure to organize the vast domains of scientific knowledge into (1) science and engineering practices, (2) disciplinary core ideas (DCIs), and (3) crosscutting concepts. The target audience for the NGSS frameworks is adult, which means we would not expect learners to benefit very much by handing this document to them. That is, students are not likely to be able to read, comprehend, and use it to accomplish proficiency in science.

In order to move to learner-friendly standards, you could use a planning template to focus on key vocabulary, definitions, and examples. The next step is to differentiate or break down the big idea or overarching standard into supporting or enabling targets. Chappuis (2012, pp. 34–35) used "grain size" as a metaphor of progress to represent different levels of standards.

> Learning targets range from simple to complex, a feature sometimes called grain size. They can be written at a pebble-sized lesson level ("Represent addition on a number line," Common Core math standard), at the rock-sized outcome of a unit of study ("Use measures of center and measures of variability for numerical data from random samples to draw informal comparative inferences about two populations," Common Core math standard), or at the boulder-sized culmination of a year's study ("Reason abstractly and quantitatively," Common Core math standard)

To continue to develop targets as learner-friendly standards, they can be converted and rewritten from the learner's perspective as "I can" statements. While the restating clear targets as "I can" statements is good, what makes this work even better is to restate them as "I can . . . this means," which helps build the bridge from standards, to criteria for success (assessing). See Figure 4.18.

The middle school science example focuses on the following NGSS (2013; see Figure 4.19).

FIGURE 4.18 ● The Bridge of Learning Targets ("I Can") to Success Criteria ("This Means") to Convert "As Is" Language to Student-Friendly "I Can . . . This Means" Statements

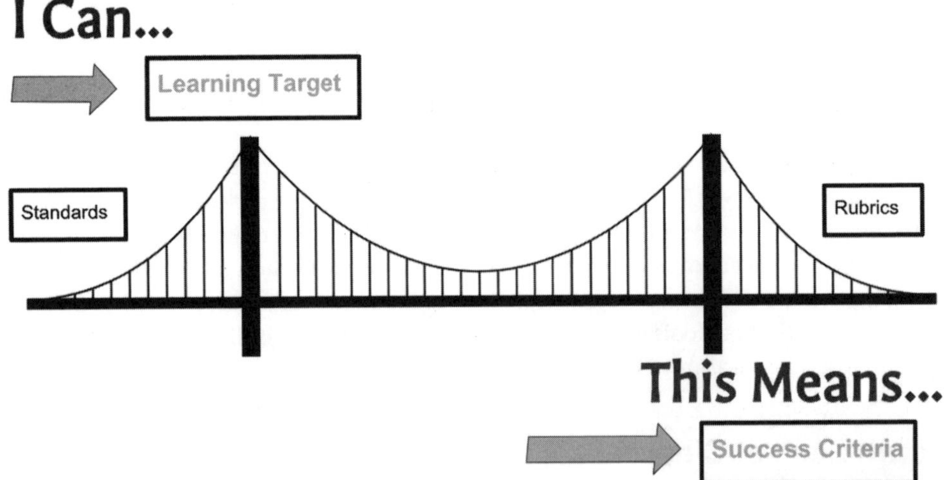

FIGURE 4.19 ● Fully Filled-in Next Generation Science Standards Model Format to Convert "As Is" Language to Student-Friendly "I Can . . . This Means" Statements for Middle School (MS-ESS1-1: The Earth's Place in the Universe)

Converting Knowledge and Reasoning Learning Targets to Student-friendly Language Earth-Sun-Moon Example

Standards written "as is.."

Learning target as written:

Develop and use a model of the Earth-sun-moon system to describe the cyclic patterns of lunar phases, eclipses of the sun and moon, and seasons. **(ESS1-1)**

Student-friendly definition(s) of word(s) to know:

Lunar phases – phases of the moon
Solar - sun

Standards written in "student-friendly language"

Student-friendly learning target:

I can/We are learning to: create a model of the Earth-sun-moon system that I can use to explain the patterns of the moon's phases and that also can be used to explain an eclipse of the sun, an eclipse of the moon, and the seasons.

This means:
*I can create a model of the Earth-sun-moon system that I can use to explain the phases of the moon.
*I can create a model of the Earth-sun-moon system that I can use to explain an eclipse of the sun and an eclipse of the moon.
*I can create a model of the Earth-sun-moon system that I can use to explain the seasons.

"Develop and use a model of the Earth-moon-sun system to describe the cyclic patterns of lunar phases, eclipses of the sun and moon, and seasons" (NGSS, ESS1-1).

- The standards statement is the "I can . . ." statement.
  - I can/we are learning to create a model of the earth-sun-moon system to describe the cyclic patterns of lunar phases, eclipses of the sun and moon, and seasons.
- The success criteria are the "This means . . ." statements
  - I can create a model of the earth-sun-moon system to explain the cyclic patterns of lunar phases.
  - I can create a model of the earth-sun-moon system to explain the eclipses of the sun and moon.
  - I can create a model of the earth-sun-moon system to explain the seasons.
- In the examples, student-friendly definitions are provided for the following terms: *lunar phases* and *solar.*

As students seek to understand "what to learn," the nested "I can" statements introduce them to the "WHY do I have to learn," and in the statement of "this means," learners get a picture of "WHAT is important to know and WHAT comes next in my learning." This differentiated view of clear learning targets is a scaffold that assists learners to understand and master their own executive functioning and strategic learning networks. The variety of strategies reflects the UDL framework, which prompts us to support learners' affective networks (the "why" of learning), the recognition networks (the "what" of learning), and the strategic networks (the "how" of learning). The clear learning targets' progression moves the learning from "why" in classroom discussions, to "what" in the "I can . . . this means" and concept maps, to the "how" in the direct use of targets for self-assessment and goal setting.

We have heard all too often from teachers, "Our students have stopped doing our 'formative assessments' because they are not graded." It is reflexive to say students are unmotivated and to blame them. We think that the first thing to do is have a conversation about clear learning targets. It is our belief that attention to clear learning targets are the touchstone for all assessment for learning strategies, since learners always return to ask, "Where am I going?"

Concept Maps and Deconstructing Standards

The idea of breaking down or deconstructing standards helps learners generate different ways to understand and present information. We have incorporated concept maps as a high-impact assessment for learning strategy that fulfils the function of unpacking and displaying clear learning targets. In Figure 4.20, the concept map represents how we see the structure of the NGSS. In this example, we added color coding of the different types of standards:

Blue = Engineering and scientific practices

Green = Disciplinary core ideas (DCIs)

Red = Crosscutting standards

We will talk about concept maps and visual thinking in more detail in Chapter 5, but the connection with clear learning targets is one that must be made to activate engagement and motivation for more learners. A complete example of the NGSS first-grade standard is shown in Figure 4.21, which contains the big standard in the "I can" statement and the concept maps as displayed along with the "this means" statements. Learners can choose one or use both to accelerate and get the most out of their learning.

FIGURE 4.20 ● Concept Map of the Three-Dimensional Next Generation Science Standards

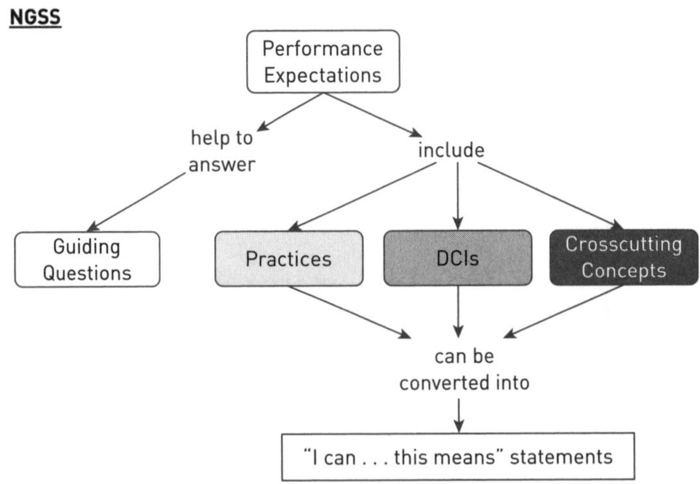

Note: DCIs = disciplinary core ideas.

FIGURE 4.21 ● Next Generation Science Standards First-Grade Example With Concept Maps

a.

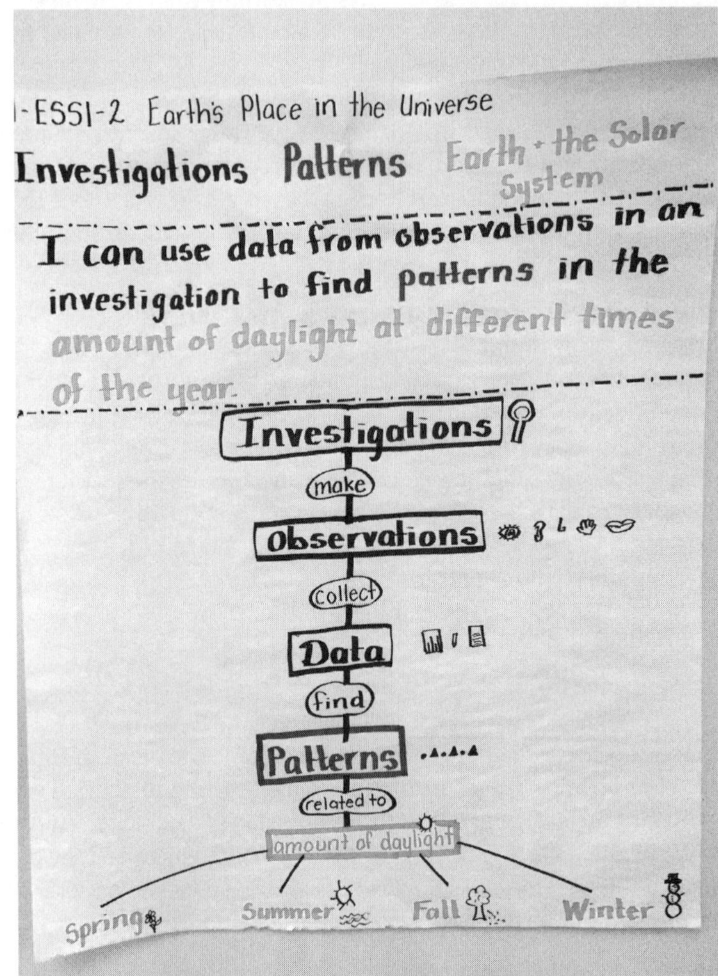

b.

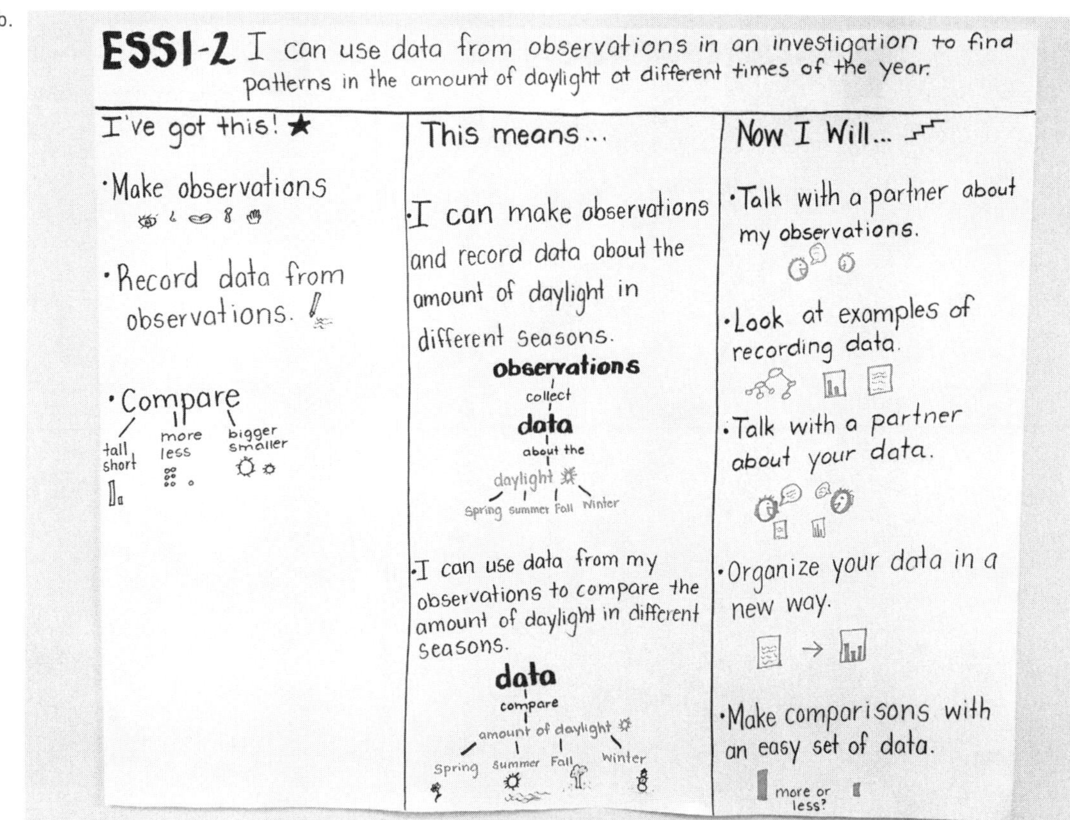

Source: Contributed by Kirsten Gould, first-grade teacher, Buxton Center Elementary School, MSAD 6.

Concept maps are an efficient, high-impact strategy (ES = 0.60), resulting in a flexible, assessment for learning product that focuses feedback, questioning, and diagnosis of learning needs. Concept maps have the greatest impact when they are created by individual students or groups, shared with others to generate feedback, and redrawn based on comments and new learning. Once teachers become fluent in the use of concept maps, the time needed to assess clear learning targets can be greatly reduced.

Combining Clear Learning Targets Strategies

With some additional work on the standards as learning progressions, we can analyze (unpack and deconstruct) standards in a concept map (a hierarchy of concepts from big standards to performance indicators and examples) and reconstruct them as "I can . . . this means" statements (success criteria), in maps (multiple pathway guides that emphasize the central ideas, overall organization and choice of pathways), and in learning progressions (Stars and Stairs).

According to Heritage (2008), "all the progressions share the characteristic of moving from less to more sophisticated understanding or skills. Where they differ is in the span of the progression, and in the level of detail or granularity" (p. 9). Expert descriptions or progressions are compelling, but in order for accurate instructional decisions to be made, we need to find out more about the effective use of learning progressions. The upward movement of stairs is the vertical conceptualization of learning and is characteristic of learning progressions (Wiliam, 2007). However, we also know that learning is not necessarily linear and sequential, which means we should be developing visual metaphors like stairs (ladder) and the journey (maps).

Some of the most exciting and promising work that we have seen is the combination of strategies to display clear learning targets (see Figure 4.22). In this model, the elementary teacher is using visual symbols to engage the youngest learners who can't read and therefore depend on visual representations and images to guide their learning. No matter the form, clear targets must be represented in well-organized, learner friendly text and in clear graphic representations like concept maps and learning progressions, such as Stars and Stairs or puzzle piece visual representations.

FIGURE 4.22 ● Concept Maps With "I Can . . . This Means" in a Learning Progression

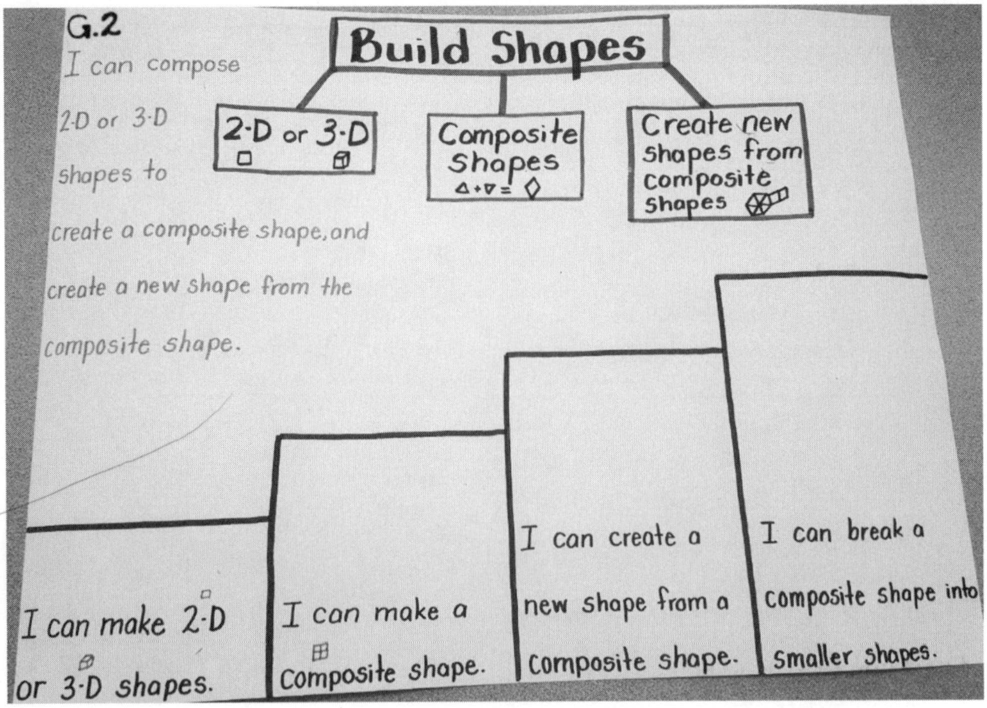

Source: Contributed by Kirsten Gould, first-grade teacher, Buxton Center Elementary School, MSAD 6.

PRACTITIONER SPOTLIGHT 4.1

LEARNING PROGRESSIONS

What?

I have used this work to create a set of learning progressions that also include a concept map and next steps for learning. As our class moves to a new standard, I begin with the concept map on a large poster. Because it's for first grade, they generally have pictures to help students access the information. Next, I post the learning progression in a form of the Stars and Stairs on the same poster. Students track their progress by using small magnets that they move up the steps as they meet their learning targets. Finally, underneath each step on the learning progression, I post next steps. This information allows students to choose their own steps for how they will help themselves progress to the next step.

So What?

The concept maps help make standards visible to students and allow them another way to access the information. When I asked my students if it's helpful for them, the majority of them said yes! They also really enjoy helping to create the concept maps as we break down the standards and talk about what they mean. This gives them a much deeper understanding of what they are being asked to show that they know and can do. One of the most exciting moments that illustrate the power in this happened when an administrator came in to do an observation. She asked several students at varying levels what they were working on and why. Each student was able to explain the standard in detail and how what they were doing related to the standard. Many of them also referred her to the concept map to show her how they knew!

The learning progressions make learning targets and growth visible to students. It shows them exactly where they are in relation to meeting the standard, what they already know, and what they are going to learn next. Because of this component, I have noticed a tremendous difference in how students respond to learning goals. Students who are struggling see that they only have to make small steps at a time, and it becomes less overwhelming to them. High achievers see that there are steps that will extend their thinking and seek to push themselves to improve. The progression also allows students to track their own progress. While students have a choice in whether or not to display their magnet for the class to see, ALL students chose to do so. I believe that speaks to the power of this tool to empower learners and foster a growth mindset.

Finally, the next steps at the bottom of the poster give students ideas for how they can move themselves forward. Because each child is committed to moving through the progression, they naturally want help in doing so. This tool gives students the information they need to be able to help themselves (and others) grow. It takes the power that the teacher once held and shifts it back to the students, giving them ownership and a sense of pride.

Now What?

I am incredibly excited to be able to continue this work. My goal is to create these tools for each of the assessed standards at my grade level and then partner with a kindergarten and second-grade teacher to make progressions that are for grade bands. If we are able to do that, we will have a tool that helps to align instruction across grade levels and gives students at all levels of learning a way to monitor and track their growth. It would allow scaffolding for students who need more practice with a particular skill and extensions for students who are ready for a challenge. I also intend to continue working with teachers in my school, district, and region to give them the support and tools they need to implement this work themselves. There is a real power in this work. As teachers, we are pulled in so many different directions, and our time is precious. I am making the commitment to put my time and effort into this. We owe it to our students to do the best we can, and this work allows us to make the kind of difference we all want to make.

Source: Contributed by Kirsten Gould, first-grade teacher, Buxton Center Elementary School, MSAD 6.

PAUSE AND REFLECT

- Here is your opportunity to do a "STOP! DROP! AND DO! (as our friends at the RiSE Center say). Take this opportunity to create visual representations of one or more of your learning targets.
- Share your visual representation with a trusted colleague for feedback.

Concerns About Creating Learning Progressions: Avoid the Traps

One of the ways that educators go about trying to accomplish clarity with regard to learning targets is to create learning progressions. There are a variety of ways to create learning progressions; however, many progressions when implemented have unintentional and harmful consequences. For instance, many learning progressions we see are outcome based, made up of a series of sequential, discrete skills or knowledge bits. The common implementation of this type of learning progression often results in the practice of summative assessments for each discrete skill or knowledge bite in the progression. Some systems even require multiple summative assessments or pieces of evidence for each discrete learning target. In doing so, the summative assessment or collection of evidence of each deconstructed chunk becomes a gatekeeper for progress toward the next step in the progression. Recall the learning progression for "Oh! The Places We Will Go!" in which students are making progress on all three standards, thus supporting all learners to keep making progress. Just because students may be struggling with one of the learning targets, they are not prevented from working on others. When systems make every step on a learning progression a summative assessment, many students are stuck at lower-level thinking or on unrelated, unmeaningful rote memory work instead of focusing on the complex work of the standards or the transferable goals of the unit of study.

As discussed also in Chapter 2, we have seen many examples of learning progressions that view the "foundational skills" as memorizing the vocabulary or practicing the isolated skill associated with the standards or unit of study. When the learning progressions become summative assessments at each step along the way, students cannot "level up," or do more meaningful work (e.g., the intention of the standards, unit goals, or larger purposes of education) until they show proficiency with memorizing vocabulary or their multiplication facts. Do students really need to be able to define similes, hyperbole, and metaphors before they engage in authentic tasks that help them use figurative language to express themselves on topics of interest and import? What we know about vocabulary development that results in concept formation and crystallized intelligence leads us to answer that question with a resounding NO!

Another harmful consequence of organizing curriculum as a series of deconstructed learning targets that must be assessed for proficiency before students can move on is that many students lose interest in learning long before they ever reach the Level 3 work—forget about the Level 4 work. Reporting out to students and parents before allowing students to move on in the progression reinforces performance or task orientation, *not* a learning orientation.

Yet another area of danger is the public display of students' progress. Putting students' names directly on learning progressions that are displayed in the classroom, such as on anchor charts or bulletin boards, is an area of concern. We need to honor students' privacy rights and ensure that the learning progressions do not become a source of demotivation and embarrassment. Our concern is that there may be consequences later for learners' self-concepts, as they quickly realize they are always at the bottom of the mountain, pyramid, rocket ship, staircase, and so forth. We encourage individualized use of learning progressions for learners to independently track their progress, while saving classroom displays for a more anonymous visual display of learning progress.

We also encourage educators to be cognizant that one goal of learning progressions or other visualizations of the standards is to help with clarity. As such, avoid lengthy, jargon-filled progressions that are typical of many content area guides and series. While these learning progressions may be helpful for teams of educators, they often require in-depth time and discussion to debrief and deconstruct into developmentally appropriate versions for use even by teachers, let alone students.

Grading, Scores, and Learning Progressions

While educators and systems may say it's all about the learning, historically the structure supports students viewing the purpose as collecting points or completing tasks. Abundant research evidence indicates that summative assessments or grading too soon shuts down learning by closing a loop for learners. Students may very well settle for a "2" because they view the work as meaningless or "good enough." Most settle for a "3" without engaging in the transfer of the standard to something authentic or novel, because it is written as Level 4 work and thus optional or unattainable. This is hardly the learning environment we want to cultivate, but nonetheless, our assessment and reporting practices often trap us (our learners and our educators) in this demotivating spiral.

Learning progressions done well—and by that we mean composed well and implemented well—serve a meaningful purpose of helping to bring clarity to what the learning might look like over time. When learning progressions show a range of typical development or performance of important understandings or the development of crucial skills, they can be quite useful. For instance, proficiency in summarizing text looks different over time. It is often helpful in developing a complex skill, as an indicator of where students are at currently, where their gaps may be, and where potential next steps in learning might be.

Conclusion

As educators, we must try every possible way to communicate our standards from our language into the minds and actions of our students. In our experience, there is always work to do on clarifying learning targets and on teacher clarity in general. Students ask, and have every right to ask, "What am I supposed to learn?" In this chapter, we have shown examples of how clear learning targets can help students build metacognitive strategies to answer their questions about "what they are supposed to learn" and "what comes next in their learning." By using tools like "I can . . . this means," standards as concept maps, learner-friendly language, visual representations, and learning progressions, students have a better chance to use the scaffolds and metacognitive learning strategies to understand how to manage and control their own learning.

Take a Deep Dive to Further Your Understanding

- Read *Knowing Your Learning Targets* by Connie Moss, Susan Brookhart, and Beverly Long (http://www.ascd.org/publications/educational-leadership/mar11/vol68/num06/Knowing-Your-Learning-Target.aspx).
- Read *Leaders of Their Own Learning: Transforming Schools through Student-Engaged Assessment* by Ron Berger, Leah Rugen, and Libby Woodfin (2014).
- Read Chapter 2 of Jan Chappuis's (2015) *Seven Strategies of Assessment for Learning.*

Mapping, Visual Literacy, and Assessment for Learning

Key Takeaways

Educators need to understand what visual literacy is and why it is so important to the learning and assessment process.

Educators need to understand the connection of visual literacy techniques like concept mapping and mind mapping with high-impact assessment for learning strategies, such as the following:

- Clear learning targets
- Descriptive feedback
- Metacognitive strategies

Educators need to understand and be able to use concept maps and graphic organizers for reading comprehension, prewriting, reasoning, and vocabulary building.

What Is Visual Literacy? Why Is It Important?

"I am no good at drawing." How many times have you heard this comment? At the same time, we know that technology, mobile devices, and the Internet continually immerse us in a digital world saturated with visual imagery, sound, and multimedia. Social media like Twitter, Pinterest, Facebook, and Instagram remind us of the combined power of visuals, text, and sound.

For us, the visualization of *assessment for learning* took many years to evolve and is instrumental to the portrayal of the connections between multiple models. The seven strategies map helped combine the seven strategies with corresponding effect sizes (or ES) from Hattie (2009, 2012) into a single concept map. For classroom teachers, a vital role for concept maps is to create and display multiple representations of clear learning targets as shown in Chapter 4. In this chapter, we go further into visual strategies to show how students and teachers can use and create concept maps and graphic organizers as products that can play a high-impact role in assessment for learning.

We believe visual literacy is no longer an option and represents the right-brain thinking that Pink (2006) suggests will rule the future. Visual literacy is a key component of the Universal Design for Learning (UDL; Rose & Meyer, 2002). UDL is a framework for educators to design learning environments for all learners, for multiple means of (1) representation, (2) action and expression, and (3) engagement. Our definition of visual literacy addresses the skills of visual representation as follows:

> Visual literacy is the ability to view, understand, analyze, evaluate, use, and design (create) visuals and visual representations for acquisition, consolidation, communication, and transfer of knowledge. Visual literacy involves both intrapersonal and metacognitive, as well as interpersonal and collaborative learning. It helps learners make more connections and create messages across multiple modes of communication. Visual literacy combines a variety of visual products (lists, tables, graphics, graphic organizers, concept maps, mind maps, argument maps, timelines, and systems maps) to support assessment *for* learning strategies like clear learning targets, feedback, self-assessment (metacognition), and diagnosis of learners' needs. (See Figure 5.1.)

We see a distinct role for concept mapping as a way to deconstruct and communicate clear learning targets, as we showed in Chapter 4, and we will discuss and show numerous examples of teachers using concept maps as artifacts that promote feedback, self-assessment, goal setting, metacognition, and diagnosis of learners' needs. One student studying microbiology for her professional licensure examination summed this up. When asked why the concept map was so useful, she replied, "I never get lost on my own map." That's the confidence we want to develop in our students.

Visual literacy has a unique and positive role as a 21st century competency, especially the development of creative problem-solving and innovative thinking. For example, teachers and learners should be able to brainstorm and generate ideas and then consolidate information into conceptual maps, effective lists, timelines (e.g., lesson plans, historical sequences), and system maps (e.g., ecological systems, organizational systems, and process diagrams). Visual literacy strategies help teachers and learners explore a variety of reasoning processes like classification, comparative thinking, as well as analysis, evaluation, and design, all of which are anchored by the visual product, the mind map. Visual literacy develops "the capacity of our pupils to use visual tools for seeking isolated definitions in context while also consciously seeking the form in text structures

FIGURE 5.1 ● Visual Literacy Mind Map

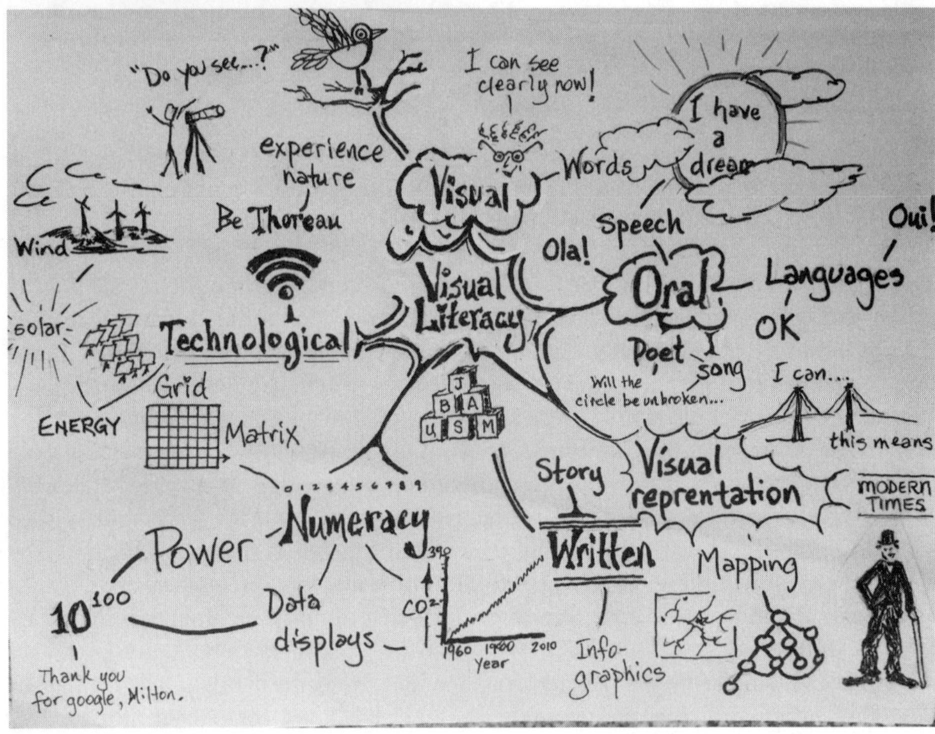

Source: Jeffrey S. Beaudry, author

across whole passages and books" to strengthen vocabulary, reading comprehension, and writing (Hyerle, 2009, p. 26). The fundamental understanding and mastery of concept maps and graphic organizers are essential competencies for educators who seek to utilize and strengthen choices in their "tool kit" of strategies.

Visual literacy is especially important in the elementary or primary school years as learners make the transition from viewing and speaking to formal language acquisition. It helps as they incorporate the rules of speaking and writing and as they move from making marks to drawing and lettering. Concept maps and graphic organizers are effective tools for meaningful learning (Novak & Cañas, 2006), critical thinking (Shedletsky & Beaudry, 2014), and products that mark the progression of knowledge for teachers and learners (Gorman & Heinze-Fry, 2014).

High-Impact Visual Learning Strategies: Mind Mapping, Concept Mapping, and Visual Representations

Concept mapping is a high-impact strategy (ES = 0.60) on a variety of outcomes, including memory, recall, comprehension, and writing (Hattie, 2009, 2012). In Marzano's model of nine instructional strategies, "nonlinguistic representations" (images and mental pictures) were identified as a high-impact strategy (ES = 0.70). Mapping has a rather large effect (approximately ES = 1.57) on student motivation (Horton et al., 1993). Learner-generated concept maps help them move from surface to deeper understanding (Fisher, Frey, & Hattie, 2016); however, teachers seem reluctant to master this strategy, and it remains underutilized (Beaudry & Wilson, 2010; Kinchin, 2001). We will present a variety of visual strategies: (1) mind mapping, (2) concept mapping, and (3) sketching. In this chapter, there are numerous examples by teachers, some of whom are first-timers at mapping. By using these tools of visual literacy, we can create ways for assessment-literate learners to make learning visible in a literal sense.

Primer: What Is a Mind Map?

Mind mapping was popularized by Tony Buzan in the 1970s as a way to combine text, graphics, and sketching to convey complex ideas on a single page (see Figure 5.2). Mind maps are a great way to introduce the creative use of text and visuals and are constructed by learners with these guidelines:

1. Place the main idea or central concept in the middle of the blank page (try 11 × 17 in.).
2. Add lines radiating out from the central image: thicker lines at the center, thinner lines as you go away from the central idea.
3. Create three or more layers of detail—for example, central concept, supporting category, and details.
4. Select keywords to represent and label each concept (text or drawing).
5. Use colors and sketches for creative, expressive representation of ideas.

PAUSE AND REFLECT

- How do you use visual representations in your current teaching?
- How do you use visual representations to assess your students' learning?
- Brainstorm these ideas, and create a mind map.
- If you are in a group, take a moment to explain your map and answer questions to others in the group.

FIGURE 5.2 ● Mind Map to Answer These Questions: Who Am I as a Learner? and Who Am I as a Researcher?

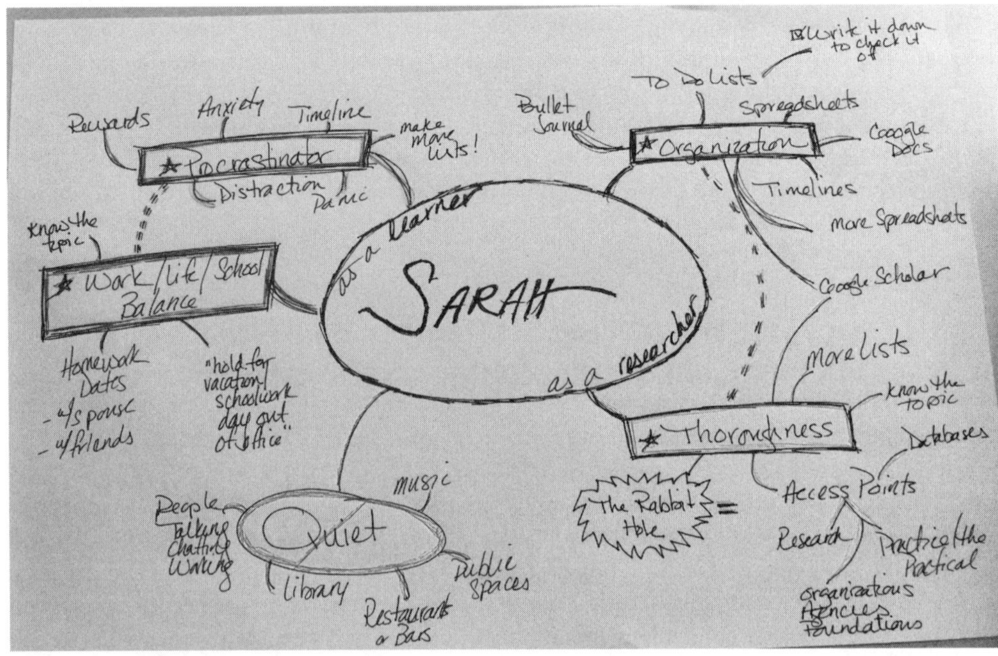

Source: Contributed by Sarah Holmes, doctoral student, University of Southern Maine.

Primer: What Is a Concept Map?

Concept mapping is an instructional technique that got its start in the field of science with the work of Novak and Gowin (1984). "Across educational levels, subject areas, and settings, it was found that studying concept or knowledge maps is somewhat more effective for retaining knowledge than studying text passages, lists, and outlines" (Nesbit & Adesope, 2006, p. 17). This statement reminds us that as educators, our repertoire of teaching tools can always be expanded. The effects of concept mapping are found consistently positive across settings, subject matter, and from elementary to postsecondary levels as well as for English language learners.

Concept maps are useful as tools for (1) language acquisition, (2) comprehension, (3) prewriting and rewriting essays, (4) creative thinking, and (5) systems thinking. Careful modeling of concept maps by educators help learners better understand this tool. Concept maps are constructed in the following way:

1. Identify a focus question. What is motion? What is a food chain?
2. Brainstorm a list of concepts on this question and create a "parking lot" or list of ideas. (Note: There is power in lists!) This is a point at which teachers can intentionally limit the number of concepts so that learners are not overwhelmed by the list.
3. Place each concept in a box or node; this could be a sticky note or a cutout piece of paper.
4. Sort and arrange the concepts hierarchically in an initial concept map. This is an opportunity for collaborative work in small groups.
5. Identify how concepts are connected and devise the linking verbs, prepositions, and prepositional phrases that help define the connection. Connections are made top to bottom, and cross-links are made between categories.
6. Add examples and details to categories.

Generally, concept maps flow (read) from top to bottom in hierarchical relationships of concepts and ideas and are constructed with shapes (nodes) and connecting lines (linking arrows). The cognitive challenge of a concept map is increased when the connecting (relational) lines are labeled with verbs or connecting words, to convey relationships, connections, and hierarchies of concepts. Overall, the strengths of concept maps are that they help learners (1) understand the main idea, (2) distinguish ideas from supporting concepts and details, and (3) make more and deeper connections between concepts. See Figure 5.3.

Concept maps are external representations of thoughts, similar to writing, but the impact of mapping is increased when learners collaboratively talk about their concept maps. Based on the feedback from teachers and/or peers, they modify and redraw a more accurate and/or expressive set of ideas to integrate prior knowledge with new knowledge. This kind of "map talk" is essential to the articulation and full expression of ideas. Concept maps were used originally as artifacts for students to use as references in interviews with teachers about challenging scientific concepts like gravity, motion, and energy. Learners constructed their own maps and then were interviewed by teachers or researchers and were asked to explain their maps. A learner's initial map represents prior knowledge, and with that, researchers could hear and see misconceptions, partial understanding, and flaws in reasoning. Most importantly, maps relieved students of the cognitive load of short-term memory so that the interview was not simply a recall activity and, thereby, focused the activity on meaningful learning. The result in learning from using a concept map is the potential increase in learners' memory and engagement versus rote memorization.

In most classrooms, we most commonly teach the use of outlining. If done right, an outline is a close approximation of a concept map; however, research has shown that maps are more effective than outlines. To provide greatest access to learning, when you are presenting important, complex ideas, we recommend that you offer teacher-constructed handouts as maps and outlines (one representation on each side of the page). By providing both formats, you allow students to choose the one that helps them best learn and understand. One caution is that learning is context dependent. Subject matter matters, and students' choices may change depending on the content, purpose, or interests.

FIGURE 5.3 • Concept Map of the Seven Strategies of Assessment for Learning With Nodes, Links, and Linking Verbs

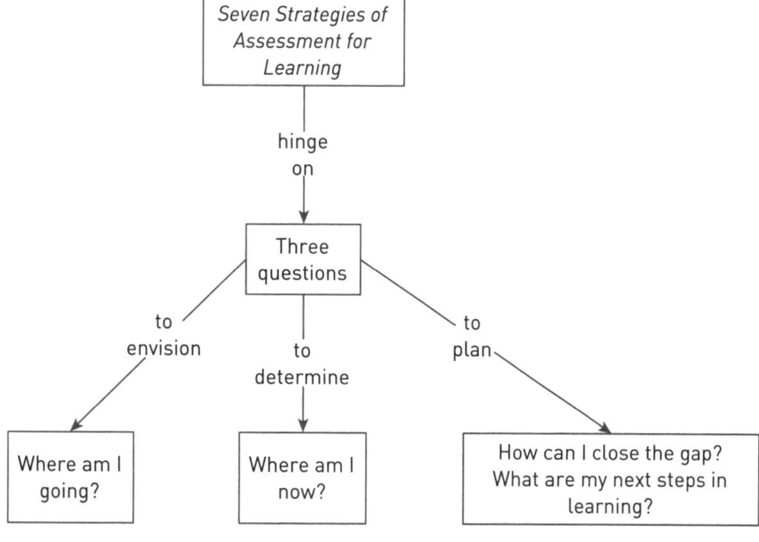

PAUSE AND REFLECT

- How do mind maps and concept maps represent students' progression from surface to deeper learning? Refer to Jim Gorman's rubric for surface and deep learning with concept maps:
- What are the next steps you could take to consolidate student knowledge and create opportunities for deeper learning?

	Criteria Comparing Final Concept Map to the First		
Depth of Learning	**Concepts**	**Linkages**	**Overall Structure**
Deep	• Original concepts remain • New concepts added	• Valid • Explanatory • Evidence of meaning in the mind of the map author	• Network and/or cycles are present • Well-defined organization • Increased number of cross-links between branches
Surface	• Significant number of new concepts but not linked with prior knowledge	• The overall number of linkages has not changed significantly	• Chain structures are present • None to few crosslinks • Explanatory power not significantly increased
Non-learning	• None to few new concepts added	• None to few new linkages made • No new cross-linking between concepts	• No change in knowledge structure or significant reorganization of concepts

Source: Contributed by Jim Gorman, high school physics teacher, Northbridge High School, Northbridge School District.

Mind Mapping in Practice

Mind maps are quick, effective ways to collect information from brainstorm activities. In Figure 5.4, first-grade students have demonstrated their prior knowledge about bats. The students worked in groups to create a collaborative mind map and have written out their ideas (invented spelling and all) using the bat symbol or illustration as the center of the mind map. This example shows how maps quickly reveal surface level knowledge, such as spelling, and deeper knowledge, such as the organization of a hierarchy. In this case, the learning targets are fused with examples in an accessible format. Having students do these by hand is a way to build basic brainstorming and visualization skills, highly valued and in constant use in design processes for both engineering and art (Kelley, 2017).

Another application of mapping is to serve the dual function as a reading comprehension tool and as a prewriting step. Practitioner Spotlight 5.1 by Heather Oakes, a fifth-grade teacher, demonstrates several assessment for learning strategies—descriptive feedback, self-assessment, and goal setting—and addresses the need to keep students focused on the task of reading and not getting lost in "think time" when creating their mind maps. The ultimate goal was to help students produce more and higher-quality writing.

FIGURE 5.4 • Mind Map for First Graders' Brainstorm of "What Do We Know About Bats?"

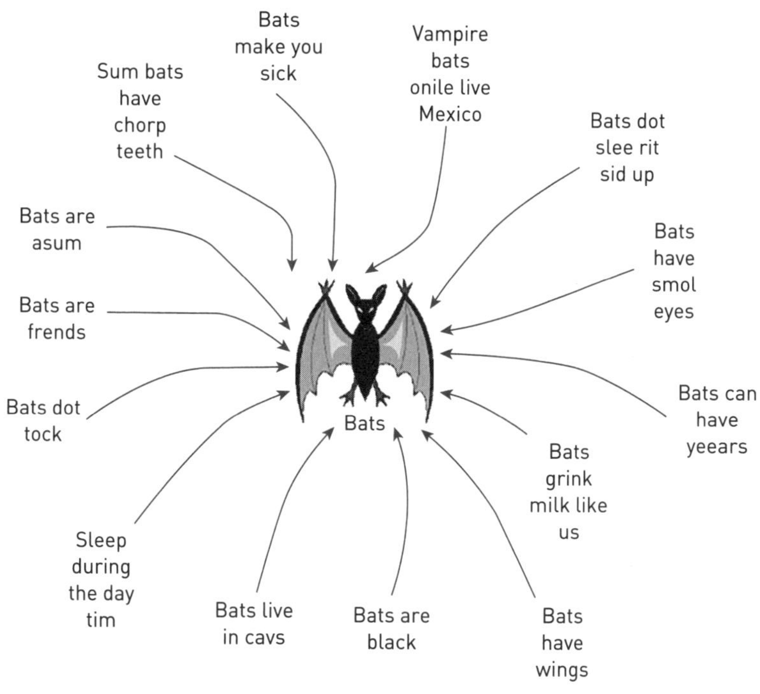

Source: Contributed by Cathlyn Langston, first-grade teacher, Falmouth Elementary School, Falmouth Public Schools.

PRACTITIONER SPOTLIGHT 5.1

USING MAPPING TO DEMONSTRATE READING COMPREHENSION

What?

While teaching a genre study with fifth-grade students, I used concept mapping to draw out students' thinking about characters' points of view and knowledge of events. I used one novel, *Number the Stars* (Lowry, 1989), in guided reading groups and the other novel, *The Boy in the Striped Pajamas* (Boyne, 2006), as a shared read. Throughout this unit, some students struggled with how to determine and analyze a character's point of view. After teaching students how to "mind map" and draw the web of connected thoughts, I asked them to create a mind map about each main character. The first time through, students used a lot of "think time." I wanted to speed up the process, so I added a time factor. I asked students to mind map as quickly as possible to get all their thoughts recorded, either in words or quick sketches, before a song (or two) finished playing. The next step was to read their mind maps, which moved closer to creating a concept map. During guided reading groups of about five or six students, each student "read" their map to the group. Using their finger, they traced their maps and connected their thoughts explaining what each part of the map meant and why they created each connection. The other students asked clarifying questions and offered supporting comments. I repeated this process, asking students to mind map about each main character's knowledge of the war, the character's friendship with a Holocaust victim, and how the characters might feel about their actions later in life. I partnered students to read their mind maps. This process took about an hour and a half. The final step was for students to write a comparative essay summarizing each book and comparing and contrasting the main characters' points of view and understanding of the war and what friendship and loyalty meant to them. The mind maps were used as prewrites.

(Continued)

(Continued)

So What?

The conversations students began having about these books were amazing. They were thinking more deeply about connecting text details to support their thoughts. Students were explaining why they thought characters behaved a certain way and why one character had a better understanding of the war. During one conversation, a struggling student made a comment that "thinking about reading really isn't as hard as it used to be" and "now that I know how to mind map my thoughts come alive." He later reported that "these were the best books I've ever read." Before that, he'd read only *Goosebumps* books. This process helped to move students toward analyzing what they've read and gaining a clear understanding about author's and character's viewpoints.

The biggest impact for me as a teacher was that I was not the one doing the talking or explaining. I became an observer and could focus on listening and asking questions. The students sharing their work with one another, reading their maps, questioning each other, and offering guidance and support for each other created a safe learning environment where all levels of learners gained academically while becoming more confident about themselves as readers. The benefits are especially evident with struggling readers. When they struggled with reading the map, I could simply ask, "Why is [that] on your map?" I could then help them connect their thoughts, which were now more specific and more meaningful.

Now What?

This will continue to be a strategy I use while teaching reading. My next step is to incorporate mind mapping into other subject areas, such as social studies and math. I plan to move the mind maps closer to concept maps by asking students to write verbs to connect the nouns or drawings on the maps. This will be an excellent prewriting activity but could also be used to prepare for class discussions.

FIGURE 5.5 ● Mind Map by Jack of the Characters in *The Boy in the Striped Pajamas*

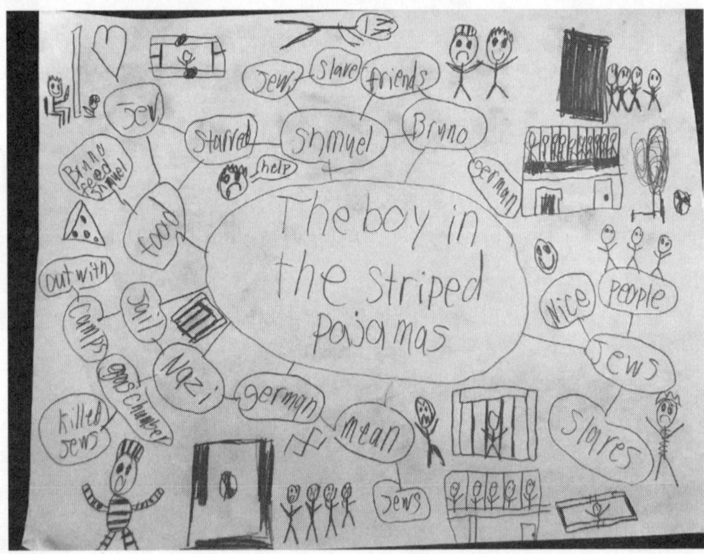

Source: Contributed by Heather Oakes, fifth-grade teacher, Granite Street School, Millinocket School Department.

There are many computer programs for creating and saving maps, but we believe that the impact of maps is more about collaboration and content than the medium. We encourage teachers to cocreate maps. Another approach to mind mapping is led by the teacher who uses chart paper or a computer program to record classroom discussion. In this example, the seventh-grade teacher is leading class discussions of the book *The Outsiders* (Hinton, 1995) and proceeds to create a comparison of the characters who are "Greasers" with the "Socs" or "Socials" (see Practitioner Spotlight 5.2). "Students who learned collaboratively by constructing concept maps outperformed those who learned from other activities such as studying texts, outlines, list and lectures" (Adesope & Nesbit, 2009, p. 238). As the teacher models this process, she adds each student's contribution. There are colors to differentiate levels of concepts from more specific details with a total of four levels to the map. While it may look messy, it is a good example of progressive development of ideas. The teacher went back to the map and added details and new categories over the course of a series of lessons.

PRACTITIONER SPOTLIGHT 5.2

MAPPING THE FLOW OF RICH, DETAILED CLASSROOM DISCUSSIONS WITH HAND-DRAWN AND COMPUTER-BASED MAPPING PROGRAMS

What?

Concept mapping has become a frequent learning activity in my classroom. Concept mapping has allowed my students an opportunity to have a learning tool that allows for visualizing and classifying ideas. Concept mapping on large sheets of paper has allowed for richer discussions with the whole class. See Figure 5.6a.

FIGURE 5.6A ● Teacher-Constructed Map From a Series of Classroom Discussions

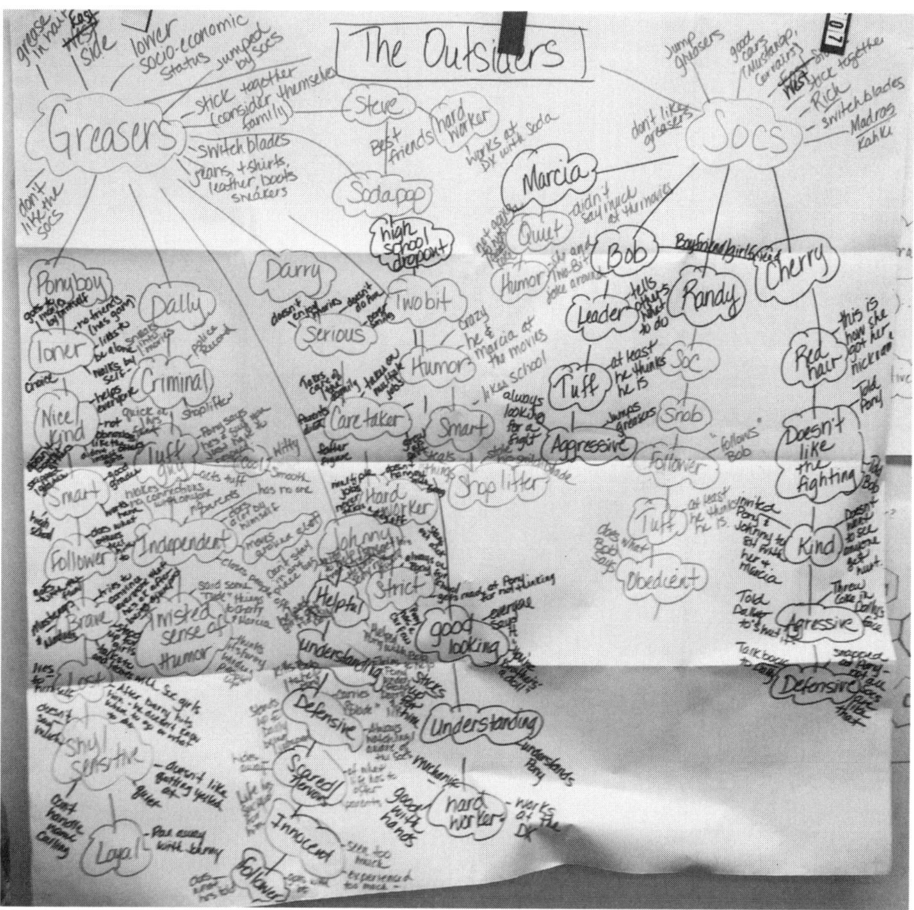

So What?

My students are more engaged and have shown a deeper understanding when using concept maps in our classroom discussions of *Esperanza Rising* (Muñoz Ryan, 2000). Concept mapping as a whole group has allowed my students to be on a level playing field, and the maps provide an opportunity for shared understanding. Results have led to more thoughtful writing and better feedback.

Now What?

Taking it to the next step, I found MindMup, a web-based concept mapping tool. The best part is that MindMup is an application that is found in Google, so maps can be saved, shared, and printed. This allows students an opportunity to create individual maps but then collaborate to revise and improve their planning leading to the same great results as group mapping on paper.

(Continued)

(Continued)

FIGURE 5.6B ● Teacher-Constructed Mind Map Used for a Series of Classroom Discussions of *Esperanza Rising*

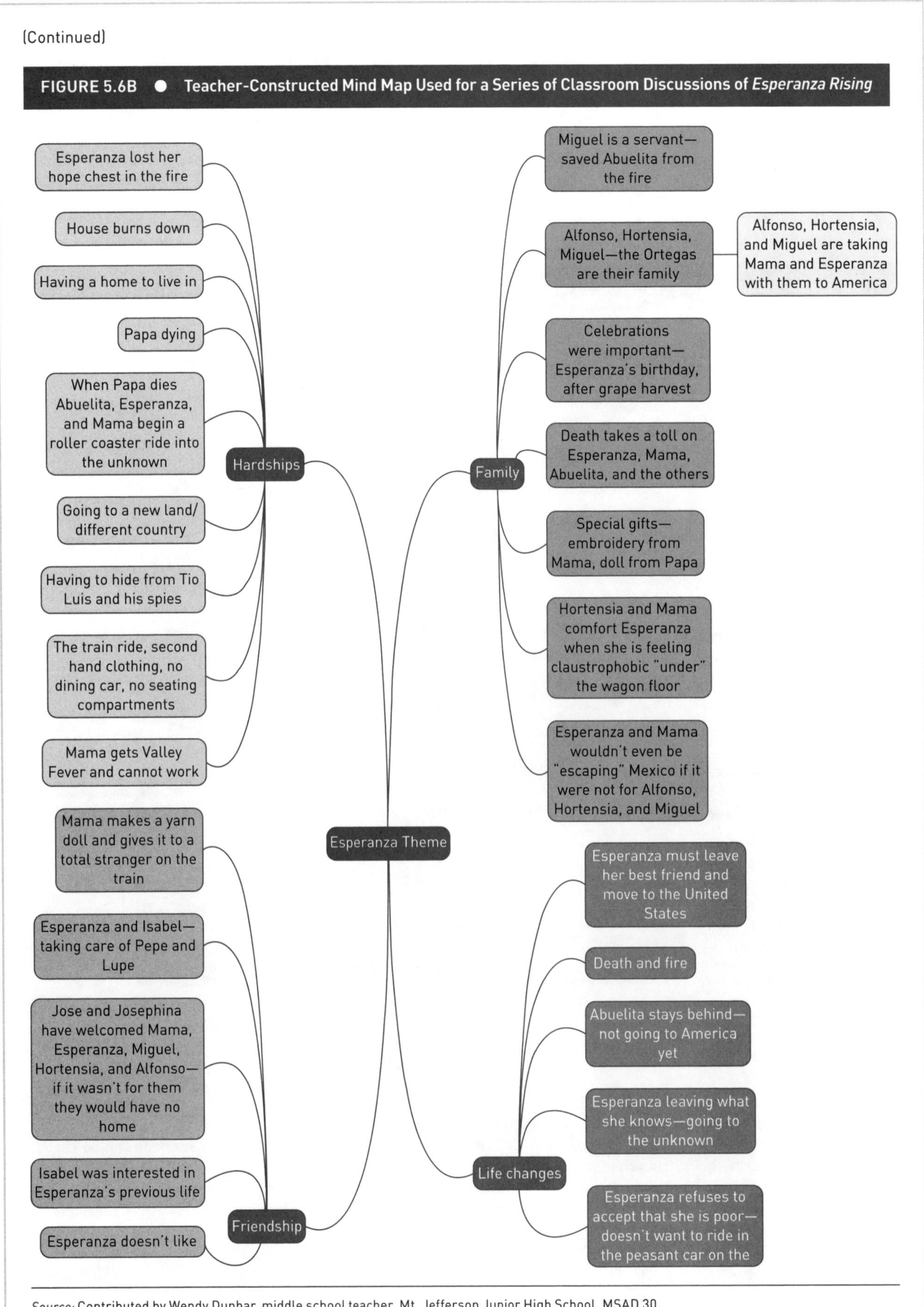
Esperanza Theme
Hardships
Esperanza lost her hope chest in the fire
House burns down
Having a home to live in
Papa dying
When Papa dies Abuelita, Esperanza, and Mama begin a roller coaster ride into the unknown
Going to a new land/ different country
Having to hide from Tio Luis and his spies
The train ride, second hand clothing, no dining car, no seating compartments
Mama gets Valley Fever and cannot work
Friendship
Mama makes a yarn doll and gives it to a total stranger on the train
Esperanza and Isabel—taking care of Pepe and Lupe
Jose and Josephina have welcomed Mama, Esperanza, Miguel, Hortensia, and Alfonso—if it wasn't for them they would have no home
Isabel was interested in Esperanza's previous life
Esperanza doesn't like
Family
Miguel is a servant—saved Abuelita from the fire
Alfonso, Hortensia, Miguel—the Ortegas are their family
Alfonso, Hortensia, and Miguel are taking Mama and Esperanza with them to America
Celebrations were important—Esperanza's birthday, after grape harvest
Death takes a toll on Esperanza, Mama, Abuelita, and the others
Special gifts—embroidery from Mama, doll from Papa
Hortensia and Mama comfort Esperanza when she is feeling claustrophobic "under" the wagon floor
Esperanza and Mama wouldn't even be "escaping" Mexico if it were not for Alfonso, Hortensia, and Miguel
Life changes
Esperanza must leave her best friend and move to the United States
Death and fire
Abuelita stays behind—not going to America yet
Esperanza leaving what she knows—going to the unknown
Esperanza refuses to accept that she is poor—doesn't want to ride in the peasant car on the

Source: Contributed by Wendy Dunbar, middle school teacher, Mt. Jefferson Junior High School, MSAD 30.

Collaborative brainstorming with students is a highly motivating strategy to generate ideas. In Figure 5.7, there is an example of a mind map done collaboratively by eighth-grade students responding to this focus question: What does "durability" mean? The art teacher was working on a project to design and build prototypes of shoes, and students added their own ideas about durability.

FIGURE 5.7 ● Collaborative Group Mind Map Used for Classroom Discussion of "Durability"

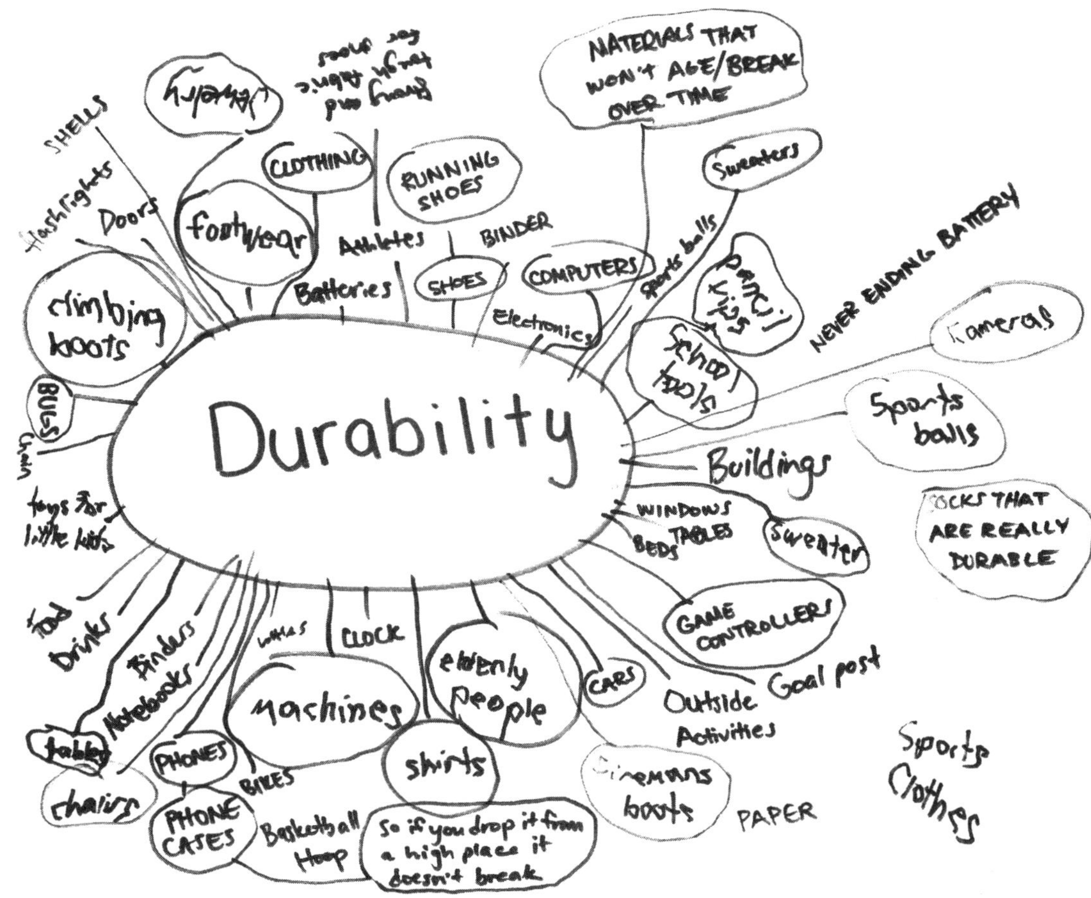

Source: The Durability Mind Map was completed as a collaborative process for an Expeditionary Learning Project for Designing Shoes and contributed by Mary Wellehan, middle school studio arts teacher, King Middle School, Portland Public Schools. Redrawn by Kirsten Nestor.

PAUSE AND REFLECT

- Imagine that you are the teacher who cocreated the mind maps in either Figure 5.6A or Figure 5.7. What could you have students do next?
- How do the seven strategies of assessment for learning connect with your suggestions?

Concept Maps in Action

We also know that there is still much to learn about how we acquire, consolidate, and communicate complex thoughts. There is ample evidence that mapping and collaborative dialogue have a vital role to play in learning, learning how to learn, and learning about who one is as a learner. Getting to know yourself as a learner through mastering and harnessing your expectations has an effect size of ES = 1.33. We see mapping as a huge opportunity for growth and impact, because we don't see nearly enough understanding and application of concept mapping by teachers. When teachers do use mapping, the results are visible and flexible and also have a positive impact on learning.

While concept mapping is not one of the seven assessment for learning strategies, it can serve as a flexible, effective, and efficient product that really does make learning visible and helps to move student thinking from surface to deep understanding (see Figure 5.8). When teachers use mapping as a strategy, it can have a multiplier effect on outcomes like reading, writing, and speaking. Mapping may seem to be an individual endeavor, but it reaches its fullest impact when each learner uses her or his map to communicate complex ideas to peers, the teacher, or a visiting school principal. In a recent case study, concept maps were compared to fully written essays in terms of the quality of content and the amount of time it took for the teacher to read and mark the final products.

FIGURE 5.8 ● The Connections of Concept Mapping to the Seven Strategies of Assessment for Learning

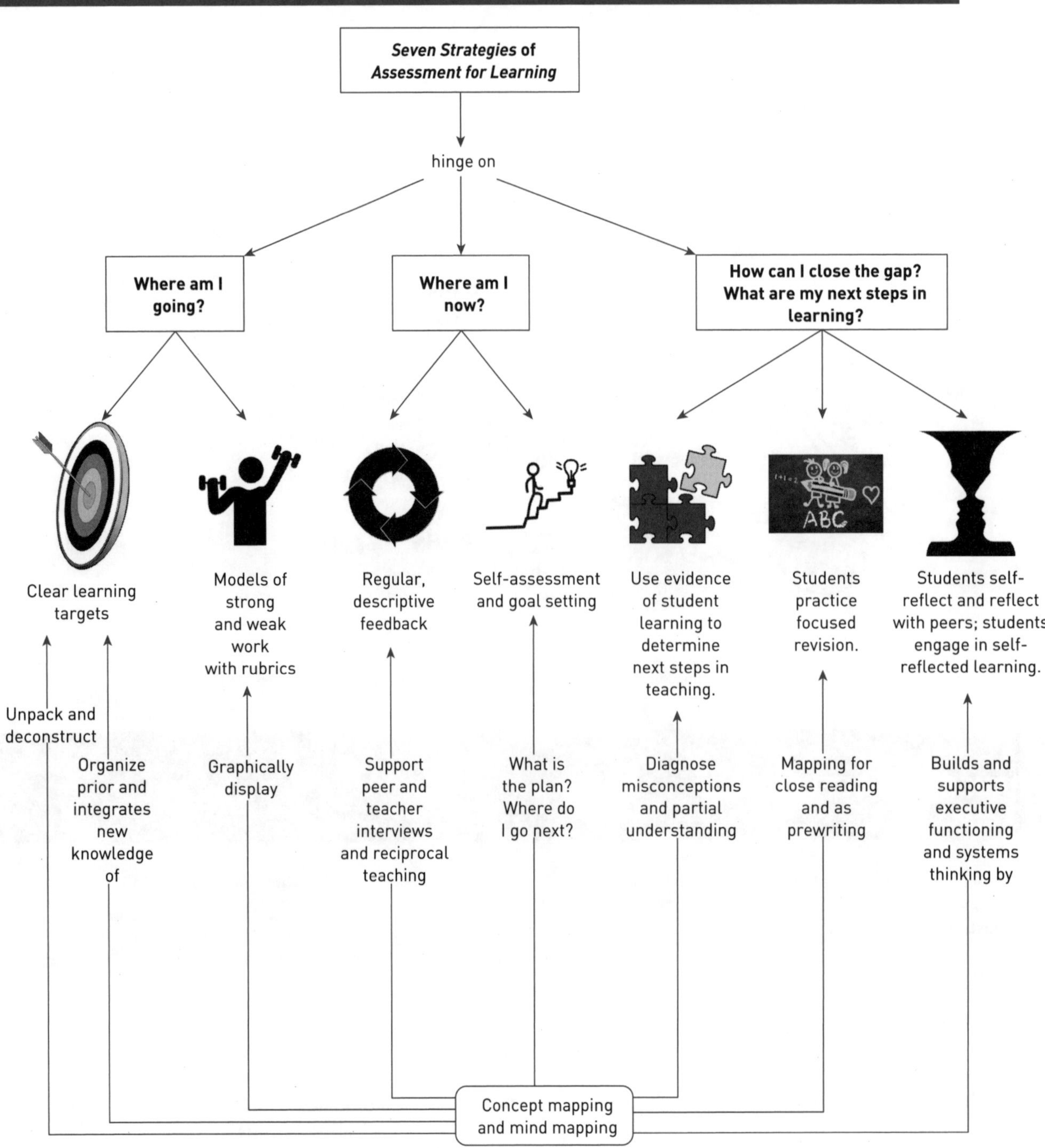

Source: Adapted from Chappuis (2015); Hattie (2009, 2012).

The study was done on adult learners in a medical evacuation program, and the results indicated that students gained a similar level of knowledge with the two approaches. A massive difference was found in the efficiency of maps. While the study was done for adult medical students, the researchers found that time was saved by a factor of 10 to 1. The case study by Gomez, Griffiths, and Navathe (2014) found that reading an essay of 1,000 to 2,000 words takes 15 to 20 minutes, while an equivalent concept map could be read, interpreted, and feedback given in 1.5 minutes. While this is exploratory research, it caught our attention and invites further study. Maybe some action research on your own is warranted to study both efficiency and impact of using concept mapping.

PAUSE AND REFLECT

- Have you compared essays to concept maps on similar topics?
- If you have used concept mapping, how does the strategy affect your time?

PRACTITIONER SPOTLIGHT 5.3

MAPPING ANALOGIES: BUILDING CONFIDENCE WITH CHALLENGING VOCABULARY

What?

Science students struggle to understand and use what may seem to them an endless amount of new vocabulary. Even after concept mapping the words, students struggle to confidently employ the vocabulary. I discovered that mapping familiar nonscience analogies, as a first step to mapping analogous science concepts, amplifies the benefit of concept mapping in science class.

So What?

To address the issue of the confusing high school biology vocabulary associated with heredity, I identified an appropriate

FIGURE 5.9A ● Teacher-Constructed Concept Map of Analogies Between Scientific Terms for Genome and Terms for Cookbook Used for Classroom Discussion

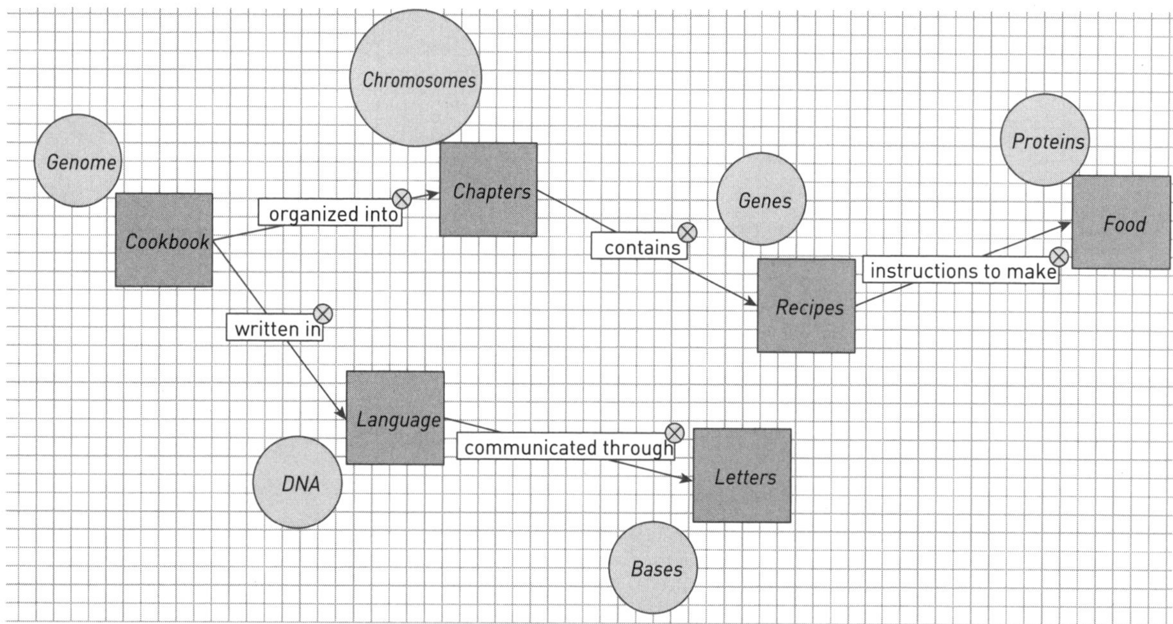

(Continued)

(Continued)

analogy and organized it into two levels. Students cooperatively mapped the first three words: cookbook, chapters, and recipes. Then, they added the second-level words: language, letters, and food. The science words were also provided in two levels: genome, chromosomes, and genes and then DNA, bases, and proteins. Students matched the science words to the analogous concepts. The links of the analogy also serve the dual purpose as the linking words for the science concepts.

When students finish mapping, they always write a narrative of their maps. The mapped concepts and linking words serve as the foundation of their paragraphs. English language learners or kids just approaching understanding construct paragraphs that closely follow the map. Students acquiring deeper understanding build paragraphs fleshed out with details and examples.

Here is an example of the basic narrative for this map.

A cookbook is organized into chapters, and a genome is organized into chromosomes. Chapters contain recipes like chromosomes contain genes. Recipes provide instructions to make food just like genes are instructions to make proteins. Cookbooks are written in a language like the genome is written in DNA. Letters are arranged to communicate language. Bases are arranged to communicate DNA instructions.

Thinking in analogies is a complex skill that high school students are generally comfortable with. Developmentally, middle school students are less skilled with analogies, so results to mapping analogies offered a few surprises and challenges. My eighth-grade science students mapped an analogy of the relationships between familiar English language words, then added less familiar analogous terms associated with matter. Most students had no problem understanding and building upon the basic analogy. A majority demonstrated knowledge by expanding the basic map narrative with examples. Interestingly, a few students really struggled with the notion of an analogy. Their paragraphs, which followed a path that their maps did not, tried to connect examples of the English language words to examples of matter.

FIGURE 5.9B ● Teacher-Constructed Concept Map of Scientific Terms for the Periodic Table and Terms for Alphabet Used for Classroom Discussion

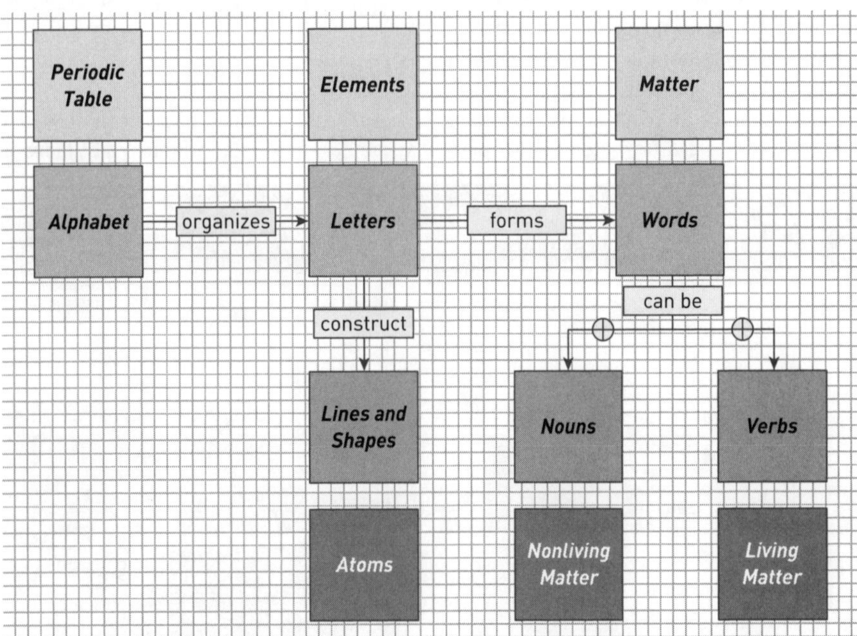

Here is an example of a correct analogy narrative:

The alphabet organizes letters just as the periodic table organizes the elements. Letters form words just as elements form matter and compounds. Lines and shapes construct letters just as different types of atoms construct elements—just as with twenty-nine protons an atom will be copper but with thirty protons it will be a zinc atom. If you add a line to a P *it becomes an* R*: words can be nouns and verbs like how matter can be living and nonliving.*

Here is an example from a student struggling to make sense of the analogy:

The alphabet consists of many letters, similar to the periodic table. For example, letters like C, N, *and* P *are used in the periodic table. The letters* C, N, *and* P *stand for carbon, nitrogen, and phosphorus.*

Now What?

Several ideas come to mind for improving mapping analogies in my middle school classes. Adding examples to the concept boxes on the maps may help students avoid confusion. I often ask students to number as well as color code each concept level on their maps so they can easily follow the map as they construct their writing. I might try experimenting with the narrative to help students think in analogies—perhaps writing the analogy narrative and the science narrative separately or maybe writing the analogy narrative even before matching the science words. In future lessons, including opportunities for students to strengthen their skill with analogies in a variety of ways can only benefit learning.

Source: Contributed by Polly Wilson, eighth-grade science teacher, King Middle School, Portland Public Schools, Portland, Maine.

Using a Concept Map to Make Comparisons and to Understand Similarities and Differences of Concepts

Making comparisons by identifying similarities and differences is one of the most powerful reasoning strategies, according to Marzano (2001). It provides an opportunity to apply concept mapping templates. We hope to improve on the Venn diagram, two intersecting circles (see Figure 5.10), with a more precise visual named the double bubble (see Figure 5.11). A suggestion would be to use the Venn diagram initially to make the comparisons between concepts and to progress to the double bubble once you have established definitions of key concepts (see Figure 5.12). The double bubble offers the next step in vocabulary development with the linking words, and the development of propositions with node-link-node connections challenges learners to integrate cognitive structures.

FIGURE 5.10 • Venn Diagram as a Template for Comparison of Volcanoes and Earthquakes

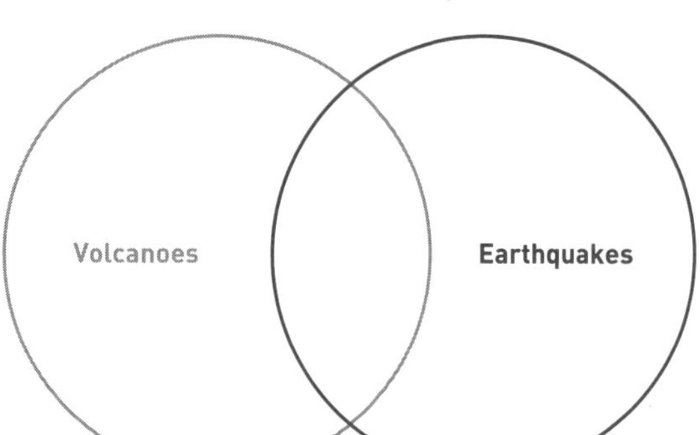

FIGURE 5.11 • Double Bubble Map as a Template for Comparison of Volcanoes and Earthquakes

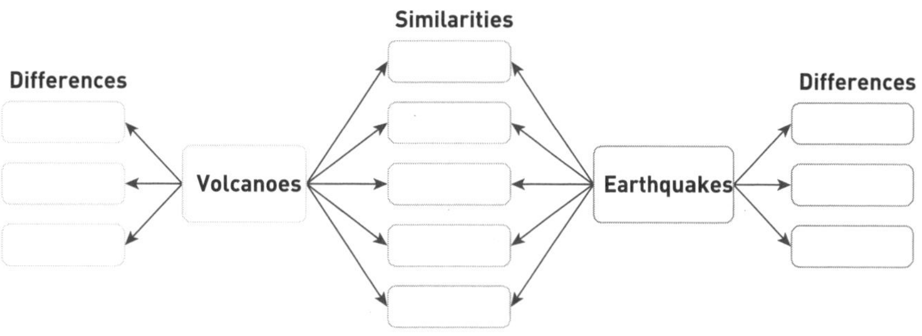

FIGURE 5.12 ● Comparison Concept Map of Volcanoes and Earthquakes

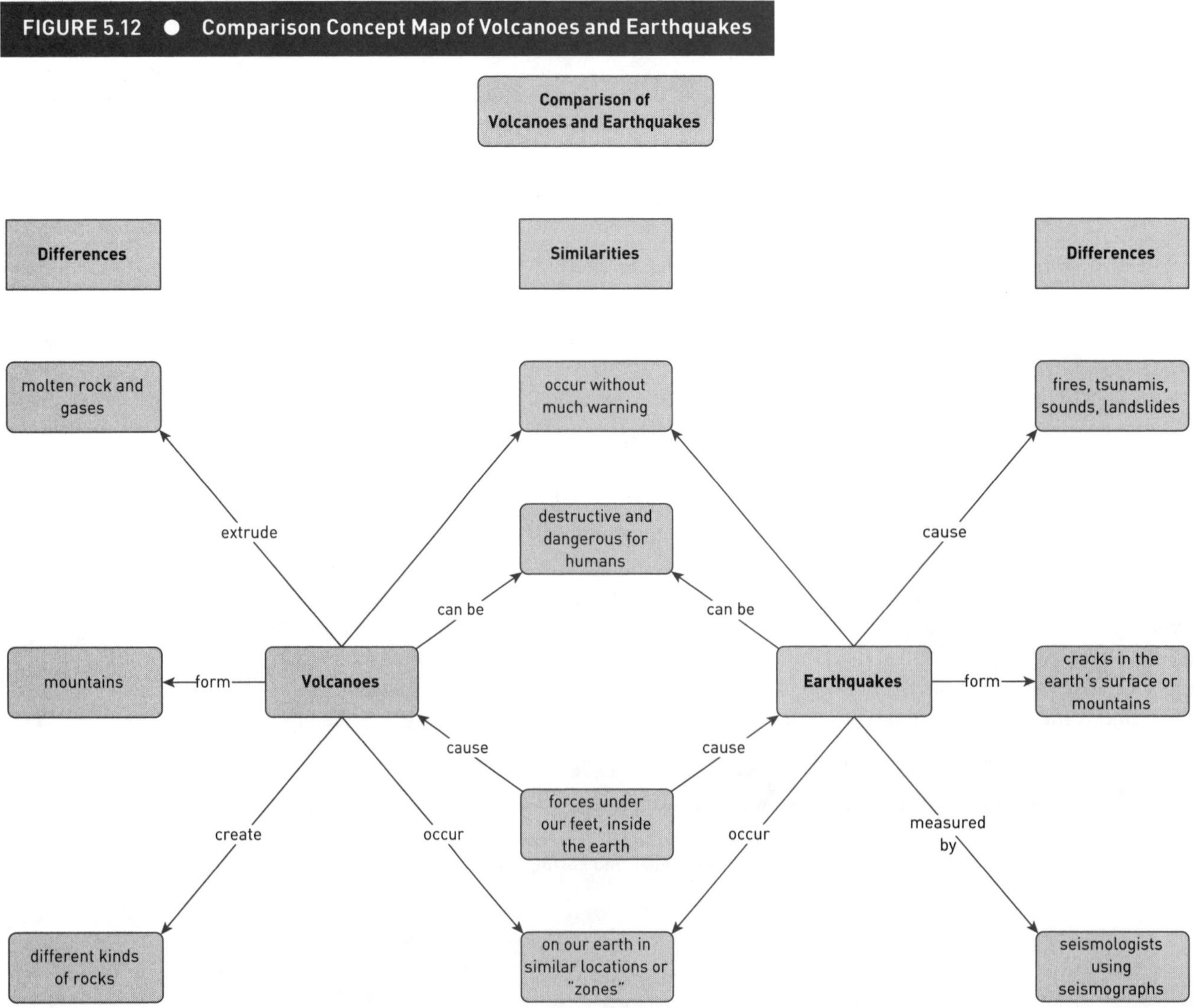

Source: Contributed by Rachel Bourgeois, elementary school teacher, Teague Park Elementary School, RSU 39.

Teachers can support and control the construction of concept maps. In Practitioner Spotlight 5.1, the teacher used the length of songs to help students manage their time with mind mapping. Another way to control the level of cognitive demand is to add concepts in groups like was shown in Practitioner Spotlight 5.3.

Graphic Organizers + Concept Maps + Sketches = Fluent Visual Literacy

Visual tools like graphic organizers, learner-generated mind maps, and concept maps can be combined with sketching and drawing to provide students a powerful set of visualization techniques.

> Sketching is a necessary fundamental area of design that includes brainstorming as well as documenting design ideas, but it is also a critical skill in communicating design ideas to others, a key 21st century skill. Ironically, sketching is also the first stage of parametric modeling (CAD) where designers first construct product parts in the 2D sketch plane. However, there appears to be little instruction and emphasis on building students' design-sketching skills in technology education. (Kelley, 2017, p. 8)

In Practitioner Spotlight 5.4 (see Figures 5.13a and 5.13b), the students utilize all three visualization tools to help themselves gain a deeper understanding of the complexities of a design challenge. As they stated, the concept maps, sketches, and the key concept graphic organizer (KCGO) were combined to help tease out key components that were lacking before they used all of the visual tools. In this case, the progression for learning went from sketching (ideation) to consolidating (concept mapping) to analyzing and then finally selecting and testing their designs. Using all of the visual tools helps to focus on the learning targets at each step, and they provide reference points and evidence of the design process.

PRACTITIONER SPOTLIGHT 5.4

FROM SKETCHING TO CONCEPT MAPPING TO THE KEY CONCEPT GRAPHIC ORGANIZER

What?

After introducing a design challenge, we would have the students sketch ideas for solutions of what they could build, given the constraints of the challenge. The sketches students would turn in were often neatly drawn but were missing some of the big key concepts of the challenge. For example, if the challenge were to design a windmill to raise a washer the quickest, some students would turn in a well-drawn windmill idea, but when we questioned how the blades would spin or how the washer would be lifted, they couldn't explain these ideas looking at what they had drawn. As a result, when it came time to test their designs, there were many groups that were not successful in achieving the goal of the challenge. Often, the group would choose one design to build rather than combine ideas, which led to the creator of the design taking over the project. Students would become frustrated when their ideas didn't pan out and would struggle to find alternative solutions to try.

FIGURE 5.13A ● Student-Generated Comparison of Two Designs

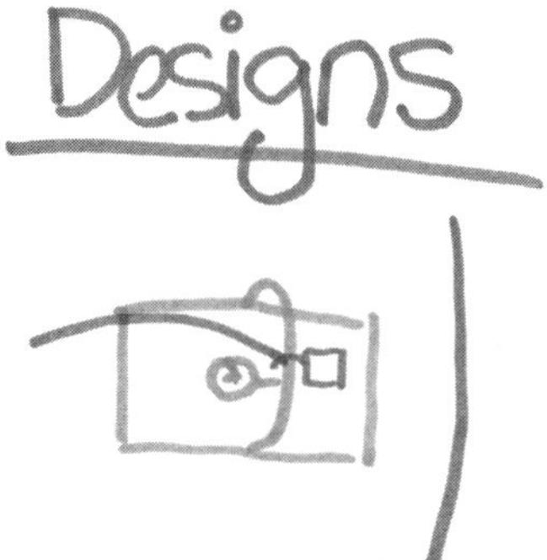

(Continued)

(Continued)

So What?

We needed a way to tease out the key components of the project that the students had to include in their design in order to be successful with the challenge. We decided to introduce the idea of concept mapping. As a whole class, we came up with the four key components of the challenge, and then as individuals, students would come up with ideas to satisfy these key concepts. Using a concept map, the students were starting to think more deeply about how each part of their design would work together to complete the given challenge, and we were starting to see the students build more successful projects. The problem we were running into, though, was the concept maps were often disorganized and hard to follow, especially if a student was struggling with a piece of the project and was trying to reference back to their concept map for a new idea to try.

FIGURE 5.13B ● Descriptive Map of Design Options for Egg Crate

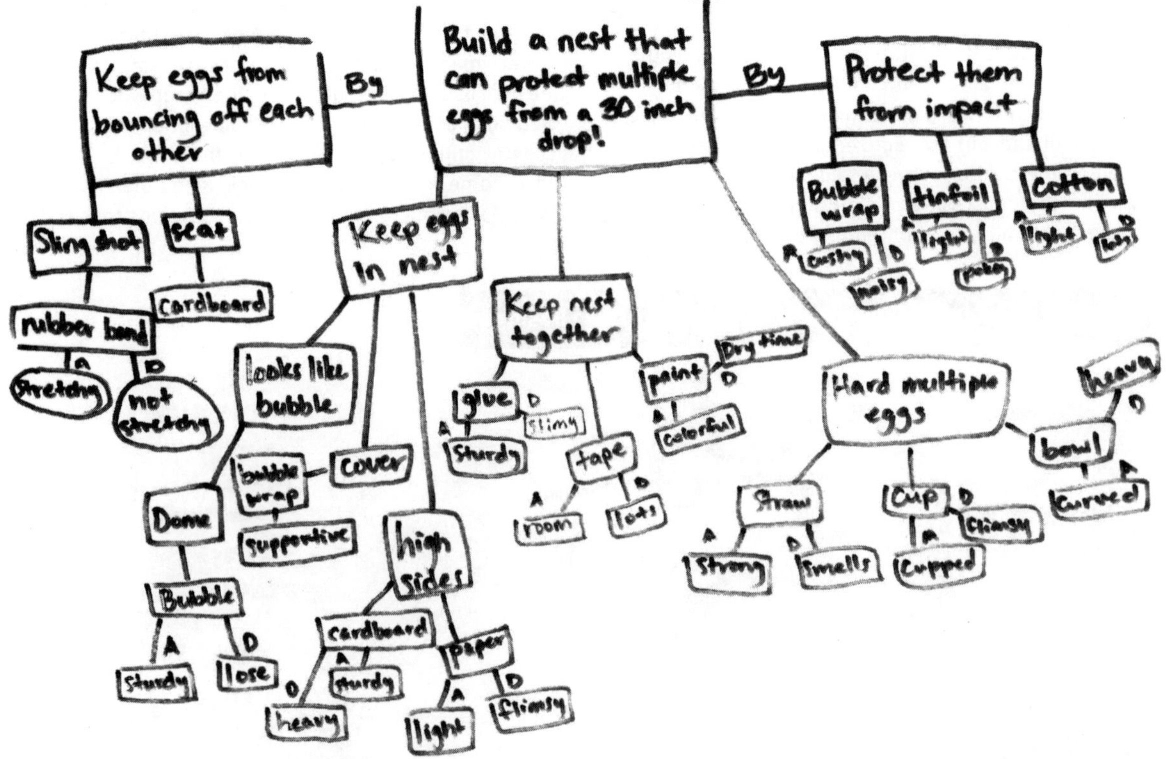

Now What?

We have now taken the idea of the concept map and created a graphic organizer we call the KCGO, or key concept graphic organizer. This graphic organizer includes all of the same information as the concept map did but in a more organized, easy-to-read way. The students can now easily reference back and see their ideas when they are struggling with building a design that is successful. Since we have started using the KCGO, 90 percent to 95 percent of groups have been able to successfully complete a design challenge. Students have become more invested in their designs and have worked better as a group. Students are more willing to look back at their KCGO to finding new or different ideas when their first plan doesn't work as they hope.

FIGURE 5.13C ● Graphic Organizer to Combine Key Concepts, Maps and Sketches, and Annotations About Design

Name: ______________________ Challenge: ______________________

Key Concept gathering tension	Idea #1 string pull back	Advantage holds tension
		Disadvantage hook needs to be in right spot to work
	Idea #2 nail for hold	Advantage just let go, string will unwrap nail releasing spoon
		Disadvantage might not hold on own
	Idea #3 rubber band on end	Advantage works to hold on own!
		Disadvantage need distance to hold spoon
Key Concept arm	Idea #1 string base	Advantage should work
		Disadvantage if overdo bad stuff happens
	Idea #2 super rubber band full!	Advantage tension not
		Disadvantage spoon might break
	Idea #3 stick band	Advantage spoon will go back
		Disadvantage spoon might break

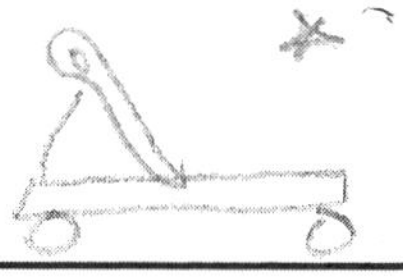

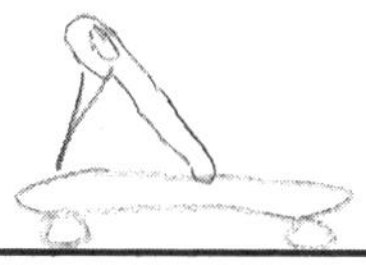

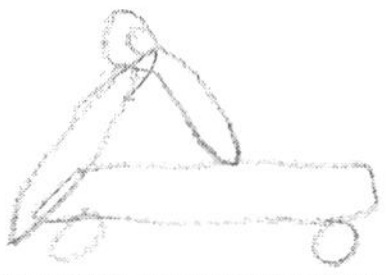

(Continued)

(Continued)

Name: ______________________ Challenge: ______________

Key Concept	Idea	Advantage	Disadvantage
Key Concept hold the projectile	Idea #1 Basket	Holds Ball	might not release ball
	Idea #2 bottom basket	Holds Ball	holding basket at bottom
	Idea #3 insert spoon *	bottom can hold string without having to hit a pom	spoon might fall out
Key Concept Base	Idea #1 Design 1: weight in front	cup: hold spoon weight: no flip over	cup: might not hold still weight: need to find a weight
	Idea #2 weight	· will hold spoon · weight on and can hold hook	· spoon can't move as much · might tip over
	Idea #3 *	· super duper hold! · super duper support!	· fragile

Source: Contributed by Kristi Raymond and Chris Hughes, middle school STEM teachers, South Portland School District.

TABLE 5.1 • Combining High-Impact Strategies With the Seven Strategies of Assessment for Learning

Where am I going?
1. Clear learning targets (ES = 0.75)
2. Models of strong and weak work with rubrics (ES = 0.57)
Where am I now?
3. Timely, descriptive feedback that directly affects learning (ES = 0.75)
4. Student self-assessment and metacognitive strategies (ES = 0.69) and goal setting (ES = 0.50)
How do I close the gap? What are my strategies to get there?
5. Teachers use evidence of student learning to determine next steps (ES = 0.60)
6. Focused practice and revision (ES = 0.71)
7. Student self-reflection (ES = 0.62), tracking and sharing learning and progress with others (ES = 0.54) (e.g., peers), learners' expectations (ES = 1.33)

Source: Chappuis (2015); Hattie (2009).

Conclusion

Whether by lack of understanding or our own familiarity with learning, the tendency for text-only communication is a problem to overcome because it limits what is possible. One concern we have heard is that given the opportunity to do mapping as a prewriting strategy, students may spend too much time on their drawing. Spending time on something you like is what "flow" in learning is all about. In Practitioner Spotlight 5.1, Heather Oakes observed this in her classroom and took action by putting limits on the prewriting time, therefore keeping the mapping strategy and using classroom management to solve the problem.

Assessment-literate learners need to be encouraged to use multiple means of expression to maximize engagement in, and communication of, themselves as learners to portray complexity, specificity, and growth, as shown in Figure 5.15. These "personal learning geographies" provide learners with the opportunity to engage in analytic and creative thinking, as is shown with the seven strategies of assessment for learning in the concept map, Figure 5.14, and in the personal learning geography in Figure 13b. Similarly, the Express-a-Book spotlights in Chapters 2 and 13 provide examples of how music and poetry can be added to the 2-D and 3-D sketching and drawing to enable deep thinking and expression of complex, intriguing concepts.

Please do not bypass visual literacy and concept mapping, strategies known to help unpack and consolidate learning of clear targets; to help display prior knowledge; to provide an efficient product for collaborative high-energy learning; and to help focus feedback. It also serves as a quick prewriting strategy that helps learners focus their writing on central topics and themes, organization, and relevant supporting evidence and details. Take a risk! This flexible, high-impact strategy is just a map away.

PAUSE AND REFLECT

- Flow—the feeling of total immersions and timeless focus—is what prompted the drawing in Figure 5.15. The image of the seven strategies and Maine helped convey the assessment literacy work we did with the Maine Center for Research in STEM Education (RiSE Center) around assessment for learning strategies and the Next Generation Science Standards (NGSS) practices.
- If you were asked to create your own visual representation of the seven strategies of assessment for learning what would it look like? What visual images might you use?

FIGURE 5.14 ● Seven Strategies of Assessment for Learning Plus Hattie's *Visible Learning* = High-Impact Assessment for Learning

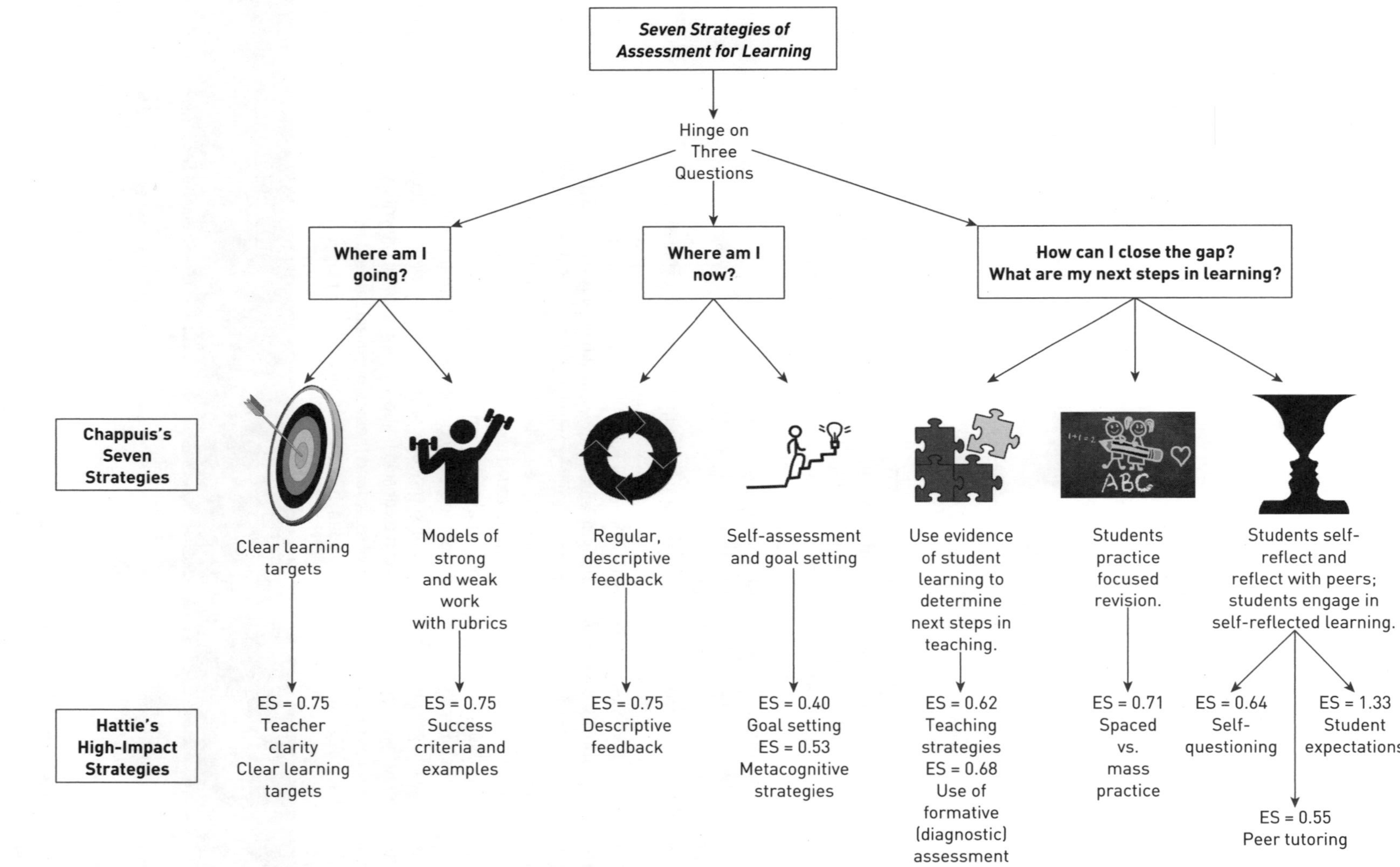

Source: Adapted from Chappuis (2015); Hattie (2009, 2012).

FIGURE 5.15 ● Visual Representation of Seven Strategies of Assessment for Learning Combined With Next Generation Science Standards Practices

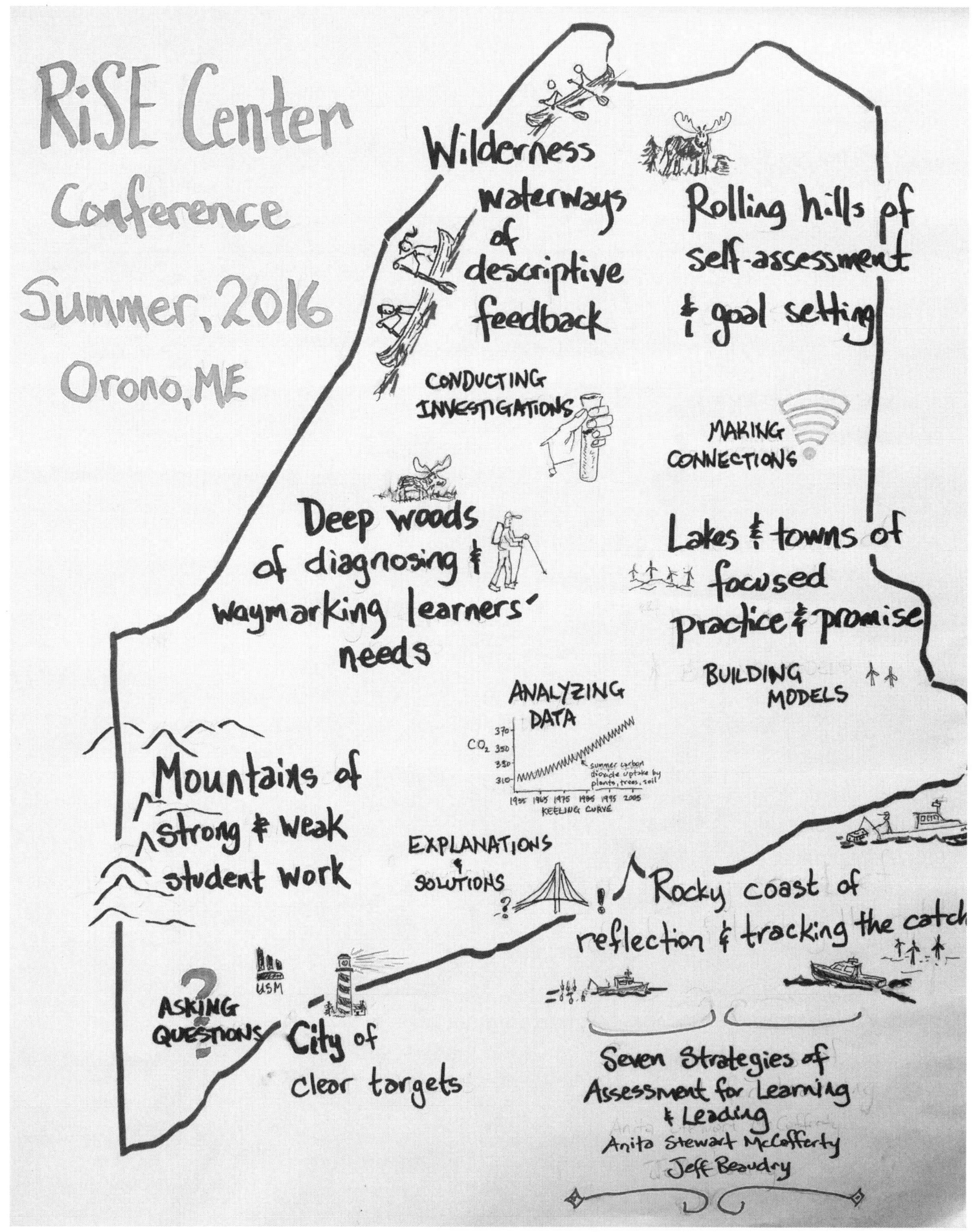

Source: Jeffrey S. Beaudry, author

Take a Deep Dive to Further Your Understanding

- Find teachers who share in-depth case studies resources and at our website: https://sites.google.com/a/maine.edu/visualliteracy20. We would like you to focus on our three webinars. They are fifteen- to twenty-minute in-depth case studies by teachers who have great stories to tell. All of these stories and many more were collected in the book *Cases on Teaching Critical Thinking Through Visual Representation Strategies* (Shedletsky & Beaudry, 2014). Happy mapping!
    - Jim Gorman, science teacher at Northbridge High School in Massachusetts, talks about the use of concept mapping for instruction and assessment of conceptual change (student growth) in "How Can Conceptual Change Be Visualized Using Concept Maps?": https://youtu.be/Ee-fGxpMa0I.
    - Dr. Amina Sadik, faculty in microbiology, Tuoro University Medical School, in "Teaching Critical Thinking to First-Year Medical Students Through Concept Mapping" carefully explains the use of concept maps for formative and summative purposes as she seeks to build knowledge of complex, interdisciplinary content—microbiology, biochemistry, and diagnosis of diseases: https://youtu.be/5dH8wX-QXqE.
    - Chigozirim Utah and Alexis Waters, University of Nebraska–Lincoln, discuss the importance of visual thinking, building, and probing concept maps. Their presentation "Confronting Critical Thinking Challenges 'In' the Classroom" is their passionate story about mapping as a way to get students to think more deeply: https://youtu.be/4U5W71JfYPk.

Putting Feedback Into Action

Key Takeaways

Descriptive feedback during the learning process is a high-impact strategy.

The way we provide feedback to our learners can reinforce or challenge their goal orientations and mindsets. Many of our feedback strategies (e.g., scoring or grading too soon, attaching points or grades to all learning tasks, overfeedbacking, vague comments, waiting until the summative assessment to provide descriptive feedback) reinforce either ego or task or performance orientations and fixed mindsets.

Only a portion of the work on effective feedback is about what the educator does or does not do in giving the feedback. Perhaps the most important part of the work on effective feedback is how receptive the learner is to feedback and what the learner does with the feedback. Assessment-literate educators create structures and environments that help learners move into a learning or mastery orientation and exhibit a growth mindset. They help learners seek feedback to improve and do not penalize mistakes during the learning process.

Teachers and principals deserve effective, timely, descriptive feedback, too, with time to act upon the feedback instead of simply receiving an evaluative rating score at the end of their evaluation cycles. An evaluative rating score is the equivalent to summative grading. High-stakes evaluation processes minimize positive risk-taking and encourage fixed mindsets.

Modeling how to *give* effective feedback is crucial. Modeling how to *receive* constructive feedback is even better. Modeling how to *seek* feedback is best still.

Although Dr. John Hattie's meta-analysis on feedback indicates that descriptive feedback is a high-impact strategy (see Figure 6.1), unless a learner puts feedback into action, it is of little value. This can be particularly disheartening to educators, especially when we have invested lots of time and energy into providing high-quality descriptive feedback to our students. It is not enough for us to provide students with descriptive feedback adhering to the characteristics of effective feedback (see Figure 6.2), although that certainly is necessary. We also have to help students develop a mind frame where they are able to receive the feedback in order to put it into action. In other words, educators have to help our students become assessment-literate learners—learners that are not only open to feedback but expect it and also give feedback to others because they realize the power it has to improve learning.

FIGURE 6.1 ● Seven Strategies Concept Map With a Focus on Descriptive Feedback

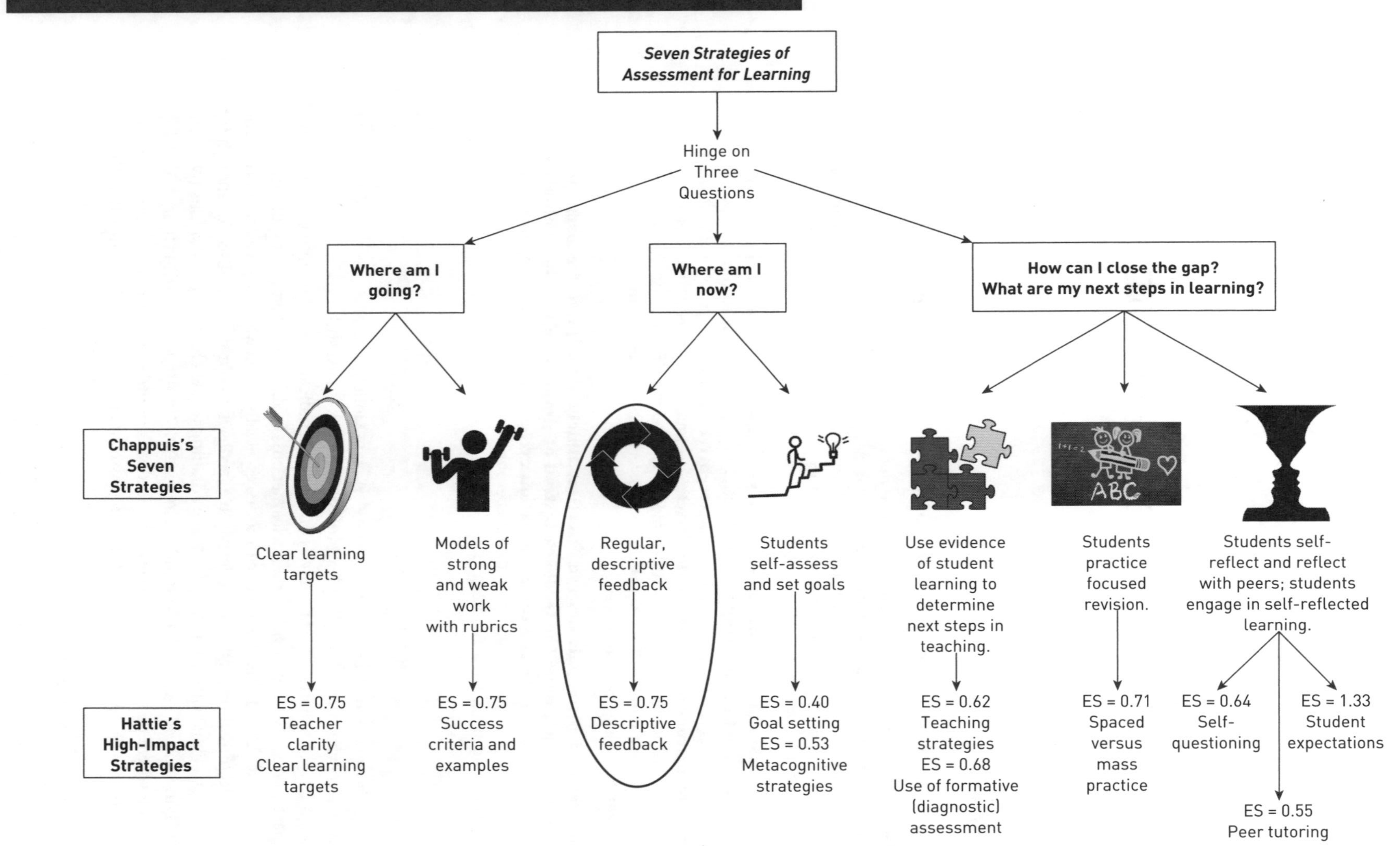

Source: Chappuis (2015); Hattie (2009, 2012).

FIGURE 6.2 ● Characteristics of Effective Feedback

Characteristics of Effective Feedback

1. Directs attention to the intended learning, pointing out strengths and offering specific information to guide improvement (e.g., success and next steps feedback)
2. Occurs during learning, while there is still time to act upon it
3. Addresses partial understanding
4. Does not do the thinking for the learner
5. Limits corrective information to the amount of feedback learners can act upon

Source: Chappuis (2015).

In our work, we cannot help but think of times where we have violated the principles of effective feedback and our efforts did not realize the learning gains for which we had hoped. For instance, Anita, one of the authors, vividly recalls her final year teaching eighth-grade social studies where she had 126 students. She remembers spending hours upon hours scoring summative work using verbose rubrics that provided analytic trait feedback to each of her students as well as a holistic score. But that wasn't enough. She also spent enormous amounts of time handwriting copious descriptive comments on each student's work. Days (perhaps weeks) later when the summative assessments were finally ready to be returned to students, she witnessed students looking for the final score or grade and not even reading the breakdown of the scoring nor the descriptive feedback. Worse, she found the majority of those assessments being stuffed into backpacks or tossed into trash cans! Anita recalls chasing students down and insisting they read the comments and take the assessments home to show their families.

Descriptive feedback was supposed to make a difference to subsequent learning. Hattie (2012), Timperley (Hattie & Timperley, 2007), and a host of other researchers indicate that feedback is a high-impact, high-leverage strategy (e.g., effect size, or ES = 0.75; see Figure 6.1). What had gone wrong in Anita's classroom? For starters, the feedback was not timely, did not occur during the learning, and was overwhelming in quantity for many of her students. Years later, upon reading Brookhart's (2008) book on effective feedback and her recount of studies on feedback along with Chappuis's (2015) work on seven strategies, Anita realized that her students had viewed the descriptive feedback as her rationale for the scores or grades she had given students. She also realized that because it had taken so long to score and provide descriptive feedback on so many projects, learners had moved on to new units of study and did not see the scores from the analytic trait rubrics or the descriptive feedback as pertinent to their current learning. Many were interested in the overall score or grade, but few were interested in little beyond that. Anita had missed opportunity after opportunity to provide actionable feedback that she then required her learners to put into action to improve worthy understandings, skills, and dispositions.

While working with the Maine Center for Research in STEM Education (RiSE Center) and their teacher leaders, we developed STEM examples using Chappuis's suggestions for providing success and next steps feedback (see Figure 6.3). One of the strategies Chappuis (2015) shared is that of providing both success and next-step (or intervention) feedback, which directs attention to the intended learning targets. We encourage teachers to collaborate with colleagues to practice providing actionable success and next steps feedback for students.

Learners often need scaffolding to help them move from receiving feedback to using feedback productively. We encourage educators to provide structures that help students put the feedback into action. For instance, a strategy that works for us is having students highlight or indicate via sticky notes or comments in a Google doc where, how, and why (or why not) the descriptive feedback has been acted upon in subsequent work. Campbell and Feldman (2017) advocated for the use of multimodal feedback, including audio and video comments, recording conferences with learners, and so on, using the wide array of technology tools now available. Their research

FIGURE 6.3 ● STEM Examples of Success and Next Steps Feedback

Success Feedback	**STEM Example**
Identify what is done correctly.	"All of your information about nonrenewable resources is accurate."
Describe a feature of quality present in the work.	"Your concept map works well to show the connections between the engineering design steps."
Points out effective use of a strategy or process.	"The table you drew really helped to solve the problem."
Next Steps Feedback	**STEM Example**
Identify a correction.	"Some of the information you gave for renewable resources is not true for all renewable resources."
Describe a feature of quality needing work.	"Your hypothesis is missing a reason explaining why you think that will happen."
Point out a problem with a strategy or process.	"Each time you use the scales, they need to be zeroed out in order to get accurate results."
Offer a reminder.	"Remember what we have learned about converting mixed numbers to improper fractions."
Make a specific suggestion.	"Try putting your CER claim, evidence, and reasoning into the graphic organizer, and look for holes."
Ask a question.	"What do you notice about these four cells that have been circled?"

Source: Adapted from Chappuis (2015).

suggests that multimodal feedback results in achievement gains for students because they can see and hear the thinking of the teacher and play it over at their own pace. We also are advocates of providing structured opportunities after feedback (whether it be oral, written, or multimodal or from peer or teacher) for the learner herself to put together an actionable plan about how to use the feedback provided. We have had success using protocols where the learner holds the pen or is in charge of the keyboard to record the feedback received and create the plan for acting upon it. In this way, the learner is empowered and more in control of the process.

Much work has been done over the past years by Carol Dweck, Jo Boaler, Angela Lee Duckworth, and others to help us better understand the idea of mindset, self-regulation, and persistence. We firmly believe in the importance of all learners—students and educators—adopting a growth mindset, where one believes that intelligence is malleable and that with effort, persistence, and the adoption of new strategies one can achieve. A mindset is a belief system; it takes diligent effort and ongoing work to move from a fixed mindset. In an effort to help students adopt a growth mindset, it is common to see posters in classrooms differentiating fixed mindset thinking from growth mindset thinking—charts illustrating "instead of this...think that," which are popular on Pinterest, Teachers Pay Teachers, and on classroom walls. We cannot underscore the importance of a growth mindset to the learning equation. However, in spite of the popularity of mindset work in our schools, we often see an apparent lack of internalization of the concept in the actions of educators, such as a continuation of labeling students, of holding low expectations for some, of penalizing mistakes, etc. Dweck (2015) warned of a "false mindset" or the misconception that praising effort alone represents growth mindset. We are encouraged by the work of researchers such as Stephanie Faye Frank and her work around teaching learners about neuroplasticity prior to growth mindset. She reminds us of the importance of understanding neuroscience and helping our learners understand how the brain works. Mistakes activate new connections in our brains and are truly to be celebrated. Teaching our learners about neuroscience and about growth mindset are instrumental steps for helping our learners receive feedback and see it as integral to the learning process. See Chapter 9 for further discussion of grit, growth mindset, and the development of specific metacognitive learning strategies.

Much work has also been done around goal orientation and how our actions as educators and learners can promote certain goal orientations or mindsets in our students. The climate, messages, and policies about learning coming from our classrooms, faculty rooms, and district conference rooms can either promote or hinder students and educators in their adoption of a learning goal orientation and a growth mindset. After sitting in what we often jokingly refer to as "prison in-service days" (where everyone is required to attend and receive the same training about a new initiative or mandate), many educators know what it is like to feel fixed in one's thinking about learning or to adopt a task or performance orientation. Many leave those professional learning experiences feeling confused about the implementation requirements, feeling underwhelmed about its importance to the everyday business of their classrooms, and feeling inadequate, overwhelmed, unmotivated, or frustrated about how she or he will be able to fit it all into an already impossible teaching or leading assignment.

Jan Chappuis, in recent conference presentations and writings, helped clarify for us and many of the educators with whom we are privileged to work, the notion of goal orientations and how our actions can promote certain orientations or mindsets to develop in our students. The three goal orientations Chappuis references from the literature are mastery, performance or task, and ego. We have noted the connections between goal orientations and mindsets: performance or task and ego orientations tend to correspond with a fixed mindset, while a mastery goal orientation has many connections with a growth mindset. The mastery learning orientation is the one we hope to promote in our students and colleagues. It incorporates and encourages a growth mindset and places less emphasis on simply completing the task or outperforming others (e.g., performance orientation). It also de-emphasizes fixed mindset thinking and ego orientation, which is promoted when feedback is about the person, not the intended learning targets.

As we pondered how feedback plays into goal orientations and mindsets in either promoting a learning or mastery orientation and a growth mindset or not, we engaged in a reflective exercise with educators. We asked ourselves and other educators to think about and identify teacher actions or feedback comments for each of the goal orientations and then to note students' reactions, their words, and their feelings. Table 6.1 represents a sampling of the results with teacher actions or comments and student talk or feelings noted for each type of goal orientation and mindset.

TABLE 6.1 ● Goal Orientations, Mindsets, and Feedback Table

	Goal Orientations, Mindsets, and Feedback		
	Mastery or Learning Orientation (Growth Mindset)	**Performance or Task Orientation (Fixed Mindset)**	**Ego Orientation (Fixed Mindset)**
Teacher Actions/ Talk	Uses five characteristics of effective feedback Teaches about neuroplasticity and the way our brains work Celebrates mistakes Models reflection on her or his mistakes Provides success and next steps feedback—focuses attention on learning Provides structures to teach and require students to put feedback into action Models seeking, receiving, and putting feedback about her or his teaching into action	Provides feedback about completing the task or the performance level "Your score is the highest in the class." "You are on track for completing your assignments for this unit by the due date." "Remember, the goal is for everyone to at least get a score of a 3. Use the rubric to see how to get a 3."	"You're a natural." "Look at you! You're the first one done!" "You are so smart!" "I can always count on you to get all the answers correct."

(Continued)

TABLE 6.1 ● (Continued)

	Goal Orientations, Mindsets, and Feedback		
	Mastery or Learning Orientation (Growth Mindset)	Performance or Task Orientation (Fixed Mindset)	Ego Orientation (Fixed Mindset)
Student Actions/ Talk/Feelings	"Oh, I see what I need to do to do better." "I'm going to try again. Mistakes are part of the learning process." "I'm going to ask for some help. I think, 'I just need to talk to a classmate who will listen and help me solve this problem.'" "Now, I want to try to figure out how to apply this idea to the bike I am trying to build at home." "I need to learn some new strategies. I'm working really hard, buy my old strategies aren't working."	"Is this what you're looking for?" "Am I done?" "What grade or score did I get?" "Did I pass?" "I'm fine with a 2.5. Guess I'm all done." "What was the top score?" "Other kids did worse than I did, so it's okay."	"Oh no! I don't know the answers. I must not be smart after all." "I'm not ever going to get this." "Why bother trying? I stink at math! It won't matter what I do." "No one in my family is musical."

Giving and Receiving Feedback: Creating a Culture Receptive to Feedback

Teaching learners to give and receive feedback is a skill that requires explicit teaching and modeling. It also takes a great deal of trust for learners to accept and seek feedback about their thinking, processes, dispositions, skills, and/or products. Carefully cultivating learning environments conducive to giving, receiving, and seeking feedback is a necessity in order to allow learners to open themselves up to taking risks. Cultivating this kind of learning environment requires a relentless effort on the part of the classroom teacher or school leader. Making mistakes and becoming stuck are part of the learning process. The way we support learners through these tenuous times is critical. Remember, actions speak louder than words. So, be careful that your procedures and policies do not penalize learning (i.e., making mistakes). Modeling how to *give* effective feedback is crucial. Modeling how to *receive* constructive feedback is even better. Modeling how to *seek* feedback is best. Without a healthy understanding that mistakes are a vital part of the learning process and truly are not a negative thing (e.g., a weakness or a deficit), learners will often resist feedback that points out next steps. If learners hold fixed mindsets or feel vulnerable in the learning environment, they are much less likely to receive or seek feedback.

If you have ever encountered or reacted to constructive feedback in a defensive manner, consider why this was so. Often there is a lack of trust established between the learner and the person giving feedback, or the feedback is seen as an evaluative judgment that will negatively affect the learner in some way. Other times, the learner may hold low self-esteem or an ego orientation, or the learner may question the credibility of the person giving the feedback. Helping learners understand mindsets and goal orientations often help them better understand and identify when they are feeling fixed or trapped in an ego or performance orientation. Spending time as teachers and leaders to develop strong relationships, acting in credible and trustworthy ways, and minimizing the negative impact of making mistakes are all helpful ways for educators to address feedback concerns.

Practitioner Spotlights 6.1 and 6.2 from Gus Goodwin and Melissa Roberts explain these educators' processes for engaging their learners in the giving of peer feedback through carefully constructed protocols and how they help their students put feedback into action. In order for peer feedback to be a positive and beneficial experience for learners, educators have to cultivate a trusting environment. Teachers and students have to be clear about what the learning intentions and success criteria look like in order to provide effective feedback to one another. As important as it is to provide time for descriptive feedback during the learning process, it is just as crucial to build in adequate time for learners to act upon the feedback.

PRACTITIONER SPOTLIGHT 6.1

STRATEGY: ROUNDS FOR PEER FEEDBACK

What?

Critique plays an important role in my engineering design class for eighth graders at King Middle School. We work on observing and sharing what we notice without judgment. So, instead of saying, "Nice project, I like it!" or "Looks good," students are encouraged to say, "I notice that your machine has a pulley system made from a yogurt cup" or "I wonder how the motor will turn on?" They can also offer suggestions such as, "You may consider having less of an angle on your ramp so the ball doesn't roll quite so fast."

So What?

We found that having the entire class critique one machine at a time was quite time consuming and resulted in the usual vocal few chiming in and offering constructive feedback, but what about everyone else? I came up with the idea for rounds from Steve Seidel's "Rounds," which he got from how doctors make their rounds. I explain to the students, "Doctors make their rounds in the hospital when they get together with other doctors and look at and talk about their patients. The doctors share and learn from one another, and you are going to make the rounds today, except your patients are your energy transfer machines, and you are engineers, not doctors."

The engineering teams get to work on their machines, and when I ring a bell one person from each team makes the rounds and looks at all of the other machines that their fellow engineers are working on. They use the rounds sheet provided, and they are not allowed to talk as they observe because I want them to really focus, and we only have seven to eight minutes per round. When I ring the bell again, that group should be finished with or wrapping up their rounds, and a new person from each group should begin. We do this until everyone has had a chance to make the rounds. The next step is where each team member shares what they saw and what they wrote on their rounds sheet. They discuss and decide if they now want to add or change anything to their own projects based on the feedback from the rounds.

Now What?

The next step for our students is to help them internalize the process of giving, receiving, seeking, and putting feedback into action.

Rounds

NAME: ____________ CLASS: __________ DATE: _____

Rounds are an opportunity to observe and examine each other's work.

DIRECTIONS:

1. When signaled, one person from each group will make the rounds by observing other groups as they work on their projects.
2. When making your rounds, you may not talk to anyone—this is your time to simply observe.
3. Fill in the boxes below with sketches and notes.

Whose project was this?

Describe something you are wondering about.

Source: Contributed by Gus Goodwin, middle school teacher, King Middle School, Portland Public Schools.

PRACTITIONER SPOTLIGHT 6.2

STRATEGY: PEER FEEDBACK

What?

While teaching in a first- and second-grade loop at East End Community School in Portland, Maine, I used a structured process of peer feedback on a regular basis. Students were taught to use these sentence stems: "I noticed that you . . . " and "It might help if you . . . " Through this process, students were taught to look at the class-built criteria and critically look at a peer's work to identify what criteria was met and what pieces were missing that would improve the piece. Students used this process during writing workshop while examining final products from our expedition and at any other time when we were looking at student work.

We began this process by looking at a piece of work as a class and working together to identify components of criteria that were in the piece and components that were missing. Students were expected to use the sentence stems and were taught to not use the words *I like*, as that tends to lead to personal preferences versus meeting criteria and class expectations. Once students were comfortable doing an example, together the class would break up into small groups or partnerships. Each student would have a feedback form to track ideas. Once the feedback was given, students were encouraged to look over their feedback and choose a next step. Students would choose one or two points from the "It might help if you . . ." side to help them revise their work.

Example of the feedback form:

I noticed that you . . .	It might help if you . . .

So What?

The benefits are widespread as students begin to take ownership of their work, recognize set criteria, and identify when it is being used and when it is missing. Students were more open to the feedback that came from peers when it was addressed in this manner. Using these sentence stems allows students to hear about what they do well, and next steps were suggested to them, which helped with the revision process. As a teacher, you were able to see if students fully understood the criteria as they were finding it in each other's work and talking about how adding it could help improve each other's work.

Now What?

With a new position comes new ways to use different techniques. A next step with this process would be to use this strategy with adults while looking at unit design work. Setting up group criteria and providing feedback in a safe, structured way would allow all to gain an understanding of how to safely give feedback to colleagues.

Source: Contributed by Melissa Roberts, professional learning and data/assessment coordinator, RSU 57.

Using Objects to Understand How One Prefers to Receive Feedback

In our work with descriptive feedback, we wanted to understand the personal dimension to assessment for learning by asking learners to reflect on this question: How do you prefer to receive feedback?

This classroom activity focuses on developing the learner's self-assessment of her or his personal, affective connection with the learning and that of self-regulated learning (Hattie & Timperley, 2007). Our purpose was to give teachers and learners a deeper understanding of feedback using a simple one-question protocol to characterize and describe how each individual preferred to receive feedback (Brookhart, 2008).

In our learning activity, we asked educators to adopt a learner's perspective about feedback with a focus on this question: How do I prefer to receive feedback? By asking the participants how they preferred to receive feedback, they were put in the position of thinking about how it was delivered as well. The activity is supported by the work of Black and Wiliam's (2009) as seeing students as the owners of their own learning, Hattie's (2009, 2012) positive learners' expectations, Stiggins's (2004) student involvement, and Brookhart's (2008) feedback strategies for reluctant learners. Black and Wiliam (2009) suggested that students become positive agents of their own learning when they learn how to collaborate and support each other as learners. Stiggins is a longtime proponent of student involvement in assessment and students as effective communicators of where they are as learners.

Each teacher selected an object to represent her or his preference and described in small groups why the object represented her or his preference for how to receive feedback. Teachers then reflected on their responses with an artifact and a series of reflective prompts. We have repeated this process with hundreds of educators and have used in-depth qualitative methods of conversations and reflections of teachers and administrators to support our inquiry. Numerous teachers remarked how much they had yet to learn about feedback and how our protocol was worthy of use with other educators and with students. Based on these initial findings, we find that educators' understandings were facilitated by the use of artifacts and has the possibility of transfer to classroom practice for students.

One of the ways to understand classroom assessment is cognitive load theory (Hattie & Yates, 2014), which points out the challenges that learners contend with as they are introduced to new learning and/or questions; and seek to connect with prior knowledge; try to be productive with strategies like feedback, self-assessment, and goal setting all while performing the internal metacognitive juggling act. To make the idea of feedback and learning more concrete, our object-focused activity helped learners by putting words and images together in a single, personalized conversation in which learners practice "the deliberate and practical use of personal pronouns" (Hattie & Yates, 2014, p. 150). For example, one participant explained that a paintbrush represents feedback "that is practical and can be put to immediate use." This shows that there are a variety of visual metaphors to represent the essential quality of feedback, that it is focused and direct (Black & Wiliam, 2009; Brookhart, 2008; Chappuis, 2012; Hattie, 2012). The most prominent category was direct, immediate feedback represented by objects like a baseball, a kangaroo boxing pen, black-and-white markers, a mirror, a flashlight, and a paintbrush. Other participants, however, preferred more indirect, multilayered objects or images represented by perfume, candles, boots, grow capsules, a silver platter, a weekly pillbox, and sunglasses. The selection of perfume represents "feedback that is soft, clear, and in small amounts." A "candle smells pleasant. At times I like feedback that is pleasant, but a candle can burn, which isn't pleasant." Be careful though, as a smoky candle in close proximity can cause surface damage, as can poorly delivered feedback even if initially it smells pleasant. We observed positive, active conversations filled with metaphors when objects and images accompanied words. The use of artifacts and this multimodality approach allowed each participant to represent her or his learning about feedback in a concrete, unique way.

Interestingly, but not surprisingly, educators often had conflicting and opposing explanations of how they liked to receive feedback. Some chose an artistic fan or a fancy ribbon bow or a glitzy bauble to represent their need to hear positive feedback first before more constructive feedback. Others chose the pliers, screwdriver, or magnifying glass to represent their desire to receive feedback about how to improve without the need for fluff, vagueness, or praise.

After the conversation with the artifacts, educators talked about their own experiences with descriptive feedback—those experiences as a deliverer of feedback to their students and/or colleagues and also as a receiver of feedback from their colleagues or administrators. This modality of combining words with images using objects or pictures promotes self-regulated learning and individual learner's self-assessment of their personal, affective connection with their learning (Hattie & Timperley, 2007). Engaging learners in self-expressive and metaphoric thinking through the use of objects or symbols is a powerful learning strategy, combining several high-impact strategies (Stewart McCafferty, 2017).

We highly recommend the use of this activity or a similar one to have colleagues in a faculty meeting or students in a classroom express their preferences about receiving feedback and how they can be more conscious of how their peers prefer to receive feedback as well.

Descriptive Feedback Symbolic Representation Task

Task Directions:

1. Please consider how you like to *receive* feedback. Think about and jot down characteristics that make for effective feedback from your perspective as a *receiver* of professional feedback.
2. Choose one or two objects that represent how you like to receive feedback.
3. Consider the following prompts and share at your table groups:

   - What is or are the object(s) you chose?
   - How does the object(s) represent how you prefer to receive feedback?
   - The last time you received professional feedback, what was the form of feedback you received?
   - Did you take action based on the feedback?
   - What could have been done to improve the feedback in order to help you take action?
   - What could have been done to improve your willingness or readiness to receive the feedback?
   - What are lessons learned (or applications) for giving feedback to your colleagues and/or to students?

PAUSE AND REFLECT

- How could you use something like the object talk to help your learners discuss how they like to receive feedback and what kinds of feedback they view as useful to their learning?

Educators Need and Deserve Formative Feedback, Too!

If we hope to improve school climate, change educators' practices, and increase student learning, then we must help our school leaders become better at giving regular, actionable, formative feedback to their teachers and staffs. School leaders must see the work of getting into classrooms daily as a priority. We understand that there are many obstacles to regular classroom observations and feedback conversations. We understand that school leaders feel torn by their immense responsibilities. We often hear that they are too busy "putting out fires" and managing their buildings to get out into the classrooms in a regular, high-quality, formative kind of way. In fact, a frightening majority of both the school leaders and their teachers that we have interviewed report that over the past decade they rarely receive summative observations and evaluations, let alone formative observations and quality formative feedback that leads to substantive changes in their classrooms and/or in the learning of their students. We often tell aspiring school leaders that unless you take proactive stances, you will still be too busy putting out fires twenty years from now to get into classrooms and engage as the instructional leader you wish to be.

As we saw in Chapter 2, providing formative feedback to teachers is a high-impact strategy (ES = 0.90). Our teachers and our students deserve for us as school and district leaders to figure out how to support their learning in substantial ways. Covey (1989) reminded us decades ago to prioritize and spend our time focused on doing the right work—or as he called it, "putting first things first." Marshall (2012) picked up on this idea as it relates to school leaders and talked about how principals can be so busy running from one task to the next. Although they are busy, they may not be accomplishing a lot in moving their schools forward, because they are not focused on the tasks that are most effective (i.e., supporting educator and student learning by being visible, engaging in ongoing classroom observations, dialoguing in formative ways with teachers on a continuous basis, participating in curriculum work, establishing effective professional learning, helping teachers set meaningful goals, and monitoring the impacts of those goals). In order for school leaders to be able to focus on the right work, they also need formative feedback, support, and a commitment from central office if they are to balance the emotionally charged work of managing their buildings *and* effectively leading the learning in their buildings.

PAUSE AND REFLECT

- How do we break the reactive cycle many of us find ourselves in and make formative feedback about learning a way of being in our organizations?

PRACTITIONER SPOTLIGHT 6.3

TEACHER EVALUATION AND FORMATIVE FEEDBACK

What?

We have been working to create a teacher evaluation system that helps align teachers' professional learning standards (Interstate Teacher Assessment and Support Consortium, or InTASC) with examining student data that results in meaningful feedback that can be used to support student learning. Anita has helped us work to devise a formative feedback tool that will deepen educator conversations and help teachers focus on student learning and professional growth. Evaluators are encouraged to be in classrooms more, offering formative feedback through a praise-probe-polish structure.

Teacher Name:

Teacher Effectiveness
Praise, Probe, and Polish

The Learner and Learning	Content	Instructional Practice	Professional Responsibility
1. Learner Development	4. Content Knowledge	6. Assessment	9. Professional Learning and Ethical Practice
2. Learning Differences	5. Application of Content	7. Planning for Instruction	10. Leadership and Collaboration
3. Learning Environments		8. Instructional Strategies	

Date:		Time
Praise:		
Probe:		
Polish:		

(Continued)

(Continued)

So What?

The simplicity of the feedback tool allows for educators and evaluators to spend more time in conversation around practices happening in the classrooms. This tool allows teachers to create goals that are meaningful to what is happening on a daily basis within their classrooms. The lack of checklists allows evaluators to give more specific feedback that is aligned to the goals of the educator and school. More frequent feedback is encouraged to allow for open communication between evaluator and educator.

Now What?

As a district, our next steps include further use of the tool while we refine forms and timelines. Teachers will receive support around goal setting and will be encouraged to spend time during staff meetings reflecting on and revising goals as needed. Evaluators will work in groups to align types of feedback given and interrater reliability. In addition, evaluators will work on consistency of implementation and expectations across the grade levels within our district.

Source: Contributed by Melissa Roberts, professional learning and data/assessment coordinator, RSU 57.

While the Stars and Stairs in Figure 6.4 was created as a tool to use for administrators and teachers when they are engaged in providing formative feedback to colleagues, it is just as applicable to students giving feedback to peers in the classroom. This Stars and Stairs is a way for learners to consider where they are on the giving of feedback continuum and what their next steps may be for improving that skill set.

FIGURE 6.4 ● Giving Feedback Stars and Stairs

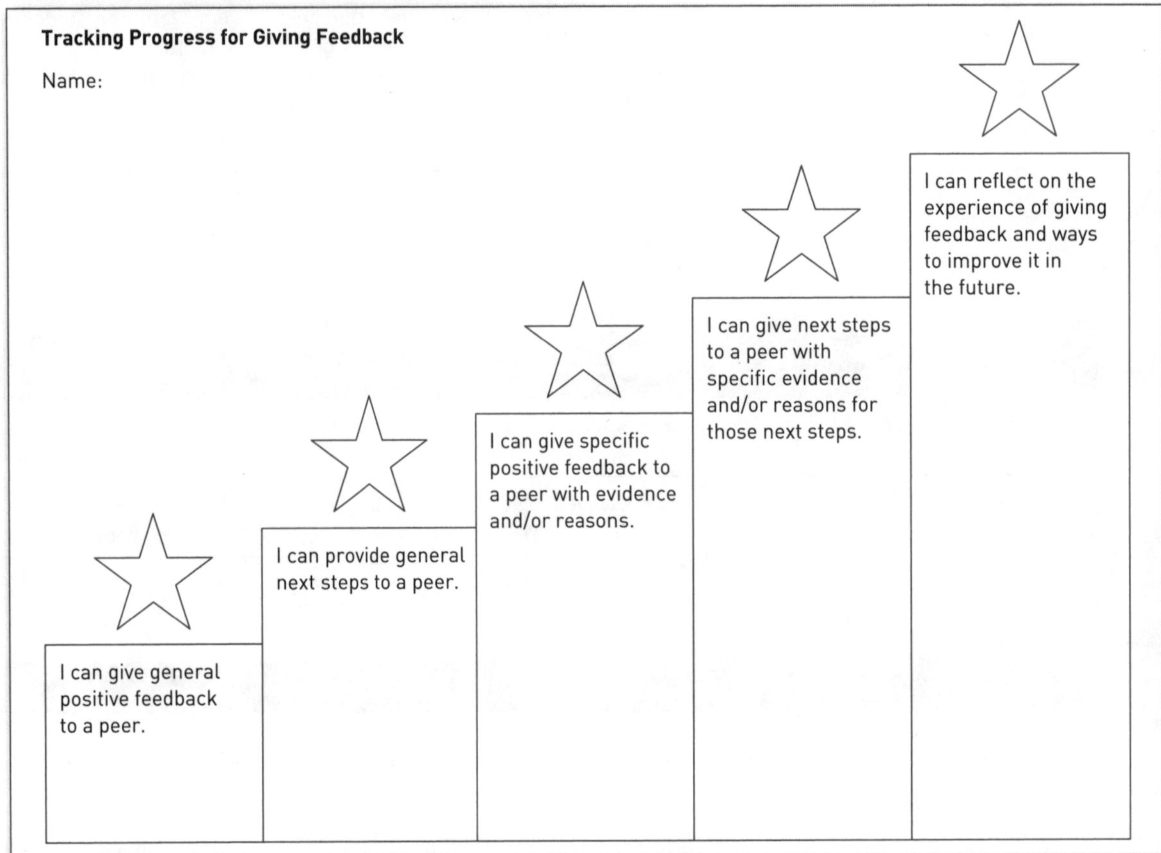

Tracking Progress for Giving Feedback
Name:
I can give general positive feedback to a peer.
I can provide general next steps to a peer.
I can give specific positive feedback to a peer with evidence and/or reasons.
I can give next steps to a peer with specific evidence and/or reasons for those next steps.
I can reflect on the experience of giving feedback and ways to improve it in the future.

Source: Contributed by Heather Rockwell, director of curriculum, RSU 67.

Conclusion

All feedback is not created equal. Research on feedback has helped identify characteristics of effective feedback that when employed on a regular basis can help improve the likelihood that the feedback given will have the desired effect of improving the learning and guiding next steps. However, the giving of feedback is only one part of the feedback equation. In order for feedback to have an impact, it must be put into action by the learner. Students and educators must be able to receive both success and next steps feedback in order for it to have the desired high impact on their learning. Creating constant feedback loops as an integral piece of the learning process in classrooms and schools helps to establish a culture of seeking feedback as a means to continual improvement. Such feedback loops are predicated on developing a climate of trust and growth mindset, where learners' mistakes are not used against them during the learning process. All learners, students, and professionals need and deserve to receive formative feedback regularly, during the learning cycle, not simply as a summative score, grade, or rating or comments accompanying an evaluative judgment.

Take a Deep Dive to Further Your Understanding

- Read Susan Brookhart's (2008) book *How to Give Effective Feedback to Your Students.*
- Read John Hattie and Helen Timperley's (2007) *The Power of Feedback.*
- Read *Thanks for the Feedback: The Science and Art of Receiving Feedback Well* (2004) by Douglas Stone and Sheila Heen.
- Watch Angela Lee Duckworth's TED Talk: "Grit: The Power of Passion and Perseverance" or read her 2016 book by the same name.
- Read Carol Dweck's (2016) updated edition of *Mindset.*
- Read Jo Boaler's (2016) book *Mathematical Mindsets*, or visit her website: https://www.youcubed.org.
- Examine Stephanie Faye Frank's website: http://stefaniefayefrank.com
- See the Chapter 6 Appendix for an in-depth look at ways a teacher could provide descriptive feedback to a student based on preassessment prompts. (The teacher's feedback is indicated in bold type.)

Chapter 6 Appendix: Earth-Sun-Moon System Pre-Self-Assessment and Teacher Feedback Case Study

Unit Pre-Self-Assessment

Earth-Sun-Moon System

Learning Target (ESS1-1): Develop and use a model of the earth-sun-moon system to describe the cyclic patterns of lunar phases, eclipses of the sun and moon, and seasons.

Step 1

Create a drawing to show what you know about lunar phases (phases of the moon; see Figure 6.5)

Describe what happens with the phases of the moon over a three-month period.

The images you have included in your drawing show how the moon changes. The white portion in your drawing, I'm assuming, is the portion of the moon that we see. These four drawings show only what the moon looks like during half of the month (twenty-nine-day cycle). You are correct that the different views of the moon repeat each month.

FIGURE 6.5 ● Step 1: Lunar Phases

FIGURE 6.6 ● Step 2: Solar Eclipse (Part 1)

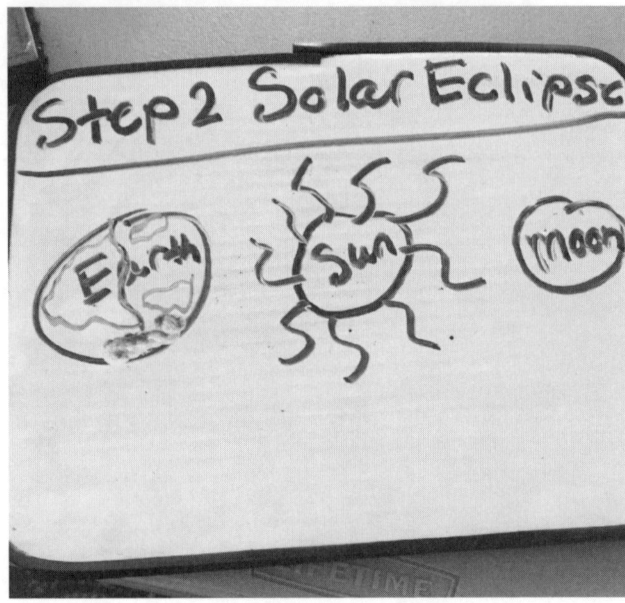

If you want to know more about this, I have put together some activities from your science book and an activity. The file is called Activity 80. A demo of this type of activity can be seen at https://www.you tube.com/watch?v=wz01pTvuMa0.

You can also watch this YouTube video: https://www.youtube.com/watch?v=NCweccNOaqo. You can't do the quizzes at the end because it is a video, but he does explain the phases and the names of the eight phases.

Step 2

Create a drawing that shows the position of the earth, sun, and moon during an eclipse of the sun (solar eclipse; see Figure 6.6).

Describe what happens during an eclipse of the sun (solar eclipse; see Figure 6.7)

Create a drawing that shows the position of the earth, sun, and moon during an eclipse of the moon (lunar eclipse; see Figure 6.8).

Describe what happens during an eclipse of the moon (lunar eclipse; see Figure 6.9).

FIGURE 6.7 ● Step 2: Solar Eclipse (Part 2)

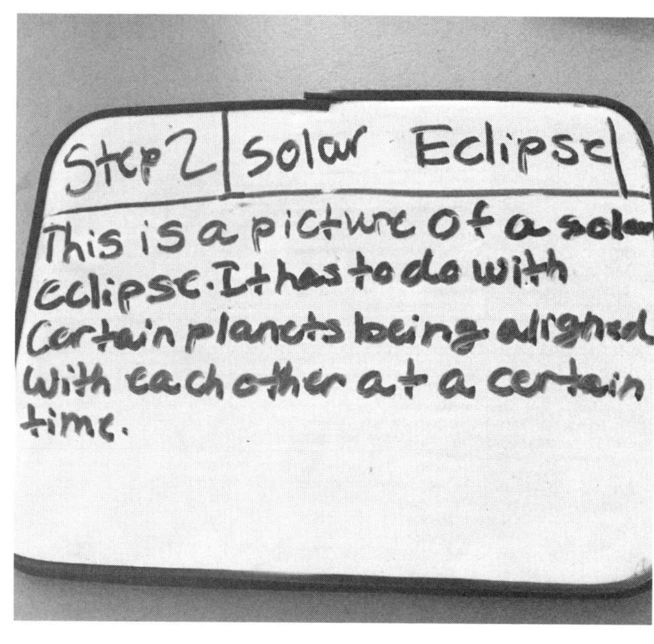

FIGURE 6.8 ● Step 2: Lunar Eclipse (Part 1)

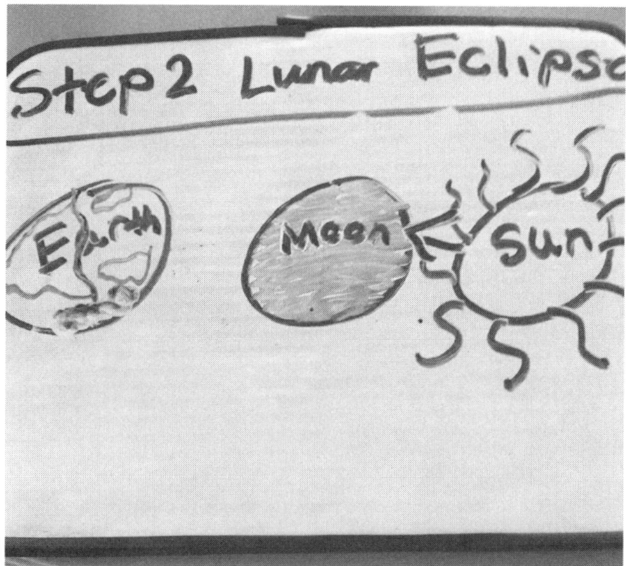

FIGURE 6.9 ● Step 2: Lunar Eclipse (Part 2)

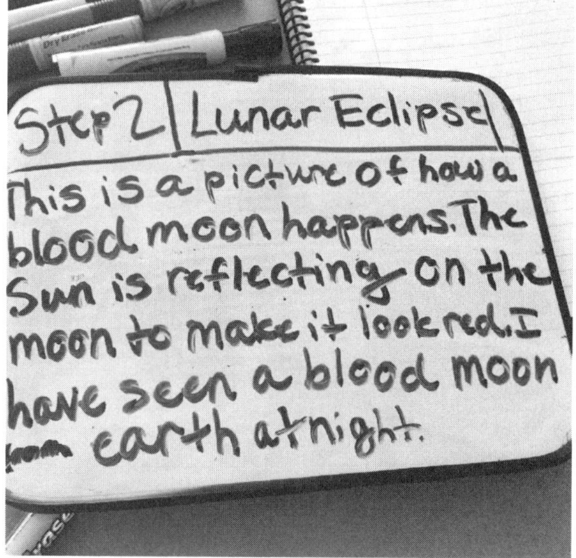

FIGURE 6.10 ● Student Model of Maine in the Summer

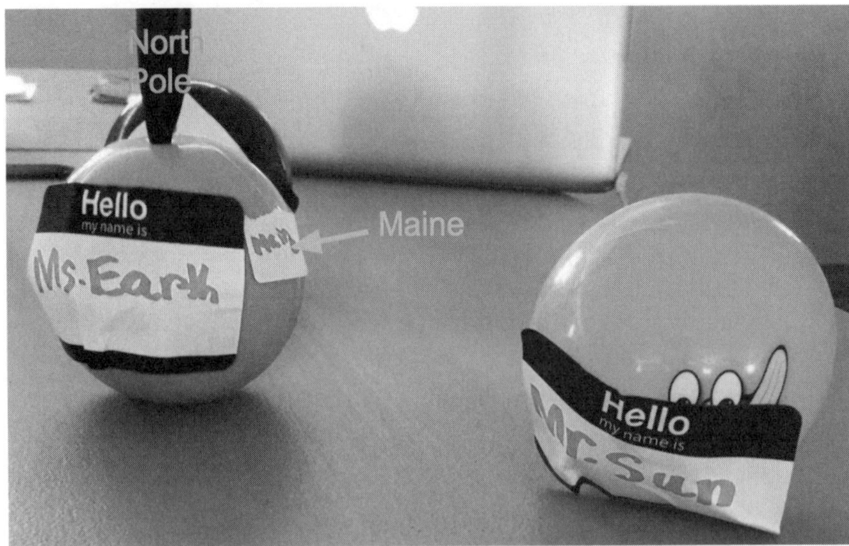

Maine in the Summer

Your drawing shows the earth, sun, and moon lined up, and this does happen during both an eclipse of the sun and an eclipse of the moon. Your drawing does share that a blood moon happens when the earth, sun, and moon are lined up during a lunar eclipse. The moon always reflects the light from the sun, so your drawing and/or explanation don't share enough about how or why this reflection and the blood color happen.

Synonyms for the term eclipse include blocking, covering, and obscuring. I think even this information will help you think about what happens during an eclipse of the sun or an eclipse of the moon. For a lunar eclipse, check out this short Khan Academy video: https://www.khanacademy.org/partner-content/nasa/measuringuniverse/spacemath1/v/lunareclipse.

This four-minute NASA video will tell you more about solar eclipses than you can imagine: http://www.nasa.gov/topics/solarsystem/features/eclipse/index.html.

Step 3

Create drawings that show the position of the earth and sun during different seasons (see Figures 6.10 to 6.14).

FIGURE 6.11 ● Student Model of Maine in the Fall and Spring

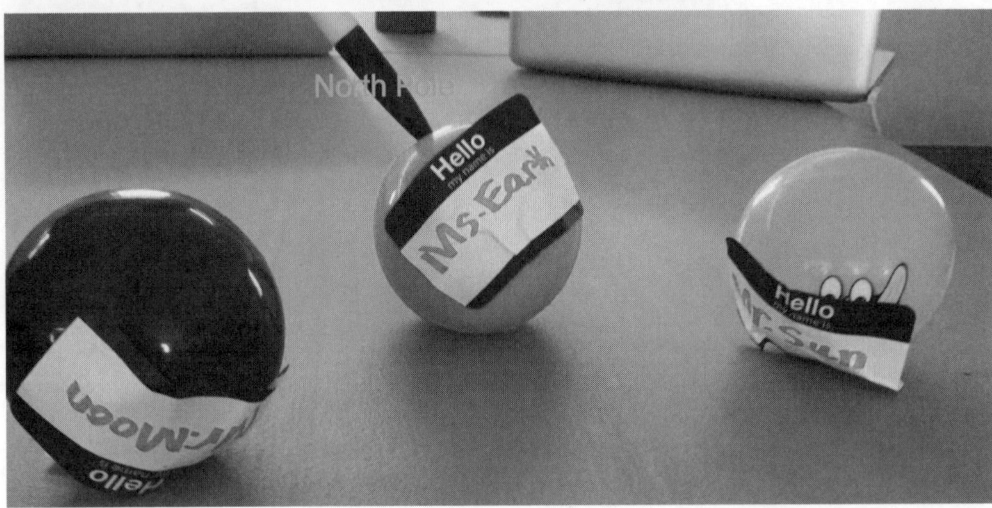

Maine in the Fall and Spring (They are the same.)

FIGURE 6.12 ● Student Model of Maine in the Winter

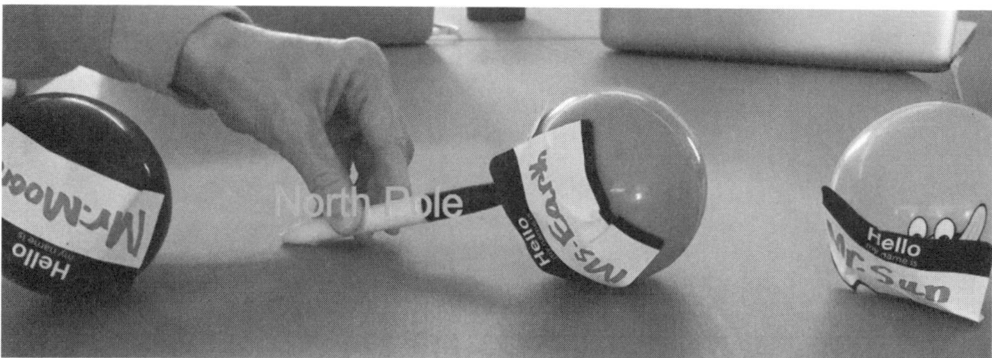

Maine in the Winter

FIGURE 6.13 ● Student Model of Maine in the Spring and Fall

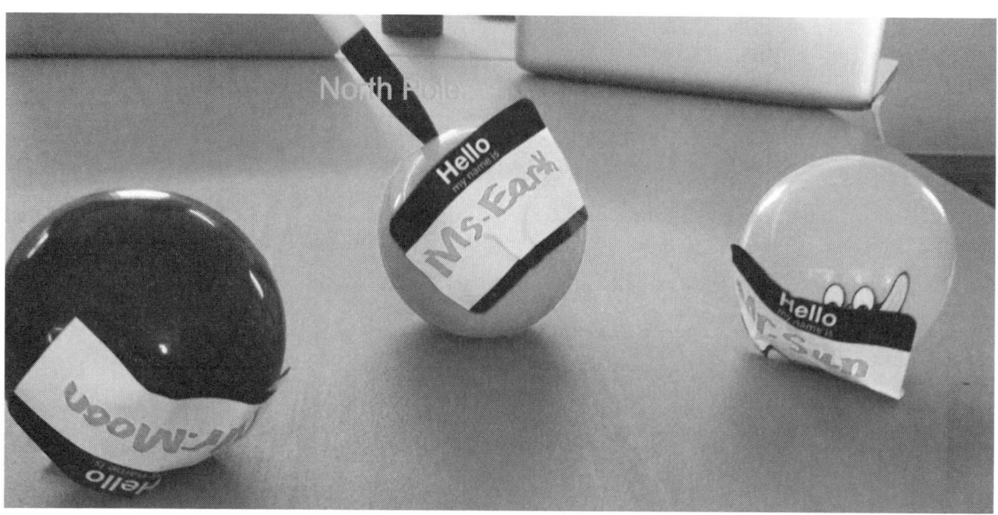

Maine in the Spring and Fall (They are the same.)

Use your drawing to explain the relationship between the earth and sun that causes seasons (see Figure 6.14).

Your explanation of seasons correctly states that when the earth is tilted toward the sun it is warmer. Your model does not correctly show how the earth tilts. This is okay because I'm sure you haven't had experience creating your own model showing the earth's tilt.

To gain experience with the tilt of the earth, see if you can find a globe. Check out the North Pole, and see if it is pointed directed upward toward the ceiling. I bet you will find that it is tilted a bit toward the wall. This is how the globe, a model of the earth, is showing the earth's tilt. Does the tilt of the globe you are looking

FIGURE 6.14 ● Step 3: Student Explanation of Seasons

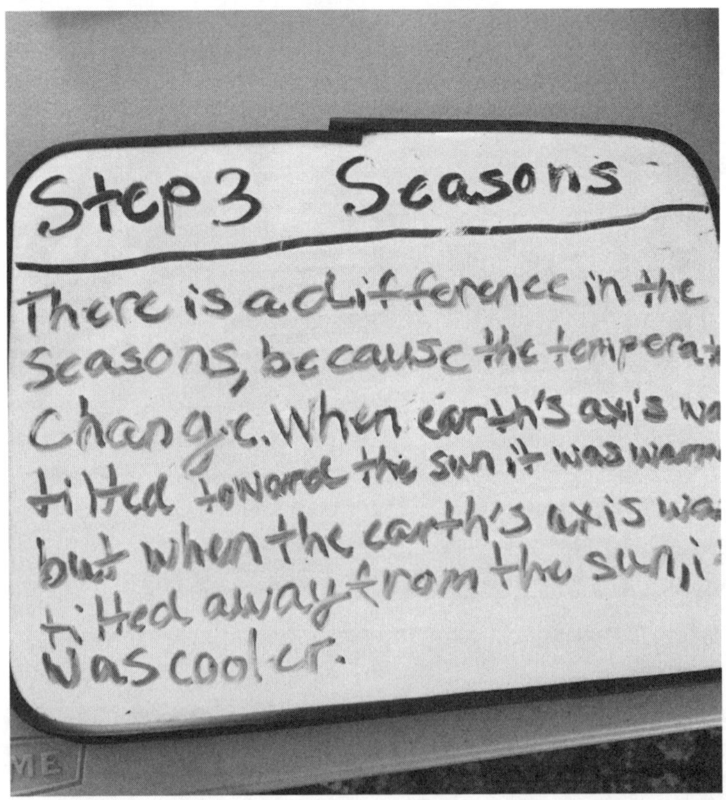

at change? Does the North Pole point toward the floor if it is sitting on its stand? What does this make you think about your model of winter in Maine?

The Kahn Academy video about the tilt of the earth is a bit long, twenty-one minutes, but it does a nice job describing the tilt of the earth and seasons: https://www.khanacademy.org/science/cosmology-and-astronomy/earth-history-topic/earth-title-topic/v/how-earth-s-tilt-causes-seasons.

Step 4

Directions: Some of the learning topic statements are true, and some are false. Carefully read each statement, and decide if you agree or disagree with each one by placing an X or check in the box for each statement. Share why you think your answer is correct in the column to the right.

Topic Statements **Some of these statements are true, and some are false.**	*Preassessment* **Agree**	 **Disagree**	*Explain and Share* **Explain your reasoning for each statement.** **Share why you think your answer is correct.**
The earth orbits the moon.		X	The earth orbits the sun, not the moon. **This is a nice, clear statement of this fact.**
The moon lights up in different parts at different times of the month.	X		There are different phases of the moon, and there are twenty-nine days until it goes back to the beginning. **The statement reads that the moon lights up. Do you agree with this?**
The moon reflects light from the sun.	X		The moon gets its light from the sun. **Your statement is true. Can you include how it actually gets light from the sun?**
The phases of the moon depend on the position of the earth in relation to the sun and the moon.	X		The earth, sun, and moon would be positioned differently. **This is a true statement, but your reasoning is unclear. Next time, please include which body (or bodies) is changing position and how it changes.**
The shadow of the sun blocks part of the moon each night, causing a pattern of different phases.		X	The earth might be causing the shadow. **You don't sound confident in your reasoning when you use the word *might*.**
The intensity of sunlight falling on a given location on the earth is the same as it orbits around the sun.		X	We tilt away from the sun. **How does the tilt of the earth away from the sun affect the intensity of the sunlight?**
The earth's axis is fixed in a direction and tilted relative to its orbit around the sun.		X	The earth's axis tilts different directions. **What causes the earth to tilt in different directions? Does something happen to cause the tilt to change?**
The seasons are a result of the earth's axis tilt and are caused by the changing intensity of sunlight.	X		The earth's axis tilts to and from the sun to create hot and cold temperatures. **I'll ask the same questions as I did in the statement prior to this one. What causes the earth to tilt in different directions? Does something happen to cause the tilt to change?**

Source: Contributed by Emma Jarvis, middle school student, Mattanawcook Junior High School, RSU 67, and Beth ByersSmall, NSF teaching fellowship program coordinator, Maine Center for Research in STEM Education (RiSE Center).

Metacognition, Self-Assessment, Goal Setting, and Reflection

GPA Matters! (Goals, Plans, and Actions, That Is!)

Key Takeaways

Rubrics are the tools that connect clear learning targets with assessment and teaching. Teachers need to understand how best to develop rubrics in their many forms. Different types of rubrics can be used to assess *for* learning and *of* learning for the purposes of scoring.

Learners need to understand their strengths and next steps according to identified success criteria of clear learning targets.

The Next Steps Rubric (NSR) is a stripped-down version of a full rubric designed to focus attention on the success criteria and evidence of learners' strengths and next steps relative to the success criteria. The NSR is one tool that intentionally brings together clear learning targets, success criteria, descriptive feedback, self-assessment, goal setting, and reflecting upon learning progress.

Self-assessment, goal setting, and reflection are metacognitive skills that need to be taught and continually reinforced. There are a host of tools that when habitually implemented and used with learners help to solidify metacognitive strategies.

Meet Our Friend Ed

Ed is a seasoned middle school teacher who feels like he has a good grasp of what rubrics are and how to use them to assess the learning of his young adolescent students. For years, he worked under the assumption that when he presented a fully developed rubric to his seventh graders, they would use it not only to self-assess their work before handing it in and to improve it for the final submission but that they would also use the rubric to self assess *during* the learning process and subsequently *after* the summative to establish goals for future learning. Ed wants his rubrics to have an impact on students' learning but has noted that the rubrics tend to be used mostly for summative purposes by both him and his students. Although Ed understands types of assessments, he is caught in a dilemma of which many educators find themselves—using a tool focused primarily on summative purposes of scoring and grading (i.e., the rubric) to meet a variety of assessment purposes.

Ed and his seventh-grade team spend much of their common planning time devoted to assessment by creating shared rubrics, common tasks, and performance assessments. They use backward design in creating the summative assessments and spend much time in wording their scoring rubrics and tasks just right for their learners. Proportionally, much less time is spent on creating and planning formative assessment experiences that teach their students *how* to self assess, *how* to give and receive descriptive feedback, and *how* to set goals and action steps to further their learning. Their emphasis on backward design translates into an imbalance of formative and summative assessment experiences for their learners. While Ed and his team emphasize that learning, not the score, is the goal, the assessment strategies and tools used send a different message to the young adolescents they teach: the score matters, and it is always looming in the forefront of the rubric used.

Like our friend Ed and his colleagues, we, too, have wrestled with this dilemma in our own practices. We have found that our rubrics or scoring guides often become cumbersome and not as learner-friendly as we had anticipated. While believing in the potential impact of a well-designed rubric or scoring guide, we have been in search of new tools and uses of traditional rubrics to help us encourage our learners to continually self-assess and establish next steps in their learning instead of using the rubric to assess their summative product or performance. Let us examine rubrics a little more closely in order to consider how we can use or adapt them to strengthen metacognitive skills of our learners during the instructional process.

Fully Developed Rubrics

Rubrics are flexible graphic organizers that combine descriptions of learning targets with levels or scales of proficiency in a simple table or matrix (Andrade, 2005; Stevens & Levi, 2005). Rubrics can serve both assessment purposes. They can provide opportunity for self-assessment and feedback from teachers and peers (assessment *for* learning or formative feedback), as well as to evaluate performances, behaviors, and products as scoring guides for grading, marking, and making decisions about student work and proficiency standards (assessment *of* learning, or summative feedback; Brookhart, 2013).

Rubrics in education are well known and have a common definition. A rubric "lists the criteria for a piece of work of what counts and articulates gradations of quality for each criterion" (Andrade, 2005, p. 27). Rubrics are an effective graphic organizer for classroom assessment, a matrix or grid, which guides analytic reasoning for students on two dimensions, the standards and the gradations in the quality of student work by which products or performances are evaluated. In the past twenty-five years, the use of rubrics in classroom assessment has increased to the point that they are a key feature of high-quality assessment practices—both for scoring student work as well as providing feedback to students. Teachers use rubrics routinely, and it is possible to involve students directly in the development and the use of rubrics; using anonymous examples of student work to determine various performance levels is one such common use of rubrics.

There are different types of rubrics—holistic and analytic as well as task-specific and general. "A scoring guide in the form of a rubric is a detailed description of the features of work that constitute quality" (Chappuis, Stiggins, Chappuis, & Arter, 2012, p. 183). Overall, rubrics are characterized as having content, a structure to the levels of quality, and specific descriptors. Though there are many examples of complex scales, the trend seems to be toward four-, five-, or six-point rubrics, as seen in the work of Dr. Marzano and organizations like the National Science Teachers Association (NSTA). Rubrics can be designed with great complexity with rows and columns filled with dense text, but how do students fare as they seek to understand and apply the rich and precise information in a rubric to her/his own work? While information about rubrics used in summative assessment *of* learning is available, there are many questions about the role of rubrics for teachers and students as tools to promote formative assessment *for* learning.

The promise of fully developed rubrics is that when done well, rubrics make targets and levels of performance clear and serve as a transparent guide to judging the quality of student work and aid in consistent scoring. Implicit within the design of rubrics are the concepts of feedback, self-assessment, goal setting, and reflecting upon learning. Bringing these elements all together using one primarily summative scoring tool, however, is a challenge for many educators and students—hence, Ed's dilemma.

Educators, such as Ed and his team, report that they use rubrics primarily for clarity of targets, to communicate learning scales to stakeholders (e.g., students, parents, colleagues, administrators), for consistency and transparency in scoring or grading (i.e., as an evaluation tool), and as a self-assessment or reflection tool.

The promise of the fully developed rubric is often not realized in ways that satisfy assessment *for* learning and assessment *of* learning. While rubrics can be transparent tools, in reality the transparency of the rubric usually means the transparency of scoring (i.e., transparency of a summative judgment of performance). In practice, rubrics simply turn into a scoring guide for the summative rather than a during-the-learning tool. The purpose of the rubric shifts to summative assessment, and it is common for students or educators to stop at a score. "I'm a 3, let me be." The message received by students often emphasizes the score at the expense of the feedback, self-assessment, and goal setting. This shift to the score is at the heart of Ed's dilemma, as he may represent educators who overestimate the effects of scoring rubrics on learners' metacognitive skills.

When teachers codevelop or show rubrics to students at the beginning of a unit or lesson as a strategy to make learning intentions clear, they often assume that students comprehend the complexity of the target and can accurately assess their current levels of proficiency and envision their goals and plans for the unit. While rubrics have the implicit elements of self-assessment and next steps (goal setting), these high-impact metacognitive strategies may not be made explicit by the teacher or appropriately scaffolded without other tools and processes being introduced into the lesson or unit mix.

The summative purpose of a rubric is to assist scorers, whether teachers, external examiners, or students, to render a score which matches the judgment or closely approximates the scores of others. These are rubrics at their best *after* learning has taken place. As learning is taking place, it is critical that teachers explore new ways to have a positive impact using assessment for learning strategies with rubrics. Rubrics are flexible and can inform learning as well as provide feedback to peers: "Students should be able to use the ingredients of the rubric to self-assess, to revise their own work, and to plan for their own next steps in learning" (Chappuis et al., 2012, p. 234). Efforts to embed rubrics into the learning process include (1) sharing the rubric with students, (2) sharing the rubric and examples of strong and weak student work with students at selected points in the lesson or unit, and (3) sharing in-depth processes for cocreating rubrics with students. Observations over time led us to conclude that even when teachers share fully developed teacher-created rubrics, complete with point scales and descriptors with students, there may be little effect on students' learning.

While showing the rubric to learners helps them understand the learning target, Andrade (2001) indicated that more is needed to be done with rubrics to improve writing. A further experimental study by Andrade, Du, and Wang (2008) showed that the student who used a model of student work in combination with the rubric had overall positive results and impact on student writing. One of the key questions about summative rubrics is whether they are the most effective way to cross the divide between formative and summative assessment. See Figure 7.1.

The Next Steps Rubric: A Bridge Between Standards and Fully Developed Rubrics

To understand the impact of rubrics on student learning, a clear distinction between formative and summative purposes must be made and a careful analysis of the empirical research must be considered. Rubrics then must be evaluated as a product used by teachers (and students) for summative grading purposes and as part of the learning process—as both a product and a part of the learning process. A great deal of time and energy went into the design and revision of a concrete tool to aid educators and their learners in their quest to advance learning. This new flexible tool is called the Next Steps Rubric (NSR) and is adapted from the single-point rubric (Fluckiger, 2010; see Figure 7.2). The NSR is an adaptation on the standard rubric format, a rubric designed to bring clear targets, self-assessment, feedback, and goal setting into a coherent graphic organizer.

FIGURE 7.1 ● Seven Strategies Concept Map With Focus on Goal Setting and Metacognition

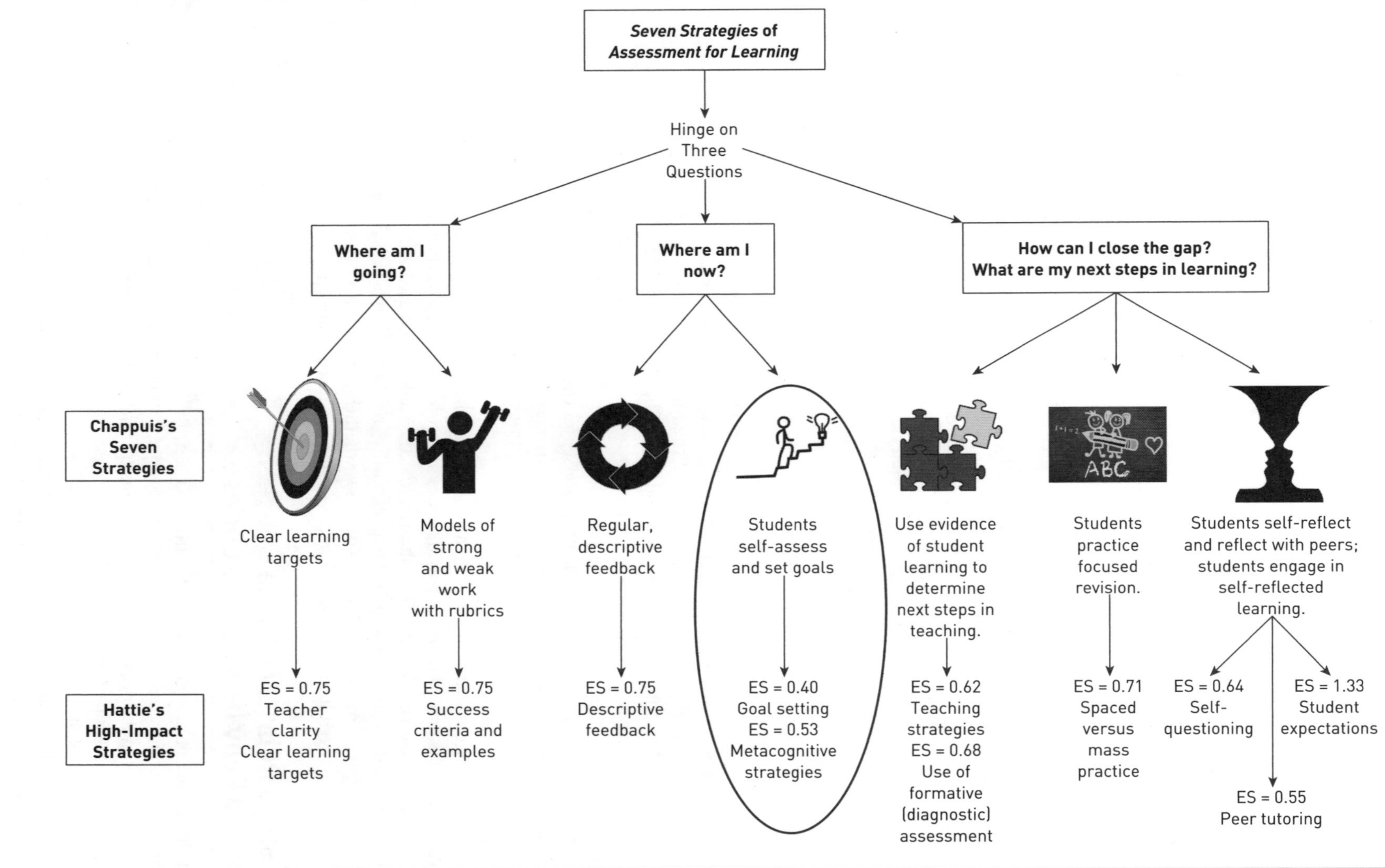
Seven Strategies of Assessment for Learning
Hinge on Three Questions
Where am I going?
Where am I now?
How can I close the gap? What are my next steps in learning?
Chappuis's Seven Strategies
Hattie's High-Impact Strategies
Clear learning targets
ES = 0.75 Teacher clarity Clear learning targets
Models of strong and weak work with rubrics
ES = 0.75 Success criteria and examples
Regular, descriptive feedback
ES = 0.75 Descriptive feedback
Students self-assess and set goals
ES = 0.40 Goal setting ES = 0.53 Metacognitive strategies
Use evidence of student learning to determine next steps in teaching.
ES = 0.62 Teaching strategies ES = 0.68 Use of formative (diagnostic) assessment
ABC
Students practice focused revision.
ES = 0.71 Spaced versus mass practice
Students self-reflect and reflect with peers; students engage in self-reflected learning.
ES = 0.64 Self-questioning
ES = 1.33 Student expectations
ES = 0.55 Peer tutoring

FIGURE 7.2 • Blank Template for the Next Steps Rubric

Blank Template for the Next Steps Rubric

Next Steps Rubric

A Self-Peer-Teacher Assessment and Goal-Setting Tool

Standard: **I can . . .**

Name: Date:

What Is Done Well ☆	**Success Criteria** **This Means . . .**	***What To Do Next*** **I Will . . . This Is How**
	□ ------------------ □	

The NSR is a during-the-learning tool that complements a fully developed summative scoring guide or rubric. The learning tool explicitly focuses on and scaffolds the following high-impact learning strategies: clear learning targets or teacher clarity, descriptive feedback, metacognitive strategies, and goal setting (Hattie, 2009, 2012).

This tool integrates strategies of assessment with teaching and learning. Simply put, the NSR is about learning. The student is the center of the process. The student assumes the essential role as learner, the one who self-assesses, sets goals, monitors progress, self-evaluates, and communicates to key audiences. The teacher is learning about and communicating about the student's needs, and the strategies of assessment for learning help guide the teacher and student toward the achievement of the learning target. The teacher supports the learning process through the display of the learning target, at the level of proficiency, the use of descriptive feedback, the diagnosis of learning needs, and the selection of teaching or learning strategies (e.g., direct instruction, classroom discussion, concept mapping, cooperative learning, reciprocal teaching, service learning, project-based learning, inquiry).

One way to interpret the impact of our teaching is to consider effect sizes, as we introduced in Chapter 3. Effect sizes are quantitative estimates of the impact of teaching, learning, and formative assessment strategies on specific outcomes like achievement or attitudes. These estimates help to summarize findings across multiple research studies. The effect size (ES) of 0.42 means that, on average, experimental groups scored higher than control groups by 0.42 standard deviations. Hattie's (2009, 2012) work on *Visible Learning* and *Visible Learning for Teachers* indicates that moderate size strategies should be above 0.40 in size, and high-impact strategies would be of a greater value. Assessment for learning strategies have moderate to large effect sizes, clear targets (ES = 0.75); samples of weak and strong work, including rubrics (ES = 0.57); descriptive feedback (ES = 0.75); self-assessment or self-reflection (ES = 0.59); goal setting (ES = 0.56); self-reported grades (ES = 1.33); and metacognitive strategies (ES = 0.69). See Figure 7.1 (earlier in the chapter) and then Figure 7.7 (later in the chapter). The synthesis of high-impact strategies with the seven strategies helps unify focus regarding thoughtful approaches to teaching and to creating an empirically based rationale for using assessment for learning strategies.

Clear Learning Targets

Educators have long sought to make rubrics friendly to learners, parents, and colleagues by clearly articulating the targets and the various levels of performance. Often the task of distinguishing between levels of performance for summative (scoring or rating) purposes results in a cluttered, language-heavy final product. The process of creating rubrics is often time consuming and an exercise in semantic "word-smithing." Clear learning targets are the bridge between standards and rubrics. As discussed in greater detail in Chapter 4, a practical process to ensure clarity for students around learning targets and standards is the employment of "I can . . . this means" statements (Chappuis, 2015; Chappuis et al., 2012).

Many educators have given us examples of "clear, student-friendly targets" that look something like this: "I can summarize complex informational text." Certainly, this is a step in the right direction in relation to the language of the Common Core literacy standard. However, by using the format of "I can...this means," educators are being asked to take the notion of clear targets one step further by answering this question: What exactly does that "I can" statement mean? The "this means" portion is in essence the success criteria that Dr. Hattie emphasized in his work around teacher clarity. The "I can" statements are a step in the right direction for teacher clarity, but the addition of "this means" clearly articulated brings an additional layer of clarity for the learner. The "this means" portion of the clear learning targets becomes the centerpiece of the NSR, a consistent learning target for all students.

Descriptive Feedback

The design spaces (the left and right columns) of the NSR allow for and encourage descriptive feedback (left column) and feed-forward or goal setting (right column) during the learning process. This rubric is designed primarily for formative purposes, using the principles of just-in-time and just-enough feedback for learning. Descriptive feedback, rather than evaluative (scoring) feedback, is the goal in order to maximize the impact of just-in-time, just-enough descriptive feedback. The feedback and feed-forward from the NSR can originate from self, peer, teacher, administrator, or parent. Opening the design space allows the NSR to be a multipurpose and a multiuser tool for descriptive feedback.

Self-Assessment and Goal Setting

While educators have grappled with clear learning targets and descriptive feedback, the next two strategies are as challenging or more so than the former. The design space to the right in the NSR is the place to record the iterative process of goal setting, and once accomplished, they determine and record next steps.

The NSR is a fluid and flexible tool rather than a static rubric. It is designed for helping the learner assess his or her progress toward reaching and even moving beyond the clearly articulated targets or criteria as the learning is occurring (while there is still time). An important note is the impact on learners who may reach proficiency but who need to keep going to the next step in the learning. The dilemma is that rubrics may communicate an end to learning, the score, rather than the next steps. Therefore, a critical element in the NSR is the explicit outcome of having learners establish next steps (goals and action steps) and commit to the attainment of those steps. To get the greatest impact from self-assessment and goal setting, the NSR must be revisited and updated with action steps to meet those next goal(s). Goal setting means students articulate what they will do (goal) and how they will do it (action steps) in each iteration.

The NSR is designed to support assessment for learning by incorporating goal setting (establishing next steps) directly into the rubric. Decades of research on goal setting gives us clear guidelines and outcomes of effective goal-setting practices. For instance, setting goals increases motivation, achievement, and one's sense of agency (Cauley & McMillan, 2009). The effects of goal setting, however, depend largely on a student's commitment to and value of the goal (Cialdini, 2009). Learners who consider the goals relevant to them and commit to their goals are much more likely to seek and apply feedback relative to their goals, to persist through challenges associated with their goals (demonstrate grit), and to take positive risks in order to meet their goals (Turkay, 2014). Self-regulation is another of the key elements related to the effects of goal setting. When learners are committed to their goals, they are more apt to practice self-regulating behaviors in order to attain their goals. Not to be forgotten or diminished is the affective side of accomplishing one's goals, especially when the goals are meaningful and relevant to the learner. The attainment of such goals results in joy, pride, and interest. Further, learners are more likely to set more challenging goals in the future as a result (Turkay, 2014). Success begets success. The attainment of goals helps to put learners on a winning or success trajectory. The cycle continues, resulting in a growth mindset toward attaining goals and increasing achievement.

Working in Concert With Fully Developed Rubrics

The NSR is every bit as much a concrete, explicit tool dedicated to engaging learners in the ongoing processes of self-assessment, goal setting, and reflection upon one's learning in addition to applying descriptive feedback to aid any learner in her or his pursuit of relevant learning goals, as it is a tool concerned with articulating content and reasoning standards. As the NSR is formative in nature, there are no evaluative scores associated with it. Regardless of a learner's level of achievement, there is still room for a next step in the learning. With that said, the NSR may complement a fully developed scoring rubric when it is the appropriate time within the learning cycle for a summative check.

How and When to Use the Next Steps Rubric for Maximum Impact

In order to maximize impact, the suggestion is not to design a NSR for every discrete learning target. In order to get the greatest impact (e.g., bang for your buck), learning intentions must be prioritized based on those targets deemed most essential to the success of learners. For example, accurately summarizing informational text is a crosscutting standard that would be developed over time with different content and learning opportunities. Goal setting for this standard would progress as students develop and demonstrate their understanding and skills. These tools are to be used at multiple points in the learning process by design to serve the idea of growth over time, especially for providing feedback around those essential targets at specific junctures of learners' education journeys.

Linking Metacognition and Student Success

Once learning targets have been prioritized appropriately and students have become familiar with the descriptive feedback, self-assessment, and goal-setting processes, the transfer of these strategies to students' understandings represent the development of their metacognitive skills. The NSR provides the student user with a learner-friendly format to identify and use concrete strategies for improvement. Most importantly, the NSR is in the hands of the learners and enables her or him to build confidence in self-evaluation (ES = 0.62) by displaying the proficiency standards and then using them for self-judgment. The NSR helps learners set goals, verbalize the next steps in a task, and use it as an ongoing tool for record keeping. As learners return to the task, the NSR is easily revised and updated to aid in reviewing her or his status and self-monitoring by observing and tracking one's own performance. While there is only informal data to support our claim, the NSR has the potential be a tool to aid in time management as well.

The Anatomy of the Next Steps Rubric: Form, Function, and Flexibility

The unique qualities of the NSR are its form and flexibility. It is a table or matrix display with three columns and at least two rows. See Figure 7.3. The middle column is used to define proficiency, the "meets standard" of the learning target. The middle column could be in formal,

FIGURE 7.3 ● Assessment for Learning Strategies in the Next Steps Rubric

Anatomy of the Next Steps Rubric

A Self-Peer-Teacher Assessment and Goal-Setting Tool

Standard: [Deconstructed Clear Targets in "I Can" Statement]

Name: Date:

What Is Done Well ☆	Success Criteria This Means . . .	*What To Do Next* I Will . . . This Is How
☐ [Self-Assessment] ☐ [Feedback from teacher or peer] ☐ [Metacognitive or Reflection]	Clear Targets [Descriptive statement(s) of proficiency; single or multiple indicators] [A rating scale, if desired, for students to use to self-assess their current proficiency status] ☐ ------------------ ☐	☐ [Self-Assessment] ☐ [Goal Setting and Action Steps] ☐ [Tracking Progress; Record Keeping] ☐ [Metacognitive or Reflection]

proficiency language "as is" but preferably in student-friendly language: "I can . . . this means." The example in Figure 7.3 illustrates how the high-impact assessment for learning strategies match with each part of the rubric.

The open or blank format has three assessment for learning spaces: (1) the learning targets in the middle; (2) on the left side is the space for students to self-assess where they are, as indicated by the "stars"; and (3) on the right side is the space for setting goals with dates and what will be done next to accomplish the goals, as exemplified by the "stairs." Figure 7.4 is a middle school chorus example of an NSR.

The example in Figure 7.5 is a NSR with scaffolding for summarization; the standard reads "I can accurately summarize complex text, and this means (1) I can make a short statement of the big ideas or main message of what I read, hear, view, or observe; (2) I can write a summary that does not include minor details or extraneous information (such as personal reflections or opinions); (3) I can write a summary that is in my own words." In addition, there is a scaffold for next step learning, which shows students what to do with the feedback with teaching and learning strategies like new learning experiences, rereading, direct instruction (reteaching), use of other resources, peer assessment strategies, reciprocal teaching, and so on. Students need to know what comes next.

With the NSR, the learner can be directly involved in assessing strengths first and then articulating goals and next steps based on clear targets and self-assessment. By either filling in the blanks or checking the boxes in the assessment for learning spaces, the learners can be more directly involved in self-regulated behaviors of mastery goal orientation. Adaptations of the NSR include its appearance, number of criteria, formatting, as well as the level of scaffolding. See Figure 7.6 for a high school science teacher's take on how to assist his learners in self-assessing and setting goals with specific learning activities to put into action.

A group of STEM (science, technology, engineering, and mathematics) teachers from the Maine Center for Research in STEM Education (RiSE Center) modified the NSR to include the learning activities and tasks with which the students would be engaged to help them learn the particular learning targets. Students used a thumbs-up, thumbs-down, or thumbs-neutral position to indicate their comfort level with the learning target and to keep track of the learning tasks

FIGURE 7.4 ● Next Steps Rubric for Proper Rehearsal Technique for Middle School Chorus

Standard: I can rehearse using proper tone techniques.

Name: Date:

What Is Done Well ☆	**Criteria** **I Can . . . This Means:**	*What to Do Next*
	Posture □ Maintains high rib cage (sitting or standing) □ Maintains elongated spine □ Maintains a level chin **Breathing** □ Abdomen expands during inhalation □ Manages and controls exhalation **Tone/Resonance/Vowels** □ Maintains space in the back of the mouth (high soft palate) □ Maintains forward placement □ Tone is clear and is not breathy throughout range □ Produce varied tone qualities, colors, and styles (bright, dark) **Intonation** □ Single with a good sense of tonality **Diction** □ Performs intelligible words □ Performs consonants clearly and rhythmically □ Vowels are formed properly resulting in a beautiful tone **Expression** □ Sings phrases with shape (direction and planned breaths) □ Sings with dynamic contrast □ Yes -------------------- □ No	

Source: Contributed by Nancy Kinkade, music teacher, RSU 67.

they completed. There is also a space for them to plan their next steps in learning and to provide evidence of their self-assessments. See Figure 7.7 for an example.

The format of the NSR ranges from minimal visual cues to varying degrees of scaffolding. Figure 7.8 illustrates a scaffolded NSR using some visual cues to aid learners. We find that many elementary teachers use the NSRs as wall charts and engage in whole group guided practice of self-assessment and goal setting.

The Whole Body Listening NSR shown in the following Practitioner Spotlight is designed for kindergarten students and contains graphics as well as language to communicate; many middle-level special education and English language learner teachers have also adapted the concept of using visual cues to support their learners.

FIGURE 7.5 ● Next Steps Rubric for Summarization With Scaffolding

Summarizing Next Steps Rubric

Self-Peer-Teacher Assessment and Goal-Setting Tool

Standard: I can accurately summarize complex informational text.

Name: Date:

What Is Done Well ★	**Criteria** **This Means . . .**	***What to Do Next*** **I Will . . . This Is How**
□ The summary states the main ideas and major points of the material to be summarized. □ The summary covers all of the material to be summarized. No big ideas or main messages are left out. □ No small details or extraneous information such as personal reflections or opinions are included. □ The summary is in the learner's own words. □	I can make a short statement of *all* of the big ideas or main messages of what I read, hear, view, or observe The summary does not include minor details or extraneous information (such as personal reflections or opinions). The summary is in my own words. □ 1 ---------------------------- □ 10	□ Reexamine or reread the text for main ideas. □ Include *all* big ideas or main messages in the summary. □ Eliminate small details or extraneous information such as personal reflections or opinions. □ Be sure the summary is in your own words, not those of the author or speaker. □ Look up or request help understanding unfamiliar vocabulary or concepts from the "text." □ Request a mini-lessons or additional guided practice. □

A. Stewart McCafferty, 2014

FIGURE 7.6 ● Using Graphs to Interpret Motion Next Steps Rubric

Learning Target: Understands how to use graphs to interpret motion

Strengths	Criteria	Next Steps
❑ Can define the terms *final velocity, initial velocity, displacement, and acceleration* ❑ Knows how to calculate displacement ❑ Knows how to calculate a velocity ❑ Knows how to calculate acceleration	**Knows the terms *final velocity, initial velocity, displacement, and acceleration*** **Can calculate displacement, velocity, and acceleration**	❑ Reviews notes or slide show. ❑ Checks book for definitions ❑ Repeats practice problems and verifies correctness ❑ Checks Khan Academy for the videos regarding topics you are struggling with ❑ Reviews lab on calculating displacement ❑ Reviews lab on calculating velocity ❑ Reviews lab on calculating acceleration

Strengths	Criterion	Next Steps
❑ Can creates a scatterplot or line graph ❑ Can uses deductive reasoning to draw conclusions about position, displacement, velocity, and acceleration when looking at a position over time graph ❑ Can use deductive reasoning to draw conclusions about position, displacement, velocity, and acceleration when looking at a velocity over time graph.	**Understands how to use graphs to interpret motion**	❑ Reviews notes and example graphs created in class ❑ Reviews motion graphs and descriptions ❑ Reviews how to create a graph and graph terminology ❑ Schedules meeting with teacher

Source: Contributed by Zach Arnold, high school science teacher, Orono High School.

FIGURE 7.7 ● Chemistry Next Steps Rubric

I can analyze and interpret data on the properties of substances before and after the substances interact to determine if a chemical reaction has occurred.

Daily Learning Target:	I did . . .	I feel . . .
I can identify physical properties of a substance.	❑ A-19 5 Separating a mixture (Student Sheet 5.1-filling in physical characteristics) ❑ A-21 6 Identifying Liquids ❑ A-26 7 identifying solids(Analysis Question 3, 3-2-1 Reaction ticket) ❑ A-36 9 Measuring Mass, Calculating Density ❑ A-41 10 Density of Unknown Solids ❑ B-14 14 Physical and Chemical Properties of Materials (Class Discussion of physical/chemical, student sheet 14.1) ❑ B-19 15 Families of Elements (student sorting during activity, analysis question 1) ❑ B-34 18 Properties of Plastic (testing chemical and physical properties, class discussion of properties) ❑ B-39 19 Creating New Materials (Analysis question 1, student sheet 19.1) ❑ B-42 20 Modeling Polymers	☐ (thumbs up) ☐ (thumbs sideways) ☐ (thumbs down)
Here's why I chose that rating . . . My next steps . . .		

Source: Contributed by Laura Matthews, middle school teacher, Reeds Brook Middle School.

FIGURE 7.8 ● Next Steps Daylight Rubric

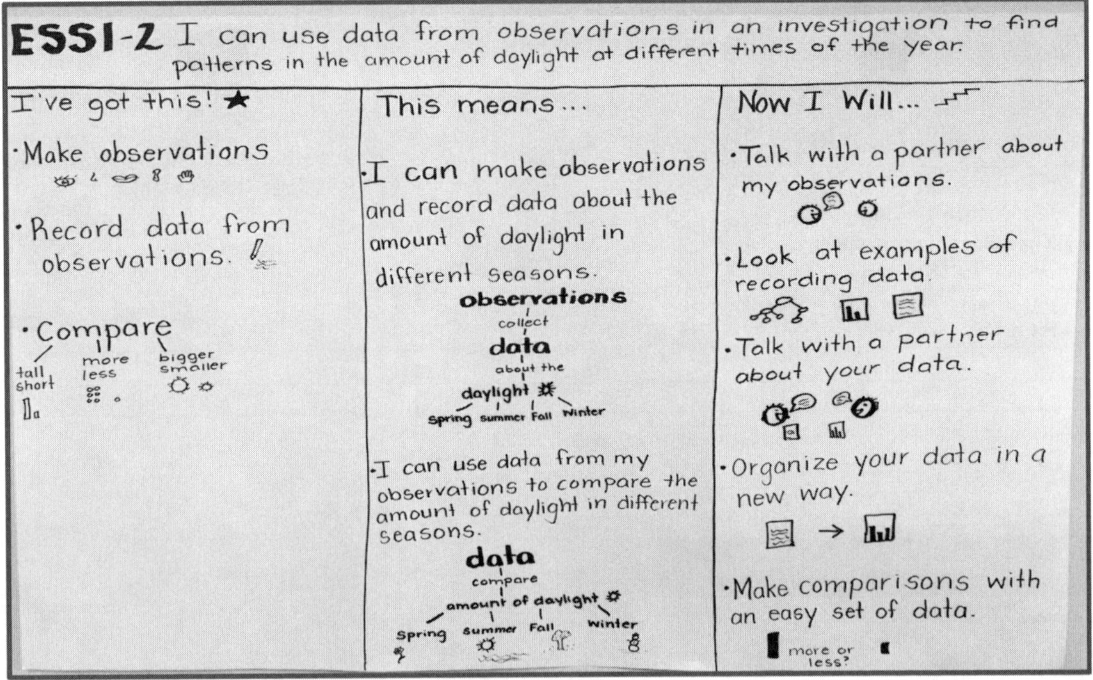

Source: Contributed by Kirsten Gould, first-grade teacher, Buxton Elementary School.

PRACTITIONER SPOTLIGHT 7.1

NEXT STEPS RUBRICS FOR WHOLE BODY LISTENING

What?

As a special education teacher, I facilitated a small group of kindergarten students working on their literacy and self-regulation skills. As a self-monitoring and goal-setting tool, I created the Whole Body Listening Next Steps Rubric (NSR), based on Hattie's research on effective learning strategies. Self-reported grades have a 1.33 effect size, being the most effective way to learn. I also created a rubric for the students to monitor their letter identification and sound progress, which was tailored to the group of letters they studied each week.

As the students learned to identify their letters and letter sounds, they also learned how to participate in a lesson by looking, being quiet, listening, and having still hands and feet. The students monitored their self-regulation progress by receiving nonverbal and verbal cues throughout the lesson. At the end of the lesson, they rated their overall progress in each of the five areas of Whole Body Listening.

So What?

Through the students' daily reflection of their Whole Body Listening, they became proficient in knowing where they were and where they needed to go. As kindergarteners, they were surprisingly honest with themselves and each other on what they needed to work on in order to improve their abilities to learn. Through our small-group reflection, we examined their Whole Body Listening and Letter Identification/Sound progress using the rubrics, and we celebrated their successes along the way. What was amazing was that the students could actually see the connection, with evidence from their rubrics, that they made the most gains in their literacy skills when they consistently demonstrated all five components of the listening skills. This process of reflection led them to become skilled in setting future goals with both rubrics.

Now What?

The students could continue to use this rubric in other academic areas to support their learning as well as other learning targets. In my new position, I hope to share these rubrics with my special education and general education teachers in support of their students' self-reported progress. I have also created rubrics for my special education teachers, as adult learners, in support of creating their student's rigorous learning plans. As an educator, I have witnessed the impact of self-reflecting and reporting, which cannot be underestimated in the process of learning. It is the key.

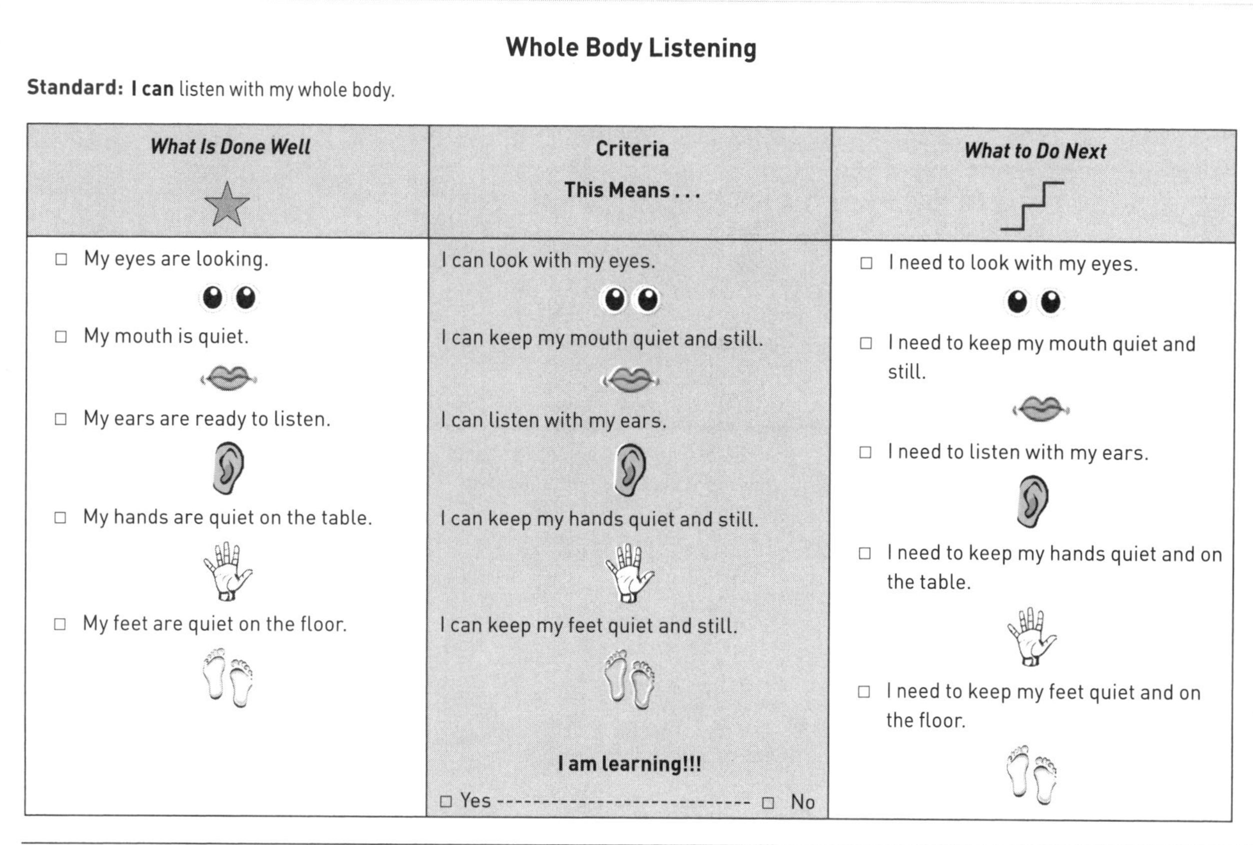

Whole Body Listening

Standard: I can listen with my whole body.

What Is Done Well	**Criteria** **This Means . . .**	***What to Do Next***
☐ My eyes are looking.	I can look with my eyes.	☐ I need to look with my eyes.
☐ My mouth is quiet.	I can keep my mouth quiet and still.	☐ I need to keep my mouth quiet and still.
☐ My ears are ready to listen.	I can listen with my ears.	☐ I need to listen with my ears.
☐ My hands are quiet on the table.	I can keep my hands quiet and still.	☐ I need to keep my hands quiet and on the table.
☐ My feet are quiet on the floor.	I can keep my feet quiet and still.	☐ I need to keep my feet quiet and on the floor.
	I am learning!!! ☐ Yes --------------------------- ☐ No	

Source: Contributed by Rebekah Drysdale, special education director, MSAD 52.

The essential information of any NSR is the learning target, the standard, or statement of proficiency. There can be single or multiple indicators for the learning target; the adjustment depends on the level of specificity in the standard and the needs of the learners. See Figure 7.9 for an example of a two-part indicator for equivalent fractions. The other two columns are the active assessment for learning spaces incorporating self-assessment on what the learner can do or feedback from the teacher confirming what the learner can do (in the left column) and the next steps in learning (in the right column). Combining students' success with next steps is the format for Stars and Stairs (Chappuis, 2015). These two assessment for learning spaces maintain students' focus on what is to be learned and how to close the gap in "what I need to know." The purpose remains formative. As we worked on the design of the NSR, the graphic icons, the Stars and Stairs, were important connections to the existing elements as they provide nonlinguistic representations that assist learners to build her or his meaning of proficiency (Dean, Hubbell, Pitler, & Stone, 2012).

Educators Benefit From the Next Steps Rubric, Too!

For example, the teacher observation rubric leaves the user fully in control of the assessment for learning strategies: clear targets, self-assessment, feedback, and goal setting. See Figure 7.10. The open assessment for learning space is used to record observations, in this case about classroom environment, as stars, and questions and suggestions in the next steps, or stairs column. While this works for one who is skilled in classroom observation, teachers told us repeatedly that providing strategies and suggestions for learners helped them better understand feedback and plan specific next steps learning. Figure 7.11 demonstrates an example of translating one of the ten Interstate Teacher Assessment and Support Consortium (InTASC) teacher standards (Standard 5: Application of Content) into an NSR. Teachers can use the NSR to self-assess and set goals relative to the standard for purpose of teacher evaluation purposes.

FIGURE 7.9 ● Equivalent Fractions Self-Assessment and Goal Setting

Name: ______________________ TARGET: Equivalent Fractions

MA.03.NSF.01.03 Equivalent Fractions

Where I Am . . .	Target Objectives	Where I Am Going. . . .
• I can tell what equivalent means. • I can list some equivalent fractions for 1/2, 1/3, 2/3, 1/4, and 3/4. • I can show, describe, or list the steps for making equivalent fractions. • I can draw fractional parts of a circle or a rectangle. • I can use drawings of circles or rectangles split into fractional parts to show that equivalent fractions are the same size. • I can mark equivalent fractions on a number line to show they are the same point on the number line.	• Knows term *equivalent*. Knows simple *equivalent* fractions for half, thirds, and fourths. Knows the steps for generating *equivalent* fractions. • Understands two fractions are *equivalent* (equal) if they are the same size or the same point on a number line.	Date: __________ Goal: Date: __________ Goal: Date: __________ Goal: Date: __________ Goal:

Source: Contributed by Betty Bickford, fifth-grade teacher, Mattanawcook Junior High School, RSU 67.

FIGURE 7.10 ● Next Steps Rubric for Observation of Classroom Environment

Classroom Environment Next Steps Rubric
Self-Assessment and Goal-Setting Tool or Peer Feedback Tool

Standard 6: I can create or maintain a classroom environment conductive to learing.

Name:

What Is Done Well ☆	**Criteria** **This Means . . .**	***What to Do Next*** **I Will . . . This Is How**
	* Learners are clear about the expectations.	☐
	*Procedures and routines are well established.	☐
	*Learners interact respectfully with one another.	☐
	*Disruptions are minimized and respectfully handled in the least intrusive manners (emotional objectivity),	☐
	*I am "with it" and tuned into my learners' needs and the classroom environment.	☐
	*I use engagement strategies effectively to include all learners.	☐
	*Content is relevant and meaningful to my learners.	☐
	*Transitions are smooth, and time is utilized efficiently or effectively.	☐
	*Learners feel safe and cared for (positive student-teacher relationship or rapport).	☐

A Stewart McCafferty, 2016

FIGURE 7.11 ● InTASC Standard 5: Application of Content Next Steps Rubric

Standard 5: Application of Content

Next Steps Rubric Self-Assessment and Goal-Setting Form

Standard: I understand how to connect concepts and use differing perspectives to engage learners in critical thinking, creativity, and collaborative problem solving related to authentic local and global issues.

Strengths Evidence	Criteria This Means . . .	Next Steps Action Plan
	I help learners see relationships across disciplines by making connections between different content areas.	
	I engage learners in applying content knowledge and skills in authentic contexts.	
	I engage learners in identifying and addressing real-world problems.	
	I connect learners in local and global resources to gather information about and solve real-world problems.	
	I engage learners in learning and applying the critical thinking skills used in the content area.	
	I guide learners in gathering, organizing, and evaluating information and ideas.	
	I engage learners in developing communication skills that support learning in the content area.	

A. Stewart McCafferty, 2016

PRACTITIONER SPOTLIGHT 7.2

NEXT STEPS RUBRICS FOR WRITTEN NOTICES AND INDIVIDUALIZED EDUCATION PROGRAMS

What?

As a special education leader, I have supported many case managers in reviewing their special education paperwork, ensuring that it meets the state and district compliance standards. For years, I provided feedback to the case managers without a quantifiable measure to track their growth, but more importantly the case managers did not have a way to assess their own level of competence. According to Hattie's research on effective learning strategies, self-reported grades have a 1.33 effect size, being the most effective way to learn. This was a problem for adult learners as they strive to develop appropriately ambitious plans for their students and follow the compliance standards. As a tool for my case managers, I developed a Self-Peer-Teacher Assessment and Goal-Setting Rubric for Written Notices (individualized education program or IEP meeting determinations and meeting notes) and a Self-Peer-Teacher Assessment and Goal Setting Rubric for Individual Education Plans. These rubrics each have a standard with an "I can" statement, What's Next?, and an overall rating of performance.

(Continued)

(Continued)

_______________________'s Written Notices (teacher)

Self-Peer-Teacher Assessment and Goal-Setting Rubric

Standard: I can adhere to the state and district guidelines in my student's written notice.

What Is Done Well ★	**Criteria** **This Means . . .**	***What to Do Next***
☐ Details are accurate. ☐ 1. State the purpose and describe the actions (disability, implement IEP, goals, services, accommodations, progress report, ESY, annual, triennial). ☐ 2. Explain why proposals are made (disability, implement IEP, goals, services, accommodations, progress report, ESY, annual, triennial). ☐ 3. Describe informal assessments, evaluations, teacher, service provider, and parent reports as a basis for the proposed actions (discussion). ☐ 4. Describe any other options considered and rejected (link to LRE). ☐ 5. Describe any other factors relevant to the proposals (i.e. counseling, medication, etc . . .). ☐ 6. Describe key points made by parents, also noted in #3.	*I can identify the reason for the meeting. *I can state the purpose of the meeting, describe the actions, and explain why they were made. *I can connect the informal assessments, evaluations and reports from the IEP team members to the proposals. *I can describe any other options considered and rejected related to the student's LRE. *I can identify and describe any other factors relevant to the proposals. *I can summarize the points made by the parents. ☐ Yes ----------------- ☐ No	☐ Details ☐ 1. ☐ 2. ☐ 3. ☐ 4. ☐ 5. ☐ 6.

Note: IEP = individualized education program; ESY = extended school year; LRE = least restrictive environment.

_______________'s Individual Education Plan (teacher)

Self-Peer-Teacher Assessment and Goal-Setting Rubric

Standard: I can adhere to the state and district guidelines in my student's IEP.

What Is Done Well ★	**Criteria** **This Means . . .**	***What to Do Next***
☐ 1. Dates are accurate. ☐ 2. Disability is accurate. ☐ 3. Secondary Transition. ☐ 3A. Parents' concerns are addressed. ☐ 3B-G. Considerations are complete and addressed. ☐ 4. A, F, and D Evaluations. ☐ 5. Developmental Performance A and B complete. ☐ 6A. Academic Strengths. ☐ 6A. Academic Needs related to performance and services.	I can identify the start and annual date of the IEP, along with the triennial review. I can identify the student's disability. I can explain the parents' concerns. I can identify the student's areas to be considered in the IEP and where it is found in the document I can analyze the student's areas of need based on evaluation results and informal assessments. I can describe the student's developmental performance (3–5).	☐ 1. ☐ 2. ☐ 3. ☐ 4. ☐ 5. ☐ 6.

The case managers began using the rubrics in the fall of that year with three student samples, identifying a baseline for themselves. They then set professional goals for the school year based on their baseline data in support of their growth as they craft their student plans. In the winter, they progress monitor their growth using three more student samples, checking and adjusting their professional goals. In the spring, they chose three additional student samples to measure their growth based on their baseline data.

This has also been a tool that their peers and I have monitored throughout the school year. The case managers pass in their rubrics with their student plans to receive feedback from their peers and myself. They use our feedback to calibrate their self-assessment and to check and adjust their progress.

So What?

In creating these self-assessment rubrics, the teachers have been able to track their growth and maintain their state and district special education compliance standards in developing appropriately ambitious plans for their students. The opportunity to self-assess and calibrate has been invaluable to the case managers growth in support of their students achievement. This has pushed all of our thinking and collaboration to develop rigorous plans that move students. It is rewarding for all of us to see that at the beginning of the year the rubrics are filled with our comments for next steps, but by the end of the year they are filled with celebrations.

As a school special education leader, the feedback that I have received from my case managers is that they love our district, but they now know that they can work anywhere in the state as a special education teacher with confidence in their skills in developing student plans to support their achievement.

Now What?

As I move to a district leadership position in special education, I plan to continue to use the Self-Peer-Teacher Assessment and Goal-Setting Rubrics in support of the special education teachers in drafting rigorous student plans. Not being in the schools every day or every week, I would like to develop a plan or protocol for teachers who are interested in using the Next Steps Rubrics (NSRs) for self- and peer assessment to support their growth. We could plan seasonal check-ins at our special education meetings to review teacher's progress, checking and adjusting as needed. This will benefit our student achievement in developing rigorous plans and in preparing for our special education audit.

Source: Contributed by Rebekah Drysdale, special education director, MSAD 52.

Summary of the Next Steps Rubric

Educators have used a variety of assessment tools that are "near" rubrics, such as checklists, product descriptors, and project templates. Rubrics used to generate scores must be aligned with well-defined learning targets and accompanied by sufficient student work to use the rubrics to score new student products and performances. Overall, the NSR is a stripped-down, sleeker, and simpler version of a full rubric. Reorganizing the graphic in this way places the emphasis on proficiency, what it takes to attain proficiency, and how one can go beyond. It is an action-oriented tool that repositions the critically important element, proficiency, in the middle of the graphic organizer. (See Figure 7.12 on the following page.)

Other Self-Assessment, Goal-Setting, and Reflection Tools

GPA Matters!

One learning organization we know has established three common talking points for all of its employees (faculty, student services, custodians, bus drivers, food service professionals, etc.) to use when they interact with students: (1) What are your goals? (2) What are your plans for reaching your goals? (3) What are the action steps you are taking to implement your plan? We have affectionately dubbed this three-step conversation starter GPA Matters! It certainly sends a strong message that active and recursive goal setting is important to achieving one's dreams.

FIGURE 7.12 ● The Next Steps Rubric With Connections to the Seven Strategies of Assessment for Learning

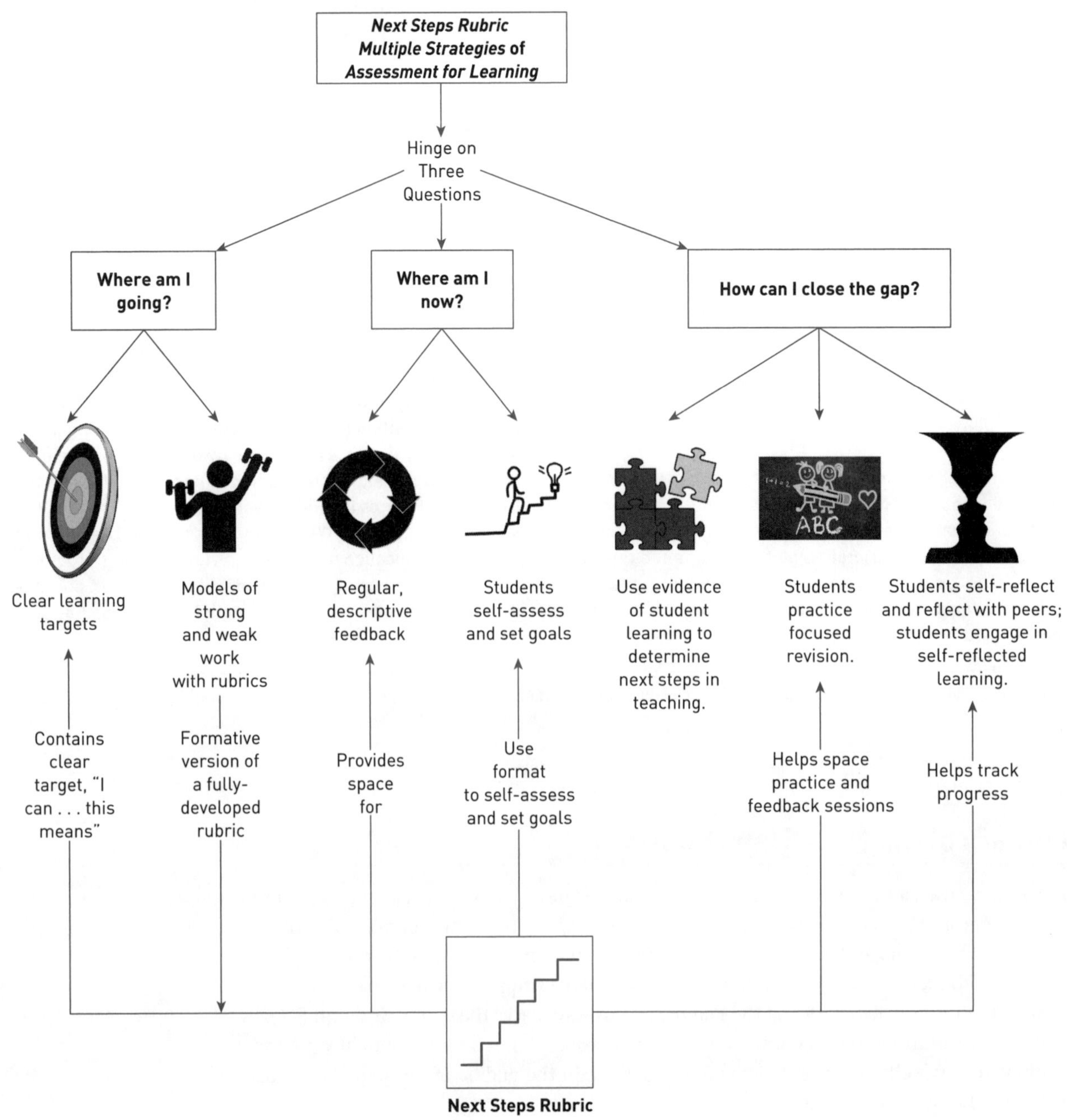

Exit Tickets

Exit tickets are widely used by many educators as a means to check for understanding. They can be useful tools to promote metacognitive skills if worded appropriately and if they are seen as more than a hoop to complete. Educators and learners must make time to reflect on their learning and take appropriate next steps to further their learning. The exit tickets can come in many formats. The formats shown in Figure 7.13 are a few of our favorites.

FIGURE 7.13 ● Sample Exit-Ticket Formats

Plus, Delta, Light Bulb Reflection Tool

What is something you understand better as a result of today's training?	What is one question you still have about the content of today's training OR one suggestion you have to improve future sessions?	What is one idea you have about how to incorporate content from today's training into your classroom, school, or mentoring experiences?

3-2-1

*Please complete the 3-2-1 activity, and be prepared to share your answers during tomorrow's class.
What are three of your strengths as an effective communicator?
What are two of your weaknesses as an effective communicator?
What is one question you still have about communicating effectively?

Stars, Stairs, and Evidence

Take a look at the Hattie's eight mind frames visual. Take some time to reflect upon these mind frames as they relate to your practices as an educator. Place a star symbol next to the mind frames you feel are your strengths. Place a stair step image next to any mind frame you feel could be next steps for you. Consider what your evidence would be for your self-assessment. Be prepared to share evidence of at least one of your Stars and Stairs with a partner.

(Continued)

(Continued)

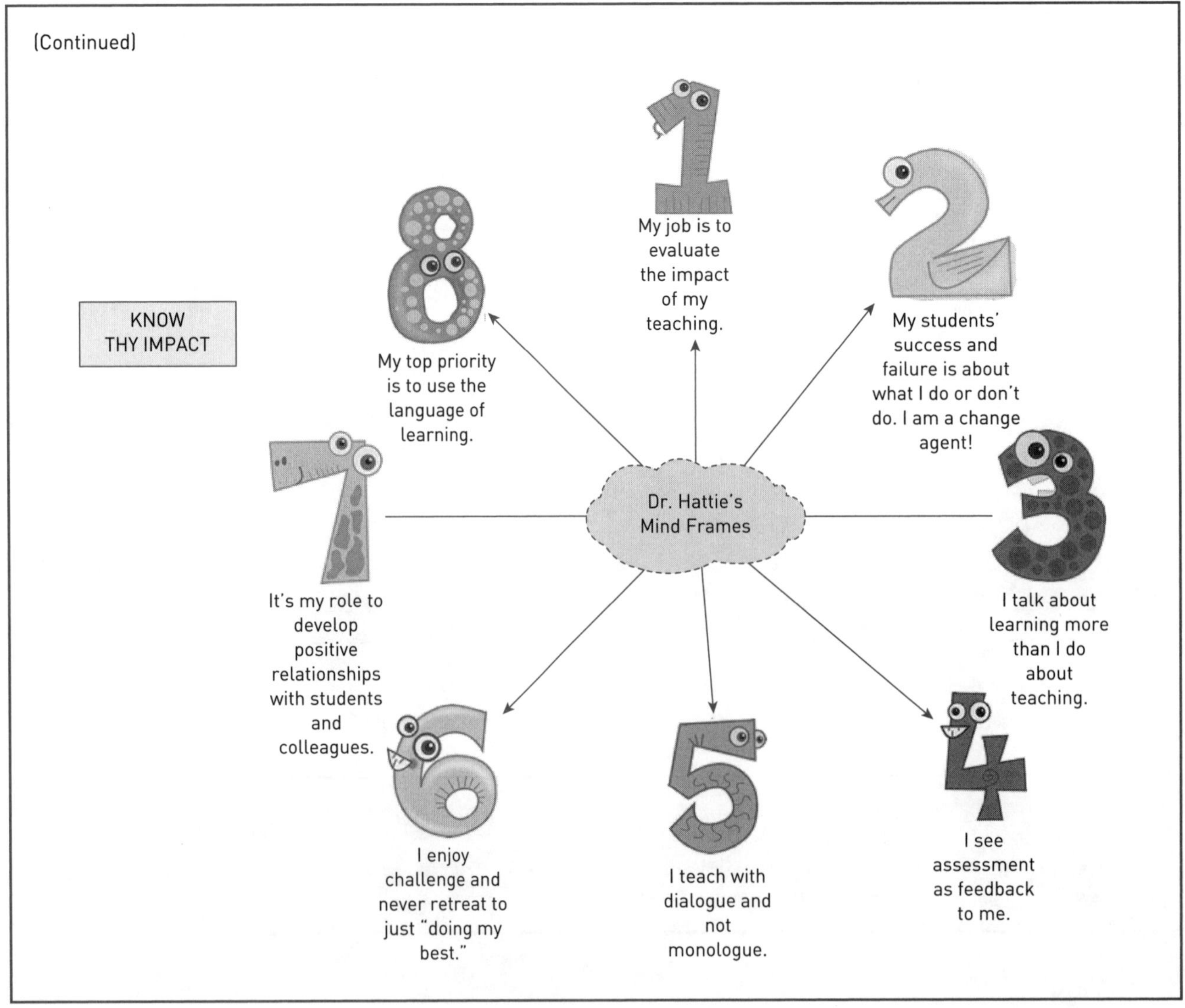

What? So What? Now What?

Video Observation Reflection

What? So What? Now What?

What?

What happened? What did you do in completing the self-observation video assignment? What did you expect? What was different than what you expected?

So What?

Why does this matter? To you? To a school? Is your experience in alignment with, informed by, and/or in conflict with our Marshall (2012) text, course readings, discussions, guest speakers, previous observation experiences, etc.?

Now What?

What have you learned from this experience? What will you do differently as a result? What will you continue doing more of as a result? How will this inform your next steps as a practitioner and leader?

And the Survey Says . . .

Use a Google Forms, Plickers, SurveyMonkey, Poll Everywhere, etc., to create a short self-assessment survey for students to take. Class results can be displayed to show how the teacher is using information to inform next steps in classroom learning.

Sticky Dots Continuum

Informed Action

On your way out of class, please choose a sticky dot, and place it on our learning target continuum to indicate your level of understanding and comfort with our learning goal of becoming more informed about the world in which we live in order to take informed action.

Triangle-Square-Circle

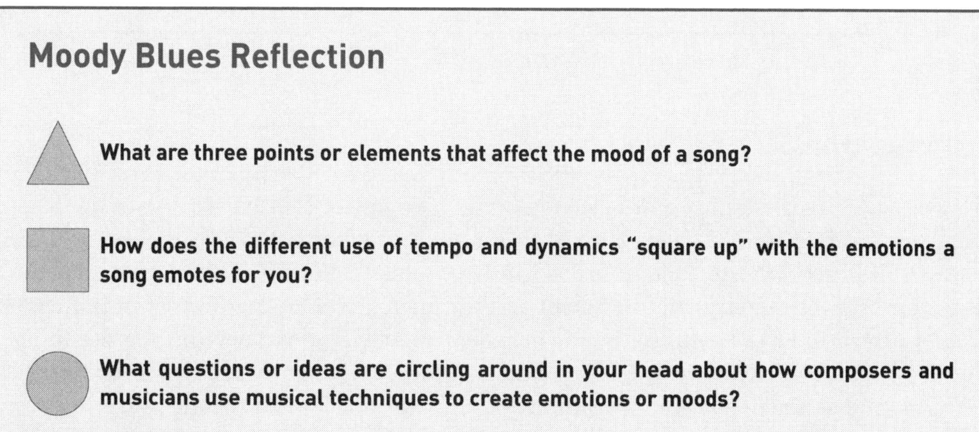

Moody Blues Reflection

What are three points or elements that affect the mood of a song?

How does the different use of tempo and dynamics "square up" with the emotions a song emotes for you?

What questions or ideas are circling around in your head about how composers and musicians use musical techniques to create emotions or moods?

Symbol Tracker

In a four-month project on designing wind turbines, students in the classroom were asked to self-assess their progress once a month. There were two dimensions to the tracker: (1) design and engineering skills and (2) how to make choices that show positive connections of technology, engineering, science, and society. The dots are the mark for the first month, and the cubes are the marks for the final assessment.

(Continued)

(Continued)

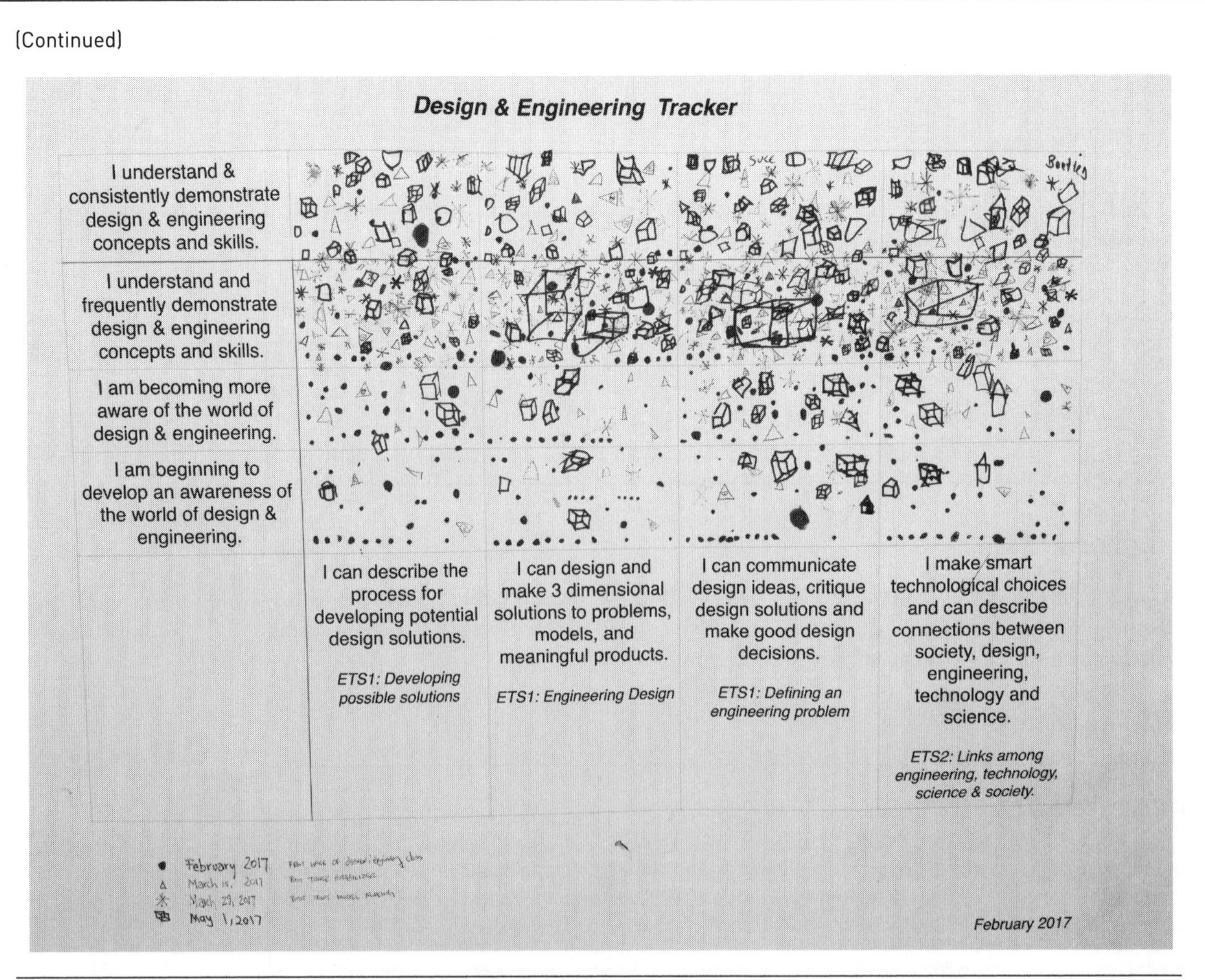

Students' Form for Design and Engineering Tracker

Source: Contributed by Gus Goodwin, middle school STEM teacher, King Middle School, Portland Public Schools.

Conclusion

Self-assessment, goal setting, and reflection are metacognitive skills that need to be taught and continually reinforced. There are a host of tools that when habitually implemented and used with learners help to solidify metacognitive strategies. Rubrics are the tools that connect clear learning targets with assessment and teaching. There are many types of rubrics; in order for them to be used effectively, teachers need to know how to develop and use formative and summative iterations with their students. Most importantly, learners need to make use of both assessment for and of learning rubrics. In order for learners to make progress, they need to understand their strengths and next steps according to identified success criteria of clear learning targets. The NSR is an example of a tool that can be used during the learning process to promote self-assessment and goal setting relative to articulated learning targets. The NSR brings together clear learning targets, success criteria, descriptive feedback, self-assessment, and goal setting in addition to reflecting upon progress in one sleek tool. In order for metacognition to be internalized, learners need ample opportunities to practice these skills.

Teachers need to understand how best to develop rubrics in their many forms. Different types of rubrics can be used to assess *for* learning and *of* learning for the purposes of scoring.

Learners need to understand their strengths and next steps according to identified success criteria of clear learning targets. The NSR is a stripped-down version of a full rubric designed to focus attention on the success criteria and evidence of learners' strengths and next steps relative to the success criteria. The NSR is one tool that intentionally brings together clear learning targets, success criteria, descriptive feedback, self-assessment, and goal setting in addition to reflecting upon learning progress.

Take a Deep Dive to Further Your Understanding

- Read "Metacognition: Thinking About One's Thinking" from Vanderbilt University: https://cft.vanderbilt.edu/guides-sub-pages/metacognition.
- Explore "Goal-Setting for Teachers: 8 Paths to Self-Improvement" from Cult of Pedagogy: https://www.cultofpedagogy.com/goal-setting-for-teachers.
- Read *Teaching Students to Drive Their Brains* by Donna Wilson and Marcus Conyers. You can read Chapter 1 at http://www.ascd.org/publications/books/117002/chapters/The-Case-for-Teaching-for-and-with-Metacognition.aspx.

8 Diagnosing Student Learning Needs During the Learning Process

Key Takeaways

What and how we question is as important as when we use questioning strategies.

How we as educators interpret learners' responses to varying prompts is crucial to the process of accurately diagnosing learners' needs.

It is important to develop students' discussion competencies in order to be able to use classroom discussion as an accurate tool for diagnosing student learning.

PAUSE AND REFLECT

- How do you check for students' knowledge, conceptual understandings, reasoning skills, dispositions, work habits, and/or skills during the learning process—while there is still time to act upon the information gathered?

Madeline Hunter included checking for understanding in her lesson plan frame more than half a century ago, so the concept of checking in on student's progress is not a new one. Educators have traditionally used a variety of techniques and tools, but none is used more regardless of format than questioning. In today's digital world, there are a variety of tools and resources that teachers can use to help them ask questions of their students: to gather, to sort, and to display the data in an effort to ensure that they sample all students in an anonymous, sensitive manner. A plethora of apps and tech sites have been developed to capitalize on our need to check our students' understandings and diagnose learners' needs. Many of our educator friends rely on Backchannel Chat, Google Classroom, Google Forms, Kahoot!, Plickers, Poll Everywhere, QR codes, Quizlet, Socrative, Vocaroo, VoiceThread, or clicker devices. And the list goes on with a host of low-tech options like individual mini-whiteboards, traffic lights, signal response such as thumbs-up, fist to five, stand and be counted, class discussions, jot or sketch an answer, and so on.

No matter how glitzy and how engaging the questioning tool or app might be for students, a teacher's information will only be as good as the question (stem), prompt, and/or

FIGURE 8.1 ● Seven Strategies Concept Map With a Focus on Using Evidence of Learning Needs

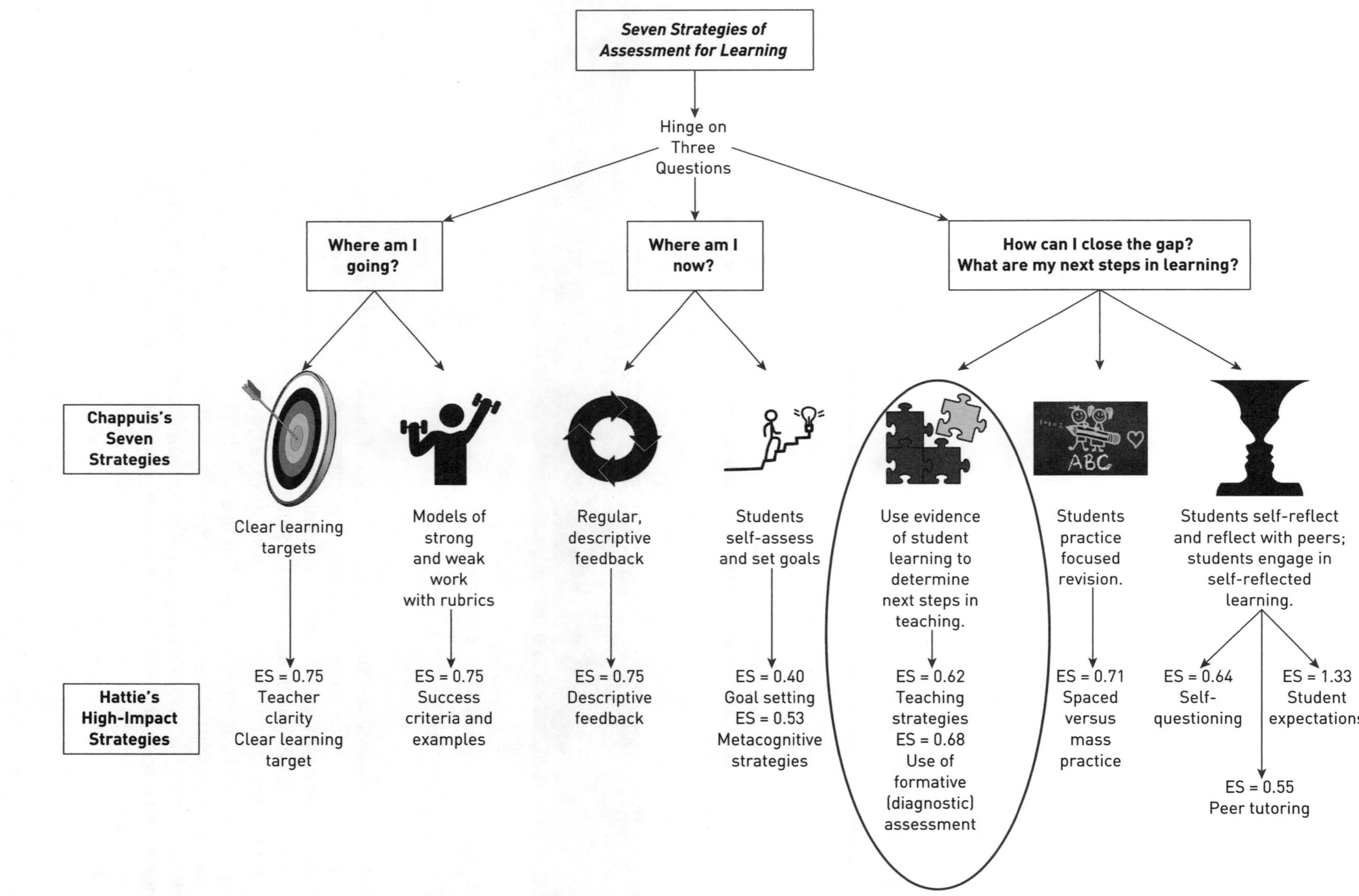

FIGURE 8.2 ● What Are My Next Steps? Learning Progression

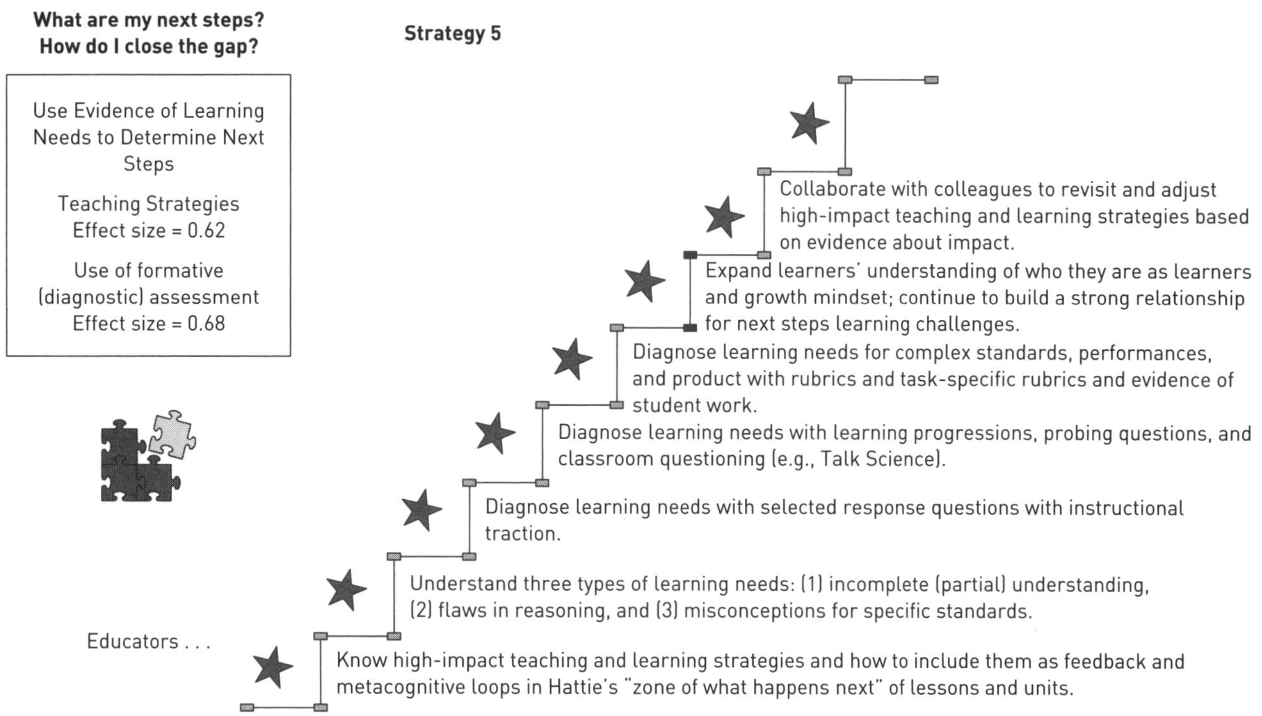

What are my next steps? How do I close the gap?

Strategy 5

Use Evidence of Learning Needs to Determine Next Steps

Teaching Strategies
Effect size = 0.62

Use of formative (diagnostic) assessment
Effect size = 0.68

Educators . . .

- Know high-impact teaching and learning strategies and how to include them as feedback and metacognitive loops in Hattie's "zone of what happens next" of lessons and units.
- Understand three types of learning needs: (1) incomplete (partial) understanding, (2) flaws in reasoning, and (3) misconceptions for specific standards.
- Diagnose learning needs with selected response questions with instructional traction.
- Diagnose learning needs with learning progressions, probing questions, and classroom questioning (e.g., Talk Science).
- Diagnose learning needs for complex standards, performances, and product with rubrics and task-specific rubrics and evidence of student work.
- Expand learners' understanding of who they are as learners and growth mindset; continue to build a strong relationship for next steps learning challenges.
- Collaborate with colleagues to revisit and adjust high-impact teaching and learning strategies based on evidence about impact.

distractors provided to students. We love the notion that the word *question* derives from the root word *quest*, which is a journey. When we pose the right questions to our students—or better yet, teach them to pose thought-provoking questions of one another—we embark upon a journey of discovery (Thoughtful Classroom, 2010). When we check in on our students' progress toward learning important content and skills, we must carefully prepare the questions that will allow us to determine their needs for next steps. Chappuis (2012, 2015)

PRACTITIONER SPOTLIGHT 8.1

WHAT? SO WHAT? NOW WHAT? A REFLECTION ON THESE QUESTIONS

We improve when we ask questions to gain understanding. It is a method that any two-year-old knows: "What's that?" they say. And who hasn't had a student say, in one form or another, "So what?" They are searching for more information. As a high school science teacher, I was grateful when those summative tests came back and the grades were good, but after a while I started asking myself, "Now what?" Could those students who begged for vocabulary lists and study guides at the beginning of every chapter or didn't read directions in a lab but constantly asking for directions do more? Was I bringing them to higher-order thinking or allowing them to stay in an elementary parrot stage? How was I to change? Because that is really what had to happen first, I had to grow up. I started by asking myself, "What is the goal?" and then considering that goal for its depth. Beyond reporting and regurgitating fact, what did it mean, and why does it happen this way? I looked at each lesson as a teacher *and* as a student. What was I to do to convey beyond the facts and allow for the students to started asking and answering themselves? So often we all look to others to fill in our gaps for us, but I had to go on the offensive and try those models and read research that could influence the hard work of advancement. It didn't happen overnight, and I was glad to sit in on a Jay McTighe webinar when he said, "Take one or two units a year, and improve on them." That is just what I did. I heard that teenager's voice in my head saying, "So what?" and I replied, "Now what?"

Source: Contributed by Joanna Martel, graduate assistant, University of Southern Maine.

posited that there are three key learner needs our check-ins should help us and our learners uncover: (1) partial understandings, (2) flaws in reasoning, and (3) misconceptions. Without first identifying typical misunderstandings, reasoning flaws, or misconceptions associated with our units of study, we have little hope that our questioning in the moment will help us appropriately diagnose learner needs.

Creating hinge questions, as Dylan Wiliam calls them, at those critical junctures in the learning help a teacher determine if the students understand the concept or skill well enough to move on to the next chunk of learning, need a brief recap of the lesson, need more practice time, or perhaps need reteaching. Wiliam reminds us that these hinge questions should be rapid response items where students can respond to them quickly and teachers can review responses quickly. Without carefully planning, administering, and analyzing results from questions posed at critical junctures in the learning, we often further confuse students or waste time with subsequent learning activities because students were missing prerequisite understandings or skill sets in order to be successful.

Using Questions to Diagnose and Improve Student Learning

Essential Questions to Consider

- How can I better use varied effective questioning techniques to enhance student learning and diagnose learning needs effectively and efficiently?
- How can I help students develop more thoughtful, well-developed, and deeper responses?

Percentagewise, questioning is one of the strategies most frequently used by teachers; in fact, most studies on the topic say that teachers spend upward of sixty percent of their instructional time asking questions, listening to answers, and providing feedback to students about their responses. Questioning has great potential when done well to greatly improve student learning and engagement. In addition to positively influencing student achievement, it also is positively connected with student success, motivation, and retention. Unfortunately, research shows that when done poorly, questioning has little effect beyond determining that a few students can recall or regurgitate key points from the lesson or unit of study.

Why Use Questioning?

Teachers use questioning in order to do the following:

- Engage learners in the lesson
- Strengthen motivation
- Promote recall of previously taught, and hopefully learned, material
- Assess student comprehension
- Help students make connections
- Activate prior background knowledge
- Develop thinking skills
- Increase students' depth of knowledge

What Does the Research Say About Questioning?

A host of researchers (e.g., Brualdi, 1998; Cotton, 1988; Dantonio, 2001; Dickman, 2009; Marzano, Pickering, & Pollock, 2001; Silver, Jackson, & Moirao, 2011; Silver, Strong, & Perinni, 2003; Wilen & Clegg, 1986) indicate the following about questioning:

- Effective questioning is positively correlated with higher achievement among students.
- On average, teachers ask forty questions per forty-five-minute class period.
- Seventy-five percent to eighty percent of questions asked are at the recall or procedure level.
- Most teachers call on students perceived as higher achievers more frequently than they call on low achievers.
- Teachers typically wait one second or less for students to respond to questions.
- Often when a student does not immediately give a correct response, the teacher answers the question herself or himself.
- On average, students ask less than five percent of the questions asked in the typical classroom.
- Students who regularly ask and answer questions in class do better academically than those who do not.
- A few carefully prepared and selected questions throughout a lesson have a greater effect on student learning than asking many questions (especially for learning anything beyond recall).

PAUSE AND REFLECT

- As you reexamine the aforementioned research on questioning and consider your own classroom experiences with questioning, what do you see as the implications for future application?

What Can I Do to Improve My Questioning Skills, You Might Ask?

As the research suggests, plan a few well-designed questions to elicit higher-order thinking or complex reasoning skills as well as to meet varied learning needs. When coupled with strong student-teacher relationships and appropriate sampling strategies, questioning has the potential to vastly improve student learning. Purposefully plan questions that ask students to engage in different ways of thinking about a concept or skill improving engagement by a wider majority of students. See Figure 8.3 and Table 8.1 for examples of questions or prompts considering different ways learners may prefer to process and express their learning and associated high-impact strategies with each type of learning or thinking process. The idea behind posing these types of questions or prompts is not to pigeonhole learners into learning style preferences but instead is used as a way to invite *all* students into the learning process and to value different ways of processing and expressing learning. Research from Thoughtful Classroom (2010) argued that teachers most often ask mastery questions (those questions that ask what, who, when, and where) and leave out other ways of processing and thinking about information—that is, the understanding learner, the interpersonal learner, and the self-expressive learner.

FIGURE 8.3 ● Types of Learning Prompts Connected With High-Impact Strategies

Mastery prompts ask learners to:	**Interpersonal prompts ask learners to:**
 ✓ Recall important facts/details ✓ Summarize key ideas ✓ Remember and describe key content and skills What? Who? When? Where? High-impact strategies: direct instruction (.59); questioning (.48); summarize (.82); note-taking (.60)	   ✓ React to, empathize, reflect upon, and explore feelings ✓ Learn about things that affect people's lives ✓ Make personal connections to the content How so? So what? High-impact strategies: classroom discussion (.82); self questioning (.64); cooperative (.59); peer influences (.53); meta-cognitive (.69)
Understanding prompts ask learners to:	**Self-expressive prompts ask learners to:**
 ✓ Ask questions ✓ Use logic, reason, debate, and inquiry to explore ideas ✓ Focus on concepts, big ideas, and generalizations Why? How? High-impact strategies: questioning (.48); problem-solving (.61); graphic organizers; note-taking (.60)	 ✓ Make connections and associations ✓ Think divergently ✓ Imagine and create ✓ Think metaphorically ✓ Generate possible solutions What if? High-impact strategies: concept mapping (.64); self-questioning (.64); metacognitive (.69); classroom discussion (.82); use of analogies & metaphors (.65)

Figure 8.3 Compiled from Silver, Strong, and Perini's The Strategic Teacher (2007); Hattie's Visible Learning (2009) for Teachers (2012) in Action (2015); and Pickering and Marzano's Highly Engaged Classroom (2010); and McREL Classroom Instruction That Works, 2nd edition Research Report (2010)

Source: Stewart McCafferty (2017).

TABLE 8.1 ● Learning Styles Exit Ticket Showing Varied Types of Questions to Promote Varied Thinking or Reasoning

Mastery	**Interpersonal**
Two learnings I will walk away with . . . 1. 2.	What is one thing you would share with a friend about the learning from today's class?
Understanding Before today I thought . . . Now I think . . .	**Self-Expressive** Was today's class (a) more like making a quilt, (b) walking in the park, (c) viewing a sunrise or sunset, or (d) climbing a mountain? Please explain your choice.

For too long, our classrooms have promoted and elevated one way of thinking and knowing over others, leaving many of our students feeling dumb, devalued, disrespected, and disengaged. The questions and prompts we pose—and the way we sample students—can either infuse our learning environment with new voices and ideas or stagnate the learning environment with few voices restating what teachers and texts have told them.

In addition to planning questions to engage various types of thinking, increase your wait time, include more turn and talk, ask students to jot a note to one's self, and make use of simple cooperative learning structures. Be sure you do not rely on sampling volunteers only. Develop sampling strategies that include cold calls, asking students to expand upon other students' answers or justify their own responses, and/or signal if they agree or disagree with a classmate's response with an explanation of their reasoning. Exit tickets, online random sampling generators, and the use of QR codes for differentiating questions are all additional ways to increase student engagement.

As educators, we make instructional decisions from the information we receive from our learners about next steps to take. When the feedback we gather comes from inappropriate sampling strategies or poorly constructed questions, we are bound to draw faulty conclusions about our students' learning and what the next steps should be to help our learners' progress. We have experienced firsthand checks for understanding that result in sampling only a small portion of our learners and assuming that the class as a whole is in good shape to move on or that all the misconceptions have been addressed by those we have sampled. We, too, have used the prompts "Any questions?" or "Is everyone all set?" often enough to know how easy it is to trick ourselves into thinking we have checked for understanding and the class is ready to move on in their learning. When we teach to the "class as a whole" and not to our learners as individuals, we settle for determining that many, if not most, students seem ready for the next chunk of learning. The amount of content to cover is overwhelming, and the pressure to teach as fast as possible is real for many of us. But if we want to go far, we have to slow down and ensure that the information we gather accurately appraises students' learning needs and helps us and them take appropriate next steps to either deepen their understandings, dislodge misconceptions, or right flawed reasoning. See Figure 8.4.

FIGURE 8.4 ● Classroom Exit Ticket Using Concept Maps—"Do a Simple Food Web (Four Biotic Factors) That Describe What the Owl Ate"

a.

Name:

Draw a simple food web (4 biotic factors) that describes what the owl ate.

owl
mouse
grass
flowers
sun

b.

Name:

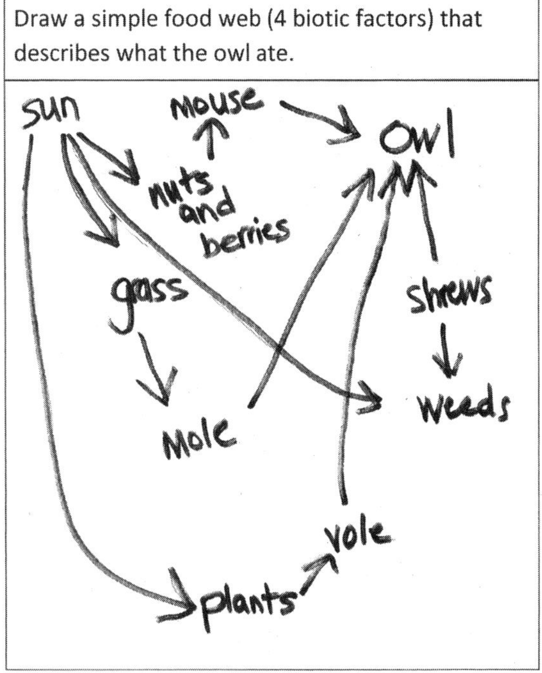

(Continued)

FIGURE 8.4 ● (Continued)

c.

Name:

Draw a simple food web (4 biotic factors) that describes what the owl ate.

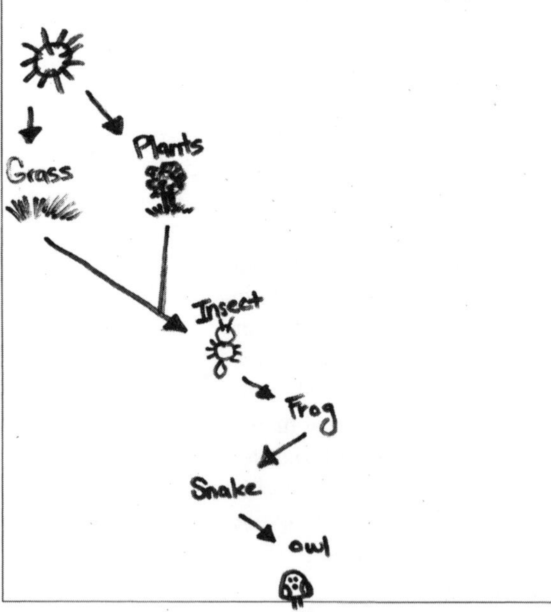

d.

Name:

Draw a simple food web (4 biotic factors) that describes what the owl ate.

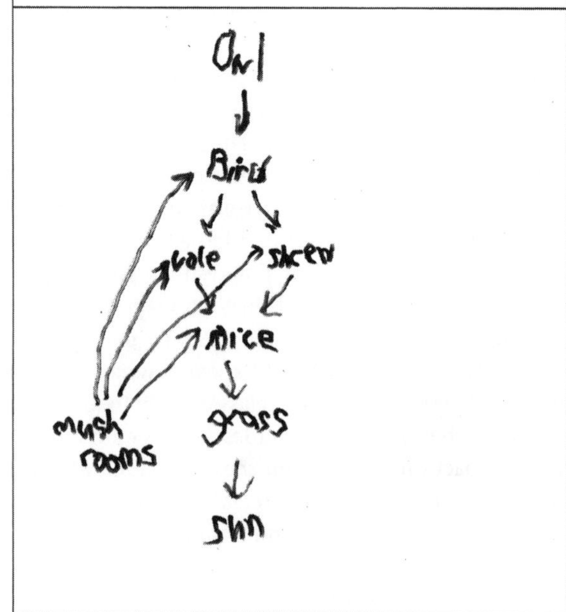

e.

Name:

Draw a simple food web (4 biotic factors) that describes what the owl ate.

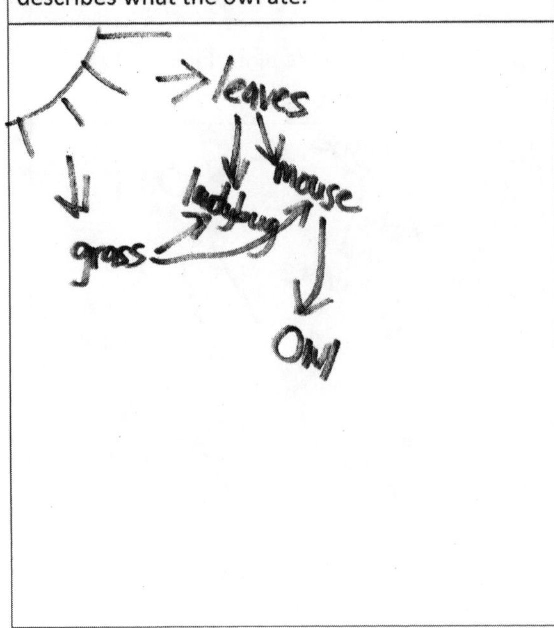

f.

Name:

Draw a simple food web (4 biotic factors) that describes what the owl ate.

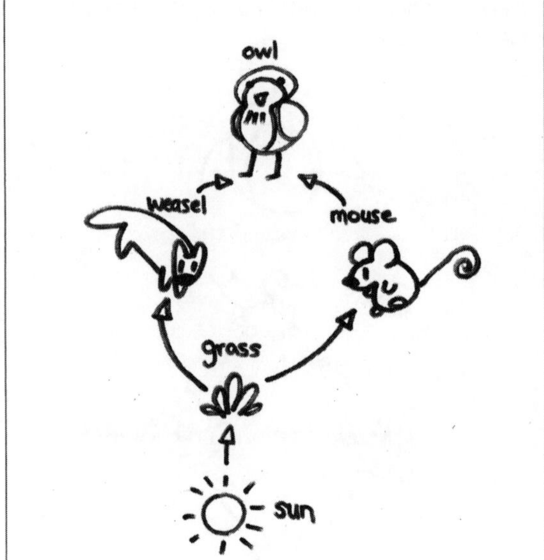

Source: Contributed by Jim Fratini, middle school science teacher, Hermon Middle School, Hermon Schools.

Teaching Productive Discourse: Using Classroom Discussions Effectively to Diagnose Learner Needs

Similar to the use of questioning, classroom discussions have been common practice in most of our classrooms with varying degrees of effectiveness and varying degrees of participation by our learners. The potential impact of classroom discussions done well is enormous (ES = 0.82;), but in order to reach this kind of impact on student learning, students have to be explicitly taught how to engage in productive discourse, or in other words the moves of academic discourse (Michaels & O'Connor, 2012). This is especially true if we wish to use classroom discussions to help diagnose learner needs and promote deeper thinking and application. Like many of our students, we often figure out through dialogue what we don't know as well as we might have thought we did, or what we might be unsure or unsettled about. In order for us to engage our students in rich discourse, they need to be skilled at talk moves. In addition, the classroom learning environment needs to be viewed as one imbued with mutual respect in order for learners to take positive risks in exposing not only what they know but also what they do not know.

Smith and Stein (2011) shared five practices for engaging mathematics learners in productive discourse: (1) anticipating, (2) monitoring, (3) selecting, (4) sequencing, and (5) connecting. In their book and professional development (PD) guide, Smith and Stein (2011) carefully outlined the importance of planning and teaching students how to engage in discourse before it can become a useful tool in diagnosing student thinking and skills.

Similarly, Michaels and O'Connor (2012) shared their findings around productive classroom talk and its impact on learning in the science classroom. Figure 8.5 explains the four goals and nine talk moves associated with the Talk Science Inquiry Project. Not all classroom discussion or academic talk is productive, and we often find ourselves posing close-ended questions to our students that have right or wrong answers and moving on to the next set of questions. A wise high school principal friend of ours uses the analogy of encouraging a volleyball game with your questions and discussion prompts instead of a tennis match. Too often the teacher asks the question, a student answers, and the teacher asks another question (similar to a tennis match where the ball goes back and forth across the net). As in a volleyball game, a worthy question posed by a teacher hopefully gets volleyed between students on either side of the net, rather than just hit back to the teacher. Michaels and O'Connor (2012) posited that there are seven key elements that help make academic talk doable: (1) a belief that students can do it, (2) well-established ground rules, (3) clear academic purposes, (4) deep understanding of the academic content, (5) a framing question and follow-up questions, (6) an appropriate talk format, and (7) a set of strategic "talk moves."

FIGURE 8.5 ● Goals and Talk Moves Associated With the Talk Science Inquiry Project

Goals for Productive Discussions and Associated Talk Moves

Goal #1: Individual students share, expand, and clarify their own thinking.

Talk Move 1: Time to Think (e.g., partner talk, think-pair-share, writing as think time, jotting a note to self, wait time, sketch time first, time to draw a concept map or mind map)

Talk Move 2: Say More (e.g., "Can you say more about that?" "What do you mean by that?" "Can you give an example?" "Can you make a connection?" "Can you add more to our discussion concept map?")

Talk Move 3: "So, Are You Saying . . . ?" (e.g., "So, let me see if I got what you're saying. Are you saying . . .?" Always leave room for the original student to agree or disagree and to say more. "Let me see if I can show what I think you're saying on our discussion concept map. Did I get it right?" "Turn and talk to a partner and tell them what you think Adam is saying . . . Now let's come back to our discussion. Who can share with Adam to see if we understood what he was saying?")

(Continued)

FIGURE 8.5 ● (Continued)

Goal #2: Students listen carefully to one another.

Talk Move 4: "Who Can Rephrase or Repeat?" (e.g., "Who can repeat what Beth just said or put it in your own words?" or after a partner talk, ask, "Please share with us what your partner said," or in a whip around activity, ask, "Before sharing your own thought, please rephrase what the previous student said.")

Goal #3: Students deepen their reasoning.

Talk Move 5: Asking for Evidence or Reasoning (e.g., "Why do you think that?" "What's your evidence?" "How did you arrive at that conclusion?" "Is there anything in the text, video, or lab that made you think that?")

Talk Move 6: Challenge or Counterexample (e.g., "Does it always work that way?" "Does your idea square with Kayleigh's example?" "Can you think of an exception to that general rule?" "Let's think about X. Would that reasoning work with X?")

Goal #4: Students think with others.

Talk Move 7: Agree or Disagree and Why? (e.g., "Do you agree or disagree, and why?" "Are you saying the same thing as Benjamin, or something different, and if it's different, how is it different?" "What do people think about what Kirsten said?" "Does anyone want to respond to that idea?" "If you agree with Muriel's thinking, please share with us your reasoning for agreeing with her.")

Talk Move 8: Add On (e.g., "Who can add on to the idea?" "Can anyone take that suggestion and go further?" "Can someone provide a different example that would add on to the idea?" "Who can add on or revise our discussion concept map?" "Who can sketch a new part to our drawing and explain why that design feature needs to be added?")

Talk Move 9: Explaining What Someone Else Means (e.g., "Who can explain what Andrea means when she says that?" "Who thinks they could explain in their words how Jedidiah came up with that answer?" "Why do you think he said that?" "Can you draw a concept map showing what Mia means when she says that?")

Source: Adapted from Michaels and O'Connor (2012).

The bottom line is that in order for classroom discussion to help us diagnose our students' thinking and learning progress, our learners have to be skilled at academic discourse and willing to engage in the discourse. Otherwise, using classroom discussions as an informal or formal assessment method provides inaccurate and faulty information. This method of diagnosing student needs is first and foremost an oral literacy assessment—similar to trying to assess social studies standards through an extended written response (e.g., essay) where the learner's written literacy skills often clouds the results, or assessing science standards through a selected response test that is first and foremost a reading test.

Visual Thinking Strategy: Classroom Discussion Protocol

As we discussed in Chapter 5, visual literacy is an important skill to develop. We can use the following protocol to help us diagnose learners' needs but only after the process has been thoroughly taught and practiced. This classroom discussion protocol, Visual Thinking Strategies (VTS), involves learners in developing their observation, thinking, inference, and communication skills by engaging in a very simple protocol involving three iterative questions:

1. What do you see in this picture or image?
2. What do you see that makes you say that?
3. What more can we find?

Adult learners, including a number of professionals beyond the ranks of art historians, museum docents, and educators, find VTS a valuable tool in helping them further develop their observation and inference skills. For instance, health professionals are also finding the simple three-question protocol valuable.

PAUSE AND REFLECT

- How might you use Talk Science, Visual Thinking Strategies (VTS), or other classroom discussion protocols to help prepare learners to engage in productive discourse?
- Once learners are taught productive discourse strategies, what are the benefits of using classroom discussion as a diagnostic tool for determining learner needs?

Conclusion

What and how we question is as important as when we question. How we as educators interpret learners' responses to varying prompts is crucial to the process of accurately diagnosing learners' needs. It is important to develop students' discussion competencies in order to be able to use classroom discussion as accurate tools for diagnosing student learning.

Take a Deep Dive to Further Your Understanding

- Read Chapter 5 from *Seven Strategies of Assessment for Learning* by Jan Chappuis (2009).
- For more information about learning styles and the connection with questioning strategies, we recommend reading this ASCD article and book chapter: http://www.ascd.org/publications/books/110129/chapters/Section-1@-Why-Task-Rotation¢.aspx.
- Read *Talk Science Primer* by Sarah Michaels and Cathy O'Connor (2012): https://inquiryproject.terc.edu/shared/pd/TalkScience_Primer.pdf.
- Read Alissa Berg's article, "Talking the Talk: Tips for Engaging Your Students in Scientific Discourse," at https://www.teachingchannel.org/blog/ausl/2014/04/21/talking-the-talk-tips-for-engaging-your-students-in-scientific-discourse.
- Explore Visual Thinking Strategies (VTS): www.vtshome.org.
- See SoundMakers: Talking About Music to Your Class—Classroom Prompts About Elements of Music at http://www.soundstreams.ca/wp-content/uploads/soundmakers_Tip_Sheet_Talking_Music_FINAL1.pdf.
- Read Anita Stewart McCafferty's (2017) article "Duct Tape and Pom-Poms: Engaging Middle-School Learners in Metaphoric Thinking Through Self-Expressive Prompts" at https://www.amle.org/BrowsebyTopic/WhatsNew/WNDet/TabId/270/ArtMID/888/ArticleID/868/Duct-Tape-and-Pom-Poms.aspx.

The Whole Learner and Nothing But the Learner

Key Takeaways

Understanding and implementing high-impact strategies help develop assessment-literate learners. Students need to understand themselves as learners and be taught habits of work and learning (HOWLs) like respect, responsibility, and perseverance.

Growth mindset and metacognitive strategies need to be translated into clear learning targets so they can be taught to students along with content and performance standards. Growth mindset, self-efficacy, and grit are linked to the notion that through effort and persistence, we can accomplish challenging, worthy goals and learning targets.

Educators need to treat growth mindset and metacognitive behaviors as clear learning targets for their students. Learners need to be able to understand, reflect on, and self-assess their own mindsets.

Teachers need to be able to use their understanding of how the assessment for learning strategies can be used to motivate reluctant learners with a fixed mindset.

Teachers can plan and lead professional learning of assessment for learning by having a shared language to represent cognitive and metacognitive strategies (see Chapter 11).

A Key Standard of Quality: Assessment-Literate Learners

Take a step back, and look again at the five keys to quality classroom assessment (see Figure 9.1). We have looked at two of the components in great detail, clear learning targets and clear purpose, to emphasize assessment for learning (forward design). The repeated emphasis on clear learning targets reinforces the message; it's all about teacher clarity and learning intentions. Also, notice that the flow of the graphic is directly through the student, what we have called the assessment-literate learner. The assessment-literate learner is an active partner in all aspects of the assessment process, an innovative notion introduced by Stiggins in *Student-Centered Classroom Assessment* (1994) and updated by Chappuis, Stiggins, Chappuis, and Arter (2015) in *Classroom Assessment for Student Learning*.

FIGURE 9.1 ● Keys to Quality Classroom Assessment

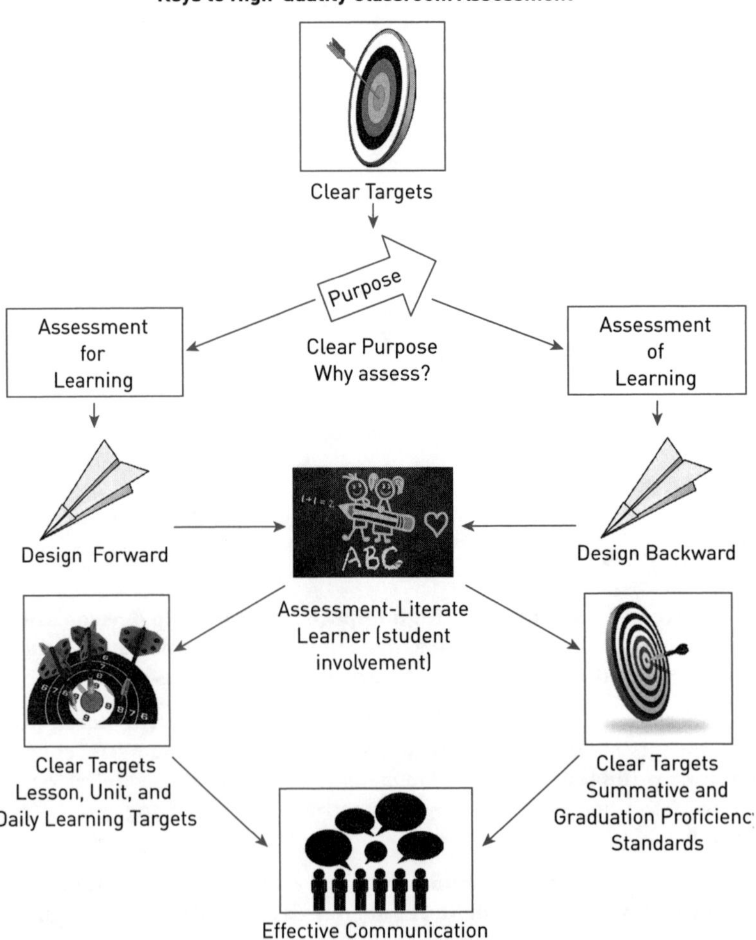

So, What Else About the Learner?

If you have a good understanding of the seven strategies for learning, you may still be asking these questions: What more is there? Why should I take the time to know deeply my students as learners? If I do take the time to get to know my students as learners, am I stealing time away from instruction and coverage of content? The time invested in building assessment-literate learners has a twofold benefit:

1. Students realize that they have their own ways to learn, to experience, to understand, and can mobilize their internal resources. They can communicate what they need to learn and what their next steps are.
2. Teachers can continue to deepen respectful, productive relationships with students and can use this to create a community of collaborative learners, modeling the growth mindset stance that we would like to see in all the students in our schools and in the citizens of our society.

In Chapters 3 through 8, there are descriptions and educators' stories about learning. These images resonate with learner-centered models like student involvement in assessment (Stiggins, 1994) and learners' expectations or self-reported grades (Hattie, Maters, & Birch, 2015). We are attempting to build a safe, responsive, learning environment where there is trust for individuals to grow and to respect peers as well as build positive, productive relationships between the teacher and students. It is all about strategies, yes! And it is all about the learners.

PAUSE AND REFLECT

- How would you define *assessment-literate learner*?
- Why is the assessment-literate learner so essential as a standard of quality for classroom assessment?
- Given the seven strategies of assessment for learning, how would you ensure that learners understand their role? Use the table in Figure 9.2 to keep track of your thoughts.

FIGURE 9.2 ● How Do the Seven Strategies of Assessment for Learning Help Build Assessment-Literate Learners?

Self-Assessment of Seven Strategies and the Assessment-Literate Learner

Directions: Reflect on the ways students are involved in and effectively communicate the seven strategies.

High-impact assessment for learning strategies	**Clear targets** (Teacher clarity & clear learning intentions) (ES = .75)	**Success criteria; models of weak and strong student work with rubrics** (ES = .75)	**Regular, descriptive feedback** and feed-forward (ES = .75)	**Student self-assess** (ES = .69) **and set goals** (ES = .50) **Metacognitive strategies** (ES = .57)	**Use evidence of student learning needs to select high-impact teaching strategies for next steps** (ES = .62)	**Students practice focused revision, spaced versus mass practice** (ES = .71)	**Self-reflection & self-questioning to monitor progress** (ES = .64), **work with peers** (ES = .55) & improve as a **self-regulated learner** (ES = 1.33)
How are you involving students? How does this strategy develop assessment-literate learners?							

(J. Beaudry and A. Stewart McCafferty, 2016)

Source: Chappuis (2015); Hattie (2009, 2012).

Let's return to our essential question: What is good learning? The greatest influence on learning is the learner (ES = 1.33; ES is the effect size). The label for this category has evolved over time; originally, Dr. Hattie named it self-reported grades. This means the learner has an accurate appraisal of her or his achievement. We are all familiar with students who either under- or overestimate their capacities; it happens all the time. An updated term, *learners' expectations*, has a similar emphasis but adds a dimension—the learner is willing to initiate, persist, and complete highly challenging tasks. Learners' expectations fit very well with more familiar descriptors like *growth mindset, self-efficacy*, and *grit*. All three are linked to the notion that through effort and persistence, we can accomplish challenging, worthy goals. Mindset can be broken down into two components: (1) growth mindset (intelligence is malleable and can grow in the process of accomplishing meaningful tasks) and (2) fixed mindset (intelligence is fixed and static and can not really change).

PAUSE AND REFLECT

- Listen to Carol Dweck's TED Talk "The Power of Yet" to hear what students say about mindset and how they can be taught strategies to persist and engage in challenging tasks: https://youtu.be/J-swZaKN2lc.
- What are your takeaways from this message?
- What are some of the strategies you use to support growth mindset in individuals?

Deep Dive: What Is Grit?

What comes to mind when you think about grit? After years of study, Dr. Angela Duckworth summarized her theory of grit like this: Grit is composed of talent (basic ability) and effort. In her theoretical schema, grit is developed in two stages, the initial interaction of talent and effort, which results in the development of basic skills. The second phase builds on the skills with renewed and relentless effort to improve on challenging tasks, which results in achievement—the belief that you have only so much talent and that it is characteristic of a fixed mindset. The belief that as a learner you can build on what you have as talent; can apply your efforts; and then build deeper skills with second, third, and fourth efforts is growth mindset.

PAUSE AND REFLECT

Take a look at Figure 9.3, the double formula for grit.

- One of the key concepts is talent. What is talent? How does talent influence your theory of learning?
- What is meant by the classic phrases about effort: "You get an A for effort" and "second effort?" How does the Duckworth theory of grit influence your interpretation of effort?
- What connections do you make between this representation of grit and fixed and growth mindset?
- Effort appears to be the driver of grit. How and when do assessment for learning strategies help build and support effort?

Making the connections between the seven strategies and grit is a crossroads of theory and practice, and in Figure 9.4, the seven strategies is combined with grit theory. The two phases of grit theory provide a meaningful addition to the seven strategies model and the three questions of assessment for learning. The acquisition of skills is the initial phase, requires the initial effort, and ties into this question: Where am I now? Knowing where learners are at the beginning is what Duckworth calls talent. In classrooms, we call it prior or background knowledge. The more we know about learners as they come into our classroom, coupled with what they know about themselves, the better. Getting a full picture of prior achievement is a high-impact strategy (ES = 0.63), especially when you consider that pretests are just one of many

FIGURE 9.3 • The "Effort Counts Twice" Theory for Grit by Dr. Angela Duckworth

GRIT: Effort Counts Twice

1 Talent × Effort = Skill

2 Skill × Effort = Achievement

strategies of assessment for learning (Hattie, 2012). Think of the strategies about teacher clarity (Chapter 4), visual representations of "What do I know about force and motion?" (Chapter 5), self-assessment and goal setting (Chapter 7), and the diagnosing of learning needs of students (Chapter 8).

The next phase is represented by this question: Where am I now? This phase reflects the initial consolidation of knowledge and skills and, with the help of teachers and peers, gives feedback for improvement as was discussed in Chapter 6. Students use strategies to seek out specific answers to this question: What do I know, and what are my goals for learning? Grit theory suggests that the second phase (skill x effort) is where learners focus their intentions, practice regularly to go further, and deepen their learning. In this phase, learners exert a range of robust metacognitive strategies. With their enhanced metacognitive skills, effort is counted twice as learners tackle the final questions: How do I close the gap? What are my next steps? Grit is more about the "stamina to go over something again and again, no matter how difficult it is" (Duckworth, 2016, p. 45).

Metacognitive Learning Strategies—A Deep Dive

Metacognitive learning strategies are essential for students to make progress toward meeting and exceeding standards we set and for them to become assessment-literate learners. These strategies represent how individuals think about their own learning and are that much-needed inner resourcefulness we would like our students to bring to classrooms. We want learners to have a quiver full of strategies, to take information and transform it into knowledge and conceptual understanding, to engage in positive reflective thinking and self-talk, and to be able to feel confident in seeking help from others. Figure 9.5 is a rank order list of metacognitive strategies (Hattie, 2012; Lavery, 2008; McGuire, 2015).

We took the list of metacognitive learning strategies and used it to create an assessment for learning tool, a Next Steps Rubric (NSR; see Figure 9.5). The list of strategies is arranged in rank order from highest, organizing and transforming information (ES = 0.85), to time management (ES = 0.44).

PAUSE AND REFLECT

- Self-control plays a pivotal role in metacognitive learning strategies, and it is a skill that can be taught. The research on self-control is evolving very quickly, and some may think we need brain scanners with biofeedback mechanisms in the classroom. This is not likely, but there are strategies to use. Here are two thought-provoking videos:

  "The Marshmallow Test" (https://youtu.be/QX_oy9614HQ)

  "Change Anything! Use Skillpower Over Willpower!" (https://youtu.be/3TX-Nu5wTS8)

- What strategies have you used to help students understand what self-control is and what they can do to make decisions?

FIGURE 9.4 ● Connections Between Seven Strategies and the "Effort Counts Twice" Grit Theory

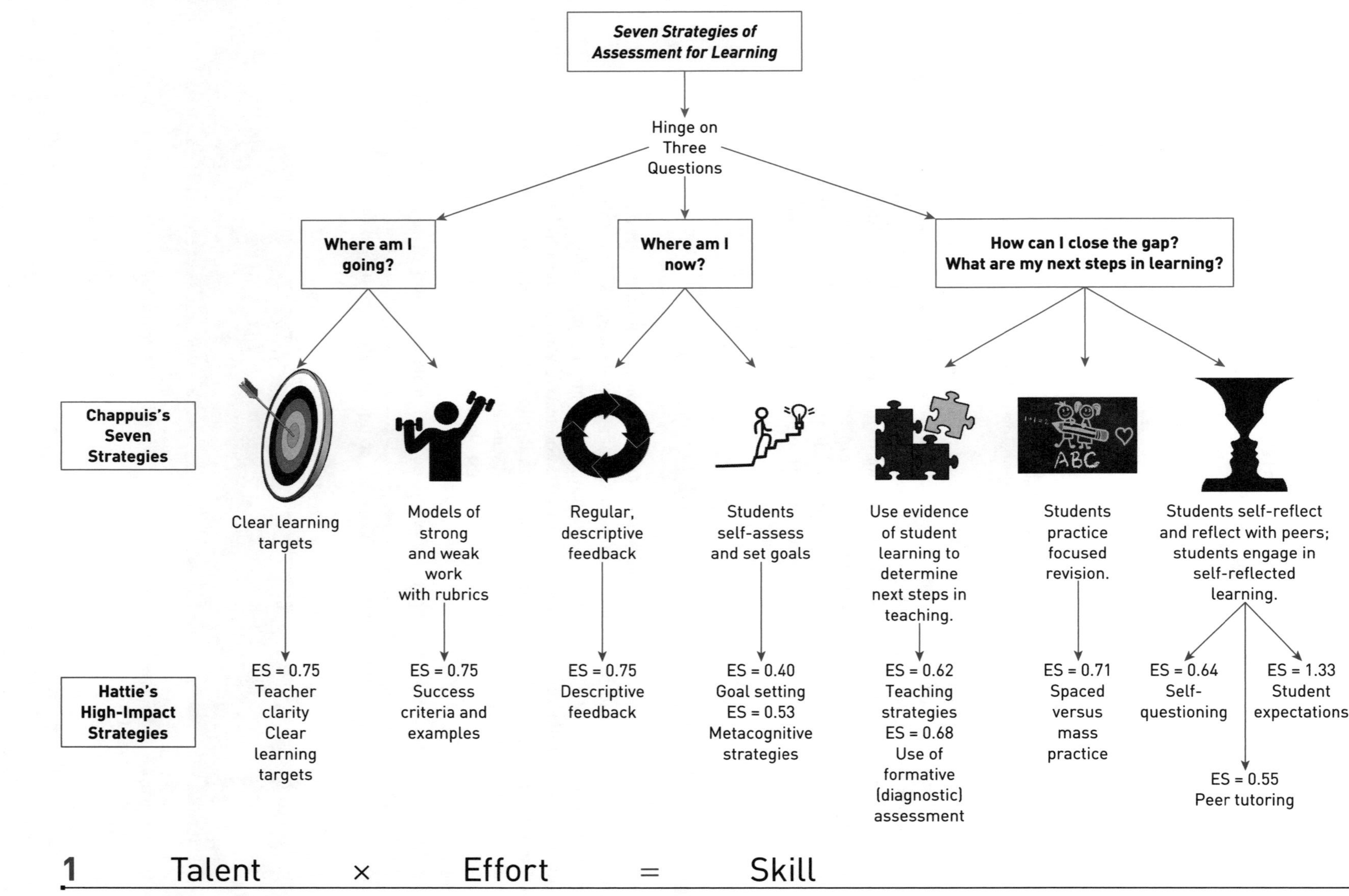

FIGURE 9.5 ● Next Steps Rubric for High-Impact Metacognitive Learning Strategies (from highest impact to moderate)

Next Steps Rubric

Using High-Impact Metacognitive Learning Strategies

Standard: I can use high-impact metacognitive learning strategies to improve my understanding, skills, and overall achievement.

What Is Done Well	**Criteria** **This Means . . .**	***What to Do Next*** **I Will . . . This Is How**
☐	I use maps and outlines to organize and transform information into knowledge.	☐
☐	I have the self-control to stay on any task. And I recognize the experience of "flow" in my learning.	☐
☐	I can engage in positive self- instruction and "self-talk."	☐
☐	I can self-evaluate and set standards for my own work (avoiding perfectionism).	☐
☐	I seek help when needed (engaging teachers, peers, parents, and community).	☐
☐	I keep records and lists, annotated in a notebook or log.	☐
☐	I practice thinking, memorizing, and rehearsing skills.	☐
☐	I plan and set goals that are realistic and about next steps.	☐
☐	I review and annotate original notes from reading, discussions, and lectures and videos.	☐
☐	☐ -------------------------------- ☐	☐

J. Beaudry & A. Stewart McCafferty (2017) USM

TABLE 9.1 ● Metacognitive Learning Strategies and Effect Sizes

Effect Sizes	Metacognitive Learning Strategies
0.85	Organizing and transforming information into knowledge (maps and outlines)
0.70	Having self-consequences (self-control to stay on task)
0.62	Self-instructing (self-talk)
0.62	Self-evaluating (setting standards for your own work, avoiding perfection/almost perfect)
0.60	Help-seeking (engaging teachers and peers)
0.59	Keeping records and lists (annotating, keeping a notebook)
0.57	Rehearsing and memorizing (practice thinking and doing)
0.49	Goal setting and planning (realistic, productive focus on next steps)
0.45	Reviewing records and notes (notes to review and annotate)
0.44	Engaging in time management (planning big blocks of time, not clock watching)

Source: Lavery (2008) in Hattie (2012, pp. 105–106); McGuire (2015).

The list of metacognitive learning skills in the appendix to this chapter goes further by adding actions to take to accomplish the desired effects. This connection of theory to practice helps identify the next moves that students and teachers can identify as "what to do next." Students need clarity from teachers to develop metacognitive strategies as well. We should be accommodating diversity with strategies that outfit learners with specific high-impact tools for learning so as to customize them and fit them to their needs. While metacognitive learning strategies involve study skills, according to the research on impact, students can be directed to other, more high-impact strategies. The checklist and NSR help teachers and students reflect on and grow as learners.

PAUSE AND REFLECT

- What is your definition of metacognition and metacognitive learning strategies?
- Look at the table in Figure 9.2 and the longer table in the chapter appendix.
- Make a list of the examples that you use to develop metacognitive learning strategies, and then share your list with colleagues and with your students.
- How do you represent these?

Metacognitive Learning Strategies in Practice—From 21st Century Skills to Habits of Work and Learning

Standards-based education is charged with developing the whole student; this means that there must be clear targets for content and performance standards, behavior, and so-called soft skills like collaboration and communication. Even though we are already well into this century, the "P21 Framework for 21st Century Learning" (www.P21.org) is a vision for student success created by a partnership of people in community organizations, businesses, corporations, and education. The core message is that learning is more than content (the 3 Rs). Learning encompasses the 4 Cs:

- Creativity and innovation
- Critical thinking and problem-solving
- Communication
- Collaboration

In addition, the life and career skills from the "P21 Framework for 21st Century Learning" go deeper into the metacognitive learning strategies and character traits:

- Flexibility and adaptability
- Initiative and self-direction
- Social and cross-cultural skills
- Productivity and accountability
- Leadership and responsibility

Next, teachers in classrooms, administrators in schools, and leaders in departments of educations are left to solve the problem of what metacognitive learning strategies to choose and to hold students and teachers accountable. There are several examples that follow. The first one is the list of core values developed by teachers at King Middle School: respect, responsibility, and perseverance. Each character trait is written from the perspective of the learner. Altogether, they are called habits of work and learning (HOWLs).

King Middle School: Habits of Work and Learning

1. I am a respectful member of the King Middle School community.
   a. I work cooperatively with others.
   b. I take care of resources and materials while acting as a steward of our community.
2. I take responsibility for my success as a learner.
   a. I arrive for each class period prepared.
   b. I participate fully and mindfully in class.
   c. I carefully and thoughtfully complete all my assignments to the best of my ability in a timely manner.
3. I persevere to produce high-quality work.
   a. I advocate for my learning by asking questions.
   b. I assess my work based on learning targets and rubrics.
   c. I learn from feedback and revise my work.

The list of HOWLs are habits that can be improved and strengthened by students with teachers and administrators who teach, model, and assess them. By taking lists and transforming them into assessment for learning tools, you can engage multiple strategies, feedback, self-assessment, goal setting, and next steps in learning. Examples of next steps rubrics for habits of mind from high school grades are seen in Figures 9.6 and Figure 9.7. Ultimately, it is the teacher and the students . . . ultimately, the students . . . who struggle to move these learning targets from paper into their minds, hearts, hands, and feet.

Practitioner Spotlight 9.1 is an example of both types of learning targets, academic and the metacognitive HOWLs. A resource for developing prompts and questions is found in Chapter 8. In Figure 8.3, you have a design framework grounded in high-impact strategies to create different types of assessment for learning prompts or questions. Teachers have grappled with the issue of fairness in grading for over one hundred years, ever mindful that they need good evidence of mastery of content and performance as well as effort and behavior. Even with the speed and power of technology, the essential daily questions are irreplaceable to make minute-to-minute instructional decisions. This example shows how evidence of HOWLs can be gathered and used efficiently by teachers and learners.

Learner's Attributes and What She or He May Be Thinking

Let's strengthen the connection between learner attributes and assessment for learning by examining a list of learner attributes that comes from Stiggins (2017) and Hattie (2012). See Table 9.2 for brief definitions of both positive and negative learner attributes.

FIGURE 9.6 ● Habits of Mind Rubric

Habits of Mind: A One-Point Rubric

Strengths		Possible Next Steps
❑ Taking time to consider options ❑ Thinking before speaking or acting ❑ Remaining calm when stressed ❑ Being thoughtful and considerate of others; Proceed carefully.	**I can manage my impulsivity.**	❑ Refer to Habits of Mind rubric ❑ Refer to classroom procedures ❑ Schedule conference with teacher ❑ Develop and follow through with action plan
❑ Sticking to the task at hand ❑ Following through to completion ❑ Remaining focused	**I can persist.**	❑ Refer to Habits of Mind rubric ❑ Refer to classroom procedures ❑ Schedule conference with teacher ❑ Develop and follow through with action plan
❑ Checking for errors ❑ Measuring at least twice ❑ Nurturing a desire for exactness, fidelity, and craftsmanship	**I can strive for quality and accuracy.**	❑ Refer to Habits of Mind rubric ❑ Refer to classroom procedures ❑ Schedule conference with teacher ❑ Develop and follow through with action plan
❑ Willing to work with others and welcome their input and perspective ❑ Abiding by decisions the work group makes even if I disagree somewhat ❑ Willing to learn from others in reciprocal situations	**I can think interdependently.**	❑ Refer to Habits of Mind rubric ❑ Refer to classroom procedures ❑ Schedule conference with teacher ❑ Develop and follow through with action plan
❑ Striving to be clear when speaking and writing ❑ Striving to be accurate when speaking and writing. ❑ Avoiding generalizations, distortions, minimizations and deletions when speaking, and writing.	**I can think and communicate with clarity and precision.**	❑ Refer to Habits of Mind rubric ❑ Refer to classroom procedures ❑ Schedule conference with teacher ❑ Develop and follow through with action plan

Source: Contributed by Zach Arnold, Ryan Crane, John Goater, Jessica Johnson, Raymond Tilton, Aaron Ward, and Carla Wright, educators, Mattanawcook Academy, RSU 67.

FIGURE 9.7 • Next Steps Rubric for Persistence and Managing Impulsivity

Student Self-Assessment and Goal-Setting Tool

Standard: I can persist on my art projects and manage my impulsivity in art class.

What Is Done Well	**Criteria** **This Means:**	***What to Do Next***
When I stay focused I do well on my art projects. I use art supplies the right way and show good skills.	**Habits of Mind:** **Persisting:** • Enter the classroom ready to work. • Be self-directed. • Stay focused on my work. • Have a "can do" attitude. • Listen during instruction and write down assignments. Refer to them to stay on task. **Managing Impulsivity:** • Think before speaking or acting. • Be thoughtful and considerate of others	Concentrate on my assignments Refrain from "I can't" or "I'm not good at art" statements. Work on a positive attitude. Respect others trying to do their work. Remain in my seat except to get supplies.

Source: Contributed by Holly Leighton, art teacher, Mattanawcook Academy, RSU 67.

PRACTITIONER SPOTLIGHT 9.1

COLLABORATIVE LEARNING, PEER FEEDBACK, AND REFLECTIVE THINKING IN THE ART CLASSROOM

What?

As an art teacher at King Middle School, I am part of the expeditionary project work that takes place across the curriculum. I need to organize the work, and students need to know what is expected—for example, their learning targets. I went to a professional development (PD) presentation about the seven strategies of assessment for learning and came away with a way to get students to see the learning targets more clearly. When I created a Next Steps Rubric (NSR) for the project on color mixing, called the mandala, I had this learning target: I can demonstrate my understanding of color through painting the color wheel. I added a focus on perseverance, which is one of our school's habits of work and learning (HOWLs).

So What?

I find these to be invaluable tools that truly guide and help the student organize their thinking around projects. I continued to create NSRs for each major project. For example, students work independently to create a series of mandalas, and the NSR helps organize their classroom time. After they have the opportunity to work on their projects for a while, I have students work in pairs to critique each other's progress. Using the NSR helps them focus

(Continued)

(Continued)

their comments and improves their feedback; it makes the feedback more about what they can do well and what they need to work at.

The additional use of the rubric is the reflection on perseverance, one of our HOWLs. Each student writes a reflection to the prompts:

1. I improve my learning by asking for help when needed and by asking questions.
2. I assess my work based on established criteria.
3. I learn from feedback and revise my work.

Each student then dates their self-assessment and rates their effort on a three-point scale. Students are honest with these ratings. One student who is usually a very focused learner gave herself a "1" and explained, "You know, it just wasn't my day." This data is part of their individual summative report and is aggregated for the school to look at HOWLs for each grade.

Now What?

Project work is a big part of the visual arts classroom, and attending to the creative process is a central focus of our standards. In previous years, when I tried doing a project without a rubric, it was a hot mess. I now have created these NSRs for other projects.

Having other students look at someone else's work and provide feedback strengthens their understanding of what the targets are and gives them opportunity to articulate what they see in someone else's work and then hopefully continue to apply that understanding to their own work. I did not use a working rubric for one project last year, and it was a hot mess without it. I will not do that again! See Figure 9.8.

FIGURE 9.8 ● Habits of Mind Rubric

Mandala Color Wheel Working Rubric

Name ______________________ Date ____________ Color ______________

Learning Target: ***I can demonstrate my understanding of color through painting the color wheel.***

What I'm doing well to reach the learning target:	***This means I understand how to:***	***What I will do next to to reach the learning target:***

★
★
★
★
★
★
	• **Mix** the primary colors thoroughly to make the secondary colors.
	• **Mix** a primary and secondary color thoroughly to get a tertiary color.
	• **Mix** white to each color thoroughly to create a tint.
	• **Mix** black to each color thoroughly to create a shade.
	• I **apply** my paint with precision.
	  ○ *Using the right sized brush for the area*
	  ○ *Holding the brush close to the bristles for control*
	  ○ *Loading only the tip of the brush with paint*
	  ○ *Painting in one direction*
	  ○ *Filling the entire shape with one color*
	• I **accurately place** my color/tint/shade in the correct space.
	• I **accurately place** my color/tint/shade in the corresponding shape.
		*
		*
		*
		*
		*

Name ______________________________

HOWL Focus: Perseverance

I Persevere to produce high quality work.

I improve my learning by asking for help when needed and by asking questions.

I assess my work based on established criteria.

I learn from feedback and revise my work.

Daily Perseverance HOWL:

Date __________ Score __________ Date __________ Score __________ Date __________ Score __________

Date __________ Score __________ Date __________ Score __________ Date __________ Score __________

Date __________ Score __________ Date __________ Score __________ Date __________ Score __________

Date __________ Score __________ Date __________ Score __________ Date __________ Score __________

Source: Contributed by Mary Wellehan, middle school studio arts teacher, King Middle School, Portland Public Schools.

TABLE 9.2 ● Learners' Positive and Negative Attributes

Learner Attributes	
Positive Attributes	**Negative Attributes**
Growth mindset—Attributes success to learning and effort	Fixed mindset—Attributes success to external factors, luck, and accident
Mastery orientation to goals—Defines success as ongoing effort for the development of competencies	Performance orientation to goals—Defines successful learning by comparing performance to others
Self-motivation—Source of learning comes from internal drive to take the next step	Self-orientation to goals—Shows that what peers think is what matters most
	Self-handicapping—Attributes failure to external causes; come to new learning with problems and prior pitfalls and less with possibilities
	Self-dependence—Shows an overdependence on adult directives and help
	Self-discounting and distortion—Dismisses all feedback and seen as an attempt to make her or him feel better
	Self-perfectionism—Sets excessively high standards; overly conscious of making mistakes and errors; reluctance to complete tasks
	Hopelessness—Demonstrates that learning is just not meant to be; there is nothing to do be done about it
	Social comparison—Compares oneself to peers' behaviors and attributes

As we try to understand these attributes, we like to give voice to what students may be thinking about and what their attributions means to them. We have selected two of the learner attributes as examples to make connections with the seven strategies. Let's walk through two examples of dispositions—(1) mindset or self-efficacy and (2) self-handicapping—and their connections to the assessment for learning strategies. We try to match what we believe learners may be thinking.

PAUSE AND REFLECT

- To get an inspiring perspective on why we need to value each learner individually, please take the time to watch the TED Talk by Todd Rose, a high school dropout and cofounder of Universal Design for Learning (UDL), titled "The Myth of Average."
- What are your takeaways from Rose's message?
- What are some of the terms you use to understand learners as individuals?
- What do you think Rose means when he said, "Design to the edge"?

Mindset (Celebrating Errors and Mistakes)

Students with growth mindsets (high levels of self-efficacy) display confidence in their learning. Their confidence leads them to believe that they can make learning happen, even in the most challenging circumstances. Failures are seen as chances to learn. Mistakes are celebrated. Reflecting on failures or mistakes is part of a greater effort and is used to look for new information next time.

Learners with growth mindsets make connections between positive actions (behaviors) and a resilient, positive, internal dialogue (state of mind). Hearing the learner's voice is important, because we want learners to reveal their internal dialogues as evidence for reflection and for action we, as educators, can help them take. Educators who generate and collect qualitative evidence from conversations and observations, so-called accountable talk, help to build and maintain a balanced, student-involved, evidence-based classroom assessment system. Conversations that focus on developing growth mindsets have a strong connection to the concept of self-efficacy and are a standard of quality assessment.

PAUSE AND REFLECT

- What would your students, both successful and struggling, say about their mindsets (see Table 9.3)?
- Think of particular students, and try to capture their words and write down what they would say.

Self-Handicapping

"When learners choose impediments or obstacles to performance that allow them to deflect the cause of failure away from their competence towards the acquired impediments" (Hattie, 2012, p. 46), we should acknowledge that not much is going to happen. Teachers need to understand that it is critical to have ways to build the cognitive with the metacognitive in our students. Being aware that students have lives outside of school should not limit or lessen the way we approach our daily activities. The effects of home and social lives can be an internalized self-handicapping that manifests itself in certain behaviors at school. Barriers may already come from their home lives—families may be struggling to stay together, may be forced to move multiple times during the school year, or may be under any one of a number of pressures. See Table 9.4.

TABLE 9.3 ● What Learners Say About Learning Depending Upon Their Level of Efficacy or Type of Mindset

What Accomplished Learners With a Growth Mindset (High Self-Efficacy) Say	What Novice Learners With a Fixed Mindset (Low Self-Efficacy) Say
"What did I do wrong, and why?" "I'd like to start over now that I see what you mean." "I want to do better."	"I can't do this." "I have never been good at this." "I really don't know how I got it right. I probably just got lucky."
"I wonder what this is connected to?" "Now this makes sense. I see the connections." "How can I challenge myself to learn more? Or what new audience or community of learners can I find to share my learning and engage in critical dialogue?"	"My mom doesn't do this either!" (e.g., speak Spanish or French or Chinese) "When will I ever use this?"

TABLE 9.4 ● Voices of Learners: What They May Say About Self-Handicapping

What Accomplished Learners Say	What Novice Learners Who Exhibit Self-Handicapping Say
"I am aware of skills that are lacking." "Can you help with this? I don't understand how to move beyond Part 4." Successful students ask specific questions: "What did I miss in the procedures of this experiment? What can I do to change the experiment to improve the results?"	"I didn't sleep last night." "It's too much work. I think I'll do the bare minimum and see what happens." "English is stupid." (Fill in your choice of subject matter.) Struggling students ask generic questions: "Your directions are horrible! How can I do this?"
"I can see how this works now. Do you have any more problems for me to try?" "I can see how the parts of the project fit together now and why I needed to practice those skills first."	"Are you going to grade this?" "How much is enough?" "I forgot my book/computer/homework." "Why am I doing this?" Continue asking why until you run out of answers.

PAUSE AND REFLECT

- **Gather resources about learners' attributes, read them, and share with your colleagues:**
- **Rick Stiggins's resources:**
  - **"Assessment Through Student's Eyes," *Educational Leadership* (2007).**
    - See http://www.ascd.org/publications/educational-leadership/may07/vol64/num08/Assessment-Through-the-Student's-Eyes.aspx.
  - ***The Perfect Assessment System* (2017) in Chapter 8.**
- **John Hattie's resources:**
  - ***Visible Learning for Teachers* (2012), especially Chapter 4, about the need to think deeply about learners' self-attributes as you prepare your lesson.**
  - ***Visible Learning and the Science of How We Learn* by John Hattie and Gregory Yates (2014)**

Deep Dive: Encounters With Learners

Let's examine two scenarios from two teachers to illustrate concrete examples of learning challenges revolving around students' attributions.

"There are . . . maybe 50 percent of my students who just don't care. I want them to learn, but they just don't want to learn." This comment was made at the beginning of a workshop series on assessment literacy by a high school teacher. The teacher was airing his sense of frustration. Is there anything more disheartening than a classroom with even one reluctant learner, let alone ten or fifteen students unwilling to engage in their own growth? As the quote from the high school teacher suggests, teachers take it personally.

A middle school teacher who began his career teaching shop class has worked hard to stay current as a teacher and leader in his school and his professional associations. He is constantly searching for ways to support all learners as they take on challenging tasks and improve. From his earliest days as a shop teacher, he has been a "maker." He gave students challenging iDesign tasks; for example, he had them design and build a model sailboat and compete with classmates in a community event to race their boats. More recently, this design task has morphed into the KidWind Challenge, a project that takes three months for teams of middle school students to design and build scale model wind turbines. In the grading system he uses, a "4" is the highest score a student can receive. His dilemma is that students were settling for a "3," and he found himself saying, "Don't you want to be a '4'?"

The search for answers is twofold. One is for the educators to adopt the learning stance that comes with a growth mindset as well as students doing the same for themselves. And second, what does it take to get and hold learners' attention? Assessment for learning strategies have greater effects on struggling learners, as measured by achievement scores (Black & Wiliam, 1998), but we need to affect all learners. Just as we know that learners will struggle, there are many who are not struggling to push themselves to go further and deeper.

PAUSE AND REFLECT

- Given what we have discussed in this chapter (as well as in Chapters 3 through 8) about learner attributes and metacognitive learning strategies, what do you think about the following two dilemmas?
  - The high school social studies teacher's dilemma: "I have a class with fifty percent of my students who do not want to participate."
  - The middle school STEM teacher's dilemma: It has become apparent that students are settling for grades and not willing to keep going. The teacher has tried saying, "Don't you want to be a '4'?" It does not seem to be working.
- Now it's your turn: Think of your students—ones who present you with intriguing, compelling dilemmas. Who is challenging your growth mindset as a teacher and learner?
  - Write two to three sentences, or create a concept map illustrating the learner and the dilemma.
  - Think deeply about how you could use the seven strategies and other high-impact strategies to come up with a plan.
  - Share your dilemmas with a small group of colleagues. Use your collaborative skills to solve the problem with evidence and insight.

Conclusion

There is a grading pit of which to be cautious. The best recommendation we have is to know the standards-based approach to teaching, learning, and assessment. Know why you need to separate reporting of academic achievement and HOWLs.

Educators have a long tradition of considering both effort and academics in their grading schemes. The discussion in this chapter is focused on the power of metacognitive learning strategies to develop assessment-literate learners. We have provided a carefully developed example of how to record and track progress on HOWLs. If standards-based education is to be effective, it is up to us to be clear about the learning targets, use backward design to ensure the alignment of instruction to assessment, and constantly examine evidence of student work to recognize and evaluate (score, grade, or mark) student work with the highest possible reliability. The paper

"A Century of Grading Research: Meaning and Value in the Most Common Educational Measure" (Brookhart et al., 2016) found that teachers' grades are more predictive of student success than standardized tests. However, the variability in teachers' grading practices penalizes and confuses too many students, and the persistent inadequacy of understanding how to assess academic and noncognitive factors leaves a lot to do.

To enhance your excitement, here is the conclusion of the one-hundred-year study of grades. They point to the essential role of the learner: "When students are taught the criteria by which to judge high-quality work and are assessed by the same criteria, grade meaning is enhanced" (Brookhart et al., 2016, p. 836). The call for assessment-literate learners is very clear.

What else do we need to know about learners and learning in order to support their growth? Everything, every day!

Take a Deep Dive to Further Your Understanding

- Take a tour of the CAST website to see more discussion about and examples of the Universal Design for Learning (UDL).
    - http://www.cast.org
    - Click on "Our Work" and then "About UDL"
    - UDL is a framework for educators to design learning environments for all learners, for multiple means of (1) representation, (2) action and expression, and (3) engagement. What connections can you make with our discussion of the assessment-literate learner?
- Take one of the many self-quizzes about growth mindset, grit, Almost Perfect, and self-efficacy. When you take a quiz, try it with assessment for learning in mind. Don't use it to label students. Have students openly talk about the questions on the survey. Some surveys are not really for kids. The Grit Scale (Duckworth, 2016), for example, asks whether the respondent has worked on a project for years. The time frame does not fit most students—even in high school.
    - Mindset quiz
    - Grit Scale
    - Almost Perfect survey
    - Self-efficacy
    - Strengths Finder
- Read *Drive: The Surprising Truth About What Motivates Us* by Daniel Pink (2009) or watch Pink's TED Talk, titled "The Puzzle of Motivation."
- Create a mind map to answer the prompt, "How do I welcome mistakes and errors in my classroom?"

Chapter 9 Appendix: Metacognitive Strategies: Definitions, Effect Sizes, and Examples

Strategy	Effect Size	Definition	Example
Organizing and transforming information into knowledge	0.85	Overt or covert rearrangement of instructional materials to improve learning	Having active reading and using visual thinking—outlines and maps Asking questions as advance organizers Making an outline and/or concept map before writing a paper (prewriting), modifying as you write
Self-consequences (Self-control)	0.70	Student arrangement or imagination of rewards or punishment for success or failure	Putting off pleasurable events until work is completed; proper sequence and proportion of healthy rewards
Self-instruction	0.62	Self-verbalizing the steps to a given task	Verbalizing steps in a math problem Paraphrasing or summarizing
Self-evaluation	0.62	Setting standards and then using them for self-judgment	Checking work before handing it to teacher (creation of questions and self-assessment rubrics) Using student-created self-assessments
Help-seeking	0.60	Efforts to seek help from either a peer, teacher, or other adult	Using a study partner Work in groups and teach to others (reciprocal teaching)
Keeping records	0.59	Recording of information related to study tasks	Taking class notes in text or concept map; organizing task timelines to complete projects Listening and note-taking skills
Rehearsing and memorizing	0.57	Memorization of material by overt or covert strategies	Writing a math formula until it is remembered Memory-building using concept maps to organize hierarchies and visual metaphors for memory "palaces"
Goal setting or planning	0.49	Setting of educational goals or planning subgoals and planning for sequencing, timing, and completing activities related to those goals	Making lists and timelines to accomplish during studying Previewing Having spaced versus massed practice
Reviewing records	0.45	Efforts to reread notes, tests, or textbooks to prepare for class or further testing	Reviewing textbook or notes before going to class Reading and rereading the book using reading comprehension strategies Taking notes
Self-monitoring	0.45	Observing and tracking one's own performance and outcomes, often recording them	Keeping records of study output with dates of completion Having learner's mastery orientation
Task strategies	0.45	Analyzing tasks and identifying specific, advantageous methods for learning	Creating memory games, strategies, and mnemonics to remember facts Doing active reading
Imagery	0.44	Creating or recalling vivid mental images to assist learning	Using images as visual metaphors for content, imagining consequences of failing to study
Time management	0.44	Estimating and budgeting use of time	Scheduling daily studying and homework time
Environmental restructuring	0.22	Efforts to select or arrange a physical setting to make learning easier	Studying in a secluded, habitual or preferred place

Source: Lavery (2008) in Hattie (2012, pp. 105–106); McGuire (2015).

High-Impact Professional Learning Principles and Communities of Practice

Let's Get It Right!

Key Takeaways

Most professional development (PD) has little impact on changing teacher practices and improving student learning. But this does not have to be the case! Studies on professional learning show us how to do professional learning well.

In order for professional learning to have an impact on teacher practices and subsequently student learning, it has to be adult-friendly. Professional learning opportunities should involve educators in active rather than passive ways as they grapple with new materials, strategies, tools, and resources.

Working with colleagues and partnerships over an extended period of time is one effective strategy for helping PD take root and become meaningful to educators. Collaborating with others builds collective efficacy and encourages stick-to-itiveness. Just as it is often more enjoyable to exercise with a friend or to engage in a hobby, professional learning is more enjoyable with others.

It is imperative that educators receive support during the implementation phase of any new learning or initiative. It is important for districts, schools, and partnerships to invest in PD for the long haul, including providing support during the many phases of implementation. Learning coaches and professional learning communities can help combat the tendency to give up on a complex strategy when it does not work right away or as well as one had hoped.

Assessment literacy is not a quick fix and requires ongoing professional learning done well!

As we turn to the last section of our book, Chapters 10 through 13, we ponder this question: What does the evidence suggest is needed to create professional learning opportunities for our educators that both improve their practices and result in improved student learning?

Because of our view of the foundational necessity of assessment-literate teachers, leaders, and students, we became very interested in how best to engage educators in professional learning opportunities that would result in an increased understanding for educators in the practices of

PAUSE AND REFLECT

In your experiences, what works well when you are learning and implementing a new teaching strategy or set of strategies?

assessment for and of learning and help to improve student learning as the ultimate outcome. As educators ourselves, we had both experienced and led a number of successful and not so successful professional learning endeavors. We wanted to get this one right! We talked to our graduate students, questioned our teacher and administrator colleagues in preK–12 and in higher education, read a lot about professional learning, chatted with assessment experts and consultants, and brainstormed our best ideas about how to engage our learning communities in assessment literacy done well.

From working with adult learners for a few decades, we knew quite a bit about how they are similar and dissimilar from other learners, including the young adolescents that we had previously taught. Learning Forward, the premier publishing wing of the National Staff Development Council, and the Center for Public Education were staples in our developing understanding of the principles of effective professional learning, as were our revered friends, authors, and consultants Jan Chappuis and Rick Stiggins. Additionally, we have been privileged to work with amazingly talented and dedicated educators at the Maine Center for Research in STEM Education (RiSE Center) and the Maine Arts Leadership Initiative (MALI). Both RiSE and MALI are organizations dedicated to building powerful professional learning opportunities and widespread teacher leadership in their respective fields. They have intentionally taken on assessment literacy for their educators as a way to improve teacher practice and student learning. We have also been privileged to work with other education partnerships, such as Penobscot River Educational Partnership (PREP), Southern Maine Partnership (SMP; which we codirect), Northwoods Partnership, Washington County Leadership, and Midcoast Superintendents Association to name a few. Additionally, we have partnered with dozens of school districts and departments who are committed to increasing educators' assessment literacy in order to improve practices and student learning. Notably, RSU 67 and MSAD 6 have invested considerable intentionality and time to implement assessment literacy as part of the fabric of their learning organizations. They have provided ample "testing ground" for systemic implementation of assessment literacy across an organization at all levels and across all roles. These aforementioned partnerships have allowed us to explore deeply how educators learn and what the common needs are of disparate educators.

Standards for Professional Learning

In 2011, in an effort to update their 2001 standards, Learning Forward published seven standards for effective professional learning. See Figure 10.1. At the heart of these standards is the belief in the importance of providing quality learning opportunities for every educator. Learning Forward adheres to the belief that improving educator effectiveness is inherently intertwined with improving student results. When the two work in conjunction with one another, a continuous improvement cycle can occur. When professional learning leads to a change in teaching practices, improved student results will follow.

In addition to the seven standards for professional learning, Learning Forward (2011) presented four prerequisites for effective professional learning.

- "Educators' commitment to students, *all* students, is the foundation of effective professional learning.
- Each educator involved in professional learning comes to the experience ready to learn.

FIGURE 10.1 ● Standards for Professional Learning

The 2011 *Standards for Professional Learning* are as follows:

- **Learning Communities**—Professional learning that increases educator effectiveness and results for all students occurs within learning communities committed to continuous improvement, collective responsibility, and goal alignment.
- **Resources**—Professional learning that increases educator effectiveness and results for all students requires prioritizing, monitoring, and coordinating resources for educator learning.
- **Learning Designs**—Professional learning that increases educator effectiveness and results for all students integrates theories, research, and models of human learning to achieve its intended outcomes.
- **Outcomes**—Professional learning that increases educator effectiveness and results for all students aligns its outcomes with educator performance and student curriculum standards.
- **Leadership**—Professional learning that increases educator effectiveness and results for all students requires skillful leaders who develop capacity, advocate, and create support systems for professional learning.
- **Data**—Professional learning that increases educator effectiveness and results for all students uses a variety of sources and types of student, educator, and system data to plan, assess, and evaluate professional learning.
- **Implementation**—Professional learning that increases educator effectiveness and results for all students applies research on change and sustains support for implementation of professional learning for long-term change.

Source: Learning Forward (2011).

- Because there are disparate experience levels and use of practices among educators, professional learning can foster collaborative inquiry and learning that enhances individual and collective performance.
- Like all learners, educators learn in different ways and at different rates."

As we work diligently to build effective professional learning for teachers and their leaders around assessment literacy, we use the professional standards and prerequisites to guide us in our planning, self-assessment, reflection, and goal setting for next steps. We also have found the *Teaching the Teachers Report* from the Center for Public Education (Gulamhussein, 2013) instrumental. See Figure 10.2, and pay particular attention to main finding #2. These main findings affirm what we have experienced, and believe to be true, about professional learning. The findings serve as an evidence-based reminder that one-off PD days—regardless of how famous and dynamic the expert flown in may be—are essentially a waste of time, money, and effort. Unless professional learning experiences have appropriate duration, active participation in learning the new strategies, and implementation support, they are doomed for failure. We have delivered enough professional development (PD) to know that "prison inservice days" where everyone in the district is mandated to attend do not work to significantly improve educator practices or student outcomes.

Let us look closer at these findings about professional learning. Our goal is to share relevant research that has helped us create more effective professional learning experiences for educators with which we are privileged to work. We hope that you will adhere to these standards and principles as you develop and implement professional learning in your own teams, schools, districts, regions, states, and organizations.

"The duration of professional development must be significant and ongoing to allow time for teachers to learn a new strategy *and* grapple with the implementation problem." (Gulamhussein, 2013). Studies indicate that it may take as many as 50 hours of professional learning, including practice and coaching, before a teacher masters and uses a new teaching strategy in their classroom (French, 1997, as reported by Gulamhussein, 2013). In order to become proficient with a

FIGURE 10.2 ● Main Findings From Teaching the Teachers Report

The main findings for providing effective professional development (PD) in an era of accountability include the following:

1. The Common Core standards focus on teaching for critical thinking, but research shows that most classroom instruction is weak in this area. Therefore, professional development needs to emphasize practices that will turn students into critical thinkers and problem solvers.
2. Most professional development today is ineffective. It neither changes teacher practice nor improves student learning. However, research suggests that effective professional development abides by the following principles:
   - The duration of professional development must be significant and ongoing to allow time for teachers to learn a new strategy *and* grapple with the implementation problem.
   - There must be support for a teacher during the implementation stage that addresses the specific challenges of changing classroom practice.
   - Teachers' initial exposure to a concept should not be passive, but rather should engage teachers through varied approaches so they can participate actively in making sense of a new practice.
   - Modeling has been found to be a highly effective way to introduce a new concept and help teachers understand a new practice.
   - The content presented to teachers shouldn't be generic, but instead grounded in the teacher's discipline (for middle school and high school teachers) or grade-level (for elementary school teachers).
3. Research estimates that pre-recession spending on professional development occupied between two to five percent of a typical district's budget. However, many districts do not track their professional development spending at all, leaving them in the dark about their costs.
4. In switching to effective professional development, the most significant cost item for districts will be purchasing time for teachers to spend in professional learning communities and with coaches.
5. Support during implementation must address the dual roles of teachers as both technicians in researched-based practices, as well as intellectuals developing teaching innovations.

Source: Gulamhussein (2013).

new teaching strategy, it is estimated that it takes at least twenty different times of practicing the skill (Joyce & Showers, 2002, as reported by Gulamhussein, 2013). These findings indicate that if we want to truly see educator practices and student results improve, we have to be willing to invest significant time in the process of learning. Thus, educators need to make sure that the strategies they are learning have the biggest bang for the buck. Assessment for learning strategies are high-impact strategies and are worthy of such investment of time and resources.

"There must be support for a teacher during the implementation stage that addresses the specific challenges of changing classroom practice." (Gulamhussein, 2013). Without support for teachers grappling with implementing the strategies in their classrooms, the likelihood of success is greatly diminished. This finding illustrates the problems inherent in flying in the expert from away for a day or two to teach the strategy or even purchasing books, training manuals, or videos for staff without providing ongoing support during the implementation phase. Limited support during the implementation phase is like asking a toddler to recite the Gettysburg Address and then write a reflection paper on it. Many times, teachers give up on complex strategies before putting them into practice in their classrooms twenty-plus times. Support is needed, especially when the going gets tough and the strategy is not having the desired impact right away. Without systemized support from colleagues, coaches, and/or administrators to help teachers make it through the learning hurdles associated with changing practice in any significant way, the hours of PD instruction will often be of little use. School leaders and PD coordinators need to spend as much time and resources, if not more, planning for implementation support as they do planning for the instruction portion of the PD process.

PRACTITIONER SPOTLIGHT 10.1

DISTRICTWIDE IMPLEMENTATION OF ASSESSMENT FOR LEARNING

What?

It is with gratitude and appreciation for the research, instruction, insights, and collaborative opportunities that Jeffrey S. Beaudry and Anita Stewart McCafferty have created for school districts that I share my experiences with Assessment for Learning (A4L). Their continuous improvement model of action research and effective teaching and learning has been (and continues to be) a remarkable experience for all of us who have evolved our thinking and implementation of best practices in A4L.

Through their diligent and exhaustive work through the University of Southern Maine's Southern Maine Partnership (SMP), Jeff and Anita have created communities of deeper learning in the area of A4L and STEAM. Since December 2014, the SMP has run three major conferences with invited guest presenters like Jan Chappuis and Rick Stiggins, recognized authorities on classroom assessment. The conferences have emphasized A4L and leading and provided our school district leadership and teacher leaders ongoing opportunities for professional growth and networking that has enabled districts such as ours to implement practices in an explicit way and with the direct assistance from Jeff and Anita. The purpose is to successfully bridge leadership practices with classroom teaching and learning needs.

In the past, our school district has been sending administrators, teachers, and instructional coaches to these SMP sessions. Over time, Jeff and Anita have worked with participants to drill further down into instruction and A4L. The resulting breakout sessions at these conferences have given our educators skills and tools for implementing A4L practices in their classrooms, and students are responding positively to new ways of learning by showing progress while being motivated to own the learning.

So What?

A key development for our district as a result of participating has been to plan a systematic approach to reaching all educators and students in our district. In June 2017, I held a meeting with Jeff, Anita, our administrators, central office leaders, and our proficiency-based education coach to discuss our next steps with A4L. The meeting was designed to have all participants understand our progress to date with proficiency education and decide on our next steps. We agreed that we would focus on A4L

SAD 6 Key Components to Focus on Formative Assessment for Learning

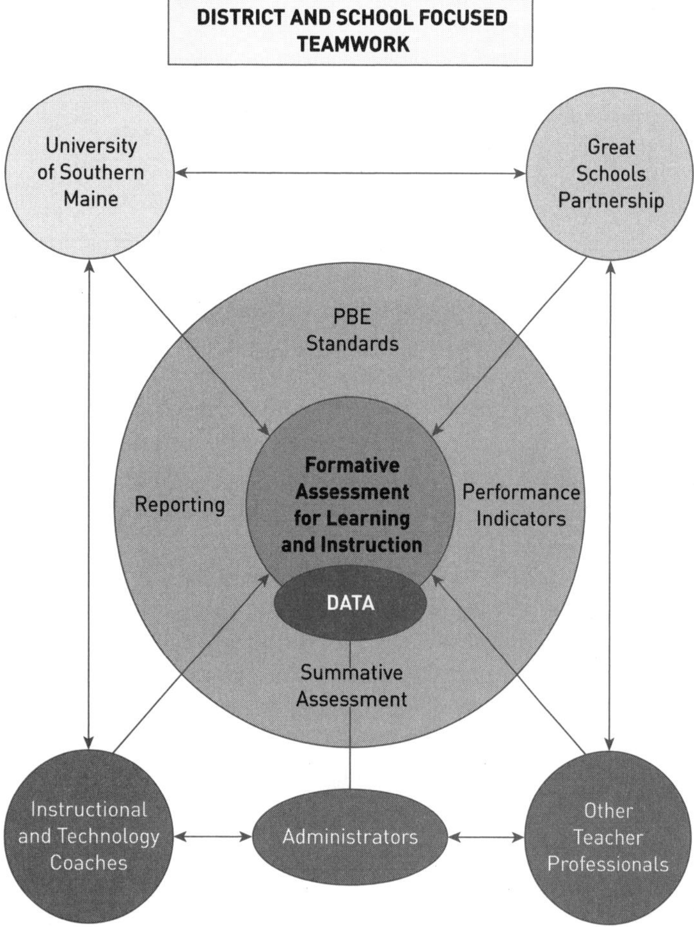

(Continued)

(Continued)

and focus on this topic at our district's administrative leadership retreat in August 2017. We also agreed to schedule three A4L all-day sessions within our district in a train-the-trainer model. Due to prior involvement in both the SMP and coursework with Jeff and Anita by several of our district teachers, they were able to blend their knowledge and experience into the first session. In fact, one of the teachers, an elementary school teacher and a certified STEM (science, technology, engineering, and mathematics) trainer who has worked extensively with the Maine Center for Research in STEM Education (RiSE Center), Kirsten Gould, cofacilitated the training.

As I worked with our leadership team on the key components, I kept trying to fit together our prior emphasis on proficiency-based education with the new focus on A4L. I began to construct a graphic representation with the various priorities and key participants, among them the University of Southern Maine, Great Schools Partnership, and instructional and technology coaches. I have gone through several iterations of this graphic after sharing it in our team meetings. See the figure that follows. The important shift was to put A4L in the center of the graphic so that it drives our conversations when we get together.

Now What?

We are now involved in a two-year project and have developed professional learning resources in the form of six online "bite-sized" modules, which can be accessed through Google Drive and customized with local examples. The modules focus on the following A4L strategies: teacher clarity and clear learning targets, self-assessment, goal setting, and descriptive feedback. Teachers and instructional coaches are trained to understand the modules and to implement them with teachers in their buildings.

As work progressed, school district leaders developed new roles and responsibilities within the school district to ensure the success of the assessment for learning work. Six instructional coaches were established, and recently a new position was designated: an A4L coach. This person will be the lead for implementation and have a greater presence in classrooms to observe, provide feedback on, and share examples of A4L processes and products. For school leaders there are two outcomes, developing a sufficient understanding of A4L and integrating A4L work into strategic planning documents for each school. Classroom visits by school leaders, from superintendent to assistant principals, will be informed by our focus on A4L and will therefore balance out our current focus on teacher evaluation.

Without developing these critical relationships over time and trying out Jeff and Anita's A4L modules, our district would have been left to a more disparate implementation of these impactful classroom practices. We are very fortunate to have put ourselves in this pathway for learning, particularly given the size of our district and the need to implement impactful practices based on solid research and student evidence of success. Through commitment and focus on applied learning, Jeff and Anita represent the epitome of an informed and enthusiastic professional learning for the benefit of our school system, teachers, and most importantly our students.

Source: Contributed by Mick Roy, assistant superintendent, MSAD 6.

In our assessment literacy work, we have worked to build local capacity for maintaining and propelling the work forward. We believe strongly in training teacher, curricula, and administrator leaders to support the assessment for learning work back in their schools. As such, we have created bite-sized assessment modules (in addition to ongoing, multiyear PD, graduate courses, workshops, etc.) complete with annotations, video clips, and examples that assessment leaders can use back in their districts to support the deepening of their own learning, so they can better support their colleagues' learning. We are very up front with district and regional leaders who wish to hire us to come in and "do" assessment literacy with their staffs that unless they invest in local support for the implementation, our best efforts will fall short. Site-based instructional leaders can, and must, be developed.

"Teachers' initial exposure to a concept should not be passive but rather should engage teachers through varied approaches so they can participate actively in making sense of a new practice." (Gulamhussein, 2013). This finding compels us to improve the ways we engage adult learners in learning more about assessment literacy. Because educators are coming to us with a variety of skill sets, experiences, beliefs, demographics, and understandings, we have our work cut out for us! In order to create active learning experiences for professional educators, we create numerous opportunities for them to discuss and apply the strategies and tools to their own contexts. We find team table talks, think-pair-share, now-you-try work time, interactive gallery walks, templates, self-assessment tools, multiple weak and strong examples of the strategies in practice, direct instruction, modeling, participant sharing, and varied resources (including multimedia, screen shares with expert others and practitioners, short video vignettes, Google Drive folders of classroom examples, chart paper posters of tools and resources, and common texts) work well for most of our adult learners.

PRACTITIONER SPOTLIGHT 10.2

ASSESSMENT FOR LEARNING SUPPORT FOR TEACHERS IN OUR STEM COMMUNITY

What?

As an organization that provides professional development (PD) opportunities to STEM (science, technology, engineering, and mathematics) teachers, there was often a request for us to help with assessment, which we did regularly. Almost exclusively, our work had been on gathering teachers together from multiple schools and districts to create summative assessments and scoring rubrics. After consulting with Anita and Jeff about assessment literacy, we decided to invest our time and energy in helping the teachers in our community gain understanding and skills around assessment for learning strategies.

So What?

It wasn't until we used the formative assessment strategies with Anita and Jeff's help that teachers came back to us and reported with enthusiasm that they now were able to help students who were struggling with STEM concepts *during* the instructional unit. The common language of strategies and tools from the modules and the ongoing support of teachers throughout the process really influenced results in classrooms. The teachers were able to provide students with additional learning opportunities for the STEM concepts they were struggling with and were seeing student grow in understanding and improved academic achievement on end of the unit summative assessments as well. The teachers in our community knew that we were all committed to helping them implement the strategies and were there to problem-solve alongside of them when things did not go as well as hoped or to help them share their resources and ideas with one another. We used videoconferencing before and after the modules to connect educators from hundreds of miles away from one another as part of the support mechanism, a website, and Google Drive folders to support one another's efforts.

Now What?

With the help of Anita and Jeff, we have built out additional assessment for learning modules and planned a second year of implementation and support for the teachers in our community.

Source: Contributed by Beth ByersSmall, NSF teaching fellowship program coordinator, RiSE Center.

"Modeling has been found to be a highly effective way to introduce a new concept and help teachers understand a new practice." (Gulamhussein, 2013). This finding reminds us of congruency once again. We are careful to model the strategies and tools we are teaching others to use in their classrooms, hoping to avoid "do as I say, not as I do!" For instance, when we teach clear learning targets, we model the processes not only with examples from various content areas and grade levels but with the content of clear learning targets itself by using learning progressions, concept maps, "I can . . . this means . . . here's how" formats, and so on. We find it particularly helpful when modeling how to use a strategy to build a tool with our learners instead of simply showing the finished product as a model or example.

"The content presented to teachers shouldn't be generic, but instead grounded in the teacher's discipline (for middle school and high school teachers) or grade-level (for elementary school teachers)." (Gulamhussein, 2013). This finding can be challenging to implement when you are trying to create assessment literate teachers and leaders at every level and content area. We have however noted the truth repeatedly of this finding. If we do not have examples or PD specific to the context of teachers or leaders, many find it difficult to transfer the examples or strategies to their own context. The strategies and tools are also easier to dismiss when they are not grade or discipline specific. We hear comments such as, "I can see how it works for middle school math, but that would never work for Grade 2 writing." So, as difficult and time-consuming as it is to tailor professional learning to the various grade spans and disciplines, the results are worth it. Two of the organizations we have worked with over a significant period of time understand this professional learning principle. They have worked hard to help their educators feel less disenfranchised or disengaged with the content provided by creating discipline-specific professional learning for and with their arts and science teachers. In fact, the RiSE Center understood this finding so well that they collaborated with us to create assessment for learning modules that included only STEM (science, technology, engineering, and mathematics) examples with each strategy and tool showing STEM examples for each grade span.

PRACTITIONER SPOTLIGHT 10.3

CREATING A COMMUNITY OF STEM TEACHER LEADERS

In Maine, we face two problems that heighten the feeling of isolation among teachers. First, we have many rural pockets in our state where schools are small and remote. This means a science teacher could be the only one in the entire school! Secondly, the state policy is local control, meaning each district determines its own instruction, curriculum, and assessments. So, not only did teachers struggle to find science collaborators within their schools but they also faced barriers of geography and common language when attempting to collaborate with teachers from other schools.

The Maine Center for Research in STEM Education (RiSE Center) at the University of Maine has been able to act as a convener for several projects and partnerships creating infrastructures to strengthen science education. We brought teachers together, along with researchers, faculty, preservice teachers, and nonprofit partners, into regional hubs to work on issues of science education. We created opportunities for common language within these regional "leading and learning communities" by either creating shared curriculum collaboratively and/or by utilizing common professional development (PD) platforms such as Talk Science (source: TERC) or assessment for learning (source: Anita Stewart McCafferty and Jeffrey S. Beaudry, authors). This common language was essential in creating an active and sustaining community. Another essential ingredient was regular in-person gatherings. We met roughly monthly throughout the academic year, and we provided a free meal and stipend for attendance at each meeting.

We knew we needed teacher leadership in these communities to give teachers a key stake and voice in their own development needs in order for the work to spread and sustain. We used a guided, scaffolded leadership model to build grassroots teacher leadership. We invited each teacher in our community to go back to their own schools and lead smaller learning communities and study groups based on the PD platforms we were working on together. During our community meetings, we spent half of the time learning together and half the time preparing to lead the next study group meeting in their local learning communities. We created study group templates, resources, and facilitation guides to support the teachers in their local leadership. When our communities would reconvene the following month, one focus of discussion was how the leadership was going in their local communities. Together, we would troubleshoot any issues or challenges. Teacher leaders heard stories from each other and were able to communicate those stories back to their local study groups, helping even the local teachers feel like they were part of something bigger.

Teachers began to be seen by their local colleagues and administrators as local leaders who were plugged into a bigger, ongoing learning community that was providing them with valuable, high-quality resources and programming. They were encouraged and supported for sharing this information back within their local communities. We positioned these teacher leaders not as experts but as liaison of information and skilled sharers of valuable experiential learning. This reduced the anxiety typically associated with peer leadership and relieved the pressure to be a "perfect teacher" in order to be an effective teacher leader.

Because we selected topics such as productive talk, higher-order thinking, and assessment for learning, we could ground the content in the context of science but ensure that the topics and strategies were relevant to teachers of other subject areas. This enabled our science teacher leaders to become local grassroots leaders of PD across their local communities.

We ended up creating a pipeline approach to leadership where leaders would check in with the leader community, get more resources or study group content, and then bring that back to their local communities—just like bees coming to the flower and then going back to the hive. As long as we offered fresh flowers via high-quality content, support for the teacher leaders, and connection with other leaders, the leaders were revered back at their hives! The model sustained because we continued to infuse high-quality flowers into our regional leading and learning communities, and our grassroots leaders continued to offer value back to their local learning communities.

Source: Contributed by Erika Allison, former project director, RiSE Center.

Conclusion

In order to change educator practices in ways that result in improved student learning, professional learning opportunities must adhere to evidence about effective practices. Assessment literacy, especially a deep and robust application of assessment for learning strategies, is foundational to educator practices. As such, it is essential when engaging in professional learning to carefully examine and plan for appropriate duration, active learning designs, varied modeling of the strategies during the learning process, discipline-specific and/or grade span-specific examples and groupings, and appropriate support during the implementation stages (Gulamhussein, 2013).

Take a Deep Dive to Further Your Understanding

- Read *Teaching the Teachers: Effective Professional Development in an Era of High Stakes Accountability*: http://www.centerforpubliceducation.org/teachingtheteachers.
- Read *Standards for Professional Learning* from Learning Forward: https://learningforward.org/standards-for-professional-learning.

Professional Learning Strategies and Tools for Creating Assessment-Literate Educators

Key Takeaways

Establish a common language, and share vetted high-quality resources with your professional learning communities.

Share and cocreate concrete examples of assessment for learning strategies in action. These examples should represent various content areas and grade spans.

Create interactive and immersive learning experiences for adult learners, such as gallery walks.

Be relentless about self-assessment, goal setting, and reflection for adult learners. Provide a variety of tools and allocate adequate time for learners to thoughtfully complete the self-assessments or reflections. Revisit goal setting periodically to determine next steps and celebrate successes.

Create (or use existing) bite-sized professional development (PD) opportunities to promote ongoing PD tied to applying strategies to the classroom. One such bite-sized PD is multimedia modules. We encourage you to borrow from those we have cocreated with—our partners—or begin to create your own. Either way, the goal is to layer in small chunks of learning over time.

Encourage collaboration amongst professional educators within districts and regional or state partnerships as well as across districts and partnerships. Such collaboration efforts should help grow leaders through widespread teacher leadership opportunities. Use a variety of collaboration strategies, such as Edcamp-style PD, screen share tools, working conferences, social media sharing spaces, and educator-created and educator-led workshops.

Embed assessment literacy in other initiatives, such as new teacher orientation, induction, mentoring, evaluation, graduation requirements, curriculum reviews, content area pedagogy or program training, etc.

In this chapter, we will share with you some of our tried and true "best bets" when it comes to professional learning strategies, tools, and resources to help create assessment-literate educators who feel empowered and efficacious! We have organized the chapter around sharing with you our take on the importance of establishing a common language and sharing vetted high-quality resources; of sharing and cocreating concrete examples from various content areas and grade spans; of creating interactive and immersive learning experiences for adult learners, such as gallery walks; of being relentless about self-assessment, goal setting, and reflection for adult learners; of creating modules or bite-sized professional development (PD); of encouraging collaboration amongst professional educators within districts and partnerships as well as across districts and partnerships; of growing leaders through widespread teacher leadership opportunities; and of embedding assessment literacy in new teacher orientation, mentoring, and evaluation.

Common Language and Vetted Resources

We recommend establishing clear common language and a set of common vetted resources as a first step in effective professional learning. Using precise common language helps clarify communication about the ideas—in this case assessment literacy. Common models, common readings, common tools, a common literature review, and a common base of evidence or research allow a starting place for all educators beyond their disparate background experiences. The idea here is not that educators have to adhere only to the common resources or models but that the resources ground or begin the collective professional learning. They provide a jumping-off place to applying the principles in concrete ways to different grade levels and content areas.

We began our own assessment literacy journeys, as mentioned in earlier chapters, a country apart from one another but both using the work of Rick Stiggins, Jan Chappuis, Steve Chappuis, and Judith Arter. Many years later, we still find their books an appropriate mix of research, theory, and practical examples. We have also been heavily influenced by the work of John Hattie, Ken O'Connor, Jay McTighe, and Grant Wiggins. As such, we begin our professional learning sessions using their work as common language for all participants. As the knowledge base becomes firm, we are then able to introduce other perspectives, scholars, practitioners, and tools into the mix with a way of thinking about and vetting ideas through a lens of practice and research.

We often begin our assessment literacy journeys with professional learning communities by sharing the following framing information:

> Essential concepts in assessment literacy for educators include: five keys of high-quality assessment (Chappuis, Stiggins, Chappuis, & Arter, 2012) accompanied by seven strategies of assessment for learning (Chappuis, 2015). We call this approach 5 + 7* = assessment literacy. Additional insights from Hattie's *Visible Learning for Teachers* (2012) will underscore the role of high-impact strategies for teaching, learning, and assessing and are represented by * as well as effect sizes (ES) laid over the assessment framework.
>
> Here are the desired learning outcomes of our professional learning:
>
> - I possess the knowledge and skills needed to (1) gather accurate information about student growth and achievement and (2) use the assessment process and its results effectively to improve growth and achievement.
> - I understand and can use the strategies of assessment for learning to ensure student growth and achievement for all of my students.

Educators will deepen their understanding of the five keys to quality classroom assessments as found in *Classroom Assessment for Student Learning* by Chappuis and colleagues (2012):

1. Clear learning targets
2. Clear assessment purposes
3. Sound design
4. Effective communication
5. Student involvement

Through immersive galleries, we share concrete examples, progressions, and takeaways for immediate application from the *Seven Strategies of Assessment for Learning* (Chappuis, 2015). Educators will deepen their understanding of the seven strategies of assessment for learning and apply the strategies to their own practices.

The seven strategies include the following:

Where am I going?
1. Clear learning targets
2. Models of strong and weak work with rubrics
Where am I now?
3. Timely, descriptive feedback that directly affects learning
4. Student self-assessment and goal setting
How do I close the gap? What are my strategies to get there?
5. Evidence of student learning to determine next steps
6. Focused practice and revision
7. Student self-reflection, tracking, and sharing learning and progress with others (e.g., peers)

See Figures 11.1 and 11.2 for examples of tables we have cocreated with professional learning communities to help consolidate our common reads and strategies or tools shared and being applied. Such tables provide a common reference point as we move deeper in our assessment literacy learning together.

Interactive and Immersive Learning Strategies

Another of the professional learning strategies we developed to teach assessment literacy to educators was that of an interactive gallery walk. The essential assessment literacy question we ask participants to consider during the gallery experience is this: How can you apply the strategies of assessment *for* learning and/or assessment *of* learning to your teaching practice in order to improve your students' learning?

With the development of participant examples, our gallery has grown and consists of over one hundred posters with accompanying interactive learning stations and spaces. Participants are encouraged to converse with colleagues as they explore the gallery and consider its applications to their practices. Learners are invited to apply the strategies and tools to their own contexts through "now you try" icons with hard copy and electronic templates and exemplars provided to aid the applications of the strategies. Participants travel with sticky notes and are encouraged to reflect and interact throughout the exhibit by responding to reflection prompts on posters along the way and/or in their gallery passports, which includes the following guiding reflection prompts for each of the seven strategies and five keys: "A question I have . . .," "I noticed . . .," and "One thing I would like to try . . ." Learners also have opportunities to self-assess about their current understanding and command of the 5 + 7 strategies using sticky dots on a series of self-assessment posters. Learners are encouraged to use their self-assessment results to establish next steps (goals) for their subsequent learning.

Some strategies, such as descriptive feedback, include hands-on self-expressive stations. In a descriptive feedback station, participants are asked to consider how they like to receive feedback during the learning process and choose two items from tables that symbolically represent those ideas. See Chapter 6 for a more complete description. Colleagues are encouraged to share their items and rationale with colleagues during the gallery walk. Additional stations include a book and article station for those who prefer to read more about particular classroom assessment concepts or strategies and a listening or viewing station that includes video clips specifically created for this professional learning purpose that further explain varied assessment literacy ideas.

FIGURE 11.1 ● Seven Strategies of Assessment for Learning—Common Language

Seven Strategies Self-Assessment

Directions: Reflect on the ways students are involved in and effectively communicate the seven strategies.

High-Impact Assessment for Learning Strategies	***Clear targets*** *(Teacher clarity and clear learning intensions) (ES = 0.75)*	***Success criteria; models of weak and strong student work with rubrics*** *(ES = 0.75)*	***Regular, descriptive feedback*** *and feed-forward (ES = 0.75)*	***Students self-assess*** *(ES = 0.69)* ***and set goals*** *(ES = 0.50)*	***Use evidence of student learning needs to select high-impact teaching strategies for next steps*** *(ES = 0.62)*	***Students practice focused revision, space versus mass practice*** *(ES = 0.71)*	***Self-reflection and self-questioning to monitor progress*** *(ES = 0.64),* ***work with peers*** *(ES = 0.55) and improve as a* ***self-regulated learner*** *(ES = 1.33)*
Strategies or Techniques: **Common Reads:** Chappuis, J., Stiggins, R., Chappuis, S., and Arter, J. (2012). *Classroom assessment for student learning.* Upper Saddle River, NJ: Pearson. Chappuis, J. (2015). *Seven strategies of assessment for learning*. Upper Saddle River, NJ: Pearson.	• Deconstructing standards into student-friendly learning targets • I can . . . this means • Learning progressions, such as Stars and Stairs or puzzle pieces and graphic displays • Concept mapping • *CASL*, Chapter 3 • *Seven Strategies*, Chapter 2	• Use of varied examples • Student-involvement in success criteria and rubric development • Use of weaker examples coupled with a think aloud of strengths and next steps (*CASL*, p. 150) • Use of formative rubrics (Next Steps Rubrics) • Use of summative rubrics • *CASL*, Chapters. 6–8 • *Seven Strategies*, Chapter 2	• Success and next steps feedback • Descriptive feedback based on success criteria/learning targets • Occurs during the learning • Three-minute conferences • Use of codes or symbols • Hold off on scoring/grading as long as possible • *CASL* pp. 30–31 • *Seven Strategies*, Chapter 3	• NSR • That's Great, Now This, or Stars and Stairs • Status, target, plan • Exit tickets • Two Stars and a Wish • Goal and Plan form • Growth mindset work • Goal orientations • *Seven Strategies*, Chapter 4	• Three Learning Needs = Partial understanding, flaws in reasoning, and misconceptions • Creating diagnostic selected response items with traction - item formulas - hinge questions (*CASL*, Chapter 5) • Agree-disagree pre-assessment (*CASL*, p. 33) • Misconception tables or charts • Review and analyze my results chart (right, wrong, fixable mistake, don't get it) • *Seven Strategies*, Chapter 5	• Use of graphic organizers to assist learners as they practice • Analysis practice opportunities to ensure they meet effective practice characteristics • Practice based on the targets and criteria identified as needs for learners • Time to act on feedback from practice before summative • *Seven Strategies*, Chapter 5	• Tracking forms by learning target • Tracking forms by assessment • Stars and Stairs with evidence • Peer review processes • Before and after reflection • I used to . . . Now I . . . Here's why and here's what I noticed • *Seven Strategies*, Chapter 6

Note: CASL = Classroom Assessment for Student Learning; NSR = Next Steps Rubrics; *Seven Strategies = Seven Strategies for Assessment for Learning.*

FIGURE 11.2 ● Five Keys to High-Quality Classroom Assessment—Common Language

Five Keys to High-Quality Classroom Assessment

Directions: Reflect upon your practice by self-assessing our mastery of each key.

	Five Keys	*Strategies or Techniques and Chapter Resources in CASL*
	Clear Learning Targets	Chapter 3; Seven Strategies, Chapter 2 • Deconstructing standards into student-friendly learning targets • "I can . . . this means" • Learning progressions, such as Stars and Stairs or puzzle pieces • Concept mapping
Purpose	**Clear Purpose, Balance of Assessment for and of Learning**	Chapter 2; Seven Strategies, Chapter 1 • Identification of key decisions and decision makers • Knowledge of the audience for the results • Understanding what kind and level of info is needed for users
	Sound Design—Backward (summative) and forward (formative)	Chapters 4–8 • Target-method match • Assessment blueprints • Use of a metarubric to assess quality of and/or design a rubric • Use of selected response guidelines—creating propositions and distractors • Use of performance task Next Steps Rubric (NSR)
	Effective Communication	Chapters 9–11 • Use of descriptive feedback (success and next steps) during learning • Communication regarding proficiency of particular standards and learning targets • Use of portfolios • Use of student-led conferences • Record keeping and tracking of student learning
ABC	**Assessment-Literate Learner (student involvement)**	Chapter 12 • Part of identifying success criteria and/or rubrics • Clear about the learning targets and what it means to achieve success • Self-assessment and goal setting for next steps • Tracking and reflection upon their learning • Creation of formative assessment items and prompts • Engagement in sharing learning with others—student-led conferences are one way

(J. Beaudry and A. Stewart McCafferty, 2016)

Another component of the interactive gallery walk is a feature we call pop-up sessions, an opportunity for participants to engage with presenters in mini lessons around specific strategies or tools, such as Next Steps Rubrics (NSRs), learning progressions, or concept mapping. Pop-up sessions generally last ten to fifteen minutes. Participants are invited to sign up for preestablished offerings and to add suggestions for topics as well. The pop-up sessions occur during the gallery walk and provide direct instruction for those who prefer that learning style.

To aid learners during and after the interactive gallery experience, we provide them with access to a host of resources, including a Google Drive with organized subfolders of supplemental materials. We also have created a virtual gallery experience using VoiceThread, where we have photographed the gallery and added narration, comments, and video clips. We invite gallery participants to use the virtual gallery as a tool for revisiting, extending the dialogue, and refreshing their learning over time. For more information about using interactive galleries as PD options, please see our article in *The Learning Professional* (Stewart McCafferty & Beaudry, 2017).

Another of the pedagogical strategies we employ, as we previously mentioned, is the use of Twitter and hashtags specific to the content or context to share the experience with participants' professional learning networks and also as a means to extend the conversation over time and beyond physical boundaries. During the gallery experience, we encourage educators to tweet their thoughts or share photos with others.

In design, we choose movement over sitting, sharing with colleagues over listening to experts, imagery over words, and short written reflections over no reflection. Based on feedback from participants, our gallery walk maximizes movement and interaction. We continually work on the organization to simplify the complex ideas and make them even more accessible to participants of varying comfort and prior knowledge of assessment literacy. Our aim is to demonstrate a differentiated approach to professional learning that places the professional educator in an active role, while providing human and material resources to facilitate each learner as he or she takes the next step in learning more about classroom assessment (or the given topic of the gallery experience). Educators deserve to engage in professional learning that models effective learning strategies in a "do as I do" manner, not a "do as I say" manner.

Once we began using the gallery walk as an immersion strategy for professional learning, the design process reflected our own growth and learning. By creating new posters and technology-rich add-ons, we added new ideas to the 5 + 7* = assessment literacy and synthesized existing concepts. The paper gallery is relatively easy to store, move, set up, and take down. The physical gallery adds an old-school feel to our cadre of professional learning strategies and helps create a 360-degree immersion of the topic of learning at hand. Coupled with technology and social media, the interactive immersion gallery walk creates a professional learning experience that employs sound principles of learning and provides an entry point for a plethora of interests, learning preferences, and professional growth.

One of the most powerful ways to begin interactive gallery walks is to have educators create a concrete example of their own or in collaboration with their colleagues of a particular aspect of assessment literacy to share with others. They then post their chart paper and circulate to see others' work. Finally, they are provided time to engage in discourse with their colleagues about what they saw, their thinking, and to develop next steps.

Self-Assessment, Goal Setting, and Reflection Tools and Strategies

As we examined in detail in Chapter 7, engaging in ongoing self-assessment, goal-setting activities, and periods of reflection are high-impact strategies and essential to creating lifelong learners. We believe in a relentless approach to strategies and tools designed to promote the development and use of these metacognitive strategies. See Figures 11.3, 11.4, 11.5, and 11.6 for additional examples.

Simplify Sources and Displays of Evidence (Quicker Prompts)

From the outset, the use of prompts for reflection with teachers has been a very effective practice. The 3-2-1 exit ticket prompt is often thorough enough and can be informative, but even its succinct nature may be too demanding for learners who struggle with writing. We are conscious of the demands of time in a PD setting. To make this efficient and effective, we have used many variations and have most success when we simply use a couple of prompts, such as the following:

- What is one thing you learned?
- What is one question you have?

FIGURE 11.3 ● Seven Strategies Self-Assessment

Seven Strategies Self-Assessment

Directions: Reflect on your assessment for learning practices by self-assessing.

	High-impact assessment for learning strategies	*I understand and am beginning to use the strategy.*	*I use it and can provide evidence or student work to show high-impact results.*	*I can link this strategy with other high-impact strategies, and here's how . . .*	*I have shared this strategy with other educators in my school or district.*
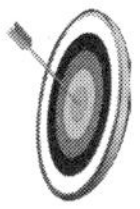	**Clear targets** (deconstructed, student-friendly, "I can . . . this means") (ES = 0.75)				
	**Models of weak and strong student work with rubrics** (ES = 0.57)				
	**Regular, descriptive feedback and feed-forward** (ES = 0.75)				
	**Self-assessment** (ES = 0.69) **and goal setting** (ES = 0.50)				
	**Evidence of student learning to select high-impact strategies** (ES = 0.62)				
 ABC	**Practice and focused revision** (ES = .71)				
	**Self-reflection and self-questioning to monitor progress** (ES = .64), **work with peers** (ES = 0.55), **and** improve as a **self-regulated learner** (ES = 1.33)				

(J. Beaudry and A. Stewart McCafferty, 2016)

FIGURE 11.4 ● Seven Strategies Reflective Prompts

	 *Clear Learning Targets*	 *Strong and Weak Examples With Rubrics*	 *Descriptive Feedback*	 *Self-Assessment and Goal Setting*	 *Instruction Based on Learning Needs Evidence*	 *Focused Practice and Revision Opportunities*	 *Self-Reflection, and Tracking and Sharing Progress*
What instructional techniques are you using for this strategy?							
How are you including students? How does this develop self-regulated or assessment-literate learners?							
How is assessment evidence increasing transparency? Communicated by teachers? Students?							

(J. Beaudry and A. Stewart McCafferty, 2016)

FIGURE 11.5 ● Assessment Literacy (Five Keys) Next Steps Rubric

Assessment Literacy (Five Keys) Next Steps Rubric

Standard: I possess the knowledge and skills needed to (1) gather accurate information about student growth and achievement and (2) use the assessment process and its results effectively to improve growth and achievement

What I Do Well	**Criteria** Five Keys to Quality Classroom Assessment **This Means . . .**	***What I Can Do Next*** ***I Will . . . This is How***
	1. Clear Purpose Assessment processes and results serve clear and appropriate purposes. *My assessments are designed to serve the specific information needs of intended user(s).*	
	2. Clear Targets Assessments reflect clear student learning targets. *My assessments are based on clearly articulated and appropriate learning targets.*	
	3. Sound Design Learning targets are translated into assessments that yield accurate results. *My assessments accurately measure student achievement.*	
	4. Effective Communication Assessment results function to increase student achievement. Results are managed well, combined appropriately, and communicated effectively. *My assessments yield results that are effectively communicated to their intended users.*	

What I Do Well ☆	**Criteria** Five Keys to Quality Classroom Assessment **This Means . . .**	*What I Can Do Next* *I Will . . . This is How*
	5. Student Involvement Students are active participants in the assessment process. *My assessments involve students in self-assessment, goal setting, tracking, reflecting on, and sharing their learning.*	

(Based on *Classroom Assessment for Student Learning* Rubric by: A. Stewart McCafferty and J. Beaudry, 2015 (Chappuis, Stiggins, Chappuis, & Arter, 2012)

Source: Adapted from Chappuis et al. (2012).

FIGURE 11.6 ● Sound Design Next Steps Rubric

Sound Design Next Steps Rubric

My assessments accurately measure student achievement.

Standard: Learning targets are translated into assessments that yield accurate results.

What I Do Well ☆	**Criteria** Sound Design **This Means . . .**	*What I Can Do Next* *I Will . . . This Is How*
	I know how to design or select assessments to serve intended formative and summative purpose.	
	I know how to select the appropriate method(s) to assess each type of learning target.	
	I create assessment plans to map the content of my assessment.	
	I understand and apply principles of sampling appropriately.	
	I can write and /or select assessment items, tasks, scoring guides, and rubrics that meet standards of quality.	
	I recognize and avoid sources of bias that can distort assessment results.	
	I know how to apply formative assessment practices within each assessment method.	

(Based on *Classroom Assessment for student Learning* (Chappuis, Stiggins, Chappuis, & Arter, 2012)

Rubric by: A. Stewart McCafferty and J. Beaudry, 2015

Source: Adapted from Chappuis et al. (2012).

Keeping the reflection prompts short and to the point allow educators to more fully engage with the reflection activity and also allow time for PD providers to analyze the data and provide feedback to participants. From a simple base of prompts, one can add an additional prompt about connections, collaboration, or leadership. We believe professional learning providers will see more participation with fewer prompts.

Input of data, as well as the analysis and communication (the output), is important. There are a number of ways to compile the responses; for instance, one might (1) read, interpret, and group the responses into themes and (2) take the responses to each of the questions and create a Wordle.

We took this idea of simplifying prompts one step further and began asking for one- to two-word responses to questions, asking similar questions in a pre- and postworkshop setting. The use of Wordles, or "word clouds" then gives you a tool to quickly summarize and display the data. For example, at the conclusion of a workshop on the need for balanced assessment, we asked teachers, "What one or two words come to mind when you think of assessment?" The responses are shown in Figure 11.7. Another strategy for the use of efficient pre- and postconference prompts and pre- and post-Wordles is shown in Chapter 12.

Another prompt asked teachers to use a word to describe themselves as a learner (see Figure 11.8). All data needs interpretation, and the strong emphasis on "visual" is a good example. To properly interpret this information, we had to go back to teachers to share the results and to ask them what they meant. Teachers told us that they need to see examples and to apply them to their own practice.

FIGURE 11.7 ● What Comes to Mind When You Think of Assessment? Wordle

FIGURE 11.8 ● Who Are You as a Learner? Wordle

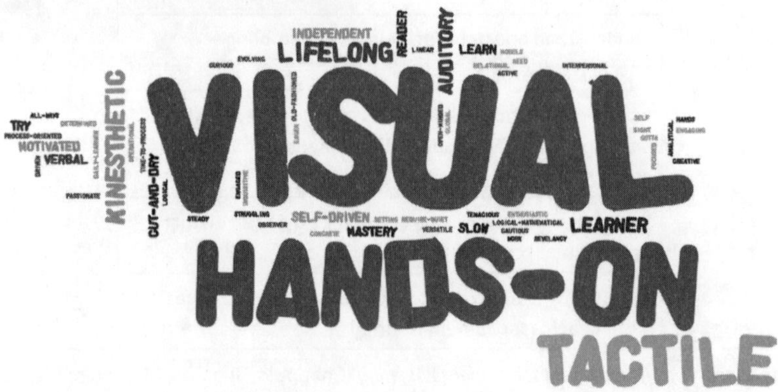

Use of Modules: Bite-Sized Professional Development

One of the professional learning strategies we have spent ample time developing, implementing, and revising is that of multimedia modules. Our investment in the creation of modules for educators, districts, and learning organizations originated from the repeated expressed need for ongoing assessment literacy PD that educators could take back to their teams, schools, and districts and use to learn with others. Districts and partnerships, such as Maine Center for Research in STEM Education (RiSE Center), Southern Maine Partnership (SMP), Penobscot River Educational Partnership (PREP), and Midcoast Superintendents' Association, contracted with us to develop and deliver ongoing full-day PD for educators. We found that in spite of participants' increased learning and application to their classroom or faculty settings, there was still a hesitancy or confusion about how to distill the ongoing intensive PD into appropriate bite-sized chunks for educators not involved in our assessment literacy professional learning experiences. The tendency was for districts and partnerships to still rely on us or other outside presenters to come to their individual settings to deliver the PD. As one of our foundational beliefs centers around promoting widespread teacher and administrator instructional leadership, we wanted to figure out a better way to empower and support educators as they took on the role of helping others become more assessment literate while they continued to become more assessment literate themselves.

We began taking our massive multimedia presentations used to accompany our PD and chunking it into smaller segments to meet the needs of various grade spans, content areas, and/or roles. We created all of our presentations in Google Drive and widely shared the presentations with any and all. We created massive collections of concrete examples of the various assessment literacy strategies, tools, and principles and housed them in Google Drive folders. Before long, this, too, became unwieldy for some educators to navigate due to the sheer volume of examples, although for others, these modules and folders of examples provided the needed boost to support districts in their efforts to help their educators become more assessment literate.

PRACTITIONER SPOTLIGHT 11.1

ASSESSMENT LITERACY MODULES

What?

Modules support the capacity building of assessment literacy staff attend out of district. The modules created by Anita and Jeff coupled with the extensive dine and discuss events and assessment conferences provide this multipronged support.

So What?

District leadership needs high-quality resources to develop and sustain assessment literacy. The impact of district work grows exponentially when the tools used are also the foundation of professional development (PD) opportunities that

Now What?

Districts can collaborate on the use of these tools and embed the continued learning regionally. It will take a sustained community focus on developing assessment literacy for the impact to show in student learning.

Source: Contributed by Anita Bernhardt, director of curriculum, instruction and assessment, York School Department.

By now, we had worked with the RiSE Center to support their assessment efforts for a couple of years. Under the directorship and leadership of Dr. Susan McKay, we began a project to tailor assessment for learning resources and PD specifically for STEM (science, technology, engineering, and mathematics). The modules were annotated with facilitator notes and complete with all the resources a teacher leader or administrator would need to engage other professionals in the learning experience. With the first year of assessment for learning modules under our belt, it was calculated that over 1,200 teachers had participated. Each module included adult-friendly learning principles, including ample opportunities to turn and talk, apply the strategy to their own setting through scaffolded guided practice, and then ongoing opportunities to try out the strategies in their own classrooms and schools and bring back their own implementation experiences to share and grow from.

Assessment for Learning (A4L) in STEM and Beyond is a multiyear PD program we created in collaboration with the RiSE Center professional learning community. The A4L program centered around one-hour modules created around an introduction to high-impact strategies and ten assessment for learning strategies (i.e., clear learning targets, effective feedback, self-assessment, goal setting, diagnosis of learner needs, effective practice, and reflection). The examples included in each module were purposefully created around Next Generation Science Standards (NGSS) from each grade span to illustrate the strategies and tools.

FIGURE 11.9 ● Overview of the Eleven Assessment for Learning in STEM and Beyond Modules

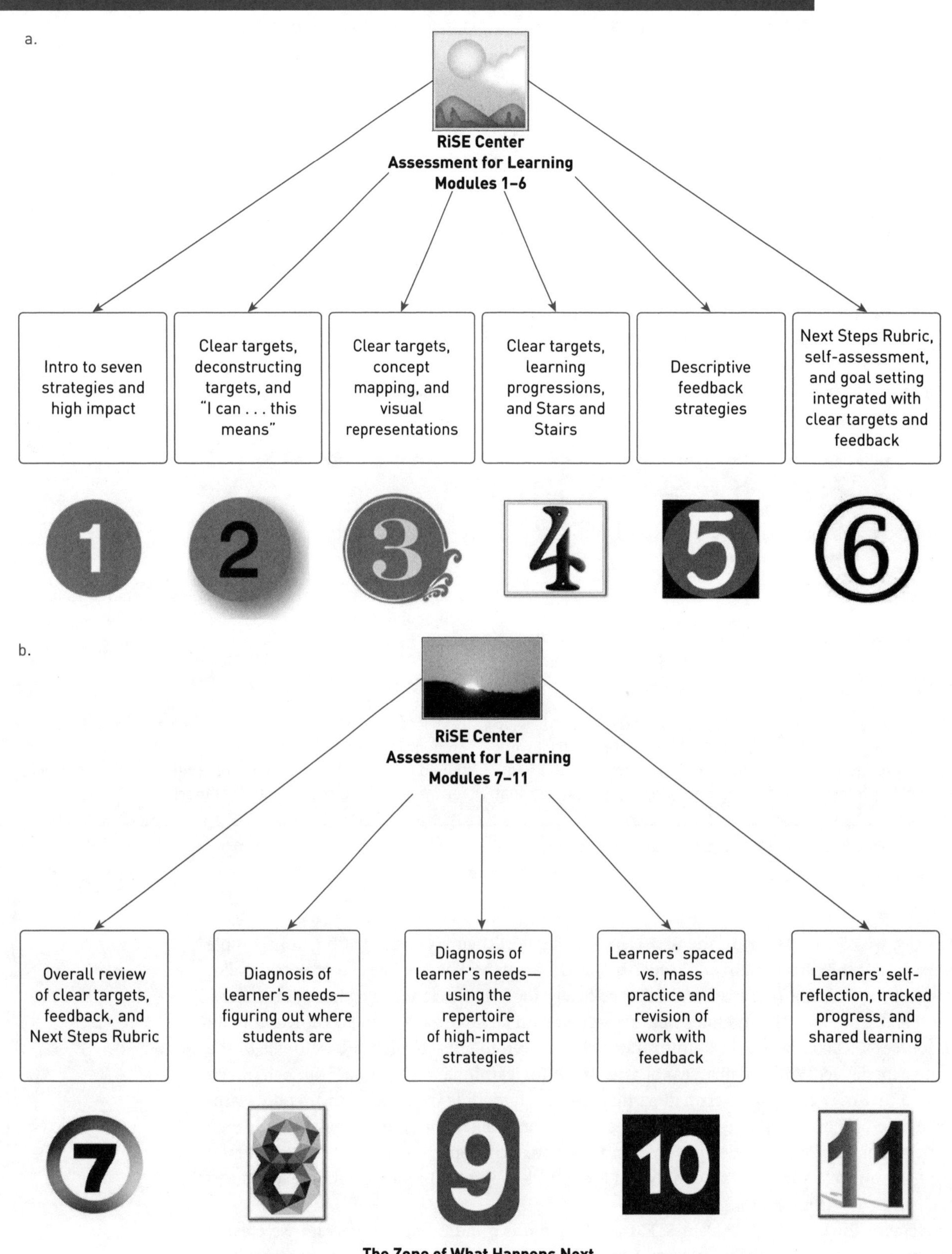

The A4L program followed a teacher-led facilitation model, where teacher leaders attended multiple professional learning sessions with us around A4L strategies, led regional cohort meetings where they taught the A4L strategies to other teacher leaders using modules we created and

examples they had tried in their classrooms. Then, all of the teacher leaders brought the modules back to their local colleagues in a study group format (one per module). The study group formats ranged in size and format from a single grade level or content area to an entire school or an entire district. Some study group formats were voluntary and open to any teacher who wished to attend, while other districts required mandatory involvement of all local educators.

The RiSE Center community has spent time in previous years building summative assessment aligned to curriculum. After surveying their community of practitioners and researchers, they decided to focus on assessment for learning strategies because of the positive impact on student achievement and because these strategies work across classrooms and curricula.

Note: RiSE = Maine Center for Research in STEM Education. The RiSE Center gratefully appreciates the support from the National Science Foundation Grant No. DRL-0962805 and the Maine Department of Education (MDOE) contracts CT20130724*0455, CT20140818*0620 and CT20150727*0363.

Grow Assessment-Literate Leaders Within and Outside of One's District and/or Partnership: Creating a Partnership of Partnerships

As previously mentioned in Chapter 2, in order for schools and districts to be effective learning organizations, there is a great need for widespread instructional leadership at all levels. See Practitioner Spotlight 11.2, written by Heather Rockwell, director of Curriculum for RSU 67, as she described their process for investing in the development of assessment-literate leaders, including their inclusion of classroom assessment "experts" and the gradual release of that expertise and leadership to leaders being grown within their district and region.

PRACTITIONER SPOTLIGHT 11.2

BUILDING INTERNAL ASSESSMENT-LITERATE LEADERSHIP CAPACITY

What?

We know that quality professional development (PD) is sustained over time. It provides educators with an opportunity to learn from experts, implement in the classroom, reflect individually and with colleagues, learn more to extend thinking and skill set, and continue to implement. If we believe this is quality PD, how do we do this in a way that works and makes sense? Another question is how do we build experts in our region so they can continue this reflective practitioner model with support from the experts but not dependence? Finally, how do we model as leaders quality learning that parallels what we would like to have in classrooms?

So What?

We decided to put into action what we knew worked for quality PD. We were blessed to have Dr. Anita Stewart McCafferty and Dr. Jeffrey S. Beaudry available as assessment experts to help us on the journey. We started with one cohort of teachers beginning the process of understanding quality assessment by meeting four or five full days during the year with our experts. They learned about quality assessment, implemented, reflected, and refined. We also had a district-wide day and a summer institute with our experts to build foundational understanding of quality assessment. A second cohort started that included other area schools after a year of foundational understanding was built. The first cohort continued to meet as a group with experts to learn more while also building their leadership skills by sharing out at workshops and staff meetings what they were learning. Both cohorts met on a regular basis to build skills and understanding, continuing to move forward.

Now What?

We now have an hour every week dedicated for teachers to learn, reflect, and work as teams to improve practice. We also have teacher leaders who are running assessment literacy professional learning community groups within their buildings and across the district to continue the learning. Our goal is to offer these teacher leaders continued PD to ask questions and continue to deepen their understanding. Our building and district leaders are also working to make sure our PD opportunities model quality teaching and learning.

Source: Contributed by Heather Rockwell, director of curriculum, RSU 67.

We also shared in Chapter 10 the importance of creating content-specific and grade-level specific professional learning opportunities. One of our missions as codirectors of SMP has been to create a partnership of partnerships around assessment literacy. In the absence of other statewide conveners, we have found it to be crucial to help grow assessment-literate leaders within schools and districts, within specific learning organizations, but even more powerful is the collective efficacy when these schools, districts, organizations, and regional partnerships come together to collectively share their understandings, resources, examples, and tools. It is often difficult for individual schools or districts to dedicate resources to appropriately support and grow assessment-literate leaders on their own. We believe districts like RSU 67 and MSAD 6 are among the minority. By tapping into other partnerships outside of school districts, as well of course as within their school districts, school organizations can more effectively capitalize on the limited human and material resources available to provide ample opportunities for educators to grow as leaders. The Maine Arts Assessment Initiative (MAAI) is one example of a statewide partnership's journey to grow assessment-literate teacher leaders in the arts and to equip them to facilitate professional learning regionally and locally. See Practitioner Spotlight 11.3 for a detailed dive into the MAAI approach to growing teacher leaders.

PRACTITIONER SPOTLIGHT 11.3

THE MAINE ARTS ASSESSMENT INITIATIVE

What?

In 2011, a leadership team was formed to address the role of visual and performing arts teachers in the era of standards-based education. Representatives on the team were full-time teachers from all grade levels, across the visual and performing arts, a university professor with background in classroom assessment, the director of an institute for arts educators, and the lead educator in visual and performing arts from the Maine Department of Education (MDOE). The purpose was to address several issues and ultimately to form a grassroots organization of arts educators to develop knowledge and skills in assessment, creativity, technology, and leadership. The result was the inception of the Maine Arts Assessment Initiative (MAAI). Assessment was one of four foci areas; leadership, creativity, and technology were the others.

Initial resistance to the emphasis on assessment was a concern. In order to provide a positive context, we used three essential questions to ensure that assessment would not be an isolated goal: (1) What is good teaching? (2) What is good learning? (3) What is good assessment?

So What?

Arts teachers from all across the state applied to be part of the MAAI, and a balanced number were selected to represent visual and performing arts and all geographic regions in the state. Each year, a new set of teachers was added to the initiative. The implementation of MAAI, since August 2011, has taken place in four parts: (1) a three-day summer institute with the initial ideation and design of workshops by teachers on an assessment topic of their own choosing, (2) independent work, (3) a structured, "critical friends" formative assessment of the workshop as a practice session with an authentic audience of arts educators who provided feedback and peer assessment, and (4) presentation of the MAAI workshop with online survey feedback from participants. See Figure 11.10.

Since the first summer institute in August 2011, there have been five more cohorts of arts educators. Participants must apply to join and are selected to maintain representation from all arts disciplines, visual and studio arts, music, dance, and theater. Currently, over 75 arts educators have joined the organization and have been directly involved in leading 150 arts-focused workshops, 6 summer institutes, over 35 regional conferences, and 2 national conferences.

On one hand, teachers accepted their role as leaders in the instruction of creativity and creative thinking. On the other hand, one third of the teachers indicated that their classroom assessment was not aligned with state standards. The surveys indicated that teachers reported that they were familiar with and used rubrics. However, both visual and performing arts teachers were less likely to include students in the development and use of rubrics.

One teacher summed up her leadership experience:

> I have already had to do a presentation informally. With the positive feedback that I got from that, I am looking forward to two more opportunities to share what I am doing in my classroom. The first workshop that I will present will be for music educators in January and the mega-regional workshop will be for arts teachers and will be held in Pointe Isle in March. This has already given me the courage to try even more things in my classroom, and I am looking forward to sharing it with others so that they know assessment doesn't have to be overwhelming and can still be managed without taking away from anything that is already being done for assessments.

Assessment may not be sexy, but it is an empowering focal point for creative collaborative group work.

FIGURE 11.10 ● Design Process for the Maine Arts Assessment Initiative Workshops

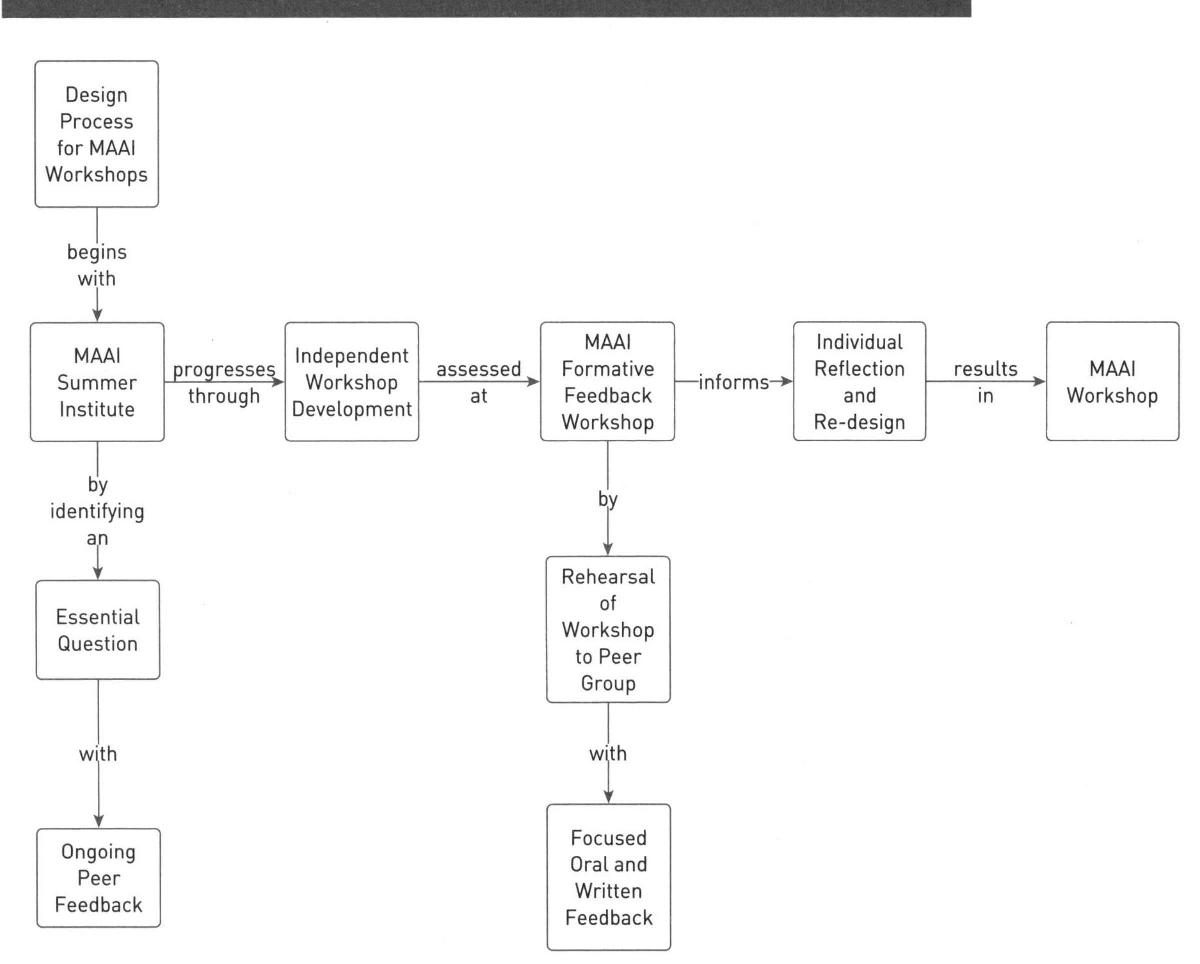

Source: Beaudry, Ritz-Swain, and Nestor (2015).

Now What?

While the work continues with the same pattern of grassroots PD, there have been several big changes. The teacher leaders voiced their readiness to embrace a new mission, and in 2015, the name of the organization there changed to Maine Arts Leadership Initiative (MALI). The areas of emphasis have remained the same—leadership, creativity, assessment, and technology—and a new emphasis, integration of the arts, was added. The aim was to integrate the arts with science, technology, engineering, and mathematics and take STEM to STEAM and beyond.

MALI has given arts educators a working group to understand policy initiatives like teacher evaluation. Several arts educators took on this challenge, and used their knowledge of high-quality assessment and evidence to create examples of their practices and share them in workshops. Some responses to the workshops called this convergence of assessment policy with classroom practice a sweet spot, a place where their work in assessment could be applied directly to professional expectations.

The cycle of PD and workshop development continues and now extends to a new membership group, a community of teaching artists. By adding teaching artists to their membership, MALI has taken on new challenges to communicate the needs of schools for proficiency-based education. The expectations for high-quality teaching, learning, and assessment now are being seen from this new perspective.

Source: Contributed by Argy Nestor, director of arts education, Maine Arts Commission; Sarah Ritz-Swain, curriculum coordinator, Connecticut; and Jeffrey S. Beaudry, author.

Finding the Sweet Spot: Embed Assessment Literacy Into Other Professional Development Initiatives: It *Is* the Plate!

In order to more effectively create assessment-literate educators, assessment literacy must be positioned within other district initiatives, such as the teacher evaluation system, new teacher orientation, the mentoring of new educators, induction programs, proficiency-based education, content-specific programs, curriculum reviews, data literacy initiatives, building intervention and enrichment blocks, and so on. By doing so, the idea that assessment literacy skills are foundational competencies important for all educators to possess and hone is solidified. After all, assessment literacy is a key component of learning and teaching.

Introduction to the Assessment for Learning Program in STEM and Beyond Project

Placing Assessment for Learning in Context

As a flavor of how we organized this project, here is the introductory video transcript where we try to place the professional development (PD) within the current context or landscape of education within our state. We believe that effective instructional leaders synthesize initiatives and help their educators understand how the PD meets multiple initiatives. In other words, it is not another thing to add to the educator's plate.

> Hello, this is Dr. Jeffrey Beaudry and Dr. Anita Stewart McCafferty from the Educational Leadership program at the University of Southern Maine. On behalf of the Maine Center for Research in STEM Education (RiSE Center), please let us welcome you to this series of exciting professional learning opportunities centered around honing educators' assessment literacy skills, specifically those around assessing for learning (e.g., formative assessment) strategies. We are excited to share the key components of the seven strategies portion of the 5 + 7* = assessment literacy framework. These assessment for learning strategies are well grounded in evidence from empirical research as well as validated by the practice of thousands of professionals like yourselves interested in improving their assessment literacy skill sets in order to positively affect student learning.
>
> The assessment for learning strategies you will practice during these modules and most importantly in your classrooms subsequently are fundamental to sound design of summative assessment, especially those focused on clear learning targets. Most importantly, these are the very instructional strategies or 'teacher moves' that propel student learning forward toward and beyond proficiency of essential learning standards. Assessment literacy is foundational to the successful implementation of any proficiency-based system.
>
> While much of assessment literacy focus, time, energy, and resources over the past decade have been spent on designing backward by building summative assessments (e.g., tasks, rubrics, selected response tests, written prompts, scoring guides), less time has been spent on designing forward using high-impact strategies of assessment for learning. The summative (i.e., the measurement) has trumped the formative (i.e., the "during the learning"). Empirical evidence strongly suggests that strategies of assessment for learning is where students see great gains in their learning *not* from taking summative assessments. These modules provide a more balanced approach to assessment literacy.
>
> The strategies we will share with you are the same strategies that you will see incorporated in all of the effective educator evaluation models (e.g., Marzano, Danielson Group, Marshall, and the Maine Schools for Excellence initiative). This is not coincidental. These strategies are widely recognized as crucial elements of any effective teaching framework. We encourage educators to explore how these modules support teacher evaluation goals; the links between clear learning targets or objectives, tracking student progress, and feedback are explicit within the frameworks and these modules.

Assessment for learning strategies promote the development of assessment-literate learners, and this means they will have increased motivation, engagement, and skills to monitor their own progress toward meeting high proficiency standards.

Thank you for being teacher leaders! We are always inspired and awed by the immense talent and dedication of Maine educators to improve not only their own crafts and profession but also their dedication to our learners. Thank you for taking time to share in this learning opportunity. We encourage you, as Dr. John Hattie exhorts, to know thy impact! The approaches you make to teaching, learning, and assessment do matter!

Conclusion

In this chapter, we shared some of our "best bets" for engaging educators in high-impact professional learning experiences designed to improve their understanding and skill sets around assessment literacy. Establish a common language and share vetted high-quality resources with your professional learning communities. Share and cocreate concrete examples of assessment for learning strategies in action. These examples should represent various content areas and grade spans. Create interactive and immersive learning experiences for adult learners, such as gallery walks. Be relentless about self-assessment, goal setting, and reflection for adult learners. Provide a variety of tools and allocate adequate time for learners to thoughtfully complete the self-assessments or reflections. Revisit goal setting periodically to determine next steps and celebrate successes. Create (or use existing) bite-sized PD opportunities to promote ongoing PD tied to applying strategies to the classroom. One such bite-sized PD is multimedia modules. We encourage you to borrow from those we have cocreated with our partners or begin to create your own. Either way, the goal is to layer in small chunks of learning over time. Encourage collaboration amongst professional educators within districts and regional or state partnerships as well as across districts and partnerships. Such collaboration efforts should help grow leaders through widespread teacher leadership opportunities. Use a variety of collaboration strategies, such as Edcamp-style PD, screen share tools, working conferences, social media sharing spaces, and educator-created and educator-led workshops.

Take a Deep Dive to Further Your Understanding

- Dive into our Assessment for Learning modules.
- Visit the Maine Arts Assessment Initiative (MAAI): https://www.maineartsassessment.com.
- Explore the Maine STEM Parnership at the Maine Center for Research in STEM Education (RiSE Center) website: https://sites.google.com/a/maine.edu/maine-stem-partnership/?pli=1.

12 Assessing Student Growth and Teacher Effectiveness

FIGURE 12.1 ● Foundational Skills for Sound Assessment of Student Growth and Proficiency

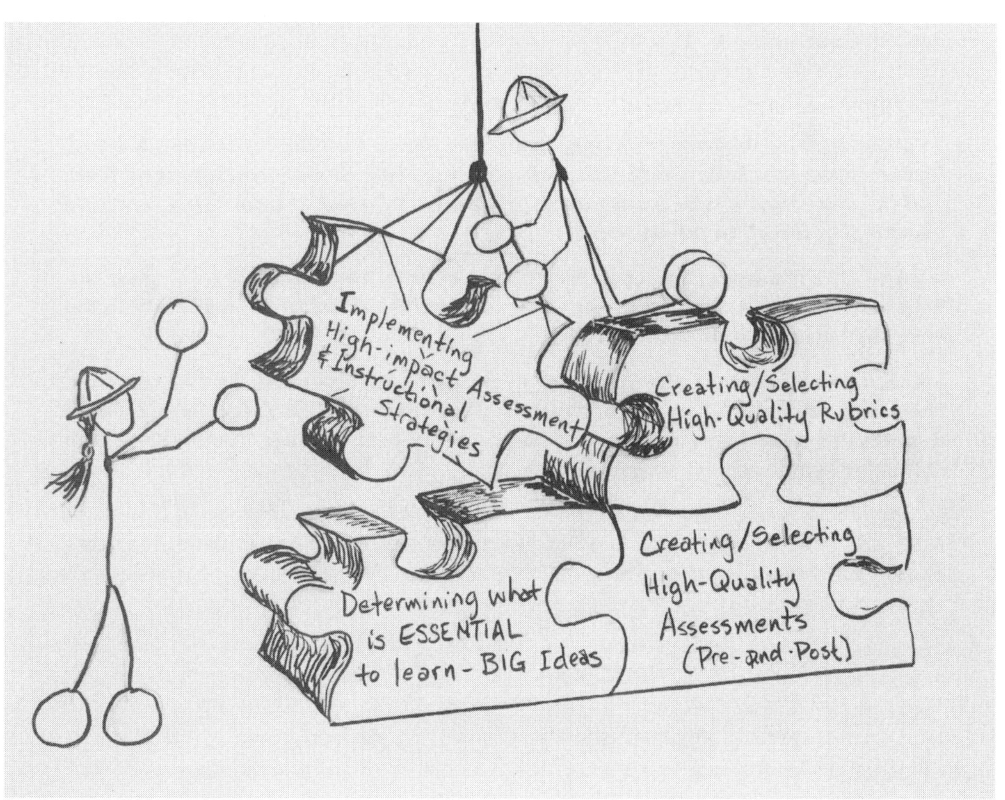

Key Takeaways

The first step in developing sound assessments for purposes of demonstrating student growth and/or proficiency is to carefully consider what is most essential for students to know and be able to do as a result of the particular course of

(Continued)

(Continued)

study. Educators should focus upon enduring understandings (big ideas), transformational goals, and standards of priority—those standards necessary for students to be successful at the next level of their educational journey or outside our school walls.

Developing the rubric and scoring criteria with clearly defined levels of student performance is essential to the process.

Keys for creating high-quality assessments are the same for preassessments as they are for postassessments.

At this stage in the process, an educator can administer the preassessment to help determine students' baseline with regard to the identified standards of priority. Consider students' strengths and weaknesses and how best to help them grow toward proficiency and/or beyond. Strong data literacy is necessary for all educators in order to accurately analyze collected data or evidence.

Formative assessment strategies and descriptive feedback during the learning process are key to student learning and achievement. The emphasis needs to be on the use of formative strategies, not just formative practice for the summative assessment.

Identifying high-impact instructional strategies for use in teaching students the standards and enduring understandings is an essential next step in creating learning experiences for students.

Educators are ready to attribute growth targets, attainable yet stretch targets, to their students. Establishing a version of SMART (specific, measurable, attainable, results-focused and realistic, and time-bound) goals as one's approach to the student learning outcome (SLO) process is a logical way to approach the task of determining growth targets.

In order for the student growth measure or SLO to become more than a hoop, leaders must carefully craft the message, the professional development (PD), and the conversations to focus on the "right work," that of improving learning experiences for *all* of our students.

Goal setting is a high-impact strategy, and as such, the SLO or SMART goal can be a process that assists educators in realizing the mission to positively influence the learning of *all* students.

Focus on the heart of the iterative cycle of learning—plan, assess, instruct, check for understanding, adjust instruction, intervene, differentiate, reteach as needed, extend learning, etc. Without a state or federal mandate, this is still the heart of what educators need to be doing.

When teachers are able to collaborate on the student growth or SLO process (including the foundational pieces), the structure of the professional learning community, team, or group may act to facilitate the growth of educators and students alike.

In education, we are no strangers to the idea of assessing student growth. In fact, many of us have long advocated for more of an emphasis to be placed upon growth as opposed to only on mastery or proficiency. Celebrating growth embraces the idea of taking each student from where she or he is now and helping each one progress further along the continuum or learning progression. Myopically focusing on proficiency sends unintended messages to learners. One demotivating message conveyed to struggling learners is that the proficiency goal is unattainable and is too far out of reach. Progress toward proficiency still results in failure to "meet the standard," and a sense of hopelessness sets in about falling further and further behind the yearly proficiency measures in spite of the progress made. An equally faulty and demotivating message sent to the able student is that proficiency or mastery is the endgame. In doing so, it de-emphasizes "drive" and the need to push one's self to grow beyond meeting the standard (emphasizing breadth over depth). The goal seemingly becomes to "collect" as many proficiency standards as one can in the shortest amount of time possible.

The inclusion of student growth as a significant factor in teacher evaluation systems forces the conversation into the arena of assessing student growth and attributing that growth to teacher performance. While there are many challenges associated with this notion of factoring student growth into an educator's effectiveness rating score, there are also many opportunities. In order to realize a positive impact on student learning, school or organizational culture, and teacher quality, systems must avoid pitfalls. Be assured that requirements around the student growth component of teacher evaluation are fraught with pitfalls!

In Maine, student growth as a significant factor in each district's teacher and school administrator evaluation plan was adopted into law and requires that teachers use a pre-post test model and not use norm-referenced or standardized tests exclusively in determining student growth for any educator. The model provided by the Maine Department of Education (MDOE) for addressing the student growth component of the teacher evaluation system is the student learning outcome (SLO) model adopted from the Teacher Incentive Fund schools and Maine Schools for Excellence work. The SLO handbook provided is closely aligned to the National Board framework, as adapted by the Maine Schools for Excellence. The SLO template provided by the MDOE asks for teachers to identify learning needs of their students, administer a pretest, determine appropriate growth projections for each student, teach the instructional unit, administer the posttest, and calculate whether or not individual students met her or his growth targets. As a state in its infancy of the creation of locally designed pre-post assessments for each teacher in every content area, one major issue with the SLO model is the growth projection for each student. Based upon what? Voodoo magic? A complicated guessing game? A mathematical formula derived from other assessments? We are concerned that angst around how to accurately determine appropriate growth for each student growth goal coupled with concerns about how miscalculating growth projections or goals may be used punitively against educators. This may derail the potential benefits of professionals (1) creating SMART growth goals around worthy understandings and skills, (2) looking at evidence of student learning, (3) considering the instructional strategies used, (4) analyzing the effectiveness of the assessment tools and methods used, and (5) establishing next steps in their professional learning to help current and future students improve achievement.

Overview of Foundational Skills for Sound Assessment of Student Growth and Proficiency

The first step in developing sound assessments for purposes of demonstrating student growth and/or proficiency is to carefully consider what is most essential for students to know and be able to do as a result of the particular course of study. Much of Chapter 2 focused on that concept. Educators should focus upon enduring understandings (big ideas), transformational goals, and standards of priority—those standards necessary for students to be successful at the next level of their educational journey or outside our school walls. Please note that the step of identifying priority standards and enduring understandings is the prerequisite to creating or selecting high-quality assessments *not* vice versa.

Once these standards or learning targets have been identified (preferably by not only grade level or content area teachers but agreed upon by the vertical teams), matching learning targets with the appropriate assessment methods or means for gathering evidence is key. The assessment task(s) created or selected needs to accurately assess the learning goals or big ideas chosen (validity).

Developing the rubric and scoring criteria with clearly defined levels of student performance is essential to the process. When considering multiple pathways to demonstrating growth and achievement, the rubric or scoring guide becomes increasingly more essential. The assessments and scoring tools need to be high quality: aligned, reliable for scoring, fair and unbiased (Center for Assessment, 2013). Please see the Next Steps Rubric (NSR) tools in Chapter 11 (Figures 11.5 and 11.6) for assistance in determining the quality of designed or selected rubrics.

Keys for creating high-quality assessments are the same for preassessments as they are for post-assessments. Preassessments should not be confused with the informal pretests often used before a unit of instruction begins to determine students' background knowledge, interests, or skills. Typical unit pretests are not rigorously aligned fully to the standards. For instance, often tools such as KWLs (a graphic organizer designed to help students identify what they already **k**now about a topic, what they **w**ant to learn about a topic, and after the unit of study is completed what they have **l**earned) are used for purposes of activating students' prior knowledge and considering how a teacher might need to differentiate based on students' prior exposure of the content or skills associated with the unit of study. In order to determine student growth accurately, the preassessment needs to adequately measure students' proficiency of the identified priority standards and big ideas and have a well-articulated scoring guide or rubric (usually the scoring tool one will also use for the postassessment).

At this stage in the process, an educator can administer the preassessment to help determine students' baseline with regard to the identified standards of priority. Consider students' strengths and learning needs and how best to help them grow toward proficiency and/or beyond. Strong data literacy is necessary for all educators in order to accurately analyze collected data or evidence. When done well, this preassessment process places the teacher and leader as action researchers, hypothesizing and investigating how best to help *all* of their students find success relative to the essential learnings identified. Hattie's (2012) research identifies this process of formative evaluation, namely teachers engaging in action research, as a high-impact strategy for improving teaching and positively influencing student learning (effect size, or ES = 0.90). Please see Chapter 2 for further information on high-impact instructional leadership strategies positively associated with improving teaching and learning.

Rarely does student learning and growth occur by accident, although certainly there are students who grow without our assistance or in unfortunate cases, in spite of us. Research tells us (as does experience) that formative assessment strategies and descriptive feedback during the learning process are key to student learning and achievement. The emphasis is on the use of formative strategies, not just formative practice for the summative assessment.

PAUSE AND REFLECT

- How will you monitor student progress during the learning and use formative assessment evidence and strategies to inform and adjust instruction?
- In other words, how will you intervene during the learning process?

Identifying high-impact instructional strategies for use in teaching students the standards, enduring understandings, and transformational goals is an essential next step in creating learning experiences for students. Please see Table 3.1 in Chapter 3 for further detail in considering high-impact instructional strategies. *Visible Learning for Teachers* (Hattie, 2012) and *Classroom Instruction That Works* (Dean, Hubbell, Pitler, & Stone, 2012) are strong sources for considering high-impact instructional strategies.

Finally, educators are ready to attribute growth targets, attainable yet stretch targets, to their students. Establishing a version of SMART goals as one's approach to the SLO process is a logical way to approach the task of determining growth targets. Let us speak frankly; the first time a teacher or group of teachers administer pre– and post–classroom-based assessments, this process is much like voodoo math! We are making our best guesses as to what might be appropriate growth targets. Ultimately, the goal should be to grow every one of our students as much as we possibly can. There is always room for improvement and growth. The effective educator and leader embrace the concepts of a growth mindset and continuous improvement and assist their students and staff in their growth to proficiency (or effectiveness in the case of teachers) and beyond. Once student work or performance evidence is collected, educators can refine the assessments, scoring tools, and growth expectations for previous iterations of the process. Figure 12.2 shows a student growth goal template we often use with educators.

FIGURE 12.2 • Student Growth Goal Template

Teacher Information:
Student Population:
Time Frame:
Standard(s) or Learning Target(s) to Assess:
Assessment(s) Used:
Student Baseline Data: **Baseline Results From Preassessment(s):**
Student Growth Targets:
Instructional and Formative Assessment Strategies Based on High-Impact Strategies:

A. Stewart McCafferty, 2016

For the past several years, we have largely left the topic of formulas for determining growth targets to others with the exception of one caveat; it troubles us when assessment philosophies do not match. For instance, if your district is operating on a standards grading scale or if your teachers are assessing using a rubric (e.g., a four-point scale), why would you promote your teachers using a traditional one-hundred-point scale for pre- and postassessments and the determination of student growth targets? Such practices are philosophically incompatible and underscore the hooplike nature of the SLO. Some states advocate a philosophically compatible four-point model for growth targets. We encourage systems to consider options other than just those proposed in a state SLO guidebook to ensure that there are no discrepancies within your messaging of sound assessment and the communication or reporting of assessment results. We have composed a philosophically compatible SLO and growth target formula; please see the chapter appendix for a concrete social studies example. Ultimately, whatever method districts use to determine student growth targets, they should be defensible and compatible with the district's philosophy and understanding of best practices in sound design of assessments. See Figure 12.3 as an example of one way to approach determining growth targets based on moving X percent of students from one performance level to the next.

In order for the student growth measure or SLO to become more than a hoop, leaders must carefully craft the message, the professional development (PD), and the conversations to focus on the "right work"—that of improving learning experiences for *all* our students. Improving teaching is in the service of positively influencing student learning. The SLO will fall flat at best and be demotivating and burdensome, detracting from the enterprise of helping our students learn at higher and higher levels in many other cases if the following foundational steps are not attended to as the heart of the work: (1) identifying priority or essential standards and big ideas, (2) creating or selecting high-quality assessments (pre and post), (3) creating or selecting high-quality scoring

FIGURE 12.3 ● Four-Point Student Growth Template

4-Point Philosophically-Compatible Student Growth Template

Teacher Information:

Student Population:

Time Frame:

Standard(s) or Learning Target(s) to Assess:

Assessment(s) Used:

Student Baseline Data:

Baseline Results From Preassessment(s):

Performance Level	4	3	2	1
# of Students				

Student Growth Targets:

The growth target established is for a minimum of X% of students from each of the baseline performance Levels 1, 2, and 3 to grow to the next performance level by xx/xx/xxxx.

Growth Targets:

Performance Level	4	3	2	1
# of Students				

Instructional and Formative Assessment Strategies Based on High-Impact Strategies:

A. Stewart McCafferty, 2015

guides and rubrics, and (4) focusing on implementing high-impact assessment for learning and instructional strategies during the learning cycle. We are convinced that if these aforementioned criteria are the focus of the work of teachers and leaders, growth and proficiency (effectiveness) will become the logical outcomes.

Once the foundational pieces are in place and the assessment and instructional strategies are piloted, setting student growth goals takes on meaning. Goal setting is a high-impact strategy; as such, the SLO or SMART goal can be a process that assists educators in realizing the mission to positively influence the learning of *all* students. Refer to Chapter 7 for more information on goal setting. Skipping the foundational steps—for example, the building blocks of effective instruction—and rushing to complete a SLO template or SMART goal will likely lead to increased confusion, frustration, resentment, and anxiety, none of which positively influences learning for anyone (educator, leader, or student). In those cases, the SLO is a hoop with little hope of improving student learning or teacher effectiveness. Without valid measurements of worthy content (e.g., the big ideas and essential standards), the potential of the goal-setting form is lost.

In 2015, we hosted a one-day conference convening educators in our state to discuss and showcase positive ways educators and systems could approach assessing student growth as part of educator effectiveness. Upon entering the conference, we asked participants to share a word or two that described how they were feeling about assessing student growth for purposes of teacher and principal evaluation. The results from over 200 teachers and administrators are portrayed in the Wordle in Figure 12.4. Upon completing only one day of professional learning where the focus was on learning, high-impact teaching, and using goal setting and assessment evidence to help us improve teaching and learning in meaningful ways, we asked participants as part of their exit ticket to once again identify one or two words that represented how they now were feeling about assessing student growth. Figure 12.5 portrays in Wordle format the results. The difference in feeling from the start of the day to the end of the day is quite startling and for us a potent reminder of the importance of focusing on the things that matter even

FIGURE 12.4 • Preconference Wordle

FIGURE 12.5 • Postconference Wordle

with the most contentious of topics. It also reminds us of the necessity of paying attention to and validating the feelings of learners as a crucial part of teaching and learning. Angry, resentful, fearful learners often have a difficult time learning, especially when their feelings are not attended to in visible and overt ways.

Our recommendation is for schools and districts to pour resources (e.g., human, financial, PD, time, energy, intellectual capital) into building a comprehensive assessment goal or plan per educator (or team of educators teaching the same content or grade level). Focus on the heart of the iterative cycle of learning—plan, assess, instruct, check for understanding, adjust instruction, intervene, differentiate, reteach as needed, extend learning, and so on. Without a state or federal mandate, this is still the heart of what educators need to be doing. For *all* students. In *every* classroom. In *every* school. No excuses.

When teachers are able to collaborate on the student growth or SLO process (including the foundational pieces), the structure of the professional learning community, team, or group may act to facilitate the growth of educators and students alike. Sadly, professional learning communities often do not fulfill their promises or potential. Some common challenges are dysfunctional group dynamics, varying levels of facilitation skill sets, and/or a lack of clarity of how to use the time well to improve teaching in ways that positively influence student learning. A wise Instructional Rounds facilitator recently relayed that in the absence of focus, professional learning communities often fall into the trap of B.S. (e.g., **b**ook **s**tudies, **b**aby **s**howers). Focusing on student growth goals and working collaboratively to improve learners' results can be an antidote to the B.S. trap of which professional learning communities often fall prey.

Assessing What Matters Most in Social Studies-Historical Thinking Example: A Case Study in Student Growth Models

When considering how to assess student growth in a pre-post test scenario, it is tempting to jump straight to an already existing assessment such as a unit project or exam, a midterm or final exam, or a purchased or mandated assessment, and so on, without first taking time as to ask yourself, of which essential skills, processes, and/or conceptual understandings is it necessary for my students to demonstrate growth? To skip over the examination of curricula is a lost opportunity to carefully consider which of the standards or skill sets are most essential for students' success in future courses or real-world applications. This essential question is best answered by a group of colleagues teaching the same content area to the same grade level or learning progression level of students. The process of wrestling with this essential question with one's colleagues has potential to be powerful in and of itself. To answer this question sufficiently, one has to be intimately aware of, and in tune with, one's standards, curriculum map, or progression of units of instruction throughout the year.

In order to illustrate this process, let us consider a typical eighth-grade social studies curriculum—the history of the United States from the 1800s to present day. When Anita left the classroom a few short years ago, this was her teaching assignment. To answer the essential questions of which essential skills, processes, and/or conceptual understandings are necessary for her students to demonstrate growth, she considered her curriculum map and her standards. See Figure 12.6 in the appendix.

What emerged from our close examination of Anita's curriculum map and deep conversations with her colleagues is the importance of historical thinking—a concept within the field that encompasses sourcing (primary and secondary), use of evidence, historical knowledge, contextualization, and corroboration. Conveniently, historical thinking is a major concept within the field of social studies as well as within the Social Studies Standards Maine Learning Results and the Common Core State Standards Initiative for history. See Figure 12.7 in the appendix.

For purposes of creating a content-specific concrete example of how to use principles of clear targets, sound design, high-impact instructional strategies, and the strategies of assessing formatively and summatively, she chose to focus her eighth-grade social studies curriculum around helping students improve their abilities to think historically, namely to accurately source, corroborate, and contextualize as well as to accurately summarize complex informational "texts."

Through the various units of U.S. history from pre–Civil War to present day, Anita provided learners with numerous opportunities to improve their historical thinking skills while gaining historical knowledge and to improve their skills in summarizing complex informational texts. The priority standards identified for historical thinking are closely aligned to the Common Core State Standards Initiative for history as well as the MLR (E. 1 Historical Knowledge, Concepts, Themes, and Patterns).

The Chapter 12 appendix leads you briefly through the process of examining Anita's unit-based curriculum map and considering what is most essential for students to know and be able to do. She shares her process for deconstructing standards around historical thinking and summarizing and shows how she converted them into student-friendly language and guiding essential questions. The example also depicts the self-peer-teacher assessment tools (i.e., NSRs, the Stars and Stairs approach, and other goal-setting forms) as well as documents to track progress. Anita also shares one rubric created by the sixth-grade English language arts curriculum team at Ashland Middle School in Oregon. The rubric used for scoring corroboration and contextualization comes from the Assessment Resource Center for History (ARCH). The rubrics are to be used for summative purposes. You can find various assessment tasks to be used both formatively and summatively at Beyond the Bubble from the Stanford History Education Group (n.d.). Anita also created a student growth goal for both historical thinking and summarizing shown at the beginning of the example.

Conclusion

As we hope one will realize, the student growth goal, or SLO, is not the foundation or the magic bullet for improving student learning and achievement. The establishing of rigorous essential priority standards and the development of an assessment evidence plan (involving preassessments, during the learning checks, and postassessments) coupled with high-impact instructional strategies is the foundation. The SLO can become essentially a SMART goal firmly grounded on a strong foundation of assessment and instructional strategies with tools used to document baseline, growth targets, and the outcomes. This middle school historical thinking example represents the kind of extensive assessment work an educator needs to do to establish and realize student growth toward proficiency and beyond.

From the following documents, we attempt to demonstrate how an educator can use sound assessment processes to document both proficiency and student growth.

Take a Deep Dive to Further Your Understanding

- Read James Popham's article "Can Classroom Assessments of Student Growth Be Credibly Used to Evaluate Teachers?" at http://www.ncte.org/library/NCTEFiles/Resources/Journals/EJ/1031-sep2013/EJ1031Can.pdf.
- Examine the "full attainment" model from AchieveNJ: Teach, Lead, Grow: Student Growth Objectives. New Jersey's approach to this process involves using baseline data (preassessments) to determine in which category students should be placed: low preparedness, moderate preparedness, or high preparedness. Specific growth targets are then assigned for each of the preparedness groups.
- Explore resources on the Center for Assessment website: https://www.nciea.org.
- Read through the Creating Smart Learning Objectives PD presentation by the Danielson Group at https://www.nsbsd.org/cms/lib/AK01001879/Centricity/Domain/769/NSBSD%20PPT%20SLO%20Intro.pdf.

To Explore More Resources Related to the Appendix Social Studies Example:

- Explore the Stanford History Education Group (n.d.) website, Beyond the Bubble, for a host of innovative assessments, interactive rubrics, and annotated student response examples: http://beyondthebubble.stanford.edu.
- Examine the resources on Assessment Resource Center for History (ARCH) at https://www.umbc.edu/che/arch/index.php.

Chapter 12 Appendix: Historical Thinking and Summarizing

Student Growth Measure or Student Learning Outcome: Example

Teacher Information:

Anita Stewart McCafferty, middle school social studies teacher, collaborative goal with eighth-grade social studies colleagues

Student Population:

Sixty-two eighth-grade students representing three sections or classes

Time Frame:

September 15–May 15

Students have fifty-minute classes five times a week with me for the duration of all three trimesters.

Assessments Evidence Used:

Classroom-based assessments and scoring guides or rubrics for historical thinking (corroboration and contextualization) have been developed as a team. Assessments were adapted from Beyond the Bubble assessments by the Stanford History Education Group (n.d.). See attached.

Classroom-based assessments and rubrics or scoring guides for summarizing informational texts were adapted and adopted from Stanford History Education Group and Ashland Middle School in Oregon. See attached.

Student Baseline Data:

Baseline student data were determined on a four-point scale for corroboration, contextualization, and summarizing.

Corroboration Baseline Results From Preassessment:

Performance Level	4	3	2	1
# of Students	2	23	31	6

Contextualization Baseline Results From Preassessment:

Performance Level	4	3	2	1
# of Students	0	16	41	5

Summarizing Information Texts Baseline Results From Preassessment:

Performance Level	4	3	2	1
# of Students	1	20	29	12

Student Growth Targets:

The growth target we have established is for a *minimum of 80 percent* of students from each of the baseline performance Levels 1, 2, and 3 to grow to the next performance level by May 15. Students performing at Level 4 on the preassessments will be expected to continue growth in both historical thinking and summarizing as demonstrated by their abilities to function at increasingly more complex and rigorous levels beyond grade-level expectations.

Corroboration Growth Targets:

Performance Level	4	3	2	1
# of Students	20	30	11	1

Contextualization Growth Targets:

Performance Level	4	3	2	1
# of Students	13	36	12	1

Summarizing Information Texts Growth Targets:

Performance Level	4	3	2	1
# of Students	17	27	16	2

Note: Because the targets of historical thinking and summarizing complex informational texts are also essential proficiency standards, the ultimate goal is for all students to reach proficiency or beyond. In order to accomplish this task, my colleagues and I will have to intervene early and often.

Once we have completed one year's cycle, we will have a better idea if our growth target goals are attainable (stretch goals yet realistic). Additionally, we will have better ideas of the professional development (PD) and structures needed to help us achieve these lofty goals with our students.

Instructional and Formative Assessment Strategies Based on High-Impact Strategies

Clear learning targets, Next Steps Rubrics (NSRs) for self-assessment and goal setting, descriptive feedback from peers and teachers, examples of weak and strong work, cooperative learning structures, direct instruction, modeling, meaningful practice, use of graphic organizers or visual representations, and teaching and practicing metacognitive skills

First Steps: Determining What Is Essential for Students to Learn

Key Question: Of which essential skills, processes, reasoning patterns, or concepts do I want my students to demonstrate growth and proficiency?

1. **While historical content will be taught throughout the units of study, the essential skill set running throughout the yearlong course is "thinking like a historian."** Skills of sourcing, corroborating, contextualizing, using evidence from sources, applying historical knowledge, and making and supporting claims will be emphasized and built upon through each of the units of study.
2. **Additionally, students will work to improve their summarizing skills of a variety of "texts," primary and secondary sources, including print, digital, visual, audio, and video texts, from varied cultures and eras.**

Priority Standards

E1 Historical Knowledge, Concepts, Themes, and Patterns

Identify and analyze major *historical* eras, major enduring themes, turning points, events, consequences, and people in the history of Maine, the United States, and various regions of the world.

RH.6-8.2

Determine the central ideas or conclusions of a text; provide an accurate summary of the text distinct from prior knowledge or opinions.

RH.6-8.1

Cite specific textual evidence to support analysis of primary and secondary sources.

WHST.6-8.9

Draw evidence from informational texts to support analysis, reflection, and research.

RH.6-8.9

Analyze the relationship between a primary and secondary source on the same topic.

Big Ideas and Essential Understandings

- The importance of examining and using varied primary and secondary sources to better understand an historical era or the human condition.
- Accurately summarizing and analyzing informational text, including primary sources, is a foundational skill of a social scientist.

Historical thinking asks students to go beyond factual recall to apply information in a specific historical context. Historical thinking is about cultivating habits of mind, ways of thinking that become *habitual*. Historians think about *when* a source was produced, *who* wrote it, and for *what* purpose.

Evaluation of evidence involves the critical assessment of historical sources. It includes the following:

- **Sourcing** asks students to consider who wrote a document as well as the circumstances of its creation. Who authored a given document? When? For what purpose?
- **Contextualization** asks students to locate a document in time and place and to understand how these factors shape its content.
- **Corroboration** asks students to consider details across multiple sources to determine points of agreement and disagreement.

Source: Stanford History Education Group (n.d.).

In Figure 12.6, major units of instruction include Introduction to Thinking Like a Historian; Life in the United States During the Mid-1800s; Conflict and Cooperation; and Struggles for Equality and Justice.

In Figure 12.7, within each of the major units of instruction or themes reside subunits examining specific content-related examples of the unit theme. For instance, during the unit on Life in the United States During the Mid-1800s, learners will explore life in the northern factories, slavery, abolition movements, and so on.

FIGURE 12.6 ● Eighth-Grade Social Studies Curriculum Map

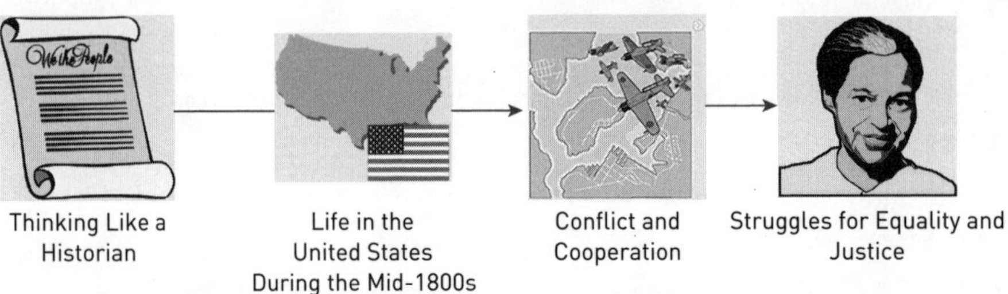

Note: This diagram and art was created using Inspiration(R) 9, a product of Inspiration Software, Inc.

FIGURE 12.7 ● Eighth-Grade Social Studies Curriculum Map Subunits

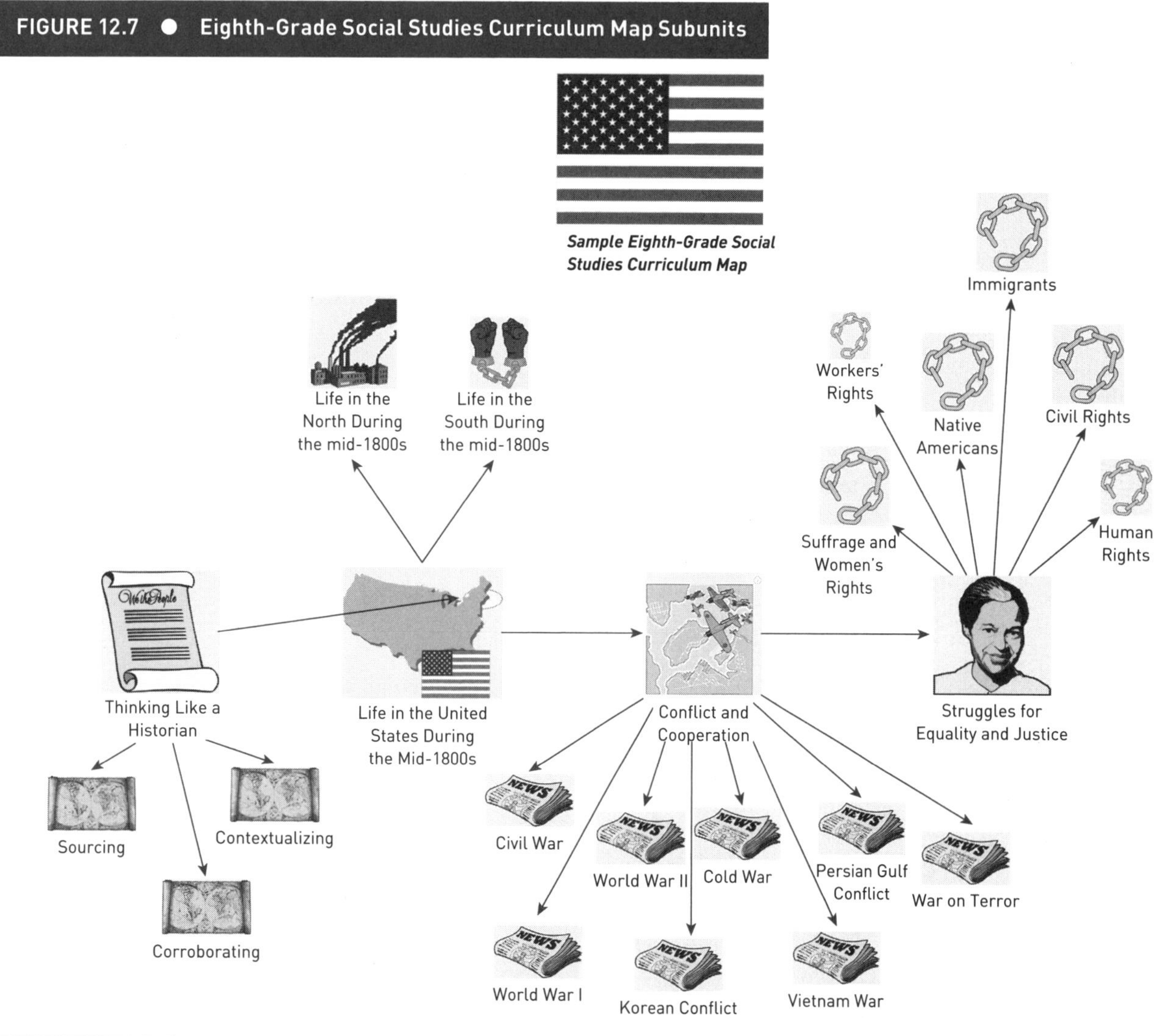

Note: This diagram and art was created using Inspiration(R) 9, a product of Inspiration Software, Inc.

Deconstructing and Converting Corroboration Into

Learner-Friendly Targets and Essential Questions

1. **Corroboration Standard (Confirmation and Comparison):**

   Able to analyze and compare a variety of multiple claims or accounts of an event (reasoning target)

   Definition: "Corroboration asks students to consider details across multiple sources to determine points of agreement and disagreement" (Stanford History Education Group, n.d.)

Essential corroboration questions to consider:

"What do other documents or sources say?

Do the documents or sources agree? If not, why?

What are other possible documents or sources to consider?

What documents are most reliable?"

(Stanford History Education Group, n.d.)

Learner-Friendly Target Using the "I Can . . . This Means" Format:

I can analyze and compare a variety of claims or accounts of an historical event. *This means* I can explain major obvious similarities and differences from the multiple sources. I can also explain more subtle (less obvious) comparisons.

Deconstructing and Converting Contextualization Into

Learner-Friendly Targets and Essential Questions

2. Contextualization Standard (Understands and Uses Context):

Able to place and interpret the evidence in the historical time (context) as opposed to present day **(reasoning target)**

Definition: "Contextualization asks students to locate a document in time and place and to understand how these factors shape its content" (Stanford History Education Group, n.d.).

Essential contextualization questions to consider:

When and where was the document created?

What was different then? What was the same?

How might the circumstances in which the document/source was created affect its content?"

(Stanford History Education Group, n.d.)

Learner-Friendly Target Using the "I Can . . . This Means" Format:

I can place and interpret the evidence from the source(s) in the historical time (context) as opposed to present day. *This means* I can use my prior background and new knowledge to determine and provide a thorough description of the historical setting of the primary source(s).

I also am able to use the historical setting of the source to interpret at least some of the evidence in historical context as opposed to through "present-day mindset or eyes."

Deconstructing and Converting Summarizing Information Texts Into

Learner-Friendly Targets and Essential Questions

3. Summarizing Informational Text Standard

Common Core History/Literacy Standard RH.6-8.2

Determine the central ideas or conclusions of a text; provide an accurate summary of the text distinct from prior knowledge or opinions. **(skill target)**

Definition: Summarizing asks students to accurately relay all of the main ideas from what they read, hear, view, or observe.

Essential summarizing questions to consider:

What are the key ideas of this "text"? Do I truly understand the main points the text is making or conveying?

If someone only had my summary to go by, would they have an accurate picture of the main ideas of the text?

Have I eliminated my opinions and ideas from the summary so that the summary truly represents the text, not my opinion of the content, topic, ideas, or author?

Does my summary demonstrate my academic honesty? Have I been careful not to plagiarize?

Learner-Friendly Target Using the "I Can . . . This Means" Format

I can accurately summarize complex informational texts. *This means* I can make a short statement of *all* of the big ideas or main messages of what I read, hear, view, or observe. The summary does not include minor details or extraneous information (such as personal reflections or opinions). The summary is in my own words.

Historical Critical Thinking Next Steps Rubric: Historians' Strategies: Corroboration

A Self-Peer-Teacher Assessment and Goal-Setting Tool

Corroboration Standard: I can analyze and compare a variety of claims or accounts of an historical event.

Name: Date:

What Is Done Well	Criteria This Means . . .	*What to Do Next* I Will . . . This Is How
	• I can explain major obvious similarities and differences from the multiple sources.	
	• I can explain more subtle (less obvious) comparisons.	

Historical Critical Thinking Next Steps Rubric: Historians' Strategies: Contextualization

A Self-Peer-Teacher Assessment and Goal-Setting Tool

Contextualization Standard: I can place and interpret the evidence from the source(s) in the historical time (context) as opposed to present day.

Name: Date:

What Is Done Well	Criteria This Means . . .	*What to Do Next* I Will . . . This Is How
	• I can use my prior background and new knowledge to determine and provide a thorough description of the historical setting of the primary source(s).	
	• I also am able to use the historical setting of the source to interpret at least some of the evidence in historical context as opposed to through "present-day mindset or eyes."	

Summarizing Next Steps Rubric

A Self-Peer-Teacher Assessment and Goal-Setting Tool

Standard: I can accurately summarize complex informational text.

Name: Date:

What Is Done Well	Criteria This Means . . .	*What to Do Next* I Will . . . This Is How
• The summary states the main ideas and major points of the material to be summarized. • The summary covers all of the material to be summarized. No big ideas or main messages are left out. • No small details or extraneous information such as personal reflections or opinions are included. • The summary is in the learner's own words.	• I can make a short statement of *all* of the big ideas or main messages of what I read, hear, view, or observe. • The summary does not include minor details or extraneous information (such as personal reflections or opinions). • The summary is in my own words.	• Reexamine or reread the "text" for main ideas. • Include *all* big ideas or main messages in the summary. • Eliminate small details or extraneous information such as personal reflections or opinions. • Be sure the summary is in your own words, not those of the author or speaker. • Look up or request help understanding unfamiliar vocabulary or concepts from the text. • Request a mini-lesson or additional guided practice.

Source: Adapted from Chappuis, Stiggins, Chappuis, and Arter (2012).

Tracking Progress by Learning Targets: Historical Thinking

Name:

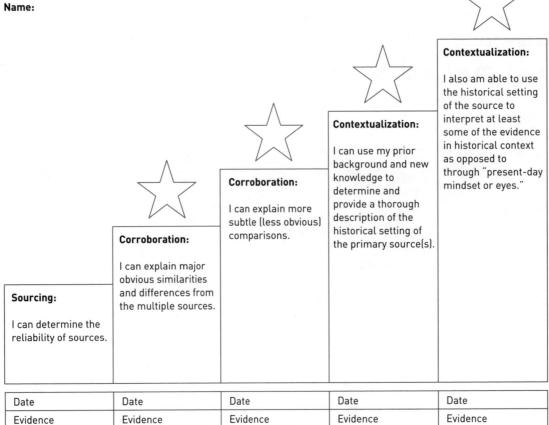

Sourcing: I can determine the reliability of sources.	**Corroboration:** I can explain major obvious similarities and differences from the multiple sources.	**Corroboration:** I can explain more subtle (less obvious) comparisons.	**Contextualization:** I can use my prior background and new knowledge to determine and provide a thorough description of the historical setting of the primary source(s).	**Contextualization:** I also am able to use the historical setting of the source to interpret at least some of the evidence in historical context as opposed to through "present-day mindset or eyes."
Date	Date	Date	Date	Date
Evidence	Evidence	Evidence	Evidence	Evidence

FIGURE 12.8 ● Summarization Rubric

Ashland Middle School Essential Learning Rubric

6th Grade Language Arts Essential Learning #3: Write a summary of the text using main events and supporting details. *CCSS ELA Literacy RL6.2*

	Mastery	Proficient	Not Yet Proficient
Identify Central Idea/ Theme 3.1	Identify central idea and/or theme in the summary. *Theme—Message author is trying to communicate to the reader.* *Central Idea—What the text is about (in one concise sentence).* ***Explain how the central idea or theme is important to a reader.***	Identify central idea and/or theme in the summary. *Theme—Message author is trying to communicate to the reader.* *Central Idea—What the text is about (in one concise sentence).*	Does not identify the central idea and/or theme in the summary.
Summarize 3.2	Compose a summary that contains the central idea ***and captures the meaning and message*** of the text. ***Isolate the most critical details which are necessary for a summary and omit all others.***	Compose a summary that contains the central idea of the text.	Summary lacks central idea or relevant support. Personal opinion is used. Unnecessary details are used instead of necessary ones.
Use Own Words 3.3	Compose a summary representative of the original text using own words. Use ***no*** non-descriptive words (a lot, stuff, things, cool, good, etc.). ***Use strong and precise verbs (new or challenge words, vocabulary from the text, etc.) to describe events and characters.*** ***When applicable, use Language Arts vocabulary (protagonist, antagonist, rising action, conflict, resolution, setting, etc.) two or more times.***	Compose a summary representative of the original text using own words. Use ***few*** (two or three maximum) non-descriptive words (a lot, stuff, things, cool, good, etc.).	Does not compose a summary using own words, or the majority of the summary is from the original text. Many non-descriptive words (a lot, stuff, things, cool, good, etc.) are used.

Source: Katherine Holden and Steve Retzlaff, sixth-grade English language arts team, Ashland Middle School, Ashland, Oregon

Sample Historical Thinking and Accurately Summarizing Goal and Plan Form

Name: Student A	**Date: 10/5/2015**
Where Am I Going?	
My goal: To improve my skills of summarizing primary and secondary sources	
Where Am I Now?	
What I can do: I do a thorough job of summarizing the main ideas.	**What I need to work on:** I need to include the most important information without including too many extra details. My summaries are often almost as long as the source itself! I need to do a better job of making sure the summaries are in my own words.
How Will I Close the Gap?	
• **With help from:** My peer revision group and my teacher • **Using these materials:** Examples of weak and strong work, the Next Steps Rubrics (NSRs), and the summarizing guide that my teacher provided • **Actions I will take:** • **What:** I will access or take advantage of the opportunities to do peer revision and to receive descriptive feedback from my teacher. • **When:** During our upcoming unit on Life in the United States During the Mid-1800s	

Source: Form adapted from Chappuis (2015).

Historical Thinking Exit Ticket

Name: **Date:**

Today's learning target:

Self-Assessment:

Evidence:

Summarizing Exit Ticket

Name: **Date:**

Today's learning target:

Self-Assessment:

Evidence:

Tracking Progress by Assessment

Learning Target 1 = Corroboration

Learning Target 2 = Contextualization

Learning Target 3 = Summarization of Informational Texts

Assignment or Assessment	*Date*	*Learning Target*	*Pre/ Practice/ Post*	*Score*	
Fredericksburg selected response: Preassessment (corroboration)		1			
Fredericksburg: Preassessment (corroboration)		1			
Post-South Civil War: Postassessment (sourcing and corroboration)		1			
Immigration: Preassessment (contextualization)		2			
Women's rights: Practice (contextualization)		2			
Civil rights: Postassessment (contextualization)		2			
Slave narrative: Preassessment (summarizing)		3			
"The Shock of Boot Camp": Postassessment (summarizing)		3			

Source: Form adapted from Chappuis (2015).

Slave Narrative Preassessment: Summarizing

Task Directions: After careful close readings of the text *Voices from Slavery* by Norman Yetman, please compose an accurate summary. Your summary may be in written format or in audio or video format. Please consult the Summarizing Next Steps Rubric as well as the rubric in Figure 12.8 to help you complete your best summarizing attempt of this complex informational text.

The Shock of Boot Camp: Postassessment (Summarizing)

Directions: Watch the following video interview clip of Ronald Winter, a Vietnam War veteran, describing his experience with boot camp. Upon viewing Winter's interview clip, "The Shock of Boot Camp," as many times as necessary and/or accessing the written transcript of the interview, please accurately summarize it. Your summary may be in written format or in audio or video format. Please consult the Summarizing Next Steps Rubric as well as the fully developed three-point summarizing rubric (Figure 12.8) to help you complete your best summarizing attempt of this complex informational text.

To access Ronald Winter's interview clip, "The Shock of Boot Camp," click the following link:

http://www.loc.gov/teachers/classroommaterials/primarysourcesets/veterans/winter.html

To access the written transcript of the interview, click the following link:

http://www.loc.gov/teachers/classroommaterials/primarysourcesets/veterans/transcript/winter.txt

For additional information on Ronald Winters, click the following link:

http://lcweb2.loc.gov/diglib/vhp-stories/loc.natlib.afc2001001.03769

13

The #assessmentliteracy Challenge

Key Takeaway

Assessment literacy is not an initiative. Assessment literacy is not another fad or bandwagon of which to jump on or off. It's a foundational essential competency for all teachers and school leaders. For us, assessment literacy is foremost about learning and secondarily about teaching.

We posit that developing assessment-literate educators is essential to the task of creating assessment-literate learners who possess the skills to learn for themselves. Educators need focused and sustained professional learning designed for adult learners in order to improve their instructional practices. When given the choice, school leaders should see teachers' time to learn and implement high-impact strategies as the focal point for ongoing investment. School leaders should refrain from, or at least carefully weigh the pros and cons of, buying formative assessment systems to replace buying time for educator development through in-depth, ongoing professional learning of formative assessment practices.

The addition of "what is good leadership?" to our essential questions helps remind superintendents, principals, policymakers, higher education institutions, and community partners of what matters—worthy curriculum, teaching, learning, and assessment evidence of that learning. It is a reminder that assessment literacy is a relatively new expectation for teachers and leaders, a set of competencies that most will still have to learn on the job. It has been our goal to show readers how to develop an understanding of and go deeper into standards of quality and high-impact practices.

We recognize that assessment literacy poses many challenges, including making the time for it, finding local expertise, sustaining the efforts for the long haul, and understanding it as a cornerstone of effective instruction. An added challenge for leaders is that of focusing not only on summative assessment creation and validation but in also helping educators and policymakers understand the importance of investing in developing appropriate formative assessment evidence and assessment for learning strategies and tools. We have devoted this book to the latter rather than the former as an intentional act to highlight the importance of and positive impact of mastering assessment for learning strategies. At the same time, we recognize the continued need for the other part of assessment literacy work—that of collecting summative evidence from sound tasks and assessments, using quality scoring criteria and/or rubrics, and of accurately reporting and communicating evaluation data in user-friendly ways to appropriate stakeholders.

Take a Creative Deep Dive: Express-a-Book, Video, Podcast, or Article

We invite you to choose an assessment literacy-related "text" to read, view, or listen to—perhaps one from our Deep Dive suggestions at the end of one of the previous chapters or a resource from the References section. We then invite you to consider a creative way to share your key takeaways with others. Please see the Practitioner Spotlight for an in-depth explanation of the idea, a protocol, and examples. The examples shared by our friends at the Maine Arts Leadership Initiative (MALI) do not involve assessment literacy texts, but we invite you to apply this innovative idea to aspects of assessment literacy. Go where your reading muse takes you. Let your inner creative self shine!

PRACTITIONER SPOTLIGHT 13.1

EXPRESS-A-BOOK

What?

The Maine Arts Leadership Initiative (MALI) is committed to the development of teacher leaders to ensure deep understanding and meaningful implementation of high-quality teaching, learning, and assessment in the arts for all students.

The MALI design team oversees the initiative and is continuously considering ideas proposed by the team and the visual and performing arts educators who serve as MALI teacher leaders and teaching artists (104 to date).

The preparatory readings for the MALI Summer Institute are rich for learning and conversation. Carol Dweck's (2016) *Mindset* provided the overarching theme and kickoff keynote for the 2017 institute. Teacher leaders indicated the desire to continue reading and reflecting in a collaborative manner beyond the institute. In response, Argy Nestor, Lindsay Pinchbeck, and Jake Sturtevant agreed to brainstorm ideas. Express-a-Book was born—an arts-integrated idea generator exploring articles, books, TED Talks, and more! It's *not* a traditional book club—the MALI approach to collaborating, connecting, and learning over what we're reading, listening to, and observing. We believe in the power to share and generate ideas through the arts!

Argy, Lindsay, and Jake planned and tried the process and presented it to the MALI participants. Argy wanted to focus on leadership, so she listened to Simon Sinek's TED Talk called "How Great Leaders Inspire Action." Lindsay wanted to read about creativity in teaching and learning, so she read the article "A Call to Action: The Challenges of Creative Teaching and Learning" by R. Keith Sawyer (2015). Jake was curious about the power of boredom. He listened to *In Defense of Boredom* on WNYC, Manoush Zomorodi's podcast *Note to Self*, and read the book *Bored and Brilliant* (Zomorodi, 2017).

Once they completed their review, they responded by creating artworks. Argy made a black-and-white illustration (shown in Chapter 2), Lindsay made a painting and wrote a poem, and Jake created a remix MP3. They shared and responded to each image or sound by giving feedback and asking questions. This provided the opportunity to learn about each of their topics in a collaborative environment.

So What?

Now in its seventh year, MALI is clear about sharing ideas and learning in a collaborative and supportive environment. This process is a great and different learning opportunity. This is what we've learned:

- The process affirms who we are as expressive beings and reinforces the power of the arts to provide a deeper meaning to what we are reading/learning about.
- When we bring people together in a collaborative environment, the potential is there to learn so much more. This process supports that notion.
- The group needs to trust each other or build trust within the process.
- Individuals must be willing to stretch and be vulnerable.
- Participants are accountable to themselves as well as to the members of the group.
- The process of Express-a-Book has practical applications for classroom learning.
- This can be applied across disciplines in professional learning communities; it can take place face-to-face or electronically, within schools or across schools, within districts or across a region or state.
- Once groups are formed, they can complete a round and join together with other groups to share their learning.
- It's an example of teachers teaching teachers.
- Express-a-Book puts teachers in the center of their learning (teacher-centered learning), empowering and encouraging them to take the leadership of their own learning.

Now What?

Small groups form and meet to decide on articles or topics of interest—set intentions and goals to meet the needs of the group. Each person selects her or his topic and what she or he wishes to read or view. Participants individually select one or more: drama, media arts, music, movement, poetry, storytelling, or visual art to express findings in books, articles, TED Talks, and more.

A suggested protocol was created so teacher leaders can guide their direction of using Express-a-Book.

Suggested Protocol for Express-a-Book

GETTING STARTED:

1. Find or be guided into a group of kindred spirits (recommended two to five people but smaller groups may work better).

Consider if the group should be an interdisciplinary one or include teachers of the same discipline or grade level.

2. Decide the format of the group.
   - Will you all read or view an article, book, video, or resource together?
   - Will you individually choose an article, book, video, or resource?
   - Will you each choose a section of a larger reading to do?
3. Decide a meeting date and time (in person, Zoom, or other digital platform).

   Recommended tool: Doodle poll

CREATE:

4. After reading or absorbing your resources, decide how you will express through creative experience.
   - What resonated with you and has you thinking?
   - Which art form(s) will you use to express your learning?
   - What medium will you select to communicate?

If you aren't sure, begin doodling, moving, writing, talking—whatever you need to do to get ideas flowing.

Consider doing several sketches, improvisations or compositions, or free play before settling on a final idea.

5. Create an artistic response that can be shared with others.

THE MEETING:

6. Give introductions and an overview of the discussion (if applicable).
7. Have each individual present (suggested protocol) the following:
   - Artistic representation of reading, video, or resource
     - Don't talk too much! It is suggested not to give a lot of insight into the reading or resource itself but allow time for others to experience what you have created.
   - Responses from others
     - Give feedback, insight, and reflection
     - Reply with "I wonder . . ., I notice . . . , What if . . . , My question is . . ."
   - Artist statement and discussion
     - Gain insight into process and product.
     - Answer some questions in the responses from others.
     - Discuss concepts presented further.
8. Wrap up, and discuss takeaways.

What are our takeaways? Give one or two sentences—from a personal response to experience.

Argy's Takeaway:

I loved being challenged to stretch myself, and because of that, I learned so much more—and differently—than I do in a traditional book club. I have so much respect for both Jake and Lindsay; it was great to have the chance to collaborate with them to develop and go through the process with a new idea. I was so encouraged and inspired by Lindsay and Jake's creations! The Express-a-Book process brought everyone's learning to a different place.

Lindsay's Takeaway:

I enjoyed learning through the arts, playing with ideas, and having a small group of trusted colleagues to engage in rich dialogue. I was motivated to keep working on my painting and poem and excited, if a bit nervous, to share but had great feedback, which motivated me to keep working, learning, and thinking more deeply about my initial ideas in the article and my artwork.

Jake's Takeaway:

It was wonderful to have the opportunity and excuse to jump in the sandbox and find ways to play with, highlight, reflect, and communicate my learning in a unique way. I also loved the rich dialogue that this sort of sharing and reflecting has to offer. When I get to see how others interpreted my own explorations of learning and how I interpret their learning expressions, it is amazing to see how this can clarify my own vision of what I learned and what I am learning.

(Continued)

(Continued)

Example:

Jake's MP3
https://soundcloud.com/sturtwars/boredom-remix

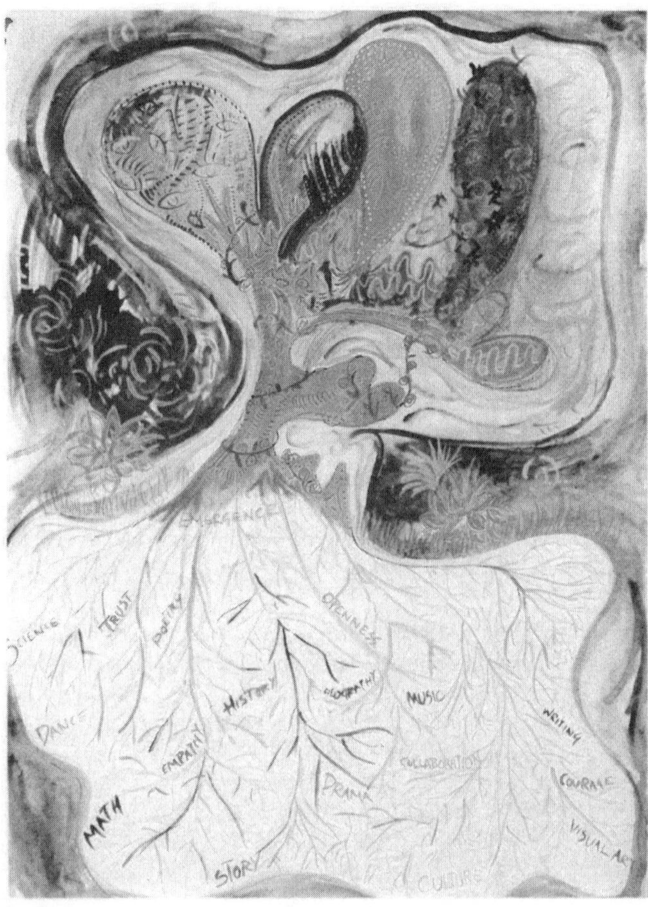

Artistic Response by Lindsay Pinchbeck

In a new time and a new place never before imagined.
Roots connect and intertwine
Leading us to new growth.
Pathways link together.

Emerging, unexpected,
Full of mistakes and magic.
Brought to life by many,
Through creative collaboration.
Careful responses, nurtured by all, together.

Perfect
with stories, surprises and experiences.
Trust, safety, openness build this complex system
held together with strong roots and the mingling of ideas.

It is all together a new creature.

Artistic Response to

A call to action:
The challenges of creative teaching and learning

R. Keith Sawyer, Washington University in St. Louis To appear in *Teachers College Record*

Source: Contributed by MALI; MAC; Argy Nestor, director of arts education, MAC; Lindsay Pinchbeck, founder and director, Sweet Tree Arts/ Sweetland School, and MALI design team member; Jake Sturtevant, music educator, Falmouth High School, and MALI design team member.

PAUSE AND REFLECT

- Let's hear from a student and get "stoked." Take twelve minutes to watch the TED Talk "Hackschooling Makes Me Happy": https://youtu.be/h11u3vtcpaY.
    - What are your "takeaways" from the presentation by thirteen-year-old Logan LaPlante?
- Have you asked your students, "What makes you happy?" lately?
- Follow up and watch "Hacker Mindset" at https://youtu.be/lV6b5dw_jug.

Following the Flow of Ideas and Finding Your Happy Place

The Map Guy (Jeff B)

Since an early age, I have been exposed to an intensely visual world. I am a big fan of creating new ways to express ideas. My "hack" of learning is to use the visual medium in as many ways as possible to experience the familiar ideas in new, unique ways. In my way, I follow the "flow of ideas" to explore the personal cognitive cartography, the mapping of ideas as they occur. I have tried to explain the power of mapping ideas over and over (see Chapter 5), and in those experiences, I am feeling a unique sense of "flow" or total immersion. You can see that in concept maps like the seven strategies there is a style and form, with clip art, that has become a graphic.

I was surprised when I started to sketch familiar places and images as visual metaphors of, you guessed it, the seven strategies. The one that follows is on the back of a postcard-size piece of paper. The images are from Seattle, the Smith Tower, Space Needle, and Mount Rainier. I wasn't trying to do this at the beginning. I was letting my words and images talk to each other; it just happened. See Figure 13.1. As I worked at it to refine and reflect, I thought how much place matters: Maine. These little sketches using Maine as a theme soon became poster-sized renderings of the seven strategies of assessment for learning, which we used to celebrate professional learning events and conferences. (See Figure 5.15 in Chapter 5.) I am not a trained artist, but I am learning to trust my creative process.

I am willing to share my passion for visual expression of ideas as I seek to make new connections. I began to explore sketching and drawing with workshop participants to address the artistic mindset in participants. I have found many who resist expressing their ideas visually, some who just think it's fun, and others who see the lost art of sketching as a 21st century skill on the rise. The sketching and mapping activities provide a shared experience to talk about how we ask students to draw and sketch in assessments but may not give them the time and training to practice. I voice a concern with teachers with this question. Do you give students enough instruction with all of the high-impact teaching strategies to be proficient in 2-D and 3-D line drawings, especially if they are using drawings for graded summative assessment? I enjoy the feeling of being immersed in the flow of ideas. They are most powerful, however, when they are shared and help to foster a collaborative, creative learning environment.

Anita's Happy Place: Experiential Learning

Like Logan and Jeff, I, too, find happiness in hacking my learning. One of my keys to happiness is pushing my learning in new and meaningful ways. In doing so, I like to create experiences for others that engage them in learning in innovative or creative ways. Teaching content has always been only one goal for me; the larger goal, the one that helps me feel joy and fulfillment, is creating experiences that teach and engage learners in practicing complex thinking skills, habits of work and learning (HOWLs), and ways of being or becoming. My passion for service learning and community engagement over the years has been one such outlet. More recently, my family and I have been turned on to escape rooms. Escape rooms center around a story or problem, take place in a themed room, and engage participants in a series of timed puzzles that you and your team members have to solve in order to "escape." In order to be successful, team members must communicate effectively, work collaboratively, be observant, and demonstrate problem-solving skills under pressure.

After trying several escape rooms, and with a little help from my middle school colleague, Lori, I discovered breakoutedu.com, a website that in its infancy shared educational "escape room ideas" for the classroom for free. As a result of exploring these resources, I began to create "breakout" and escape room experiences for children, youth, and adult learners in a variety of settings. For instance, my husband and I created a series of escape rooms for our church summer camp, Camp Can Do. These immersive rooms allowed us to help participants be transported to a unique setting while they worked together to solve a variety of puzzles while trying to beat the clock. We were inspired (and exhausted!) by the challenge of differentiating the same room for toddlers through teenage and adult participant groups.

FIGURE 13.1 ● Seattle Meets Seven Strategies of Assessment for Learning

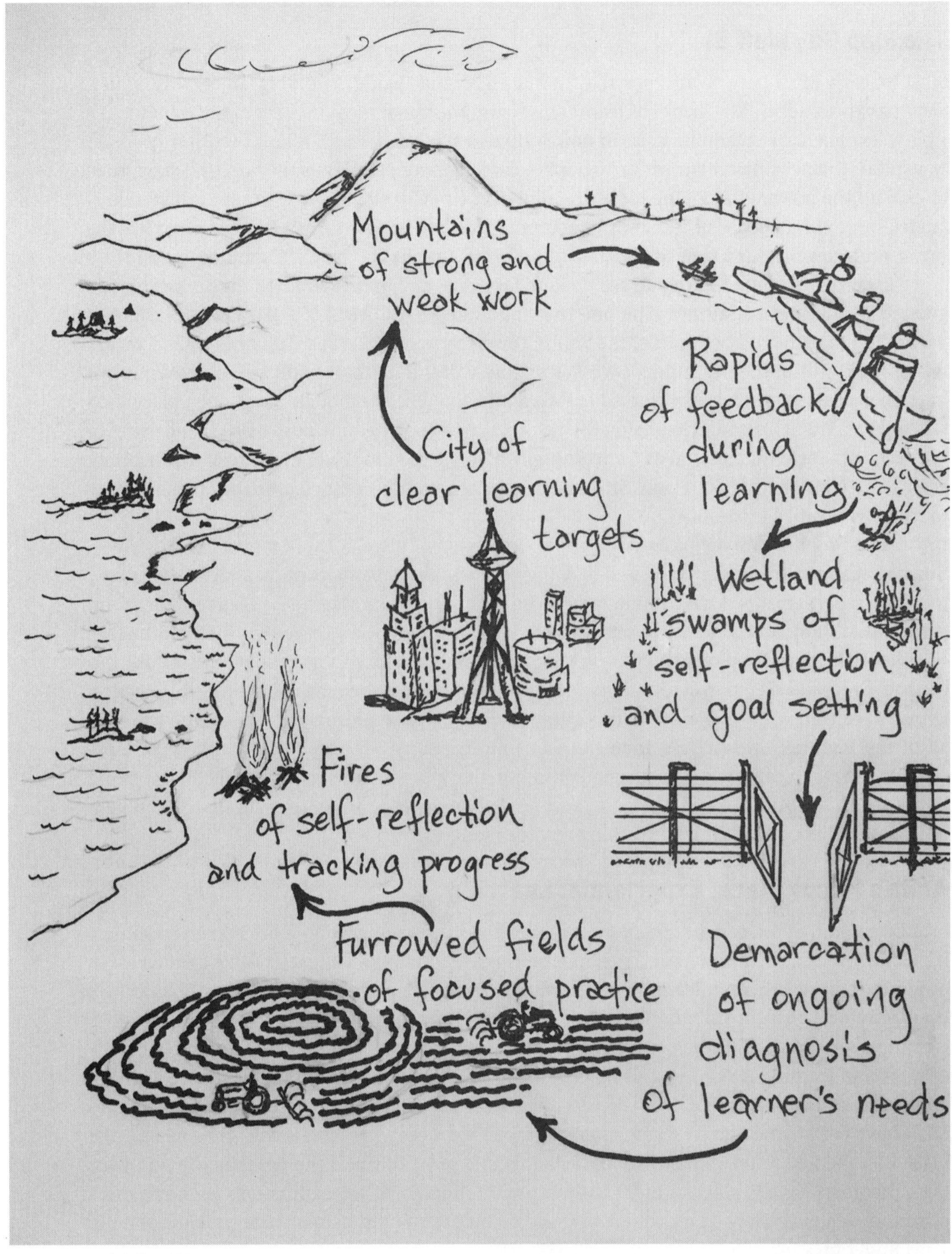

I have enjoyed creating and using escape room experiences for professional development (PD) as a way to engage educators in learning more about a topic in a manner that challenges them to innovate and problem-solve with their colleagues. These breakout experiences center around such themes as high-impact teaching strategies, assessment for learning, and service learning. These PD experiences look quite different than traditional PD. Some simply involve a room full of locked boxes, while others involve a decorated or themed room with props; costumed characters; locked boxes, safes, and/or doors; a timer; and a problem to solve in a specified period of time. The dilemma might be something as straightforward as "unlocking the keys to learner success." Participants use relevant books, handouts, QR codes, digital clues, black lights, magnifying glasses, decoders, and so on, to solve the various puzzles to begin unlocking the varied types of locks in the room (e.g., number locks, letter codes, directional codes, padlocks). Creating and differentiating the escape rooms to teach content while engaging educators in experiential learning that emphasizes critical thinking, collaboration, communication, and problem-solving in addition to teaching them about assessment for learning keeps me energized...and happy. I enjoy the challenge of creating something new and helping others "hack" their learning as well. Engaging others in experiential learning is my way of making sure I stay congruent with my message about high-impact pedagogy. My goal is to avoid the trap of "teach as I say, not as I do."

PAUSE AND REFLECT

- What is quality? That is the essential question of *Zen and the Art of Motorcycle Maintenance* by Robert Pirsig (1974). The argument is made that it comes down to how you use student work to help learners. See Appendix A, which is an activity guide for this book.
- How did the weather get all those rubrics, like hurricanes (the Beaufort scale) and tornado levels (the Fujita scale)? It all began with the development of the Beaufort scale by the British Navy. This story is told in Sebastian Junger's *The Perfect Storm*(1987). The story shows how a rubric helped save lives of sailors using the best data available to make critical judgments. Think of how these rubrics and many other rubrics are used in our daily lives.
- The authors of *Art and Fear* are teachers, and they have a great story about an experiment they did in their ceramics class (Bayles & Orland, 2001). The question was this: How do you get the best ceramics products from your students? See Appendix B, which is an activity guide for *Art and Fear*.

What Will Be Your Next Steps in Your Assessment Literacy Journey?

We encourage you to apply the assessment for learning strategies and tools we have shared in this book to your classrooms and faculty rooms. As we have shared in this chapter, do so in a way that works for you, in a way that engages you. Dare we say, have fun with assessment? Share the results of your learning with your colleagues—near and far. Watch the impact the consistent use of these strategies have on your learners, whether your learners are students or educators. Share your assessment literacy ideas with others through face-to-face opportunities as well as through social media outlets such as Twitter. We invite you to post your thoughts, questions, and hacks to @AnitaStewartMcC or @BeaudryJeff or leave a message at ***#assessmentliteracy.***

Chapter 13 Appendix A: What Is Quality? High-Impact Teaching Strategies Meet *Zen and the Art of Motorcycle Maintenance* by Robert Pirsig (1974)

Deep Dive

As a reader, do you find stories that help you with insights and examples to better understand what assessment means? The book by Robert Pirsig (1974), *Zen and the Art of Motorcycle Maintenance*, contains a classic classroom vignette that hit the target. The scenario is about an undergraduate philosophy professor, Dr. Phaedrus, who is trying to find a suitable definition of "quality," the pursuit of aesthetics (what is good?), and axiology (what is beautiful?). The author struggles throughout the book and finally provides this story, presumably his story, about his insight into quality—we know it when we see it. He provides evidence for this insight by employing several high-impact strategies. If you want to read the entire scenario, it is in Chapter 12 of Pirsig's book. Here is a summary.

The Scenario

In order to find out what students thought about quality, he gave a writing assignment with the prompt, "What is quality in thought and statement?" (Pirsig, 1974, p. 204). Dr. Phaedrus then goes on to talk about the reactions from his students. There was a great deal of frustration expressed by the students who felt that he should give them the answer, as an expert should. Many students felt that the "search for the truth was an imposition" (p. 204).

In the classroom discussion, the professor countered that he was very excited by the fuss and anger. Such a display of cognitive dissonance signaled to him that they had "stumbled on a genuine question" (p. 205). In the pursuit of truth, he provided two examples of student's essays. "The first was a rambling, disconnected thing with interesting ideas that never built into anything. The second was a magnificent piece by a student who was mystified himself about why it had come out so well" (p. 203). The discussion that followed focused on a comparison of the characteristics of each essay. With the evidence provided by examples of student work, there was full agreement on what quality looked and sounded like.

- What high-impact assessment for learning strategies were used? See Chapter 3 for a list and other chapters for in-depth examples.
- Which of these strategies do you use in your teaching?
- What feedback would you give to Dr. Phaedrus?

Chapter 13 Appendix B: Art, Fear, and High-Impact Teaching and Learning Strategies

Deep Dive

Classroom teachers continuously confront the moment with students when you need to move from first signs of student work, early drafts, or models. This scenario was written from the perspective of a ceramics teacher. He wanted his students to produce ceramics' products but had a dilemma, a question. Based on prior teaching experiences he saw the potential value two different approaches. The following is a retelling.

A ceramics teacher had a question about two different teaching approaches and stopped to do some action research on this question: How should you orient your students towards learning to produce high-quality ceramics?

> The ceramics teacher announced on opening day that he was dividing the class into two groups. All those on the left side of the studio, he said, would be graded solely on the quantity of work they produced, all those on his right solely on its quality. His procedure was simple: on the final day of class he would bring his bathroom scales and weigh the work of the "quantity" group: fifty pounds rated an "A," forty pounds a "B," and so on. Those being graded on "quality," however, needed to produce only one pot—albeit a perfect one to get an "A." Well, came grading time . . . (Bayles and Orland, 1993, p. 29)

Pixabay

Pixabay

For this action research experiment, there was a stark difference in quality. The group that was asked to produce the fifty pounds created higher quality and a far greater variety of work, making far more mistakes and errors as well. "In the end they had little more to show for their efforts than grandiose theories and a pile of dead clay" (Bayles and Orland, 1993, p. 29). The group that discussed quality had much less to show, as they had spent time talking about the perfect pot and bowl.

- What high-impact assessment for learning strategies were used? See Chapter 3 for a list of strategies and other chapters for in-depth examples.
- Which of these strategies do you use in your teaching?
- What feedback would you give to the ceramics teacher?

• References •

Adesope, O. O., & Nesbit, J. C. (2009). A systematic review of research on collaborative learning with concept maps. In P. L. Torres & R. C. V. Marriott (Eds.), *Handbook of research on collaborative learning using concept mapping* (pp. 238–255). Hershey, PA: IGI Global.

Anderson, L. W., & Krathwohl, D. R. (2001). *A taxonomy for learning, teaching, and assessing: A revision of Bloom's taxonomy of educational objectives*. New York, NY: Pearson.

Andrade, H. (2005). Teaching with rubrics: The good, the bad, and the ugly. *College Teaching, 53*(1), 27–31.

Andrade, H., Du, Y., & Wang, X. (2008). Putting rubrics to the test: The effect of a model, criteria generation, and rubric-referenced self-assessment on elementary school students' writing. *Educational Measurement: Issues and Practice, 27*(2), 3–13.

Bayes, D., & Orland, T., (1993). *Art and fear: Observations on the perils (and rewards) of artmaking*. Minneapolis, MN: Consortium Books.

Bayles, D., & Orland, T. (2001). *Art and fear: Observations on the perils (and rewards) of artmaking* (2nd ed.). Minneapolis, MN: Consortium Books.

Beaudry, J. S., & Miller, L. (2016). *Research literacy: A primer for understanding and using research*. New York, NY: Guilford Press.

Beaudry, J. S., Ritz-Swain, S., & Nestor, A. (2015). The Maine Arts Assessment Initiative: Uniting assessment and professional development in arts education. *Journal of Maine Education, 31*, 68–76. Retrieved from http://publications.catstonepress.com/i/567263-journal-2015

Beaudry, J. S., & Wilson, P. (2010). Concept mapping and formative assessment: Elements supporting literacy and learning. In R. Marriott & P. Torres (Eds.), *Handbook of research on collaborative learning using concept mapping*. Hershey, PA: IGI Global.

Berger, R., Rugen, L., & Woodfin, L. (2014). *Leaders of their own learning: Transforming schools through student-engaged assessment*. San Francisco, CA: Jossey-Bass.

Black, P., & Wiliam, D. (1998). Inside the black box. *Phi Delta Kappan, 80*(2), 139–148.

Black, P. J., & Wiliam, D. (2009). Developing the theory of formative assessment. *Educational Assessment, Evaluation and Accountability, 21*(1), 5–31.

Boaler, J. (2016). *Mathematical mindsets: Unleashing students' potential through creative math, inspiring messages and innovative teaching*. San Francisco, CA: Jossey-Bass.

Boyne, J. (2006). *The boy in the striped pajamas*. New York, NY: Random House Children's Publishers.

Brookhart, S. (2008). *How to give effective feedback to your students*. Alexandria, VA: ASCD.

Brookhart, S. (2013). *How to create and use rubrics for formative assessment and grading*. Alexandria, VA: ASCD.

Brookhart, S., Guskey, T. McMillan, J., Smith, J., Smith, L., Stevens, M., & Welsh, M. (2016). A century of grading research: Meaning and value in the most common educational measure. *Review of Educational Research, 86*(4), 803–848.

Brualdi, A. (1998). Classroom questions. *Practical Assessment, Research & Evaluation, 6*(6).

Butler, R. (1988). Enhancing and undermining intrinsic motivation: The effects of task-involving and ego-involving evaluation on interest and performance. *British Journal of Educational Psychology, 58*, 1–14.

Campbell, B., & Feldman, A. (2017). The power of multimodal feedback. *Journal of Curriculum, Teaching, Learning, and Leadership in Education, 2*(2).

Cauley, K. M., & McMillan, J. H. (2009). Formative assessment techniques to support student motivation and achievement. *Clearing House: A Journal of Educational Strategies, Issues and Ideas, 83*(1), 16.

Center for Assessment. (2013). *Student learning objective toolkit*. Dover, NH: National Center for the Improvement of Educational Assessment.

Chappuis, J. (2009). *Seven strategies of assessment for learning*. Portland, OR: Educational Testing Services.

Chappuis, J. (2012, September). How am I doing? *Educational Leadership, 70*(1), 36–41.

Chappuis, J. (2015). *Seven strategies of assessment for learning* (2nd ed.). Upper Saddle River, NJ: Pearson Education.

Chappuis, J., Stiggins, R., Chappuis, S., & Arter, J. (2012). *Classroom assessment for student learning*. Upper Saddle River, NJ: Pearson Education.

Chappuis, S., Commodore, C., & Stiggins, R. (2016). *Balanced assessment systems: Leadership, quality, and the role of classroom assessment*. Thousand Oaks, CA: Corwin.

Cialdini, R. B. (2009). *Influence: Science and practice* (5th ed.). Boston, MA: Pearson.

Cizek, G., & Andrade, H. (2010). *Handbook of research on formative assessment*. New York, NY: Routledge.

Cotton, K. (1988). *Classroom questioning in school improvement research series*. Portland, OR: Northwest Regional Educational Laboratory.

Covey, S. R. (1989). *The 7 habits of highly effective people.* New York, NY: Simon & Schuster.

Crooks, T. J. (1988). The impact of classroom evaluation practices on students. *Review of Educational Research, 58,* 438–481.

Dantonio, M. (2001). *Collegial coaching: Inquiry into the teaching self* (2nd ed.). Bloomington, IN: Phi Delta Kappa.

Dean, C., Hubbell, E., Pitler, H., & Stone, B. J. (2012). *Classroom instruction that works: Research-based strategies that improve student achievement* (2nd ed.). Alexandria, VA: ASCD.

Dickman, N. (2009). The challenge of asking engaging questions. *Currents in Teaching and Learning, 2*(1), 3–16.

Duckworth, A. (2016). *Grit: The power of passion and perseverance.* New York, NY: Scribner.

Dweck, C. (2015). Carol Dweck revisits the "growth mindset." *Education Week, 35*(5), 20, 24.

Dweck, C. (2016). *Mindset: The new psychology of success: How we can learn to fulfil our potential.* New York, NY: Ballantine.

Fisher, D., Frey, N., & Hattie, H. (2016). *Visible learning for literacy impact: Implementing the practices that work best to accelerate student learning, grades K-12.* Thousand Oaks, CA: Corwin.

Fluckiger, J. (2010). Single point rubric: A tool for responsible student self-assessment. *Teacher Education Faculty Publications.* 5. Retrieved from http://digitalcommons.unomaha.edu/tedfacpub/5

Gomez, G., Griffiths, R., & Navathe, P. (2014). Concept maps as replacements of written essays in efficient assessment of complex medical knowledge. In L. Shedletsky & J. Beaudry (Eds.), *Cases on teaching critical thinking through visual representation strategies* (pp. 223–271). Hershey, PA: IGI Global.

Gorman, J., & Heinze-Fry, J. (2014). Conceptual mapping facilitates coherence and critical thinking in the science education system. In L. Shedletsky & J. Beaudry (Eds.), *Cases on teaching critical thinking through visual representation strategies* (pp. 296–334). Hershey, PA: IGI Global.

Gulamhussein, A. (2013). *Teaching the teachers report: Effective professional development in an era of high stakes accountability.* Alexandria, VA: Center for Public Education. Retrieved from http://www.centerforpubliceducation.org/Main-Menu/Staffingstudents/Teaching-the-Teachers-Effective-Professional-Development-in-an-Era-of-High-Stakes-Accountability/Teaching-the-Teachers-Full-Report.pdf

Hattie, J. (2009). *Visible learning: A synthesis of over 800 meta-analyses relating to achievement.* New York, NY: Routledge.

Hattie, J. (2012). *Visible learning for teachers: Maximizing impact on learning.* New York, NY: Routledge.

Hattie, J. (2015). High-impact leadership. *Educational Leadership, 72*(5), 36–40.

Hattie, J., Maters, D., & Birch, K. (2015). *Visible learning into action: International case studies of impact.* London, England: Routledge.

Hattie, J., & Timperley, H. (2007). The power of feedback. *Review of Educational Research, 77*(1), 81–112. Retrieved from https://doi.org/10.3102/003465430298487

Hattie, J., & Yates, G. (2014). *Visible learning and the science of how we learn.* New York, NY: Routledge.

Heritage, M. (2012). *Using the formative assessment rubrics and observation protocols to support professional reflection on practice.* KSDE Annual Preconference. Retrieved from http://ksde.org/Portals/0/Learning%20Services%20Documents/Using%20the%20Formative%20Assessment%20Rubrics%20and%20Observation%20Protocols%20-%20October%202nd%202012.pdf

Hinton, S. E. (1995). *The outsiders.* New York, NY: Penguin Group.

Horton, P. B., McConney, A. A., Gallo, M., Woods, A. L., Senn, G. J., & Hamelin, D. (1993). An investigation of the effectiveness of concept mapping as an instructional tool. *Science Education, 77,* 95–111.

Hyerle, D. (2009) *Visible tools for transforming information into knowledge.* Thousand Oaks, CA: Corwin.

Junger, S. (1987). *The perfect storm.* New York, NY: Harper Perennial.

Kelley, T. (2017). Design sketching: A lost skill. *Technology and Engineering Teacher, 76*(8), 8–12.

Kinchin, I. (2001). If concept mapping is so helpful to learning biology, why aren't we all doing it? *International Journal of Science Education, 23*(12), 1257–1269.

Lavery, L. (2008). *Self-regulated learning for academic success: An evaluation of instructional techniques* (Doctoral dissertation). University of Auckland, New Zealand. Retrieved from https://researchspace.auckland.ac.nz/handle/2292/16530/browse

Learning Forward. (2011). *Standards for professional learning.* Retrieved from https://learningforward.org/docs/pdf/standardsreferenceguide.pdf

Lowry, L. (1989). *Number the stars.* New York, NY: Sandpiper.

Marshall, K. (2012). *Rethinking teacher supervision and evaluation: How to work smart, build collaboration, and close the achievement gap* (2nd ed.) San Francisco, CA: John Wiley.

Marzano, R. (2001). *Designing a new taxonomy of educational objectives.* Thousand Oaks, CA: Corwin.

Marzano, R. J., Pickering, D. J., & Pollock, J. E. (2001). *Classroom instruction that works: Research-based strategies for increasing student achievement.* Alexandria, VA: ASCD.

McGuire, S. (2015). *Teach students how to learn: Strategies you can incorporate into any course to improve student metacognition, study skills, and motivation.* Sterling, VA: Stylus.

McMillan, J. H. (2004). *Classroom assessment: Principles + practice for effective standards based instruction* (3rd ed.). Boston, MA: Pearson.

Mehrabian, A. (1972). *Nonverbal communication.* Chicago, IL: Aldine.

Michaels, S., & O'Connor, C. (2012). *Talk science primer.* Cambridge, MA: Teaching Educational Research Centers.

Molnar, M. (2017, June 7). Market is booming for digital formative assessments. *Education Week, 36*(32), 28–31. Retrieved from http://www.edweek.org/ew/articles/2017/05/24/market-is-booming-for-digital-formative-assessments.html?cmp=eml-enl-eu-news1-RM

Moss, C., & Brookhart, S. (2012). *Learning targets: Helping students aim for understanding in today's lesson*. Alexandria, VA: ASCD.

Moss, C., Brookhart, S., & Long, B. (2011). Knowing your learning targets. *Educational Leadership, 68*(6), 66–69.

Muñoz Ryan, P. (2000). *Esperanza rising*. New York, NY: Scholastic.

National Association of Secondary School Principals and National Association of Elementary School Principals. (2013). *Leadership matters: What the research says about the importance of principal leadership*. Alexandria, VA: National Association of Elementary School Principals.

Nesbit, J. C., & Adesope, O. O. (2006). Learning with concept and knowledge maps: A meta-analysis. *Review of Educational Research, 76*(3), 413–448.

NGSS Lead States. (2013). *Next generation science standards: For states, by states*. Washington, DC: The National Academies Press.

Novak, J. D., & Cañas, A. J. (2006). *The theory underlying concept maps and how to construct and use them*. Pensacola, FL: Institute for Human and Machine Cognition. Retrieved from http://cmap.ihmc.us/docs/theory-of-concept-maps.

Novak, J. D., & Gowin, D. B. (1984). *Learning how to learn*. New York, NY: Cambridge University Press.

Oosterhof, A. (1999). *Developing and using classroom assessments* (2nd ed.). Upper Saddle River, NJ: Prentice Hall.

Pink, D. H. (2006). *A whole new mind: Why right-brainers will rule the future*. New York, NY: Riverhead Books.

Pink, D. H. (2009). *Drive: The surprising truth about what motivates us*. New York, NY: Riverhead Books.

Pirsig, R. (1974). *Zen and the art of motorcycle maintenance*. New York, NY: William Morrow.

Popham, J. (2013). Can classroom assessment of student growth be credibly used to evaluate teachers? *English Journal, 103*(1), 34–39.

Robinson, V. M. J., Lloyd, C. A., & Rowe, K. J. (2008). The impact of leadership on student outcomes: An analysis of the differential effects of leadership types. *Educational Administration Quarterly, 44*(5), 635–674.

Rose, D. H., & A. Meyer (2002). *Teaching every student in the digital age: Universal design for learning*. Alexandria, VA: ASCD.

Sawyer, K. (2015). A call to action: The challenges of creative teaching and learning. *Teachers College Record, 117*(10).

Shedletsky, L. J., & Beaudry, J. S. (2014). *Cases on teaching critical thinking through visual representation strategies*. Hershey, PA: IGI Global.

Silver, H., Jackson, J., & Moirao, D. (2011). *Task rotation: Strategies for differentiating activities and assessments by learning style*. Alexandria, VA: ASCD.

Silver, H., Strong, R., & Perini, M. (2003). *So each may learn: Integrating learning styles and multiple intelligences*. Alexandria, VA: ASCD.

Sinek, S. (2009). *Start with why: How great leaders inspire everyone to take action*. New York, NY: Portfolio.

Silver, H., Strong, R., and Perini, M. (2007). *The strategic teacher*. Alexandria, VA: ASCD.

Smith, J., & Smith, R. (2015). *Evaluating instructional leadership: Recognized practices for success*. Thousand Oaks, CA: Corwin.

Smith, M. S., & Stein, M. K. (2011). *5 practices for orchestrating productive math discussions*. Reston, VA: NCTM.

Stanford History Education Group. (n.d.). *Beyond the Bubble: A new generation of history assessments*. Stanford, CA: Stanford University. Retrieved from http://beyondthebubble.stanford.edu

Stevens, D. D., & Levi, A. J. (2005). *Introduction to rubrics*. Sterling, VA: Stylus.

Stewart McCafferty, A. (2017). Duct tape and pom-poms: Engaging middle-school learners in metaphoric thinking through self-expressive prompts. *AMLE Magazine*. Westerville, OH: Association for Middle Level Education.

Stewart McCafferty, A., & Beaudry, J. (2017, December). "The gallery walk: educators step up to build assessment literacy." *The Learning Professional: The Learning Forward Journal, 38*(6), 47–53.

Stiggins, R. (2004). New assessment beliefs for a new school mission. *Phi Delta Kappan, 86*(1), 22–27.

Stiggins, R. (2007). Assessment through the student's eyes. *Educational Leadership, 64*(8), 22–26.

Stiggins, R. (2017). *The perfect assessment system*. Alexandria, VA: ASCD.

Stiggins, R. J. (1994). *Student-centered classroom assessment*. Princeton, NC: Merrill.

Stiggins, R. J, & Conklin, N. F. (1992). *In teachers' hands: Investigating the practices of classroom assessment*. Albany: State University of New York Press.

Stone, D., & Heen, S. (2014). *Thanks for the feedback: The science and art of receiving feedback well (even when it's off base, unfair, poorly delivered, and frankly, you're not in the mood)*. New York, NY: Penguin.

Thoughtful Classroom. (2010). *Questioning styles and strategies* [Video]. Retrieved from https://www.youtube.com/watch?v=5uKqs3D0Z0M

Turkay, S. (2014). *Setting goals: Who, why, how?* Cambridge, MA: Harvard Initiative for Learning & Teaching.

Wallace Foundation. (2011). *The school principal as leader: Guiding schools to better teaching and learning*. Retrieved from http://www.wallacefoundation.org/knowledge-center/school-leadership/effective-principal-leadership/Documents/The-School-Principal-as-Leader-Guiding-Schools-to-Better-Teaching-and-Learning.pdf

Waters, T., & Cameron, G. (2007). *Balanced leadership framework: Connecting vision with action*. Aurora, CO: Mid-Continent Research for Education and Learning.

Wiggins, G., & McTighe, J. (1998). *Understanding by design*. Alexandria, VA: ASCD.

Wiggins, G., & McTighe, J. (2005). *Understanding by design* (2nd ed.). Alexandria, VA: ASCD.

Wiggins, G., & McTighe, J. (2011). *The understanding by design guide to creating high-quality units*. Alexandria, VA: ASCD.

Wilen, W., & Clegg, A. (1986). Effective questions and questioning: A research review. *Theory in Research & Social Education, 14*(2), 153–161.

Wiliam, D. (2007). Content then process: Teacher learning communities in the service of formative assessment. In D. B. Reeves (Ed.), *Ahead of the curve: the power of assessment to transform teaching and learning*. Bloomington, IN: Solution Tree.

Wilson, D., & Conyers, M. (2016). *Teaching students to drive their brains*. Alexandria, VA: ASCD.

Yetman, N. (1972). *Voices from slavery*. New York, NY: Holt, Rinehart and Winston.

Zomorodi, M. (2017). *Bored and brilliant: How spacing out can unlock your most productive and creative self.* New York, NY: St. Martin's Press.

• Index •

CORWIN
A SAGE Publishing Company